THE BLOOMSBURY GROUP

THE BLOOMSBURY GROUP

A Study of E. M. Forster, Lytton Strachey,
Virginia Woolf, and their Circle

by J. K. Johnstone

OCTAGON BOOKS

A DIVISION OF FARRAR, STRAUS AND GIROUX

New York 1978

Reprinted 1978

OCTAGON BOOKS
A DIVISION OF FARRAR, STRAUS & GIROUX, INC.
19 Union Square West
New York, N.Y. 10003

Library of Congress Cataloging in Publication Data

Johnstone, John Keith, 1923-
The Bloomsbury group.

Reprint of the 1954 ed. published by Noonday Press, New York.
Bibliography: p.
1. Bloomsbury group. 2. English literature—20th century—History and criticism. I. Title.
PR478.B46J6 1978 820'.9'00912 78-17490
ISBN 0-374-94262-5

History and critism. I. Title.

Manufactured by Braun-Brumfield, Inc.
Ann Arbor, Michigan
Printed in the United States of America

CONTENTS

CHAPTER PAGE

Introduction ix

PART I
THE BACKGROUND

I. Bloomsbury 3
II. Bloomsbury Philosophy 20
III. Bloomsbury Aesthetics 46

PART II
VALUES

IV. E. M. Forster, Lytton Strachey, Virginia Woolf 99

PART III
COMPOSITION

V. E. M. Forster 159
VI. Lytton Strachey 267
VII. Virginia Woolf 320
Conclusion 375
Bibliography 377

ACKNOWLEDGMENTS

This book was written as a thesis at the University of Leeds. A generous Scholarship awarded by the Imperial Order Daughters of the Empire, an organization well known in Canada for its goodwill towards scholarship in the Humanities, made possible my study at that University.

I am greatly indebted to Professor Bonamy Dobrée, of the University of Leeds, who first suggested to me the possibility of considering the Bloomsbury Group as a subject for study, and who, while the work was in progress, showed a warm interest in it. Mr. N. G. Annan, of King's College, Cambridge, read the typescript of the thesis and made several useful suggestions. The interest of both Professor Dobrée and Mr. Annan was of that most helpful kind which assists a student to develop and criticize his own views without attempting to force other views upon him.

My wife, who was a constant and patient critic of my writing, helped me to improve my style throughout the book.

J. K. J.

INTRODUCTION

"BLOOMSBURY" is the name of the close group of friends who began to meet about 1906 and included, among others, John Maynard Keynes, Lytton Strachey, Virginia and Leonard Woolf, Vanessa and Clive Bell, Duncan Grant, E. M. Forster, and Roger Fry. The term was applied derisively to the group before the First World War, because their hostesses, Virginia and Vanessa Stephen (who became Virginia Woolf and Vanessa Bell), lived in the London district of Bloomsbury.

"Bloomsbury" meant a number of things—snobbish, "high-brow", "arty", "Bohemian"—all rolled into one word. It was intended to smack, all at once, of the British Museum, of untidy art studios, of an exclusive, "unconventional" life, of pale aesthetes who met to read esoteric papers in some ivory tower.

This derisive epithet had, of course, a grain of truth in it. Bloomsbury was "arty" in that its members believed art to be the most important thing in the world, the highest expression to which man has attained. What is more, they practised this belief. They infused new life into the novel, the biography, and art criticism; and they have made important contributions to British painting. But they were not exclusively "arty". They have made contributions at least equally important to economics and to international affairs.

They were, in a sense, "high-brows" too. Their approach to problems was intellectual. They were fastidious and highly civilized; yet their life was, no doubt, rather "Bohemian"—the one probably demanded the other. But they were not snobs. Certainly they did not wish to keep the good things of life, among which they believed the creation and appreciation of works of art to be the best, to themselves. Rather, they did a great deal to publicize and popularize art, and it is largely to them that we owe the Arts Council. Their political beliefs ranged from Liberal on the Bloomsbury right to Socialist on the Bloomsbury left. Their religious beliefs, in so far as they can be said, as a group, to have had any, were non-Christian.

Bloomsbury was not, as the epithet " Bloomsbury " was at first meant to imply, a group of irresponsible, " high-brow " *poseurs* ; it was a nucleus from which civilization has spread outwards. To deal with that nucleus in all its aspects would require many books. There would be a book on Roger Fry's aesthetic theory and art criticism, another on Vanessa Bell's and Duncan Grant's painting ; a book on Keynesian economics, and another on Leonard Woolf's studies of international affairs and communal psychology, to name a few. This book proposes to deal only with an aspect of the literature of Bloomsbury. It will attempt to see the novels of Virginia Woolf and of E. M. Forster, and the biographies of Lytton Strachey, in their relation to the Bloomsbury milieu. And in this attempt it will, of course, see something of that milieu itself.

PART I

THE BACKGROUND

CHAPTER I

BLOOMSBURY

"BLOOMSBURY" began shortly after the death of Sir Leslie Stephen in 1904. Stephen, with other eminent Victorians, had, by his bold thinking, helped to prepare the way for Bloomsbury. It was ironic, though in the nature of things, that Stephen's death should have been required before the way was finally clear.

Leslie Stephen's life, which neatly straddled Victoria's reign (he was born in 1832), was an epitome of a facet of the intellectual life of that era. He was brought up by Evangelical parents in the faith of the Established Church ; he went to Cambridge, and in good time received a Fellowship from his college and entered Holy Orders. But after eight years of the life of a Cambridge don, his reading caused him to question the teachings of his Church. As a result, he resigned his Tutorship and before long withdrew from Cambridge to take up a literary career in London, to become editor of *The Cornhill Magazine*, and to begin the *Dictionary of National Biography*. He was a friend of many of the writers and intellectual leaders of his time ; his masters were Mill, Darwin, and Huxley ; he explained and defended his position as an agnostic.*

As a father, Leslie Stephen gave his children a training which he had not had. They *began* to think, as it were, at the point that he had reached when he left Cambridge, and, freed from the Articles of the Church, began to follow the bent of his own mind. If they were given a religion at all, it must have been one that maintained the value of human relationships. "Though [Leslie Stephen] was an agnostic", says his daughter Virginia, "nobody believed more profoundly in

* For an account of Leslie Stephen's thought and of his relation to the Clapham Sect and the Bloomsbury Group, see Noel Gilroy Annan, *Leslie Stephen : His Thought and Character in Relation to His Time.*

the worth of human relationships." And she tells us more of her father :

> The relations between parents and children to-day have a freedom that would have been impossible with my father. He expected a certain standard of behaviour, even of ceremony in family life. Yet if freedom means the right to think one's own thoughts and to follow one's own pursuits, then no one respected and indeed insisted upon freedom more completely than he did. His sons, with the exception of the Army and Navy, should follow whatever professions they chose ; his daughters, though he cared little enough for the higher education of women, should have the same liberty.

And so his daughter Vanessa was allowed to paint, and Virginia read anything she would in his library at the age of fifteen.

Leslie Stephen's influence upon his daughters was strong. Their mother, Stephen's second wife, died suddenly in 1895 when Vanessa was sixteen and Virginia thirteen. The two girls were educated at home, and for a time after their mother's death Stephen was their schoolmaster. He was not suited to the task, and had to give it up, for he could not adapt himself to the formal teaching of young, undeveloped minds. His informal teaching was more successful. Each evening, for an hour and a half, he would recite poetry or read fiction to his children. Scott's novels were the most popular and were all read through. There were also times when Stephen, like some of the fathers and elderly gentlemen that Virginia was later to create in her novels, was preoccupied with his thoughts ; but " when, suddenly opening his bright blue eyes, and rousing himself from what had seemed complete abstraction, he gave his opinion, it was difficult to disregard it ", Virginia tells us. She gives us other glimpses of her parent : " Sometimes with one word—but his one word was accompanied by a gesture of the hand—he would dispose of the tissue of exaggerations which his own sobriety seemed to provoke." But he was capable of his own exaggerations. He sometimes cast himself in a tragic rôle, and a small incident which caused him discomfort might assume extraordinary proportions in his mind.

Often the girls were left to themselves while Stephen worked in his study. " As [my father] wrote he smoked a short clay pipe, and he scattered books [around his low rocking chair] in a circle. The thud of a book dropped on the floor could be heard in the room beneath."

In 1902 Stephen's health broke down, and he became more dependent upon his daughters, on whom the responsibilities of housekeeping had fallen. He suffered from internal cancer, and was an invalid until his death in 1904. It was perhaps memories of this period, of the secluded life in her parental home, and of the forceful parent who must often have dominated the girl, that prompted Virginia in later years to write bitterly against the conception of the daughter as, as she calls it, " The Angel in the House ", who is to stay at home, sacrificing herself to others, while the sons go up to university and out into the world. At any rate, Leslie Stephen's death was necessary to Vanessa's and Virginia's freedom,* though it was he who had taught them to demand freedom and, once gained, to put it to use.

After their father's death Virginia and Vanessa left his home, at 22 Hyde Park Gate, to set up house with their brothers, Thoby and Adrian, at 46 Gordon Square, Bloomsbury. The duties of Hyde Park Gate were left behind ; they had a remarkable degree of freedom for young women of their generation, and the opportunity, since they were financially independent, to make of their lives what they chose.

Virginia chose to write ; Vanessa to paint ; and both of them made new friends. Thoby Stephen had been to Cambridge, and his University friends came to his new home. This was Thoby's one contribution to Bloomsbury, but it was a vital one. He was handsome, charming, and admired ; among the friends that he brought to Gordon Square and introduced to his sisters were some of the most gifted and original young men of his generation. He had little more than introduced them when he died of typhoid fever in 1906, while on holiday in Greece with his brother and sisters.

One of Thoby's best friends was Clive Bell, that " gay and

* There is a situation similar in this one respect in Virginia Woolf's novel *The Years.*

amiable dog ", as Maynard Keynes has called him.* Bell was enamoured of the visual arts ; he believed aesthetic experience to be " the end of existence " ; but he was also, in these days at least, " concerned for the fate of humanity ", and he planned, in one of those dreams of youth that are never realized, to write a " *magnum opus*, a book to deal with nothing less than every significant aspect of our age, a book to be called *The New Renaissance* ". Though not a deep or original thinker, his conversation and writing were spirited, and he was often acute enough to express an idea more clearly than its originator had succeeded in doing—a gift which is too useful to be belittled. Above all, he had a sense of humour, and this, as he himself has said, is " one of the qualities that most clearly distinguish a civilized man from a savage . . . ; and . . . is in the last analysis nothing but a highly developed sense of values ".†

Clive Bell married Vanessa Stephen a few months after Thoby's death, in 1907. To allow the newly-married couple to live at 46 Gordon Square, Virginia and Adrian moved to 29 Fitzroy Square, nearby. Around these four a group of young, talented intellectuals, who were all interested in art, began to form. Duncan Grant, a neighbour and close friend of the Stephens and Bells, describes the gatherings at Fitzroy Square :

> [Adrian's] study on the ground floor had the air of being much lived in. It was to this room that [Virginia's and Adrian's] friends came on Thursday evenings—a continuation of those evenings which began in Gordon Square before Thoby died and before Vanessa married. It was there that what has since been called " Bloomsbury " for good or ill came into being.
>
> About ten o'clock in the evening people used to appear and continue to come at intervals till twelve o'clock at night, and it was seldom that the last guest left before two or three in the morning. Whisky, buns and cocoa were the diet, and people talked to each other. If someone had lit a pipe he would sometimes hold out the lighted match to Hans the dog, who would snap at it and put it out. Conversation ; that was all.

* " My Early Beliefs ", *Two Memoirs*, p. 81.

† *Enjoying Pictures*, p. 96 ; *Civilization*, pp. v and 111.

> Yet many people made a habit of coming, and few who did so will forget those evenings.
>
> Among those who constantly came in early days were Charles Sanger, Theodore Llewelyn Davies, Desmond Macarthy, Charles Tennyson, Hilton Young (now Lord Kennet), Lytton Strachey.
>
> It was certainly not a " salon ". Virginia Stephen in those days was not at all the sort of hostess required for such a thing. She appeared very shy and probably was so, and never addressed the company. She would listen to certain arguments and occasionally speak, but her conversation was mainly directed to someone next to her. Her brother's Cambridge friends she knew well by this time, but I think there was always something a little aloof and even a little fierce in her manner to most men at the time I am speaking of. . . .
>
> I do not think that her new existence had " become alive " to Virginia's imagination in those first years. She gave the impression of being so intensely receptive to any experience new to her, and so intensely interested in facts that she had not come across before, that time was necessary to give it a meaning as a whole. It took the years to complete her vision of it.*

The quiet life at Hyde Park Gate must inevitably have continued to have its effect upon Virginia Stephen, and there was, as well, the shadow of mental illness, which had manifested itself for a time in 1905. But if these evenings of conversation and discussion with young people were a new experience for her, they were not new to Lytton Strachey and his Cambridge friends.

Strachey and several others of the Cambridge men who came to Fitzroy Square had been members of the Cambridge " Society " which was begun by F. D. Maurice, Tennyson, and Hallam in the 1820s, whose members came to be known as " Apostles ", and whose affairs were supposed to be kept secret. The Apostles were a select group. Their numbers were small—sometimes as few as six undergraduates were included. New members were chosen with extreme care. As a result, and due in some measure too, no doubt, to the nature of the Society itself, many of Cambridge's most distinguished

* " Virginia Woolf ", *Horizon*, Vol. III, No. 18 (June 1941), pp. 403–4.

men have been Apostles. All of them, from Tennyson and Dean Merivale, to Henry Sidgwick and to Maynard Keynes, are unanimous in their affection for the Society and in their testimony to the value they attach to the rôle it played in their lives. The Society was the centre of Cambridge life for its members. They were seldom apart. They dined in one another's rooms ; they went on boating parties and on vacations together ; and, above all, they talked. Once a week, on Saturday evenings, they met to read and discuss a paper that one of them had written. Sidgwick tells us of the spirit of the Society and of these discussions :

> I can only describe it as the spirit of the pursuit of truth with absolute devotion and unreserve by a group of intimate friends, who were perfectly frank with each other, and indulged in any amount of humorous sarcasm and playful banter, and yet each respects the other, and when he discourses tries to learn from him and see what he sees. Absolute candour was the only duty that the tradition of the society enforced.*

This spirit and tradition endured throughout the years in the Society and were brought from Cambridge to Bloomsbury.

Lytton Strachey and his friend Maynard Keynes were two of the most prominent undergraduate members of the Society in the first years of the present century. In appearance they could scarcely have been more dissimilar. Sir Max Beerbohm has described Strachey as he saw him, several years later, in 1912 : " an emaciated face of ivory whiteness, above a long square-cut auburn beard, and below a head of very long sleek dark brown hair. The nose was nothing if not aquiline, and Nature had chiselled it with great delicacy. The eyes, behind a pair of gold-rimmed spectacles, eyes of an inquirer and a cogitator, were large and brown and luminous." † And this face and head surmounted a very tall, very thin body, so loosely knit that it appeared disjointed. Keynes was much more solidly built than his friend. His easy air of physical relaxation made him appear athletic in contrast to Strachey, whose body, when in repose, seemed entirely beyond his control.

* See R. F. Harrod, *John Maynard Keynes*, to which this section is indebted.

† *Lytton Strachey*, p. 5.

Keynes's eyes, piercing, yet reflective, were set beneath overshadowing brows. A decisive nose led to a neat moustache that fully covered his upper lip. His lower lip was full; his chin receded slightly; his head was set forward on his shoulders. Keynes looked poised, ready to give his attention at once to any problem that might confront him. His whole appearance, though not handsome, was urbane. His voice, one may be sure, was suave. Strachey's voice "went into a high pitch on the emphatic termination of a sentence".*

But Keynes and Strachey had enough in common. They were also different enough to complement one another. They both came from solid Victorian homes to which they owed a debt at least as great as Virginia and Vanessa Stephen owed to theirs. Keynes's father was a Cambridge don and official; Strachey's father a great Indian administrator. Both Strachey and Keynes were gay, and each had a sharp sense of humour. Deep in both, well masked, perhaps, were passionate natures. They were very interested in human relations, and, as their letters to one another testify, they spent a good deal of time in character analysis. What was X really like? Why had he done such and such? And in what subtle ways did his character reveal itself? They gained practical experience in this sort of character-study, no doubt, as they scouted the undergraduates for new members for the Society. They were both intellectual. Keynes exercised his mind in logic and mathematics, and soon interested himself in political economy. Strachey was more active in his study of history than in these sciences, but they met on common ground in their interests in philosophy and in literature. They had fine minds, and, inevitably and rightly, they were aware that they had, and trusted their own abilities. They intended to revalue things for themselves, and in making their judgments they did not hesitate—and this was in part an outcome of their love of character analysis—to criticize their predecessors or to ridicule those in authority. But it would be wrong to think of them as revolutionaries in the intellectual world. They stood squarely within a tradition, and they carried that tradition a step or two farther. To do that it is necessary to diverge somewhat

* Harrod, *Keynes*, p. 85.

from the past in order to keep the essential continuity. Keynes and Strachey did not want to burn down the Victorian house ; they wanted to sweep out some trash, move in some new furniture, and rearrange the rooms.

The Society was the centre of their intellectual life. It gave them an opportunity to discuss and mature their ideas ; and, although their Apostolic friends were sharp enough critics, Strachey and Keynes could develop their ideas more boldly within such a circle than they could have done elsewhere. The Society gave them shelter, and the feeling of security and superiority that the closed, exclusive brotherhood always generates among its members. And in the Society they found, as well, a philosopher, G. E. Moore, who seemed to them to have swept out the materialist, utilitarian, and moral trash of the Victorians, and to have formulated a logical, idealist philosophy based upon premises that the twentieth century could accept.* "The influence", says Keynes, "was not only overwhelming ; but it was the extreme opposite of what Strachey used to call *funeste* ; it was exciting, exhilarating, the beginning of a renaissance, the opening of a new heaven on a new earth, we were the forerunners of a new dispensation, we were not afraid of anything." It was the same feeling, no doubt, that caused Clive Bell to plan his *magnum opus*, *The New Renaissance*.

And this was the feeling that came to Bloomsbury to enliven the hitherto quiet lives of Vanessa and Virginia Stephen. Strachey soon found, at Fitzroy and Gordon Squares, the centre that he had found in the Society. Bloomsbury was never quite as important to Keynes as to Strachey, if only because the profession of economics, which Keynes adopted, took him into a wider, busier world, less related to Bloomsbury than Strachey's profession of letters. But Keynes was important to Bloomsbury, particularly perhaps, during its first ten or fifteen years, as a friend who could give authoritative advice on almost any matter. In 1908 he took up a Fellowship at his college, King's, in Cambridge ; but he kept rooms in London with his friend Duncan Grant so that he might come regularly to London and to Bloomsbury.

* See Chapter II.

Duncan Grant, whom we have already met briefly as a Bloomsbury neighbour of Virginia and Adrian Stephen, was a cousin of Lytton Strachey. He was brought up partly in the Strachey household, while his family were in India. Lady Strachey encouraged his aptitude for painting and persuaded his parents to allow him to take up painting as a profession. After Keynes's undergraduate years Duncan Grant became his best friend, and remained so throughout Keynes's life. Grant was conscientiously devoted to painting, but his interests were not narrow, and to any discussion he brought intelligence and the level-headed outlook of the craftsman who works with material things and knows their limitations.

Interest in the creation and appreciation of paintings became a dominant characteristic of Bloomsbury. Lytton Strachey and Clive Bell, who had championed the visual arts at Cambridge and had aroused Keynes's lively interest, retained their enthusiasm. Clive Bell wrote on art and became a well-known critic. Vanessa Bell and Duncan Grant painted together. (The Bells and Grant still work together at Charleston, near Lewes, in Sussex.) There was scarcely anyone in the group who did not have a lively interest in the visual arts; and the leader in this interest was Roger Fry.

Roger Fry matured late. Unlike Strachey and Keynes, who as undergraduates seemed already to be in possession of powers that only required development to become the powers of great men, Roger Fry was not able until middle age to control and direct the abilities that made him a great art critic. But in middle age he had many of the finest qualities of youth—qualities that are even more lovable, because they are rarer, in a man than in a boy.

Fry was fifteen years or so the senior of most of the other members of Bloomsbury. He was born in 1866 to rather austere Quaker parents, and he was brought up, of course, in the Quaker faith. His father, Sir Edward Fry, was a judge. After an unhappy, tortured existence at a private school, Roger went to a public school at Clifton, where the years were dull and monotonous, relieved only by the friendship of John Ellis McTaggart, a fellow schoolboy who was later to become a famous Cambridge philosopher. It was not until he came up to Cambridge and entered King's College to read for the science tripos that Roger Fry discovered that life could really be a very pleasant affair.

Fry's Cambridge was the Cambridge of the youthful McTaggart, Goldsworthy Lowes Dickinson, and Nathaniel Wedd. It is best epitomized for us in E. M. Forster, another Bloomsbury associate and member of the Society, who is now a Fellow of King's. Forster came up to Cambridge in 1897, twelve years later than Fry ; but the spirit that Fry knew still endured ; and Forster, much more, for example, than Maynard Keynes, who entered King's in 1902, seems to belong to the last century. McTaggart was at Trinity, Dickinson and Wedd were Fellows of King's College, when Forster was an undergraduate. " Wedd ", Forster says, " taught me classics and it is to him . . . more than to anyone that I owe such awakening as has befallen me. It is through him that I can best imagine the honesty and fervour of fifty years back.* Wedd was then cynical, aggressive, Mephistophelian, wore a red tie, blasphemed, and taught Dickinson how to swear too—always a desirable accomplishment for a high-minded young don, though fewer steps need be taken about it now."† It is indicative of Dickinson's character, as well as of the times, that he had to be taught to swear and yet was willing to learn. One cannot imagine that he was a very adept student of the art. " He was ", Forster agrees with Dickinson's former bedmaker at Cambridge, " the best man who ever lived." His creed is perhaps expressed best in his *Letters from John Chinaman* : " To feel, and in order to feel to express, or at least to understand the expression of all that is lovely in Nature, of all that is poignant and sensitive in man, is to us in itself a sufficient end ". He believed that the pursuit of this ideal was becoming more and more difficult throughout the world, because the modern governments and industrialists of the West were spreading " ugliness, meanness, and insincerity ". He looked longingly to Ancient Greece, where he believed that the real had been close to the ideal ; but at the same time he worked, in the " League of Nations Society ", to bring the League of Nations into being. And with Wedd and others he founded a maga-

* Written about 1933. † *Goldsworthy Lowes Dickinson*, pp. 73–4.

zine, *The Independent Review*, which Forster, who was a contributor, tells us was " not so much a Liberal review as an appeal to Liberalism from the Left to be its better self ". In his broad Liberalism Dickinson differed from his friend McTaggart, a traditionalist who became more and more reactionary as he grew older. But he could agree with McTaggart that the human relation of love (in its broadest sense) is the best thing we can know, and he shared McTaggart's faith in reason while trying, like McTaggart, to gain knowledge in other, more intuitive ways.* In these beliefs of Dickinson's, Forster, who became an intimate friend, concurred with few reservations.† Through Forster and Roger Fry, at least, Dickinson had his effect upon Bloomsbury.

Dickinson, Wedd, and McTaggart were Fry's close friends at Cambridge ; Dickinson the most intimate. They were all four members of the Society ; they rowed and holidayed together ; their philosopher in these early days was, of course, McTaggart. Cambridge, Forster says in his biography of Dickinson, " acquired a magic quality. Body and spirit, reason and emotion, work and play, architecture and scenery, laughter and seriousness, life and art—these pairs which are elsewhere contrasted were there fused into one. People and books reinforced one another, intelligence joined hands with affection, speculation became a passion, and discussion was made profound by love." Like the hero of one of Forster's novels, Roger Fry found at Cambridge that " his boyhood had been but a dusty corridor that led to the spacious halls of youth ".

Fry graduated in 1888 with a first-class degree. His father saw prospects of a brilliant scientific career for him ; but Roger had become so interested in art as to think it his " only possible job ". He compromised with his father by staying at Cambridge for a few more terms in order to study painting and anatomy, while trying, half-heartedly and unsuccessfully, for a Fellowship. Sir Edward was bitterly disappointed, and Roger was for years sensitive to the fact that his father regarded

* McTaggart was subject to mystic experiences. Dickinson hoped for moments of mystic vision and dabbled in psychical research (Dickinson, *McTaggart*, pp. 92–8 ; Forster, *Dickinson*, pp. 54 and 121–2).

† See Chapter IV.

him as a failure. Their relationship, though a break between them was never threatened, was made the more difficult because at Cambridge Roger's religious faith had slipped from him.

Cambridge and its spacious halls were left behind. The next decade or so Roger Fry spent learning his art: studying in Italy and France, painting at home. In December 1896 he married Helen Coombe, a fellow art student; and there followed one of those rare, perfectly complete periods that came now and then in a life that had enough anxieties and disappointments. But in the spring of 1898 Helen Fry became mentally ill, afflicted with, as it was later learned, an incurable thickening of the skull.

Money was badly needed, and Fry, whose painting had not brought him success, set out to earn it by writing and lecturing on art. He was at once successful. He loved art enough to choose it as his "only possible job" when that choice was a very difficult one to make; and he had found art to be the one thing of real value that time and life's misfortunes could not destroy. He wished, for he was nothing if not sympathetic, generous, and sociable, to share that discovery and his love of art with others. He would stand before a picture (and his sensibility was great), submitting himself to his sensations. Then, in a tentative, unassuming style that seemed to take his listeners or readers on a quest with him, and with a voice, if he was lecturing, that another great lecturer, Bernard Shaw, believed was worth listening to for its own sake, he would try to describe his feelings and convey them to his audience. Finally—for had he not been a fellow Apostle of McTaggart and Dickinson?—he would subject his feelings to a rigorous intellectual examination in an attempt to learn what, in the painting, had caused them. He had found his vocation (though he continued his practice of painting and considered it of more importance than criticism), and he became famous.

Meanwhile there were respites in Helen Fry's illness, intervals when she and Roger thought that they could plan life together once more, and that the disease which they fought might be beaten. There were two children. In 1905 Fry was appointed Director of the Metropolitan Museum in New York; and he had to spend two or three months of each of the next five years in America. His hopes were to be disappointed there too, for he could not agree with the President of the Museum, Pierpont Morgan, and he left his position in 1910. In the same year Helen Fry entered an asylum, where she remained until her death in 1937.

It was in 1910 that Roger Fry became a member of the Bloomsbury family. He looked, Virginia Woolf tells us, much older than his age of forty-four ; but he was about to begin the most important and, if one may speak so without too great danger of paradox, the most youthful phase of his career. To the consternation of the English public, he introduced them in November 1910, by means of an exhibition which he called " Manet and the Post-Impressionists ", to the new movement in French art. The public were aghast or thrown into fits of laughter before the paintings of such men as Cézanne, Van Gogh, Matisse, and Picasso ; some of them believed that Fry was out to dupe and to swindle them, and many were indignant. But there were others, a small number and most of them young, who were inspired by the Post-Impressionist paintings. Bloomsbury was foremost among this group. Its painters were enthralled by the pictures ; its writers and thinkers by Fry's explanation of why these pictures were great works of art. There was a new feeling of excitement in Bloomsbury, and it was liveliest in Roger Fry himself. " I feel ", he wrote to an art critic, " that I . . . have an altogether new sense of confidence and determination which I shall stick to as long as it will last." * He believed, as Maynard Keynes and Clive Bell had believed ten years earlier, that the world was about to witness a renaissance. He arranged a second Post-Impressionist Exhibition in the autumn of 1912. In July 1913 he opened the Omega Workshops in Fitzroy Square, where he employed young artists to design textiles, furniture, and other household articles. He hoped to improve interior design and decoration, and to give artists an opportunity to make a living that would leave them free to paint as they wished.

Shortly after the first Post-Impressionist Exhibition, Leonard Woolf, who had been an Apostle at the same time as Lytton

* For quotations in this section see Virginia Woolf's *Roger Fry*.

Strachey and Maynard Keynes, returned to London after seven years in Ceylon in the Civil Service. In 1912 he married Virginia Stephen. Woolf was a student of history; he had had practical experience in government in Ceylon; and he was convinced that socialism is the only answer to the world's problems. In a group that leaned, if anything, to the left side of centre, he was the only member who was solidly leftist—though if we use that term we should remember that he envisioned the introduction of socialism as a step forward in the progress of civilization, not as a revolution or break with the past. And he carried the Bloomsbury trait of respect for reason to its furthest extent. In an unfinished work, *After the Deluge*, he attempts to give an account of " the communal psychology which developed between the French Revolution and 1914 and ended in the war ". He believes that the communal psychology of the First World War and of the Treaty of Versailles should be investigated as well, and that, after these investigations are complete, the historian should be able to " place " the war in the past history of the human race and in relation to the future. He would then be better equipped to do his job, which should be, Woolf believes, to tell men what will happen if they move in certain directions. But Woolf was not occupied only with such broad, historical matters. He was also concerned with more immediate affairs, such as colonial administration, social welfare at home, and the establishment of the League of Nations, for which he worked, with Lowes Dickinson, in the League of Nations Society. And in 1917 he and Virginia Woolf founded the Hogarth Press—at first a hand-press that they operated themselves—to publish work, whether didactic or purely artistic, which contained new ideas.

Leonard Woolf brought these social and political interests into Virginia's life, and he shared with her an interest in literature. He respected and encouraged her talents as a writer, while introducing her to a world less fastidious, more concerned with the basic needs of life, than she had met before. He helped her to satisfy, one may imagine, both her desire to explore her mind in solitude and to commune with others —an ambivalent desire that we all share, but which was intense in Virginia Woolf, perhaps because of her vivid awareness of two worlds, " one flowing in wide sweeps overhead, the other tip-tapping circumscribed upon the pavement ". And thanks to his care and vigilance she had less to fear from attacks of mental illness. As the years passed, the shy, aloof, rather fierce girl, who had listened to her brother's friends in Fitzroy Square, became, in the words of T. S. Eliot, " the centre . . . of the literary life of London ". According to another witness, she was, among people whose company is a delight, in a class apart.

Virginia Woolf's development owed much to Bloomsbury, as well as to her married life. As an artist or as an individual she could scarcely have found a more suitable milieu than she did in this society of equals, who had a similar background, who had few worldly pretensions, and who, although each member was an individual with a distinctive contribution to make to the group, had common interests and shared a point of view.* All Bloomsbury believed in reason, and this belief was leavened or balanced by sensitiveness and a love of beauty. Every one in Bloomsbury was interested, directly or indirectly, in the production of works of art ; and no one, with Leonard Woolf and Maynard Keynes in the group, could be unaware of contemporary social and political problems. This awareness did not mean, however, that Bloomsbury thought it necessary to mix art and politics. Bloomsbury was gay ; it was sceptical ; it was polite. Friendship was the basis of the society ; friendship had drawn its members together ; and Bloomsbury depended on a family feeling for its continued existence. Friendship made possible a frank exchange of views, which, Bloomsbury found, enlarged the individual. For this, conversation was necessary ; and because Bloomsbury loved beauty, and found conversation to be of great value, conversation became an art in its midst and was more important than it had been, perhaps, since the days of Dr. Johnson. Bloomsbury was a society in which the artist could test his ideas, develop

* The above review of Bloomsbury members does not pretend to be complete. Among others, the names of Francis Birrell, Sir Desmond Macarthy (who is referred to by Duncan Grant in a quotation above), and Raymond Mortimer should be mentioned.

his personality, and perfect his art. It was not unlike the society that Virginia Woolf, in her biography of Roger Fry, says Roger Fry envisioned shortly before the First World War :

> At last, he felt . . . a time was at hand when a real society was possible. It was to be a society of people of moderate means, a society based upon the old Cambridge ideal of truth and free speaking, but alive, as Cambridge had never been, to the importance of the arts. It was possible in France ; why not in England ? No art could flourish without such a background. The young English artist tended to become illiterate, narrow-minded and self-centred with disastrous effects upon his work, failing any society where, among the amenities of civilization, ideas were discussed in common and he was accepted as an equal.

Bloomsbury gave its artists the advantage of a society of this sort. In its sheltered, invigorating climate they gained strength and confidence. They felt that the world was about to experience a new renaissance, and, what is more, that they were to be leaders in the reawakening. They had not long enjoyed this feeling when " suddenly, like a chasm in a smooth road ", as Virginia Woolf describes it, " the war came ". Maynard Keynes was plunged into the business of financing the war, and then into what he found to be the chicanery at Versailles. Leonard Woolf and Lowes Dickinson began to investigate the causes of the war and to work for peace. E. M. Forster served as a non-combatant in Egypt. Duncan Grant, Vanessa Bell, Virginia Woolf, and Lytton Strachey continued to write and paint as best they could. Life, art, the amenities of civilization were threatened ; and security was scarcely regained in the two feverish decades that followed the war and preceded the second catastrophe. But Bloomsbury had formed its values in a calmer era and recalled happier days. It remembered when there had been more time for long, leisurely evenings of conversation ; it remembered listening to G. E. Moore as he expounded an idealist philosophy at Cambridge ; it remembered boating parties and summer days when all the good things of life seemed to have coalesced ; and it remembered, rather ruefully, no doubt, its belief that a golden age was about to dawn. It had to change some of its conceptions, but it was more certain than ever before that art was necessary to civilization ; and it carried this belief into the troubled years that lay ahead.

CHAPTER II

BLOOMSBURY PHILOSOPHY

BLOOMSBURY'S values, or at least, the values of those of its members who were undergraduates at Cambridge in the early years of the century, were formed under the influence of G. E. Moore, whose *Principia Ethica* defined Bloomsbury's attitude to life and guided its actions to a quite astonishing degree. *Principia Ethica* is the book that Helen Ambrose, who is wise in the ways of life, reads in Virginia Woolf's first novel.* It is the book that caused Lytton Strachey to declare, " The age of reason has come ! " In fact, one might almost say that *Principia Ethica* was Bloomsbury's Bible in the group's younger, if not in its older years. Its publication is described by Maynard Keynes in a paper that he read, shortly before the Second World War, to a " Club " composed mainly of Cambridge and Bloomsbury friends :

> I went up to Cambridge at Michaelmas 1902, and Moore's *Principia Ethica* came out at the end of my first year. I have never heard of the present generation having read it. But, of course, its effect on *us*, and the talk which preceded and followed it, dominated, and perhaps still dominate, everything else. We were at an age when our beliefs influenced our behaviour, a characteristic of the young which it is easy for the middle-aged to forget, and the habits of feeling, formed then, still persist in a recognizable degree. It is those habits of feeling, influencing the majority of us, which make this Club a collectivity and separate us from the rest. They overlaid, somehow, our otherwise extremely different characters.

And Keynes says that the teaching of *Principia Ethica* is still (in 1938) his religion " under the surface ".

The book that Keynes and his friends read with such

* *The Voyage Out*, p. 82.

excitement in 1903 begins with the assertion that the treatment of ethics has hitherto been inadequate and muddled. Moral philosophers have, rightly, tried to answer two questions: What kind of things ought to exist for their own sakes? and, What kind of actions ought we to perform? But, "they have almost always confused [these two questions] both with one another and with other questions". The first concern of ethics must be to answer the first of these questions clearly, to determine "what things have intrinsic value and in what degrees"; for until we know what is good we cannot know what we should strive to attain, nor can we value correctly what we have. But this "primary and peculiar business of Ethics . . . has received no adequate treatment at all". Moore sets out to put the matter right, and to enunciate what he believes to be "a scientific Ethics".

Previous philosophers, Moore points out, have identified "good" with other things or defined it in terms of something else. They have confused it with natural phenomena, such as pleasure; they have said that it is defined by the mental attitude that we take towards it and is "that which is desired for its own sake"; or they have supposed that it is some supersensible reality. But, Moore says, good is nothing but itself, and is indefinable. Like "yellow", "good" is a simple notion that cannot be analysed: "just as you cannot, by any manner of means, explain to anyone who does not already know it, what yellow is, so you cannot explain what good is". "It is one of those innumerable objects of thought which are themselves incapable of definition, because they are the ultimate terms by reference to which whatever *is* capable of definition must be defined."* Moore is careful to point out that "What is thus indefinable is not 'the good', or the whole of that which always possesses the predicate 'good', but this predicate itself." And he decides that "Our first conclusion as to the subject-matter of Ethics is . . . that there is a simple, indefinable, unanalysable object of thought by reference to which it must be defined." Therefore, "the fundamental principles of Ethics must be *synthetic* propositions, declaring

* The italics, as throughout in quotations from *Principia Ethica*, are Moore's.

what things, and in what degree, possess a simple and unanalysable property which may be called ' intrinsic value ' or ' goodness ' ".

The failure to recognize these facts, Moore believes, leads moral philosophers astray ; and he says they have overlooked another difficulty which complicates the problem of judging the intrinsic values of wholes, namely, that the value of a whole may differ in amount from the sum of the values of its parts. That is to say, that two parts, for example, of little or no value may form a whole of great value. Moore calls this principle " the principle of organic unity ", and a whole so formed he calls an " organic " whole. " It seems to be true ", he says in his illustration of the relation that exists in an organic whole, " that to be conscious of a beautiful object is a thing of great intrinsic value." Yet the beautiful object by itself, if no one be conscious of it, has comparatively little value, or, as many would hold, no value at all. Similarly, the value of mere consciousness appears to be very small. Therefore, consciousness of a beautiful object is a whole, composed of consciousness and a beautiful object, possessing a value greater than the sum of the values of its parts. Consideration of the principle of organic unity leads Moore to believe that all things of great intrinsic value are likely to be highly complex wholes.

Moore is now ready to proceed to the examination of intrinsic values. He has defined a method that the science of ethics should follow ; he has asserted as a postulate that " good " is indefinable (he presents a long list of strong arguments to support this assertion and to dispose of contrary views) ; and he has explained the principle of organic unity. If advantage is taken of these gains and a correct method continues to be followed, it should be possible to go on to decide the fundamental question of ethics : " What things have intrinsic value, and in what degrees ? " The method to be employed is simple. " In order to arrive at a correct decision on the first part of this question," Moore says, " it is necessary to consider what things are such that, if they existed *by themselves*, in absolute isolation, we should yet judge their existence to be good ; and, in order to decide upon the relative *degrees* of value of different things, we must similarly consider what comparative value seems to attach to the isolated existence of each." Means are not to be mistaken for ends (and will not be if they are considered in complete isolation) ; and the principle of organic unity, which demonstrates the intrinsic value that a whole, as a whole, may have over the sum of the values of its parts, is to be borne in mind. Moore thus appeals to intuition, to reason, and to knowledge, or, as he says, to " reflective judgment ", to assist in the recognition of what is intrinsically good. Reason devises the method and approves (Moore hopes) its soundness ; intuition, since good is an ultimate term of reference, is expected to recognize goodness, when that which is good in itself is held in isolation, just as yellowness is recognized ; and knowledge helps intuition in the classification of various goods.

The most important question of ethics now appears, Moore says, to be much less difficult.

> Indeed, once the meaning of the question is clearly understood, the answer to it, in its main outlines, appears to be so obvious, that it runs the risk of seeming to be a platitude. By far the most valuable things, which we know or can imagine, are certain states of consciousness, which may be roughly described as the pleasures of human intercourse and the enjoyment of beautiful objects. No one, probably, who has asked himself the question, has ever doubted that personal affection and the appreciation of what is beautiful in Art or Nature, are good in themselves ; nor, if we consider strictly what things are worth having *purely for their own sakes*, does it appear probable that any one will think that anything else has *nearly* so great a value as the things which are included under these two heads. . . . I regard it as indubitable . . . that [the] mere existence of what is beautiful has value, so small as to be negligible, in comparison with that which attaches to the *consciousness* of beauty. This simple truth may, indeed, be said to be universally recognized. What has *not* been recognized is that it is the ultimate and fundamental truth of Moral Philosophy. That it is only for the sake of these things—in order that as much of them as possible may at some time exist—that anyone can be justified in performing any public or private duty; that they are the *raison d'être* of virtue ; that it is they—these complex wholes *themselves*, and not any

> constituent or characteristic of them—that form the rational ultimate end of human action and the sole criterion of social progress : these appear to be truths which have been generally overlooked.

" Personal affections and aesthetic enjoyments ", Moore concludes, " include *all* the greatest, and *by far* the greatest, goods we can imagine."

Moore points out that all the things which he means to include under his general description of great goods are highly complex organic unities. Beautiful objects themselves, to deal first with aesthetic enjoyments, are, for the most part, organic unities. A painting, for example, is a whole of great complexity which is of more value than the sum of the values of its parts. Yet, a painting, or any other beautiful object, can be a part only of a great intrinsic good ; and it is so in the highest degree only when it is contemplated by some one who both recognizes and enjoys its beautiful qualities—who sees truly, that is to say, and feels appropriately. Good taste is, therefore, of the utmost importance to Moore's ethics. He considers two errors that may lead one to see beauty in that which has no beauty. The error of attributing beautiful qualities to an object that does not in fact possess them is much less damaging to the intrinsic value of a whole, Moore believes, than the error of feeling towards qualities, which the object does possess but which are not beautiful, an emotion appropriate only to beautiful qualities. " The former ", Moore says, " may be called an error of judgment, and the latter an error of taste ; but it is important to observe that the ' error of taste ' commonly involves a false judgment *of value* ; whereas the ' error of judgment ' is merely a false judgment *of fact*." Indeed, an error of taste may lead to one of the classes of great intrinsic evils that Moore considers, which " consists of those evils, which seem always to include an enjoyment or admiring contemplation of things which are themselves either evil or ugly ". But true belief in the beautiful qualities of the object cognized, even though not as important as good taste, is still of great importance to the intrinsic value of a whole. It is " an absolutely essential constituent in the highest goods ", Moore says ; and he believes that knowledge that the object really exists, and that its exist-

ence is truly good, is equally important. " Indeed all knowledge, which is directly concerned with the nature of the constituents of a beautiful object, would seem capable of adding greatly to the value of the contemplation of that object, although, by itself, such knowledge would have no value at all." * So Moore, with the help of the principle of organic unity, brings knowledge in by the back door, as it were, to form part of his conception of the good. And since he believes that knowledge of the real existence of the object cognized is an important part of the greatest intrinsic goods, he holds that " a just appreciation of nature and of real persons may maintain its equality with an equally just appreciation of the products of artistic imagination, in spite of much greater beauty in the latter ".

The appreciation of beauty, however, occupies a more important position than knowledge in the wholes which Moore believes to be great intrinsic goods. The appreciation of beauty is a *sine qua non* of such goods ; knowledge merely enhances them, and is essential only to the greatest intrinsic goods. " A great positive good " may exist, Moore says, even though beautiful qualities are mistakenly attributed to an object (by the error of judgment already considered), provided that an appropriate emotion is felt towards the beautiful qualities which the object is so believed to possess. It would be better, of course, if the belief were true ; but the first essential of great intrinsic value is that beauty should be appreciated. In fact, Moore thinks that " the beautiful should be *defined* as that of which the admiring contemplation is good in itself ". He believes that " beautiful " is an " objective predicate of value ", and that judgments of taste should not, therefore, be subjective.

> The question, whether [a thing] is *truly* beautiful or not, depends upon the *objective* question whether the whole in question is or is not truly good, and does not depend upon the question whether it would or would not excite particular feelings in particular persons. This definition has the double recommendation that it accounts both for the apparent connection between goodness and beauty and for the no less

* Moore admits, of course, that knowledge is " immensely valuable *as a means* " (p. 196).

> apparent difference between these two conceptions. It appears, at first sight, to be a strange coincidence, that there should be two *different* objective predicates of value, "good" and "beautiful", which are nevertheless so related to one another that whatever is beautiful is also good. But, if our definition be correct, the strangeness disappears; since it leaves only one *unanalysable* predicate of value, namely "good", while "beautiful", though not identical with, is to be defined by reference to this, being thus, at the same time, different from and necessarily connected with it. In short, on this view, to say that a thing is beautiful is to say, not indeed that it is *itself* good, but that it is a necessary element in something which is: to prove that a thing is truly beautiful is to prove that a whole, to which it bears a particular relation as a part, is truly good.

Moore believes, in fact, that the appreciation of beauty is the most essential constituent of the good.

The truth of this belief is less obvious, Moore realizes, when one turns, as he does now, to a consideration of his second group of great intrinsic goods, personal affections. Nevertheless, personal affection, to be good in the highest degree, must, Moore holds, have all the attributes that are necessary to the best aesthetic enjoyments. "Appropriate emotion, cognition of truly beautiful qualities, and true belief," he says, "are equally necessary here." And he believes, therefore, that the person who is the object of such affection must be physically beautiful in some degree. To this extent the situation is the same as in the case of aesthetic enjoyments; but there is, Moore says, an "additional complication" in that the person has, as a beautiful object has not, great intrinsic value, which resides in the mental qualities of the person. The appreciation of mental qualities must therefore be added to the appreciation of physical beauty to form the most valuable whole of personal affection; but the appreciation of beauty is basic, indirectly if not directly, even to this good; for, Moore says, it follows from the conclusions reached in the consideration of aesthetic enjoyments, that admirable mental qualities themselves "consist very largely in an emotional contemplation of beautiful objects; and hence the appreciation of them will consist essentially in the contemplation of such contemplation".

> It is true that the most valuable appreciation of persons appears to be that which consists in the appreciation of their appreciation of other persons : but even here a reference to material beauty appears to be involved, *both* in respect of the fact that what is appreciated in the last instance may be the contemplation of what is merely beautiful, *and* in respect of the fact that the most valuable appreciation of a person appears to *include* an appreciation of his corporeal expression. Though, therefore, we may admit that the appreciation of a person's attitude towards other persons, or, to take one instance, the love of love, is far the most valuable good we know, and far more valuable than the mere love of beauty, yet we can only admit this if the first be understood to *include* the latter, in various degrees of directness.

Moore goes on to describe the complexities, as he sees them, of personal affection :

> . . . the mental qualities of which the cognition is essential to the value of human intercourse . . . include, in the first place, all those varieties of aesthetic appreciation, which formed our first class of goods. They include, therefore, a great variety of different emotions, each of which is appropriate to some different kind of beauty. But we must now add to these the whole range of emotions, which are appropriate to persons, and which are different from those which are appropriate to mere corporeal beauty. It must also be remembered that just as these emotions have little value in themselves, and as the state of mind in which they exist may have its value greatly heightened, or may entirely lose it and become positively evil in a great degree, according as the cognitions accompanying the emotions are appropriate or inappropriate ; so too the appreciation of these emotions, though it may have some value in itself, may yet form part of a whole which has far greater value or no value at all, according as it is or is not accompanied by a perception of the appropriateness of the emotions to their objects. It is obvious, therefore, that the study of what is valuable in human intercourse is a study of immense complexity ; and that there may be much human intercourse which has little or no value, or is positively bad. Yet here too, as with the question what is beautiful, there seems no reason to doubt that a reflective judgment will in the main decide correctly both as to what

are positive goods and even as to any *great* differences in value between these goods.

It follows from Moore's account that the best goods of human intercourse, which offers such great opportunities for good but demands so much if advantage is to be taken of them, will result from friendship and love, or, as he says, from personal affection. And this relationship, it is clear, must be close, fine, and intelligent. The persons between whom affection is felt (for Moore believes that affection is enhanced if it is reciprocal) must be physically beautiful, at least to the degree that their looks, their words, and their actions are expressions of their characters ; their mental characteristics must be good ; their relationship must be so intimate that they are aware of the qualities—exactly these and no others—that each possesses (for true belief, it will be remembered, contributes to the value of a good whole) ; and they must have intelligence and taste exquisite enough to appreciate these qualities and to value them correctly. All this is necessary if personal affection is to be good in a high degree. Friendship, it will be seen, becomes, in Moore's ethics, an exacting discipline and an art of great value.

This discussion of personal affection completes *Principia Ethica*'s account of great intrinsic goods. Two conclusions may now be drawn, Moore says, as to the nature of the Ideal, or the greatest good that we can conceive. First, this good must be mental ; it will consist, in fact, of states of mind. So the spiritual is found to be superior to the material. But, second, the material is none the less an indispensable part of the Ideal. For let it not be forgotten that the appreciation of beauty in art and in nature is the most essential constituent of good states of mind, and that the cognition of material qualities is necessary to this appreciation. It therefore follows, Moore says, that " To deny and exclude matter, is to deny and exclude the best we know " ; for it is to exclude the good itself.

Though Moore is confident that a " reflective judgment " can decide correctly as to what is intrinsically good, even in such an immensely complicated thing as human intercourse, he is much less sure that correct decisions as to good conduct, which he defines as the means to intrinsic good, can be made with any certainty. Intuition, he says, will not serve us here, for moral laws are not self-evident : " they are capable of being confirmed or refuted by an investigation of causes and effects ". But this investigation is so complicated that it is, in the present state of our knowledge, impossible to carry out. Moore is, therefore, sceptical of so-called " duties " and " virtues ", and he thinks that moralists have attached an undue importance to these concepts. He maintains that in order to prove that one is duty-bound to perform, or that it is virtuous to perform, a particular action, it would have to be shown, by an examination of a wide choice of actions and of the total effects of each, that the action concerned will produce a greater amount of good in the universe than any other action that could be performed instead. And this is clearly an impossible task. The most that can be done, Moore believes, is to prove the general usefulness in a given state of society of certain rules which are approved by common sense and are widely observed. These are the only rules, he says, to which the individual should always conform. In all other cases he should not follow rules of conduct at all, but, " guided by a correct conception of what things are intrinsically good or bad ", he should decide for himself what positive good he, in his particular situation, is likely to be able to effect so far as he can see. For, Moore says, " The extreme improbability that any general rule with regard to the utility of an action will be correct seems, in fact, to be the chief principle which should be taken into account in discussing how the individual should guide his choice." The individual who has a sound knowledge of intrinsic values should therefore he left free to make his own decisions as to right and wrong. This belief goes a long way to explain why Moore devotes most of *Principia Ethica* to an attempt to define the greatest intrinsic goods, and why the consideration of conduct takes a decidedly secondary position in his book. The former is the fundamental business of ethics, Moore believes : conduct will look after itself to a large extent if men know what is good.

This was the philosophy that Moore expounded to the

Cambridge "Society" when Maynard Keynes, Lytton Strachey, and Leonard Woolf were Apostles. Of course, his philosophy underwent a few changes as it was interpreted in the Society, but these were much fewer than might have been expected, and resulted rather from the development of tendencies implicit in *Principia Ethica* than from alterations to the philosophy itself. The pursuit of knowledge evidently came to be regarded as a great intrinsic good, and was raised to somewhat the same status as personal affection and the appreciation of beauty.* And Moore's belief that there were some rules of conduct that the individual should follow was ignored.

> We entirely repudiated a personal liability on us to obey general rules, *Keynes says in the paper from which quotation has already been made.* We claimed the right to judge every individual case on its merits, and the wisdom, experience and self-control to do so successfully. This was a very important part of our faith, violently and aggressively held, and for the outer world it was our most obvious and dangerous characteristic. We repudiated entirely customary morals, conventions and traditional wisdom. We were, that is to say, in the strict sense of the term, immoralists. The consequences of being found out had, of course, to be considered for what they were worth. But we recognized no moral obligation on us, no inner sanction, to conform or to obey. Before heaven we claimed to be our own judge in our own case.

These were, after all, no great departures from Moore's teaching ; and in other respects the Society followed *Principia Ethica* closely.

> Nothing mattered, *Keynes says,* except states of mind, our own and other people's of course, but chiefly our own. These states of mind were not associated with action or achievement or with consequences. They consisted in timeless, passionate states of contemplation and communion, largely unattached to "before" and "after". Their value depended, in accordance with the principle of organic unity, on the state of affairs as a whole which could not be usefully analysed into

* So we may gather from Clive Bell and Maynard Keynes, who, in their interpretations of Moore's philosophy, give the pursuit of knowledge this rank (Bell, *Art*, pp. 88 and 107–14 ; Keynes, "My Early Beliefs", *Two Memoirs*, p. 83).

> parts. For example, the value of the state of mind of being in love did not depend merely on the nature of one's own emotions, but also on the worth of their object and on the reciprocity and nature of the object's emotions ; but it did not depend, if I remember rightly, or did not depend much, on what happened, or how one felt about it, a year later, though I myself was always an advocate of a principle of organic unity through time, which still seems to me only sensible. The appropriate subjects of passionate contemplation and communion were a beloved person, beauty and truth, and one's prime objects in life were love, the creation and enjoyment of aesthetic experience and the pursuit of knowledge. Of these love came a long way first. But in the early days under Moore's influence the public treatment of this and its associated acts was, on the whole, austere and platonic.

Though some attention was given to the visual arts, especially by Lytton Strachey, it was to be expected that in the Society friendship and love (the two terms should not be separated from one another in this context, as they often are in everyday usage) should come " a long way first ", as Keynes says they did. To reinforce the emphasis that Moore gives to personal affection, there was the close association in which the members of the Society lived with one another, the careful consideration that they gave to the selection of new members, and the penchant, shared by Keynes and Strachey at least, for character analysis. Besides, there was no more ready or attractive field that offered such scope for the fine distinctions and precise definitions taught by Moore's ethics than the immensely complicated business of human intercourse. And Bertrand Russell's *Principles of Mathematics*, which came out in the same year as *Principia Ethica*, furnished a method, Keynes says, which assisted the Apostles in estimating the value of a given friendship. A discussion society of clever undergraduates could scarcely have had a more intriguing, or inexhaustible, subject ; though it would be wrong to think that the Apostles merely discussed friendship, and did not practise it as well.

In addition to a credo and matter and method for discussion, Moore's philosophy gave the Society something that is harder to define. Moore's Ideal is spiritual. There is a certain mysticism associated with his rational, scholastic method ; and this characteristic was evidently more apparent when one saw and heard Moore present his philosophy in person. We have already seen Keynes's testimony to the Apostles' interest in states of mind that were unassociated with action, achievement, or consequences. Their contemplation of the good that Moore described was disinterested and unworldly. And though they regarded this contemplation as rational and scientific, and Moore's method gave them a pretext for thinking so, there was an element of mysticism in it which, together, no doubt, with a certain amount of ritual that they had inherited from previous generations of Apostles, served the members of the Society as a religion. So, at any rate, Keynes calls it. It was, he says, " some sort of relation of neo-platonism ". And he describes the atmosphere of the Society in his undergraduate days :

> Thus we were brought up—with Plato's absorption in the good in itself, with a scholasticism which outdid St. Thomas, in calvinistic withdrawal from the pleasures and successes of Vanity Fair, and oppressed with all the sorrows of Werther. It did not prevent us from laughing most of the time and we enjoyed supreme self-confidence, superiority and contempt towards all the rest of the unconverted world. But it was hardly a state of mind which a grown-up person in his senses could sustain literally.

When Keynes and Strachey came to Bloomsbury, some of the habits of thought and feeling that originated in the Society were left behind. The " sorrows of Werther ", however real, or unreal, they may have been at Cambridge, did not afflict Bloomsbury. And the pleasures of scholastic hair-splitting were not so attractive now as they had been to the undergraduate mind. What remained was more mature ; and enough did remain to make of Bloomsbury, in a sense, a more adult and more varied development of the Society. But here, in exchange for the peace of Cambridge, the traffic of London clattered by on the pavements just outside. The world was closer, and there was certain to be a new awareness of it.

The Apostolic ideal of friendship was important to Bloomsbury, and everything that might stand in the way of the intimate communion of friends was suspect. Desire for worldly success and honours Bloomsbury considered a deadly sin, not only because they believed that it might lead to the misdirection of energy, but because they thought that robes and titles, medals and distinctions, surround one with barriers that are difficult to penetrate, and often pass current for character itself. Pomposity they disliked equally, because it veils one from oneself and from others. Prudery, insincerity, and that kind of " good manners " that consists of evasion and concealment may also make honest friendship impossible. These sins had been veritable traits of the Victorian Age, Bloomsbury thought, and had segregated the sexes and isolated individuals. Bloomsbury resolved that there should be absolute sincerity and freedom from prudery in their midst. Nothing should interfere with the frank exchange and discussion of states of mind.

This decision was harder to make in the early years of the century than it might be to-day, and harder to follow in Bloomsbury, where both sexes met on equal terms, than it had been in the Society. It was possible only, perhaps, because the Apostles had repudiated customary morals, and convention had not been allowed to stand in the way of knowledge in the Stephen household. In any case, there was complete freedom from moral prejudice in Bloomsbury ; and however much this freedom may have aroused the suspicion of the outside world, there can be no doubt that on the whole it stood Bloomsbury's members in good stead, both as artists and as individuals. It made a fuller examination of human nature possible : Bloomsbury knew how hollow it would be to discuss states of mind and pretend that sex does not exist. And it enabled one to be more honest both with others and with oneself. There is a good deal of indirect testimony in Virginia Woolf's writing to the help that free discussion gave her in her development as an artist ; and other artists in the group must have gained somewhat similar benefits. What this freedom might mean to a woman, who is, or was, more surrounded by the taboos of sex than a man, we may gather from the meditations of the heroine of Virginia Woolf's second novel, to whom the hero has just offered a frank and sincere friendship. The passage is of central importance in the book, giving, as it does, the best clue to the intention of the title, *Night and Day* :

> . . . as in her thought she was accustomed to complete freedom, why should she perpetually apply so different a standard to her behaviour in practice? Why, she reflected, should there be this perpetual disparity between the thought and the action, between the life of solitude and the life of society, this astonishing precipice on one side of which the soul was active and in broad daylight, on the other side of which it was contemplative and dark as night? Was it not possible to step from one to the other, erect, and without essential change? Was this not the chance he offered her—the rare and wonderful chance of friendship?

The offer, of course, is accepted.

Keynes indicates that Bloomsbury's freedom from the restraints of convention was not intellectual only. Moore's Ideal, after all, includes matter as a necessary constituent ; and in Bloomsbury, belief and action, theory and practice, were close companions. " As the years wore on towards 1914," Keynes says, " . . . there was . . . some falling away from the purity of the original doctrine [which at Cambridge had been, ' on the whole, austere and platonic ']. Concentration on moments of communion between a pair of lovers got thoroughly mixed up with the, once rejected, pleasure. The pattern of life would sometimes become no better than a succession of permutations of short sharp superficial ' intrigues ', as we called them." And Keynes speaks of a " thinness " and " brittleness ", which was combined, apparently, with a feeling of superiority, a feeling that one was " in the know " and above the petty conventions and superstitions that cramped the souls of others. This was one side of the matter ; but Bloomsbury also held a belief, which was mystic in its intensity and found philosophic justification in *Principia Ethica*, in the value of love. Roger Fry expresses it in an account of the " tragic story " of a French lady who had been dear to him and had taken her own life. Fry had given her, her relatives told him, the greatest happiness she had known ; and he believed the relationship to have been of great value. The account, written probably in 1924, shortly after the lady's death, is in French that is Anglicized and haltingly punctuated, but that transmits, none the less, the intensity of his feeling. " Par l'amour et seulement par l'amour ", he says, " nous touchons ou croyons toucher à une réalité solide, à un monde peuplé de vraies substances, des âmes, des substances, indestructibles, éternelles, définitives. Dans tout le reste de notre vie règne une rélativité complète." In the expression of a strongly felt experience, Fry has evidently forgotten for a moment his belief, elsewhere expressed, in the spiritual value of art ; but, with this reservation only, there can be no doubt that he enunciates here a faith in love that was shared by others in Bloomsbury. Bloomsbury believed that love gives almost every one glimpses of the Ideal, that though it may have a physical basis, it is a spiritual exercise, and is, as they might say, the most direct way to " reality ". But they knew, or learned, that it is a way that may not be permanently open to one. The wings of love, Clive Bell says, wear out quickly ; love, though " the most intense of all human experiences, . . . is unluckily also the most unstable ". So Bloomsbury turned more and more from love to art ; for art too is a method of communication, a medium for the exchange of states of mind ; but it is less subject to the exigencies and accidents of time and space, less exclusive than love, and a more enduring, if less absolute, way, Bloomsbury believed, to " reality ".

The creation and appreciation of works of art became, in the literal sense of the word, a religion in Bloomsbury. These activities were more and more closely associated in Bloomsbury belief with the good, and they were pursued in a spirit akin to that of the Apostles' unworldly and mystic contemplation of good states of mind. Aesthetic enjoyments were studied and analysed as personal affection had been ; the search for the essential constituents of this class of goods was taken up where Moore had left it :

> I very early became convinced, *says Roger Fry*, that our emotions before works of art were of many kinds and that we failed as a rule to distinguish the nature of the mixture and I set to work by introspection to discover what the different elements of these compound emotions might be and to try

> to get at the most constant unchanging and therefore I suppose fundamental emotion. I found that this " constant " had to do always with the contemplation of form. . . . It also seemed to me that the emotions resulting from the contemplation of form were more universal (less particularized and coloured by the individual history), more profound and more significant spiritually than any of the emotions which had to do with life (the immense effect of music is noteworthy in this respect though of course music may be merely a physiological stimulus). I therefore assume that the contemplation of form is a peculiarly important spiritual exercise.

Clive Bell agrees that art is " a spiritual necessity " ; and he considers art as a religion :

> It is the entanglement of religion in dogma that still keeps the world superficially irreligious. Now, though no religion can escape the binding weeds of dogma, there is one that throws them off more easily and light-heartedly than any other. That religion is art ; for art is a religion. It is an expression of and a means to states of mind as holy as any that men are capable of experiencing ; and it is towards art that modern minds turn, not only for the most perfect expression of transcendent emotion, but for an inspiration by which to live.*

Roger Fry's opinion is similar, if more measured :

> If religions made no claim but what art does—of being *a* possible interpretation without any notion of objective validity all would be well—that's what the artist does—but religions all pretend to do what science tries to do—namely discover *the* one universally valid construction and hence comes all the trouble and hence it is that religions have always obstructed the effort towards more universal validity. . . . I think what I feel is that for the most part religions are so deeply dyed with wish-fulfilment that more than anything else they have stood in the way of the disinterested study (science) and vision (art) of the universe.†

To Roger Fry and Virginia Woolf, at least, among the members of Bloomsbury, vision of the universe was the most important thing of all. Perhaps because he was a painter, Roger Fry believed that this vision was best attained by artists in the

* *Art*, p. 277. † *Fry*, p. 271.

visual arts. He thought that writers were moralists and propagandists ; and " propaganda . . . shuts off the contemplative penetration of life before it has found the finer shades of significance. It simplifies too much." Virginia Woolf believed that the writer too might have, and transmit, his vision :

> The writer, as I think, has the chance to live more than other people in the presence of . . . reality. It is his business to find it and collect it and communicate it to the rest of us. So at least I infer from reading *Lear* or *Emma* or [*A*] *La Recherche du Temps Perdu.* For the reading of these books seems to perform a curious couching operation on the senses ; one sees more intensely afterwards ; the world seems bared of its covering and given an intenser life.*

Lytton Strachey praises Racine in like terms : " One might be tempted to say that [Racine's] art represents the sublimed essence of reality, save that, after all, reality has no degrees." Certainly it was believed in Bloomsbury that it was the artist's business to catch this thing that they sometimes called " reality ", and that " reality " lay behind great works of art. Virginia Woolf's account of Roger Fry's critical method casts more light on this matter, and describes, as well, some of the best characteristics of Bloomsbury's faith in art :

> Pervading all [the writings of Roger Fry] is the character of the critic himself, with its strange mixture of scrupulous sincerity and fervent belief. He will reason to the last moment, and when that limit is reached he will admit honestly : " I feel unable at present to get beyond this vague adumbration." But if reason must stop short, beyond lies reality—if nothing will make him doff his reason, nothing will make him lose his faith. The aesthetic emotion seems to him of supreme importance. But why ?—he cannot say. " One can only say that those who experience it feel it to have a peculiar quality of ' reality ', which makes it a matter of infinite importance in their lives. Any attempt I might make to explain this would probably land me in the depths of mysticism. On the edge of that gulf I stop." But if he stops it is in the attitude of one who looks forward.

And in the meantime, he was sure that art is " a necessary

* *A Room of One's Own*, p. 166.

and culminating function of civilized life . . . indeed the great refining and disinterested activity, without which modern civilization would become a luxurious barbarity." Bloomsbury agreed.

Though there was something mystic in Bloomsbury's faith in the value of art, Bloomsbury had too great a respect for reason not to keep this element in correct perspective. Roger Fry says that mysticism is " the attempt to get rid of mystery ", and so in Bloomsbury in a sense it was.

> To the primitive mind, *Fry explains,* there is no mystery—[the primitive man's] mysticism is so complete and is capable of such indefinite extension that he can always explain every phenomenon. Science can only begin when you accept mystery and then seek to clear it up. But the effect of science is nonetheless always to increase the mystery for with every new avenue that's cleared up you get a fresh vista into the world beyond. To have science one has both to accept mystery and to dislike it enough to try to clear it up which is so complicated a balance that there is no wonder that it's rare, and that nearly everyone is even now at heart a primitive.

This balance Bloomsbury tried to keep by using reason to control mysticism and intuition strictly. We have seen that they rejected convention, tradition, and authority, and distrusted any sort of long-range or universal ethical calculus. They depended on intuition and mysticism, which is the extension of intuition to the unseen, to establish first principles. But they subjected the findings of intuition to a rigorous intellectual examination before they accepted them ; and they were always ready, on sufficient evidence, to revise their opinions. Nor did they believe that a few first principles were sufficient basis for a rational system : rationalism and sensibility, reason and intuition, must go hand in hand, for there were always fresh discoveries to be made. Bloomsbury knew that life is very complicated, but they trusted in the ability of intellect to solve its problems. " It is just the advantage of our highly self-conscious and critical age ", Roger Fry says, " that we can by a deliberate effort change our character. We can fix our minds on those defects which from long-inherited custom have become not only traditional but instinctive, and by so fixing our minds we may ultimately correct them altogether." * Perhaps it is a false faith, but it is the only one that is possible if man is not to relinquish all hope of helping himself.

But to know how to improve one must have a sense of values ; and since authority and convention are not reliable guides, good taste, as Moore had recognized, is indispensable to this sense. Here again, art, that " great refining and disinterested activity ", may help us.

> I cannot doubt the importance of perfecting our sensibility [before works of art], *says Roger Fry,* since art is one of the essential modes of our spiritual life. There are innumerable shades of feeling, overtones of our normal life of which we should never become aware if the artist did not bring them to our consciousness. And the possession of such a sensitive apprehension is one of the marks of a man of culture, a necessary complement to the possession of a well-stored and logical mind.

The civilized man, as Bloomsbury conceived him, trusts reason, and has a sound sense of values that is cultivated by, and evidenced in, a fine appreciation of works of art. From these primary characteristics, in the words of Clive Bell,

> may spring a host of secondaries : a taste for truth and beauty, tolerance, intellectual honesty, fastidiousness, a sense of humour, good manners, curiosity, a dislike of vulgarity, brutality, and over-emphasis, freedom from superstition and prudery, a fearless acceptance of the good things of life, a desire for complete self-expression and for a liberal education, a contempt for utilitarianism and philistinism, in two words —sweetness and light.

This was Bloomsbury's ideal of the gentleman, and of the lady.

These beliefs led Bloomsbury to certain social and political views. The best and most highly civilized society, Bloomsbury had no doubt, would be that in which conditions were most favourable to the creation of works of art, and to the appreciation of art by the masses. All other political and social considerations should be secondary to this, and all acts of good

* *Architectural Heresies,* pp. 46–7.

government should be the means to this end; for art is not only an index of civilization : it is itself a civilizing agency. Artists and critics, therefore, men and women of a fine and disciplined sensibility who are capable of artistic vision, should be given every freedom, both material and spiritual, to follow their own interests, and should be supported by the state if need be. They are the guardians and disseminators of civilization, who will leaven the society in which they live and lead it to the good life. As was their custom, Bloomsbury put this belief into practice. They thought, and they discussed ; they painted, and they wrote. The Hogarth Press was meant to spread civilization ; the Omega Workshops to bring new beauty into everyday life. Roger Fry in his lectures tried to teach people " the art of looking at works of art with the most sensitive and vivid response possible ", to enjoy the life of the spirit, and to exercise " all those human faculties and activities which are over and above our mere existence as living organisms ". Maynard Keynes, amongst numerous other projects with which he was concerned for the assistance and dissemination of the arts, was responsible for the building of the Arts Theatre at Cambridge, which he presented to a Trust to be administered by representatives of the town and University. He was Chairman from 1942 of the wartime " Committee for the Encouragement of Music and the Arts ", and he became the first Chairman of the Arts Council. His broadcast talk on the inauguration of the Arts Council in 1945 could serve as a Bloomsbury manifesto.

> At last, *he says*, the public exchequer has recognized the support and encouragement of the civilizing arts of life as a part of their duty. But we do not intend to socialize this side of social endeavour . . . everyone, I fancy, recognizes that the work of the artist in all its aspects is, of its nature, individual and free, undisciplined, unregimented, uncontrolled. The artist walks where the breath of the spirit blows him. He cannot be told his direction ; he does not know it himself. But he leads the rest of us into fresh pastures and teaches us to love and to enjoy what we often begin by rejecting, enlarging our sensibility and purifying our instincts. The task of an official body is not to teach or to censor, but to give courage, confidence and opportunity.

This for the artist ; and for the public :

> Certainly in every blitzed town in this country one hopes that the local authority will make provision for a central group of buildings for drama and music and art. There could be no better memorial of a war to save the freedom of the spirit of the individual. We look forward to the time when the theatre and the concert-hall and the gallery will be a living element in everyone's upbringing, and regular attendance at the theatre and at concerts a part of organized education.
>
> *　*　*　*　*　*
>
> The purpose of the Arts Council of Great Britain, *Keynes concludes*, is to create an environment, to breed a spirit, to cultivate an opinion, to offer a stimulus to such purpose that the artist and the public can each sustain and live on the other in that union which has occasionally existed in the past at the great ages of a communal civilized life.*

It is evident that Bloomsbury lived according to its beliefs and carried them out as fully as possible in action. And these beliefs were nearly all derived from, or at least, expressed in, *Principia Ethica.* The whole of Bloomsbury's philosophy and action may be regarded, with little exaggeration, as a development of the central passage (which has been quoted once before but will bear quoting again) of Moore's book :

> By far the most valuable things, which we know or can imagine, are certain states of consciousness, which may be roughly described as the pleasures of human intercourse and the enjoyment of beautiful objects. . . . it is only for the sake of these things—in order that as much of them as possible may at some time exist—that anyone can be justified in performing any public or private duty ; . . . they are the *raison d'être* of virtue ; . . . it is they . . . that form the rational ultimate end of human action and the sole criterion of social progress. . . .

It must be asked, therefore, whether Moore's philosophy is valid, and whether the effects that it had upon Bloomsbury were good.†

* *The Listener*, 12 July 1945.

† This discussion considers Moore's philosophy only as it is set forth in *Principia Ethica*, since this is the book which affected Bloomsbury.

Although Moore devotes much of *Principia Ethica* to a refutation of hedonism, yet pleasure creeps into his own philosophy: he rejects hedonism, but decides that aesthetic enjoyment and the pleasures of human intercourse "include *all* the greatest, and *by far* the greatest, goods we can imagine".

Moreover, it appears, from the layman's point of view, that Moore's philosophy is too narrow: that there are states of mind of great value for which he makes no allowance at all. The satisfaction derived from a task well done, the contemplation of a just and well-ordered community, are two such states of mind that may be mentioned. And Moore takes too little account of the life of action. It follows from his ethics that a life occupied wholly with the pleasures of friendship and love and the just appreciation of beautiful objects must be regarded as a life of superlative excellence; though it is doubtful if the "reflective judgment" of many would approve such a life, at least in the present condition of our society. Bloomsbury recognized, in practice if not in theory, this weakness of *Principia Ethica*, for they were all creators or men and women of action. But Moore's philosophy is in this respect academic and cloistered, a university ethic that takes no account of the social and political framework in which the university is set.

In another respect, however, Moore's view is much less restricted and his field of reference is broader: he set out to value things anew at a time when the younger generation thought that a revaluation was badly needed. From the vantage-point of the first decade of this century, at least, Victorian values appeared to be materialistic and utilitarian. And no doubt the Victorians had often laid greater stress on moral obligation than on the natural affections, on propriety than on real personal relations. No doubt too they had often regarded art as a moral exercise. In 1903 it was well worth insisting, as Moore did, that things are themselves, and not something else, and that "duties" and "virtues" should be thoroughly examined before they are accepted as guides to action and criteria of value. Moore swept away many moral encumbrances, and in their place he set an Ideal that was spiritual and unwordly and yet included the appreciation of beautiful material things. It was this work of Moore's that

Bloomsbury admired most. His values seemed to them more real and honest than those of the Victorians ; and his ethics held the promise of a richer and fuller life than the Victorian moral code had allowed.

Nevertheless, Moore was working in the tradition of some of the greatest Victorian thinkers. His philosophy, and Bloomsbury's, in its respect for beauty and truth, is, in a sense, an extension of the thought of Ruskin and Matthew Arnold. And his endeavour to set forth a " scientific ethics ", to remove superstition, taboos, and traditional sanctions from moral philosophy in order to give it a more certain basis, is in line with T. H. Huxley's contribution to the philosophy of science, though it is, of course, much less successful than Huxley's work.

Indeed, Moore had excellent precedent for drawing an analogy between science and ethics. The determined attempt to base ethics on biology, which still continues, began soon after the publication of *The Origin of Species.* T. H. Huxley, who was a leader in this attempt, perhaps accommodated his ethics rather too much to his view of the evolutionary process and of the future decline and fall of our solar system. Samuel Butler and Bernard Shaw, on the other hand, tailored their views of biology and the universe to fit their ethics. But *Principia Ethica* appears to be unaware of these currents of thought that swirled around it. It takes no account of evolution. Moore is from first to last the professional philosopher ; but it was likely because science and ethics were so closely associated when he wrote that he wished to enunciate a " scientific ethics ". And no doubt this desire added to his book's appeal among his contemporaries. To those who did not examine too closely its claims to be scientific, *Principia Ethica* might appear to provide a scientific basis for an idealistic philosophy.

In one instance, however, Moore's analogy between science and ethics is so close that it leads him to doubtful conclusions. The case in point is his conception of " good ". Even if it be granted for a moment that, as Moore claims, " good " is a simple, indefinable object of thought, it is not clear that it is recognized by intuition as yellow is recognized by the eye. Moore's comparison here of a mental faculty and a physical organ is faulty and dangerous. It cannot be demonstrated that we have a mental faculty capable of recognizing goodness with anything like the accuracy of the eye in its recognition of yellowness ; nor can science say, " This is good," as it can say, by measuring the wave-lengths of reflected rays of light, " This is yellow."

Partly in an effort to overcome this difficulty (and partly because he relates beauty and goodness so closely), Moore places what seems to be an undue reliance on taste. Though he believes that reason and knowledge are also guides to what is good, " taste ", in his usage, often seems to mean " intuition of the good ". But even if taste might perform this task, it is doubtful if the taste of many of us is highly enough developed to do so. Indeed, the greatest weakness in Moore's ethics results from his trust in taste. And although one must agree with Moore that we have ultimately to depend on reason, knowledge, and taste, these three together, if we are to know what is good, still it appears that taste, knowledge, and reason are not yet widespread enough to enable many to choose good for themselves without other help. Here again Moore's ethics is influenced by his university environment and takes too little account of the outside world. It might do well enough for Moore and for Bloomsbury, but it would not do for any large part of society.

As a further result of the analogy that Moore draws between the physical and the spiritual in his explanation of the fundamental concept of his ethics, it is inevitable that, struggle as he may against it, his notion of " good " has the appearance of a metaphysical entity—of something as objective as a physical object, though it has no existence in the physical world. Some of the mysticism associated with Moore's philosophy may thus be explained ; and Bloomsbury's conception of reality, which seems somehow to have got behind Moore's description of the Ideal (a comparatively straightforward account of the greatest good imaginable), may come in part from the same source. A new doctrine of the elect, a belief that certain individuals are born gifted with the ability to recognize goodness infallibly, might have been the result of this kind of mysticism ; and there are hints that such a belief was toyed with occasionally in Bloomsbury. On the whole, however, Bloomsbury was little affected by this tendency inherent in their creed. They were protected from it by a genuine concern for the welfare of their fellows, and by their belief that art may help almost any one to recognize what is good.

But Bloomsbury did not believe that art is valuable because they thought that it has a good effect upon conduct and public morality. They believed, as we have seen, that the creation and appreciation of works of art are exercises that heighten one's sensibilities and increase one's awareness of life. But they denied that art is to be judged by its moral value or by its reaction upon life. In short, they could not and would not regard art as a means. All their experience, and the whole of Moore's philosophy, taught them that art is an intrinsic good—" one of the chief organs ", as Roger Fry puts it, " of the spiritual life "—which is valuable in and for itself and needs no other justification. This is the central belief of Bloomsbury's philosophy : a belief in art for art's sake. And, as a group, Bloomsbury's main contribution to twentieth-century thought may prove to have been that they regained a considerable degree of respect for the creed of art for art's sake at a time when it had fallen into disrepute. The reaffirmation of this creed by a group of serious artists and critics, aware, as Bloomsbury was, of the world's social and political problems, has been of value to our age, in which spiritual goods are often enough disregarded, and art is sometimes ordered to debauch itself for the purposes of propaganda.

Without *Principia Ethica* Bloomsbury could not have defended their belief in the intrinsic value of art so confidently as they did. Moore's teaching, in spite of its inadequacies—perhaps even, to some extent, because of them, for it seems often to consider only the needs of cultured intellectuals of the first decades of the twentieth century—served Bloomsbury well. It helped to make Bloomsbury possible by strengthening the Apostles' belief in the value of friendship. It gave Bloomsbury a philosophic basis for their faith in art ; and it left them ethically free to practise this faith as fully as they might.

CHAPTER III

BLOOMSBURY AESTHETICS

WHETHER or not *Principia Ethica* sets forth a sound moral system, there can be no doubt that it affords an excellent starting point for the study of works of art and for the formulation of a theory of aesthetics. Moore's belief that " beautiful " is an " objective predicate of value " is a necessary postulate of aesthetics, for the aesthetician must hold that it is possible, in some degree, to account for tastes. And Moore's definition of " beautiful "—" to say that a thing is beautiful is to say, not indeed that it is *itself* good, but that it is a necessary element in something which is [good] " —at once makes art moral and frees it from morals.* Indeed, since, as we have seen, Moore believes good taste to be very important to morals, and since the appreciation of beauty is the most essential constituent of the good that he describes, a theory of aesthetics is necessary to complete his ethics. Bloomsbury provided this theory. Its principles were set forth by Roger Fry, with some help from Clive Bell. These two were, of course, concerned first of all with the visual arts, but Fry, at least, believed that his theory would hold for the other arts as well, and his aesthetics influenced E. M. Forster, Lytton Strachey, and, especially, Virginia Woolf.

As we might expect from our consideration of Bloomsbury's philosophy, Roger Fry believes that works of art are autonomous. They should be " completely self-consistent, self-supporting and self-contained—constructions which do not stand for something else, but appear to have ultimate value and in that sense to be real ".

Suppose, *he says*, . . . that we are looking at a Sung bowl; we apprehend gradually the shape of the outside contour,

* p. 26.

> the perfect sequence of the curves, and the subtle modifications of a certain type of curve which it shows ; we also feel the relation of the concave curves of the inside to the outside contour ; we realize that the precise thickness of the walls is consistent with the particular kind of matter of which it is made, its appearance of density and resistance ; and finally we recognize, perhaps, how satisfactory for the display of all these plastic qualities are the colour and the dull lustre of the glaze. Now while we are thus occupied there comes to us, I think, a feeling of purpose ; we feel that all these sensually logical conformities are the outcome of a particular feeling, or of what, for want of a better word, we call an idea ; and we may even say that the pot is the expression of an idea in the artist's mind. Whether we are right or not in making this deduction, I believe it nearly always occurs in such aesthetic apprehension of an object of art. But in all this no element of curiosity, no reference to actual life, comes in ; our apprehension is unconditioned by considerations of space or time ; it is irrelevant to us to know whether the bowl was made seven hundred years ago in China, or in New York yesterday.

Again, speaking of Courbet's painting of *La Blonde Endormie*, Fry says, " This plastic unity holds us entirely within its own limits. . . . Everything here is so transmuted into plastic terms and finds therein so clear a justification that we are not impelled to go beyond them or to fill them out, as it were, by thinking of the model who posed more than half a century ago to M. Courbet in Paris, or of any other woman whatever." While travelling in Spain one summer, Fry found himself peculiarly impressed by the interior designs of the churches, and he asked himself why this should be so. He decided that it was because, in entering a building, he was able to do physically what in other works of art he could only do spiritually :

> Every work of art which one enjoys with complete aesthetic apprehension becomes for the time being the spirit's universe. No conscious reference to anything outside the work of art is relevant ; we are absorbed and englobed within it. But in the interior of a great building this spiritual isolation is happily symbolized and as it were incarnated by our being physically shut off from all other life. It is as though when

> one looked at a picture one could enter into its space corporally as well as ideally.

Fry is sure that "art has its own specific function, that it conveys experiences which are *sui generis*, not to be defined or valued by anything outside—experiences which have immense, but quite inexplicable, value to those who are sensitive to them. . . ."

Art, then, according to Fry, is distinct from ordinary life, and to appreciate rightly a work of art we must, while contemplating it, cut ourselves off completely from the affairs of life. In everyday life, Fry says, we do not look at our surroundings. We see things and react instinctively to them or label them for practical use; we take enough visual note of them to recognize them quickly—we understand their appearances in shorthand, as it were; but beyond this superficial knowledge we are ignorant of what they look like; so it may happen that when an artist pauses before an object and, after looking disinterestedly at it, reproduces faithfully what he sees, we are indignant, and say that his picture is humbug. Vision, in life, often causes emotion and results in some appropriate instinctive action. If we see a wild bull in a field we experience the emotion of fear, and, unless we sternly control our instinctive reaction, we flee. We have little knowledge of our visual and emotional experiences in this situation, for the whole of our attention is occupied by the action required to escape from the bull. But we may later relive the experience in memory, or "in imagination". "In the imaginative life", Fry says, "no . . . action is necessary, and, therefore, the whole consciousness may be focussed upon the perceptive and the emotional aspects of the experience. In this way we get, in the imaginative life, a different set of values, and a different kind of perception." We see things that we do not see in everyday life, and our emotions "though they are likely to be weaker than those of ordinary life, are presented more clearly to the consciousness".

Fry believes that art is "the chief organ of the imaginative life", and that it is therefore free of the instinctive, practical, and moral demands of actual life. "Art . . . is an expression and a stimulus of [the] imaginative life, which is separated from actual life by the absence of responsive action. Now this responsive action implies in actual life moral responsibility. In art we have no such moral responsibility—it presents a life freed from the binding necessities of our actual existence." Whereas morality appreciates emotion only if it results in appropriate action, art appreciates emotion for itself alone : art is, in fact, " an expression of emotions regarded as ends in themselves ".

Just as art depends upon cutting off the ordinary responses of everyday life, so it arouses, Fry says, a response of its own, which he calls the " aesthetic state of mind " or the " aesthetic emotion ". He believes that

> whenever we make a favourable aesthetic judgment—whenever we say that a work of art is beautiful—we imply by that statement that it is of such a kind as to produce in us a certain positive response, and . . . if we compare in our minds responses experienced in turn in face of different works of art of the most diverse kinds—as, for instance, architectural, pictorial, musical or literary—we recognize that our state of mind in each case has been of a similar kind, we see in all these different experiences a general similarity in our attitude, in the pattern of our mental disposition, and . . . the attitude common to all these experiences is peculiar to them and is clearly distinguishable from our mental attitude in other experiences.

It is distinguished by a free, " pure and as it were disembodied functioning of the spirit ".

It has not been commonly recognized that all the various kinds of art, literature and sculpture, as well as architecture and music, call forth the same special response, Fry says, because many structures which claim to be works of art do not provoke this response at all, while many others, which do provoke it, evoke responses of ordinary life as well. Perhaps no absolutely " pure " work of art, no work which arouses the aesthetic emotion only, exists ; and the " impurities " in works of art may arouse other emotions which tend to obscure the aesthetic emotion. Furthermore, even the purely aesthetic characteristics of a work of art may become associated for us with things " in the outside world " and so arouse feelings which blur the aesthetic emotion. *God Save the Queen* has some aesthetic characteristics, but their existence has been overlaid and obscured for us because this piece of music is associated in our minds with many other things, with feelings of patriotism and memories of solemn occasions. It is little wonder then, especially since the aesthetic sensibilities of most men are not highly developed, that the aesthetic emotion has not been widely recognized as a distinct and peculiar response to works of art.

But, Fry says, if we will compare a number of our experiences before works of art of different kinds, we will find that one characteristic is common to them all : " in all cases our reaction to works of art is a reaction to a relation ". This is the distinguishing mark of the aesthetic emotion. It " is not an emotion about sensations, however necessary a responsive sensualism may be for our apprehension of aesthetic wholes. Nor is it an emotion about objects or persons or events." It is an emotion about the relations that are seen to exist between these things in a work of art. If we asked only for sensations from art we could have an art based upon the sense of smell. We have no such art, Fry says, because we do not know how to relate smells to one another in aesthetic wholes. Again, if art merely titillated our senses we would always prefer ornate architecture. In fact we usually prefer simpler kinds. Sensations, objects, persons, events are the counters that the artist borrows from life and builds into a structure that is significant, not because of the counters, but because of the relations that the artist has established between them—relations which have nothing at all to do with the everyday meaning-for-life of the things represented. It is these relations that arouse the aesthetic emotion, which is, then, an emotion about form, and depends upon " a special orientation of the consciousness, and, above all, a special focusing of the attention " in the contemplation of a work of art.

It comes as no surprise to learn that Fry has little respect for artists who engross themselves in " childish problems of photographic representation ". Such artists, he believes, are not really concerned with the business of art at all. They are not making structures which are autonomous and have significance and value in and for themselves ; they are merely giving us reports about other things. " It will be noticed ", he says, " that the full value of the representational element almost always depends on a reference to something outside the actual work of art "—so life is brought in ; its values are substituted for aesthetic values ; and the work arouses the instinctive, moral, and practical responses of life rather than the aesthetic emotion. The artist who aims only at realism of the photographic sort seldom penetrates beneath the surface of appearances : his vision is not an artist's vision at all, but the perfunctory, commonplace vision of the man in the street. Some of Courbet's work illustrates this failing, Fry says :

> [In many of his poorer pictures] Courbet has taken the view of reality which is almost that of the unsophisticated man. That is to say, the accent is mainly on those details which give the idea of verisimilitude, those marks which separate the object, which enable us, as it were, to read its label and say, that is a dog, a stone, a tree. It happens that these accents are not those which have the greatest visual significance, partly because, by isolating things one from another, they tend to break up that unity of the whole-appearance which is essential to a work of art. In fact, in pictures like these Courbet was creating the formula for the popular Academy and Salon pictures of succeeding generations with its insistence on a trivial verisimilitude. He was using his powers not to interpret experience but to state what things look like to the casual, uncontemplative regard which we use in the practical affairs of life.

In contrast to those paintings of Courbet's to which this criticism applies is Turner's *Petworth Interior* as described by Clive Bell :

> For Turner the ballroom at Petworth had ceased to be a room full of furniture possessing a value for life, and had become a congeries of luminous masses possessing aesthetic value of their own ; life, in the common sense of the word, had been eliminated. The subject is seen purely in terms of art.

For the artist, Bell concludes, " the labels on things are

essential, . . . all that matters is their significance as forms and colours ".

Fry, and Bell, believe that the artist who is preoccupied with exact representation is likely to neglect the form of his work. While he strives to represent every detail of an object with photographic accuracy he may forget to relate the object to other objects on his canvas : he is unable to see the wood for the trees, and his painting will lack those significant relations that are the essence of art. Realistic representation, they believe, may be either good or bad. It is good if it subserves the formal requirements of the painting—if it is an integral part of the design. If it exists for itself alone it ruins art. For this reason, a ready facility in representation, if it leads to ostentation of skill, may be " even more fatal " to the artist, Fry says, than " downright incapacity ". Fry and Bell's main concern is to dispose once and for all of the belief that the purpose of painting and drawing is mere imitation.

> For, I suppose, *Fry says*, it must be admitted that if imitation is the sole purpose of the graphic arts, it is surprising that the works of such arts are ever looked upon as more than curiosities, or ingenious toys, are ever taken seriously by grown-up people. Moreover, it will be surprising that they have no recognizable affinity with other arts, such as music or architecture, in which the imitation of actual objects is a negligible quantity.

But drawing and painting, and, one should add, sculpture, are related to the other arts : their purpose is something other, and much greater, than imitation.

Creation in these arts begins, certainly, with vision—vision of a special and penetrating kind.* The artist pierces beneath the trivial, obvious characteristics of his subject, beneath the surface appearance, to seize, perhaps, the profound, internal, plastic rhythms of a human head, or to come to an intimate, intuitive understanding of animal life. He expresses what he sees in forms that are clearly related to one another ; and this is something more, Fry says, than a " realistic " account, given by the anxious delineation of wrinkles or fur, of what the man or the animal " looks like ".

* See p. 36.

Just as the artist, through vision, comes to a closer understanding of living things, so too he finds a new significance in objects and in landscapes—in fact, in all that surrounds him. Perhaps the way people take their place in the space of a room has at moments a special meaning for him ; perhaps he finds a new value in a particular view of a building, and so tells us something of " the universal and fundamental meanings of our physical situation in a spatial world ". Or, like Cézanne, the artist whom Fry admires most, he may discover in landscapes an " underlying structural unity which answer[s] a profound demand of the spirit ". His business is to discover universal principles beneath the particular forms that confront him.

The experiences that the artist has before nature have an emotional and spiritual meaning so important to him that he feels them to be more real and permanent, Fry says, than anything else he knows. He wishes to hold them and examine them until he has exactly appreciated their quality, and to do this he creates a work of art which externalizes his experience for him and, at the same time, communicates it to others. The work may ostensibly be a painting of a saucepan or a view of Honfleur, but it is really an account of the spiritual experience that Chardin, or Corot, or whoever the artist was, had one day at Honfleur or in his kitchen. Art—art of all kinds—Fry says, is " the only means by which human beings can communicate to each other the quality and quiddity of their experiences ". This, together with its closely related power to help us to understand the universe, is its *raison d'être.*

Art, then, complements science. The scientist asks what happened and why it happened. If the solution turned blue at a certain point, why did it turn blue ? The artist is interested in his experience of the event. What did the sensation of blue feel like ? What was its emotional significance ? And as the scientist discovers " causal harmonies " in nature, so the artist discovers emotional harmonies. Furthermore, the scientist and the artist are equally concerned with reality. It is true, Fry says, that there is a pseudo-art which " is mainly preoccupied with creating a fantasy-world in which the fulfilment of wishes is realized ". But real art " is concerned with the contemplation of formal relations "—with "the distinctive aesthetic activity". This activity is "as much detached from the instinctive life as any human activity that we know; [it is] in that respect on a par with science".

The artist is "obsessed by the love of truth and beauty". Far from indulging in wish-fulfilment, he expresses "the highest aspirations and the deepest aversions of which human nature is capable". Fry would no doubt question Shelley's belief that the artist is a legislator; he would agree, however, that he is a prophet, "the articulate soul", as he says, "of mankind". But if art is in this sense communal, it is also highly individualized. It is the direct expression of "impassioned thought and feeling", and conveys to us the artist's state of mind—a very complicated and valuable thing which has at least as much to do with the subconscious as with the conscious.

> What the artist brings to the particular experience, *Fry says*, is much more than his immediate consciousness of it. His reaction is coloured by all sorts of subconscious associations and feelings, of which he is naturally unaware, but which affect profoundly the form taken by the work of art and which have the power to stir up corresponding subconscious feelings in the spectator. It is this fact that the work of art acts as a transmitting medium between the artist's subconscious nature and our own that gives it its peculiar, and as we say "magic", power over us. It is magic because the effect on our feelings often far transcends what we can explain by our conscious experience.

Art is not greatly affected, Fry believes, by "the most primitive and fundamental part" of the subconscious, by "those emotional patterns which are laid down in the first years of infancy". It is affected much more by

> those parts of the subconscious being which have filtered down through our conscious life and consist of the abiding residue of innumerable sensations, feelings, predilections, aspirations, desires, judgments, in fact all those things which constitute our spiritual life.
>
> The mere length of time that an artist has lived has then inevitably an influence on the work of art. When we look at

> the late works of Titian or Rembrandt we cannot help feeling the pressure of a massive and rich experience which leaks out, as it were, through the ostensible image presented to us, whatever it may be.

Perhaps it is something similar that gives the paintings of Cézanne their " grave authority ". They seem to be " revelation[s] of the highest importance ", and, like all great works of art, they add something to our experience.

The artist's problem is to relate his state of mind, his intuition about things, to his vision in a coherent, self-contained work of art—to express, in fact, feeling in form. To do this he disengages and arranges in a system of his own certain elements of natural form—mass, space, light and shade, colour, and, perhaps, inclined planes—which, because they are so intimately and universally connected with our physical existence, have, Fry says, emotional effects upon us. As these elements take their place in the painting they are impregnated, as it were, by the artist's feeling, which finds expression not only in the way that he arranges them, but also in the rhythm of his line and in the whole texture and tone of his work. This process, the process of incorporating the data of vision in a " spiritual whole ", Fry calls " interpretation " or " transformation ".* He tells us a good deal about it in his description of the artist's " creative vision ":

> Almost any turn of the kaleidoscope of nature may set up in the artist this detached and impassioned vision, and, as he contemplates the particular field of vision, the (aesthetically) chaotic and accidental conjunction of forms and colours begins to crystallize into a harmony ; and as this harmony becomes clear to the artist, his actual vision becomes distorted by the emphasis of the rhythm which has been set up within him. Certain relations of directions of line become for him full of meaning ; he apprehends them no longer casually or merely curiously, but passionately, and these lines begin to be so stressed and stand out so clearly from the rest that he sees them far more distinctly than he did at first. Similarly colours,

* " By the word ' Transformations '," Fry says, " I wish to suggest all those various transmutations which forms undergo in becoming parts of esthetic constructions " (*Transformations*, Preface).

> which in nature have almost always a certain vagueness and elusiveness, become so definite and clear to him, owing to their now necessary relation to other colours, that if he chooses to paint his vision he can state them positively and definitely. In such a creative vision the objects as such tend to disappear, to lose their separate unities, and to take their places as so many bits in the whole mosaic of vision. The texture of the whole field of vision becomes so close that the coherence of the separate patches of tone and colour within each object is no stronger than the coherence with every other tone and colour throughout the field.
>
> In such circumstances the greatest object of art becomes of no more significance than any casual piece of matter ; a man's head is no more and no less important than a pumpkin, or, rather, these things may be so or not according to the rhythm that obsesses the artist and crystallizes his vision.

So the artist, in order to express himself, presents natural objects in such a way that the emotional elements inherent in them " are elicited with an order and appropriateness altogether beyond what Nature herself provides ". While keeping always in close touch with nature so that he will not neglect its infinite variety and its emotional significance, he builds a world which has a significance and " reality " of its own because it suggests " the inevitability and orderliness of our intellectual life ", and expresses the artist's feeling and intuition. Since the artist's " visible harmonies " clothe his emotion, they speak directly to the mind, and (if the work is great) " the deepest emotions . . . exude, like a perfume . . . from form considered in its pure essence and without reference to associated ideas ".

This quality Fry and Bell believe to be the " purely aesthetic quality " that exists, in greater or less degree, in all works of visual art. Bell calls it " significant form "; Fry adopts Bell's term.* " I think we are all agreed ", Fry says, " that we mean by significant form something other than agreeable arrangements of form, harmonious patterns, and the like. We feel that *a work which possesses it is the outcome of an endeavour to*

* Fry described significant form without giving it that name in 1909. (See " An Essay in Aesthetics ", reprinted in *Vision and Design*.) Bell introduced the term in 1914 in his book *Art*.

express an idea rather than to create a pleasing object." * It is the idea, the state of mind, behind a work of art that gives it its significance, and causes us to feel, if the idea is well expressed, that everything is in its appointed place, that not a colour could be changed or an object disturbed. This is what Fry means when he speaks of emotional harmonies in art or of the emotional unity of a work of art.

> In a work of art, *he says*, what gives us the special aesthetic pleasure is the recognition that the matter of which the work is made has been, as it were, penetrated and impregnated by an idea with which we associate ourselves. We see something akin to our spiritual being penetrating and moulding matter. The fullest pleasure occurs when, having realized the general idea, the main relations of the members of a building, the main composition of a picture, the disposition of the limbs of a sculptured figure, we are able to consider the interior relations of the parts, proceeding always from larger to smaller relations, without finding any point at which the informing idea breaks down, until we come to the matter of the work, the grain of the stone or the canvas. It is important that we should feel at every point this impregnation of matter by the idea. The presence at any stage in this process of any mechanically precise statement of form causes a gap ; we feel that a link in the chain that binds matter to the informing spirit is broken. . . . What we desire in a work of art is the feeling of an inexhaustible wealth of significant relations which lie ready to hand for our investigation. We feel at once that a work of art has an idea that is intelligible, and that it is infinite in its possibilities. It is this feeling of infinity which gives to the embodied idea its organic completeness and uniqueness, and distinguishes it from a geometrical figure which is finite and capable of repetition.

Abstract art, then, will not do. (Fry disagrees with Bell on this point.) Art comes somewhere between photography and geometry, and expresses, as neither photographs nor geometric figures do, its creator's sensibility. Thus Cézanne's " interpretation of natural form always seems to imply that he is at once thinking in terms of extremely simple geometrical forms, and allowing those to be infinitely and infinitesimally modified at each point by his visual sensations ". The geometrical

* My italics.

forms served him as a "kind of intellectual scaffolding" which brought order to his vision of nature. He did not push geometric construction to its logical extreme, as some of his followers, the Cubists, have done. But his paintings are more "solidly articulated" than those of the Impressionists, who were more interested, Fry believes, in discovering nature's diversity (much of which they revealed to Cézanne) than in building solid pictorial structures.

It follows that the greatest art will reveal to us the most complex, surprising, and yet, absolutely inevitable relationships. We are startled as we contemplate it, but we feel at once that it is right, that nothing within it could be otherwise than it is.

The painter has perhaps more means at his disposal than any other visual artist for creating significant relations. He may use colour harmonies, or relate patches of light or shade to one another. Certain directions of line and dispositions of space may become meaningful in his work. The way that he situates volumes in space may, perhaps, because of the three-dimensional relations of these plastic forms to one another, and the sense of solidity, volume, and weight that they give us, be the most moving and significant element in his work. And all the elements in his work may be bound together by flow and continuity of line, rhythm of design, and unity of texture. When a master uses these means successfully to express a spiritual experience, his picture reaches to the depths of the imaginative life.

Fry believes that the visual artist can reach these depths only if he is true to the medium of his art and abjures psychological and dramatic suggestions in his work in order to concentrate wholly upon visual relations. He thinks that "the spaceless world of psychological entities and relations" has its own proper medium in literature; and he approves the suggestion, put forth by a French friend of his, Charles Mauron, in an essay that Fry translated in 1926 for the Hogarth Press, that there are in literature "psychological volumes" which correspond to the plastic volumes of visual art and between which the literary artist establishes significant relations. Mauron seems to owe much of his aesthetics to

Fry, but his application of it to literature is interesting, especially when seen in relation to the art of Virginia Woolf, which will be considered in a later chapter. By a " psychological volume " Mauron means a sensation, an emotion, a state of mind—any psychological reality that the writer may describe. " The simplest entities that literary art admits ", he says, " are states of mind, or perhaps one ought to say moments of the spirit. They are what we are given at a moment. . . . The external reality blends [in the mind] with the interior, or rather there is only one reality. Those divisions, useful enough for the life of action, into external objects, sensation, and sentiment,* are abolished. [This] is the central principal of all lyric poetry." The state of mind described by lyric poetry need not, Mauron says, be sentimental. The effect of a poem on the sadness of death, for example, is not due to its expression of the emotion of sadness : " sadness is only the pretext, the poem is not sadness ; it is something different ; a new direct experience of the spirit (not of the ear) ; an unforeseen mixture of sensations, ideas, memories, and emotions which find themselves miraculously in unison, and compose, one knows not how, a single whole. This choice and this situation of common psychological values (as the painter does spatial value), herein lies the poet's art." " The reality of a poem is in the spiritual shape that it offers us." Besides " moments of the spirit ", literature uses, Mauron says, characters, situations, and their complexes. The relations that are established between these elements are, he believes, the vital principle of literary art.

However, Fry was interested in the aesthetics of literature long before he translated Mauron's essay. We have seen that he believes that the same emotion is aroused by all works of art. He would agree with Clive Bell that " the supreme quality in [all] art is formal ; it has to do with order, sequence, movement and shape ". In 1913 he wrote to Lowes Dickinson that he was " attacking poetry to understand painting ". He frequently discussed aesthetics with Virginia Woolf, and these discussions were so equally concerned with literature and painting that he spoke to her in terms that might apply to

* One questions Fry's translation here.

either art. " I know ", he writes of Rilke in a letter which Virginia Woolf quotes in her biography of Fry and which appears to be to Virginia Woolf herself—" I know that [Rilke's] the other side of a big dividing line between our ways of taking things. You like the overtones to sound more than the main note. I want a construction made out of solid blocks first and then let the overtones modify it. . . . It's something like that isn't it ? " Fry regretted (elsewhere) that " comparatively few novelists have ever conceived of the novel as a single perfectly organic aesthetic whole ". " Why ", he complained to Virginia Woolf, as she tells us, " was there no English novelist who took his art seriously ? Why were they all engrossed in childish problems of photographic representation ? " He believed that the Post-Impressionist painters had shown the way by returning to " the ideas of formal design which had been almost lost sight of in the fervid pursuit of naturalistic representation ". He hoped that writers would follow their example. " But he never found time ", Virginia Woolf says, " to work out his theory of the influence of Post-Impressionism upon literature, and his attempts to found a broad-sheet, profusely illustrated, to be sold for one penny at all the bookstalls, in which the two arts should work out the new theories side by side, failed—the money difficulty floored even him."

Fry quotes with approval A. C. Bradley's statement that poetry's nature " is to be not a part, nor yet a copy, of the real world (as we commonly understand that phrase), but to be a world by itself, independent, complete, autonomous ". " This passage at least suggests to us ", Fry says, " that the purpose of literature is the creation of structures which have for us the feeling of reality, and that these structures are self-contained, self-sufficing, and not to be valued by their references to what lies outside." We see, then, that Fry's objection to naturalistic representation in literature is precisely the same as his objection to it in painting : literature,* like painting

* " Literature " must be understood to mean in this chapter, unless otherwise specified, poetry, drama, the novel, the short story, and certain kinds of biography—works of literary art, in the aesthetic sense of the word, as opposed to writing of a purely informatory, expository, or persuasive kind.

and all art, is not a copy of the outside world. Fry says that this truth was brought home to him at a cinema as he watched, in a news-reel, a difficult work of rescue from a ship wrecked just off the coast of Portugal. Here was a dangerous situation from real life, highly charged with emotion. It should have been, Fry reflected, at least as significant as great tragic drama.

> But, in point of fact, *he says*, the experience, though it was far more acute and poignant, was recognizably distinct [from great tragedy] and was judged at once as of far less value and significance than the experience of a great tragic drama. And it became evident to me that the essential of great tragedy was not the emotional intensity of the events portrayed, but the vivid sense of the inevitability of their unfolding, the significance of the curve of crescendo and diminuendo which their sequence describes, together with all the myriad subsidiary evocations which, at each point, poetic language can bring in to give fullness and density to the whole organic unity.

The essential of the novel, Fry believes, is something very similar. Novels that endure, he says,

> depend . . . for their effect upon a peculiar detachment from the instinctive life. . . . they note the inexorable sequence in life of cause and effect, they mark the total indifference of fate to all human desires, and they endeavour to derive precisely from that inexorability of fate . . . the pleasure which consists in the recognition of *inevitable sequences* ; a pleasure which . . . corresponds to the pleasure . . . in marking the inevitable sequence of the notes in a tune ; in fact again a pleasure derived from the contemplation of the relations and correspondences of form.

In a letter (to Virginia Woolf?) Fry notes, as Maupassant did before him, that we accept chance in life more readily than we do in art :

> I think there's a real reason why novelists should be very sparing in violent action—it increases the element of mere chance [which] one knows the author can turn either way he likes—whereas if you remain within the ordinary course of civilized life the situation whatever it is develops with some appearance at least of logical inevitability—of course chance is

> always at work but its effects are minimized and one's sense of inevitable sequences is heightened.

And in a note on André Rouveyre's caricature of *La Duchesse d'Uzès douairière,* Fry hints that biography may attain an emotional unity akin to that of a drawing. Rouveyre's caricature, he says, " puts us at once in the position that we might be in had we read a brilliant short biography of such a person, and had had time for all the facts to fade from our memory and leave only the quintessence, the psychological experience, as it were, which gives significance to the facts ".

But if literature achieves a unity of this sort, it does so, as Fry implies, only when seen in retrospect. Like those Chinese paintings on long rolls of silk, whose unity, Fry tells us, " depends upon the forms being presented to us in such a sequence that each successive element is felt to have a fundamental and harmonious relation with that which preceded it ", or like music, literature's unity is a " successive unity ". So, at any rate, with a special emphasis upon its analogies with music, E. M. Forster sees the novel.

Forster deplores one aspect of the novel's kinship to the painting on a roll of silk. He wishes that it did not appeal to the primitive, unaesthetic, unintelligent desire to know what happens next, to know what is on the next wind of silk. The story, which Forster believes to be the backbone of the novel, relates the life of the characters in time ; it is a narrative of events arranged strictly according to their time sequence : and then . . ., and then . . ., and then . . . If only the novelist were free to drop the story altogether, and to give his whole attention to the values that we attach to things—values that are quite removed from the life in time. But, Forster says, the novel cannot express values alone : without the time sequence that the story provides it would be unintelligible. " Yes—oh dear yes—", he says, " the novel tells a story. That is the fundamental aspect without which it could not exist. That is the highest factor common to all novels, and I wish that it was not so, that it could be something different —melody, or perception of the truth, not this low atavistic form."

Yet, in spite of the story, Forster believes that the novel is, or should be, an aesthetic whole. Though it gathers its material from life, from the " outside " world, and though words, which are often used only to give information, are its medium, yet the novel (like the poem, which shares these characteristics) stands apart, both from its author and from life, as a created object : it is self-sufficient, or, as Forster puts it, it " tends towards a condition of anonymity ": it " wants " not to be signed because it is alive. For words, Forster says, may do more than convey information ; they may create an atmosphere and build a world which seems " more real and solid " than the world in which we live from day to day. He gives the classic example of the *Ancient Mariner* : " When we are reading the *Ancient Mariner*, or remembering it intensely, common knowledge disappears and uncommon knowledge takes its place. We have entered a universe that only answers to its own laws, supports itself, internally coheres, and has a new standard of truth." * The poem, the novel—all art is " based on an integrity in man's nature which lies deeper than moral integrity ".

Form and the artist's individual vision are as important in literature, Forster believes, as in any of the arts. The artist looks about him at the muddle and incompleteness of the world. He understands it, passionately (to understand, Forster says, is our deepest desire) ; he feels things that have not been felt before—or, if they have been felt, have not been expressed ; and he expresses his feeling and interprets the disappointing scene before him by giving it (and here form comes in) a coherence and beauty and completeness that life itself does not possess. Art, and perhaps mystic contemplation, alone, Forster says, make any meaning out of life.

Forster agrees with Fry that the artist's feeling and understanding, his intuition about things, is based as much upon the subconscious mind as upon the conscious. In the creative state, he says, " a man is taken out of himself. He lets down

* Bloomsbury's aesthetics has not a little in common with Coleridge's and with Wordsworth's. Coleridge's belief that a poem should contain within itself the reason that it is so and not otherwise and so cause us willingly to suspend our disbelief, and Wordsworth's belief that the poet recollects emotion in tranquillity, are shared by Bloomsbury (see p. 88).

as it were a bucket into his subconscious, and draws up something which is normally beyond his reach. He mixes this thing with his normal experiences, and out of the mixture he makes a work of art. . . . When the [creative] process is over, when the picture or symphony or lyric or novel (or whatever it is) is complete, the artist, looking back on it, will wonder how on earth he did it. And indeed he did not do it on earth." * Forster's conjectures as to the nature of the subconscious, it will be seen, lean more towards mysticism than Fry's. "The lower personality", he says, "is a very queer affair. . . . There is something general about it. Although it is inside S. T. Coleridge, it cannot be labelled with his name. It has something in common with all other deeper personalities, and the mystic will assert that the common quality is God, and that here, in the obscure recesses of our being, we near the gates of the Divine. It is in any case the force that makes for anonymity." ". . . there are no names down there," Forster continues, "no personality as we understand personality, no marrying or giving in marriage. What there is down there—ah, that is another enquiry, and may the clergymen and the scientists pursue it more successfully in the future than they have in the past." † At any rate, because writers draw their inspiration from the subconscious they have all through history felt more or less the same while writing. (This is why Forster, in his *Aspects of the Novel*, envisions the novelists of all ages writing their novels at the same time in a round room.) And if their works are successful, their readers will feel, as they read,

* J. L. Lowes' *Road to Xanadu*, an account of how the *Ancient Mariner* and *Kubla Khan* grew in Coleridge's subconscious, lends support to Bloomsbury's belief that the process of artistic creation takes place largely in the subconscious. "As Professor John Livingston Lowes has shown," Forster says, "many fragments of Coleridge's day-to-day reading are embedded in *Kubla Khan*, but the poem itself belongs to another world, which he was seldom to record" (*Two Cheers for Democracy*, p. 123).

† Speaking of Arnold Toynbee's *Study of History*, Forster says: "Professor Toynbee comes to the conclusion that [civilizations] rise and fall in accord with a religious law, and that except the Lord build the house their labour is but lost that build it; or, if you prefer the language of Freud to that of the Old Testament, that the conscious must be satisfactorily based on the subconscious" (*Two Cheers for Democracy*, p. 283).

somewhat the same as the authors felt while they wrote. " I would not suggest ", Forster says, " that our comprehension of the fine arts [in which Forster includes the novel] is or should be of a nature of a mystic union. But, as in mysticism, we enter an unusual state, and we can only enter it through love. Putting it more prosaically, we cannot understand music unless we desire to hear it. And so we return to the earth."

And once back on earth we remember that the artist expresses his feeling and intuition in a work of art. So Beethoven's Fifth Symphony (as Helen Schlegel, one of Forster's characters, interprets it in *Howards End*) tells us that panic and emptiness always threaten the splendour of life and often overwhelm it. As the third movement of the symphony begins goblins steal across the universe and observe that there is no splendour or heroism in the world—nothing but panic and emptiness. Beethoven scatters them, and they are replaced by heroes and heroism, glory and splendour. But the goblins return ; the glorious world is dissolved ; and again there is panic and emptiness in the universe. Beethoven makes it all right in the end. He scatters the goblins for the second time ; he brings back " the gusts of splendour, the heroism, the youth, the magnificence of life and of death "—and so his symphony has a completeness that life can never have. But we know that the goblins are there and that they may return : Beethoven has told us so plainly enough. The Fifth Symphony has given us his view of the universe.

Music may be " untrammelled and untainted " by reference to things outside itself ; * the novel, a humbler art, must gather its material directly from life. Yet music, Forster says, is the novel's " nearest parallel ". So, " after one has read *War and Peace* for a bit, great chords begin to sound, and we cannot say exactly what struck them ". The novelist, of course, may give us his views of life and the universe by direct comment. (Forster thinks this is permissible.) But his deeper, more

* Since Forster believes that it is the nature of music to express the composer's feeling and intuition, he would not regard, for example, the interpretation just given of Beethoven's Fifth Symphony as outside reference. The interpretation, of course, only approximates what Beethoven tells us.

significant intuitions, the intuitions that come from the subconscious, are expressed in other ways. Thus, Forster believes, the great chords that sound in *War and Peace* come mainly from Tolstoy's feeling for, and sense of, space : " they come from the immense area of Russia, over which episodes and characters have been scattered, from the sum-total of bridges and frozen rivers, forests, roads, gardens, fields, which accumulate grandeur and sonority after we have passed them ". The novelist's creative imagination accretes round the things of life until they are transformed and become part of a whole. Perhaps he chooses places and space, as Tolstoy does ; perhaps, as in Virginia Woolf's *To the Lighthouse*, one of the things from life is a " great dish of Boeuf en Daube which forms the centre of [a] dinner of union . . . round which all that section of the book coheres " ; or perhaps it is an orange such as D'Annunzio's characters discuss in his drama *The Dead City*, an orange which, passing " as a tangible presence behind the veil of their prose ", lends " importance to their fate, like the peaches and pears surrounding a Crivelli Madonna ". Forster describes this process, the process of creating literature from the things of life, as he believes it is evidenced in the works of Virginia Woolf :

> [Virginia Woolf] liked receiving sensations—sights, sounds, tastes—passing them through her mind, where they encountered theories and memories, and then bringing them out again, through a pen, on to a bit of paper. Now began the higher delights of authorship. For these pen-marks on paper were only the prelude to writing, little more than marks on a wall. They had to be combined, arranged, emphasized here, eliminated there, new relationships had to be generated, new pen-marks born, until out of the interactions, something, one thing, one, arose. This one thing, whether it was a novel or an essay or a short story or a biography or a private paper to be read to her friends, was, if it was successful, itself analogous to a sensation. Although it was so complex and intellectual, although it might be large and heavy with facts, it was akin to the very simple things which had started it off, to the sights, sounds, tastes. It could be best described as we describe them. For it was not about something. It was something.

So, Forster says, he sometimes sees her work gleaming as a row of little silver cups. " 'These trophies', the inscription runs, 'were won by the mind from matter, its enemy and its friend.' "

Each novelist has, no doubt, his or her own method of composition which differs from the methods of others. But the differences are individual; the underlying principle is the same; for all novelists, to be successful, must build self-contained structures that have internal harmony. And though, Forster says, to explain how words build worlds that are real and solid "would be to explain the secret of the universe"; though the tools of criticism break as soon as they encounter living tissue—yet it is possible, he believes, to discover some of the ways in which the novelist, in spite of the story, in spite of the novel's close attachment to life, makes his book an aesthetic whole. He conducts the search in his *Aspects of the Novel.*

As the novelist turns from the story to the characters of his book, Forster says, "a new emphasis enters his voice: emphasis upon value". He no longer appeals merely to our curiosity, but also to our intelligence and imagination; we need not ask what happens next, but to whom does it happen. The novelist has begun to move out on the tether that ties him to the story, and to escape, so far as he can, from the tyranny of time. And though he depends upon life for his material, he creates something that is not life—or that is life within the pages of a book. He pays little attention to birth and to the early years of childhood; his characters "come into the world more like parcels than human beings". On the other hand, he may, with the help of imagination, describe death more fully than witnesses of a death, relying only on the evidence of their senses, could describe it. He treats food and sleep perfunctorily: his characters seldom want either. But he gives an inordinate amount of attention to love and to human aspirations, and his characters are tirelessly occupied with their relationships with one another. No; on the whole, Forster says, people in fiction are not at all like us or like our friends—yet, they are real. When they are well done they are, in a sense, more real than our friends, for the novelist knows all about them, about their secret inner life as well as the life that reveals itself in action, and he may explain them completely to us if he chooses. So, because the creator and the narrator of the characters in fiction are one, we get a reality of a kind that we can never get in life. " Were we equipped for hyperbole," Forster says, " we might exclaim at this point : ' If God could tell the story of the Universe, the Universe would become fictitious.' For this is the principle involved." And once more art completes life :

> For human intercourse, as soon as we look at it for its own sake and not as a social adjunct, is seen to be haunted by a spectre. We cannot understand each other, except in a rough and ready way ; we cannot reveal ourselves, even when we want to ; what we call intimacy is only a makeshift ; perfect knowledge is an illusion. But in the novel we can know people perfectly, and, apart from the general pleasure of reading, we can find here a compensation for their dimness in life. In this direction fiction is truer than history, because it goes beyond the evidence, and each of us knows from his own experience that there is something beyond the evidence, and even if the novelist has not got it correctly, well—he has tried. . . .
>
> And that is why novels, even when they are about wicked people, can solace us ; they suggest a more comprehensible and thus a more manageable human race, they give us the illusion of perspicacity and power.

In this respect, even the characters that Forster calls " flat ", characters who are created around a single idea or quality, who are always the same, and who can be summed up in one sentence, make an important contribution to the reality of a novel. " All of us, even the sophisticated, yearn for permanence, and to the unsophisticated permanence is the chief excuse for a work of art. We all want books to endure, to be refuges, and their inhabitants always to be the same, and flat characters tend to justify themselves on this account."

But the novel should have " round " characters as well as flat—characters who have the incalculability of life about them, who are capable, or seem to be capable, of taking affairs into their own hands at times, and who surprise us in a convincing way. They must not be given control of the book, however, for their author has to adjust them to one another and adapt them to the story, the plot, the atmosphere of his novel, and so on. While keeping his eyes always upon human nature, he must relate it to the structure of his book as a whole : this is the novelist's major problem, Forster believes. We are reminded of Fry's belief that the artist should bring order to his vision of nature by relating it to a sort of intellectual scaffolding.

The main intellectual scaffolding of the novel, according to Forster, is the plot. It is a narrative of events in which the emphasis falls not, as in the story, upon the time-sequence, but upon causality ; it is " the novel in its logical intellectual aspect ". With it the characters fight the hardest : they wish to go their own way, and the plot would make them conform to a preconceived plan. Here indeed is a dilemma for the novelist, for he wishes everything in the novel to be founded on human nature, to develop from character and be, in that sense, intentional ; and, at the same time, he wants his book to convey a sense of inevitability, to have that air of predetermination which may come from the plot because he has planned it beforehand. He cannot quite have it both ways. Free will and fatality struggle within his creation, and he is continually negotiating between character and plot. When he is most successful incident springs out of character and, having occurred, alters character to connect people and events closely. But he cannot work this mechanism as freely as the dramatist may, because by no means all the emotions of the secret life, which the novelist reveals to us much more fully than the dramatist, result in action. Though this increases the difficulty for the novelist, it perhaps gives him the opportunity of creating a richer organic whole. At any rate, if his plot is good we will feel, as we watch it develop, much as we do as we discover significant relations in a painting. It will surprise us, and yet convince us that it is inevitable.

> Over it, *says Forster,* as it unfolds, will hover the memory of the reader . . . and will constantly rearrange and reconsider, seeing new clues, new chains of cause and effect, and the final sense . . . will not be of clues or chains, but of something

aesthetically compact, something which might have been shown by the novelist straight away, only if he had shown it straight away it would never have become beautiful. We come up against beauty here—for the first time in our enquiry: beauty at which a novelist should never aim, though he fails if he does not achieve it.

The novelist may, if he wishes, substitute fantasy for, or perhaps add it to, plot, and then, if he is successful, he achieves beauty in another way, in a way that is more akin to music, insofar, at least, as it is less closely attached to life. The fantasist, Forster says, asks us to pay something extra, to accept things that could not possibly happen. He may, as Forster himself does in his experiments with fantasy in the short story, deal with Fauns and Pans and Dryads; he may draw his material from " all that is mediaeval this side of the grave ". There is a sense of mythology in his work, but he is not, as a rule, overtly serious. Another kind of novelist who also deals in myth is serious—very serious. He does not glance about as the fantasist does; his face is towards unity. " His theme is the universe, or something universal ", though he may not say anything directly about the universe. He has " gone ' off ' more completely than the fantasist, he is in a remoter emotional state while he composes ". Forster calls his work " prophecy ".

Prophecy, when it occurs at all, Forster says, is an addition to plot and people and other aspects of the novel. It is an accent in the novelist's voice; it is like song. We find ourselves in the ordinary world of fiction, but somehow that world " reaches back "; the people and things in it have a universal significance. Forster illustrates prophecy with an excerpt from Dostoevsky's novel *The Brothers Karamazov*. Mitya Karamazov, who is spiritually but not technically guilty, is being accused of the murder of his father. While a protocol is drawn up, he lies down on a large chest and immediately falls asleep. He dreams he is somewhere on the Steppes, where he had once been stationed, driving with a peasant through sleet and snow. A village has been half destroyed by fire; and the women are standing near the road, begging. One, tall and thin and wasted, with breasts dried up, holds a baby, who cries and holds out its bare arms, its fists blue with cold.

"Why are they crying? Why are they crying?" Mitya asked as they dashed gaily by.

"It's the babe," answered the driver. "The babe weeping."

And Mitya was struck by his saying, in his peasant way, "the babe", and he liked the peasant calling it "the babe". There seemed more pity in it.

"But why is it weeping?" Mitya persisted stupidly. "Why are its little arms bare? Why don't they wrap it up?"

"Why, they're poor people, burnt out. They've no bread. They're begging because they've been burnt out."

"No, no," Mitya, as it were, still did not understand. "Tell me, why is it those poor mothers stand there? Why are people poor? Why is the babe poor? Why is the steppe barren? Why don't they hug each other and kiss? Why don't they sing songs of joy? Why are they so dark from black misery? Why don't they feed the babe?"

And he felt that, though his questions were unreasonable and senseless, yet he wanted to ask just that, and he had to ask it just in that way. And he felt that a passion of pity, such as he had never known before, was rising in his heart, that he wanted to cry, that he wanted to do something for them all, so that the babe should weep no more, so that the dark-faced dried-up mother should not weep, that no one should shed tears again from that moment, and he wanted to do it at once, at once, regardless of all obstacles, with all the recklessness of the Karamazovs. . . . And his heart glowed, and he struggled forward towards the light, and he longed to live, to go on and on, towards the new beckoning light, and to hasten, hasten, now, at once!

And then he is wakened to hear the protocol and to sign it. As he rises he finds that some one has put a pillow under his head as he slept.

"Who put that pillow under my head? Who was so kind?" he cried, with a sort of ecstatic gratitude, and tears in his voice, as though some great kindness had been shown him.

He never found out who this kind man was, perhaps one of the peasant witnesses, or Nikolay Parfenovitch's little secretary had compassionately thought to put a pillow under his head, but his whole soul was quivering with tears. He went to the table and said he would sign whatever they liked.

" I've had a good dream, gentlemen," he said in a strange voice, with a new light, as of joy, in his face.

In this passage we have as clear a glimpse as we are likely to get of the working, of which Fry and Forster speak, of the subconscious in artistic creation. Perhaps this is so because Mitya's subconscious is, in a sense, Dostoevsky's, and so the artist's mind is externalized for us for a moment. Mitya's feeling of compassion that would embrace with joy the whole world to comfort it, is Dostoevsky's feeling. It is akin to that feeling of spiritual well-being, of passionate understanding and exhilaration which we all have at times, but which has its roots so deep in the subconscious that we cannot say why we feel as we do. Here we see the feeling coming into being and can identify some of the elements which, at any rate, externalize it for Dostoevsky—elements both spiritual and material, elements from the conscious and from the subconscious mind. In the conscious mind are the room in which the investigation is held, the people in it, and the emotions aroused by the accusation of parricide. In the subconscious is the dream that seems utterly remote from the real scene, and yet is profoundly related to it. The feeling of compassion, which is really a spiritual readjustment, begins and grows as Mitya sees the women and the child, is pleased that the peasant calls the child " the babe ", and asks questions and experiences an emotion which reach far beyond the group of women, out into the universe. The subconscious and the conscious are adjusted to one another, or, rather, the subconscious flows over into the conscious. The pillow, the peasant witnesses, Nikolay Parfenovitch's little secretary, might be a part of Mitya's dream. " He went to the table and said he would sign whatever they liked. ' I've had a good dream, gentlemen,' he said. . . ."

To be a person in Dostoevsky, Forster says, " is to join up with all the other people far back ". " In Dostoevsky the characters and situations always stand for more than themselves ; infinity attends them, though they remain individuals they expand to embrace it and summon it to embrace them ; one can apply to them the saying of St. Catherine of Siena that God is in the soul and the soul is in God as the sea is in the fish and the fish is in the sea ". Recalling Forster's remarks on the subconscious, we may paraphrase : " The subconscious is in us and we are in the subconscious as the sea is in the fish and the fish is in the sea." Through the subconscious (" the force that makes for anonymity ") we reach out to others and share something with them.

Of course, what we have to share will not always be joy and well-being. Herman Melville, who is also, Forster says, a prophet, " reaches straight back into the universal, to a blackness and sadness so transcending our own that they are indistinguishable from glory ". They transcend Melville's characters and Melville himself. " What one notices in him is that his apprehensions are free from personal worry, so that we become bigger not smaller after sharing them. He has not got that tiresome little receptacle, a conscience "—which belongs, no doubt, to the surface personality and so will not do for the prophet. If Dostoevsky had been impeded by his conscience Mitya might have stopped to comfort the women instead of going on to embrace humanity—Forster does not say this, but it is something of the sort that he means.

Forster notes in passing the intermittent realism with which the prophet occasionally illumines the objects of common sense more vividly than they are ever seen in life. D. H. Lawrence, he says, " irradiat[es] nature from within, so that every colour has a glow and every form a distinctness which could not otherwise be obtained ". The process is somewhat similar, perhaps, to the way in which Corot embodies a spiritual experience in a view of Honfleur, or Chardin expresses himself in a painting of a saucepan.

When Forster sees such possibilities for the novel, it is not surprising to find that he does not believe it should be cut to a rigid pattern, to a formal plan conceived in the abstract before flesh and blood is allowed to come in. Forster's objection to rigid pattern in the novel is analogous to Fry's dislike of Cubism in painting. " Pattern ", Forster says, " springs mainly from the plot (though it is not the plot), and the characters and all else in the novel contribute to it." Sometimes it is so definite that it enables us to sum the shape of the novel up in a simple image. Thus *Thaïs*, by Anatole France, Forster says, is the shape of an hour-glass. Paphnuce the saintly ascetic meets Thaïs the courtesan. As a result of their meeting, she devotes her life to religion and he is damned. The shape of Henry James' *TheAmbassadors* is the same, though here Paris gleams at the centre of the hour-glass. Strether and Chad, like Thaïs and Paphnuce, change places. Strether, the middle-aged American who is sent to bring Chad home from Paris, is captured by the city. Chad, who had been enamoured with Paris, returns to his family's manufacturing business in the United States. After examining these novels, Forster decides that rigid pattern cannot be combined with the immense richness of the material that life provides. " It shuts the doors on life ", and though it may be beautiful, its beauty is tyrannous and demands too many sacrifices. The verdict of most readers will be, Forster says, " Beautifully done, but not worth doing ".

However, Forster believes there is another way by which beauty, in addition to the beauty of the plot, may be introduced into the novel. Turning once more to music to consider its analogies with fiction, he speaks of " rhythm ". He says there are two kinds of rhythm, illustrated in the symphony by the phrases to which we can all tap (the " diddidy dum ", for example, with which Beethoven's Fifth Symphony begins), and the " rhythm " of the symphony as a whole—due mainly to the relation between its movements—which some people can hear but no one can tap to. In fiction rhythm of the first kind is illustrated, Forster says, in Proust's *A la Recherche du Temps Perdu* by the " little phrase " in the music of Vinteuil which appears and reappears at intervals throughout the novel. Vinteuil is an obscure provincial organist who gains posthumous fame from his music. After his death his daughter and a Lesbian friend desecrate his photograph. We do not hear of him again for a hundred pages, when a phrase in a violin sonata catches the ear of another character, Swann, and enters his life. It attends his love affair, and then his jealousy when the affair is ended. We learn, with Swann, that the sonata is by Vinteuil. " That seems all. The little phrase crosses the book again and again, but as an echo, a memory ; we like to encounter it, but it has no binding power." Then, hundreds and hundreds of pages on, another work of Vinteuil's is performed, a septet.* The hero, Marcel, who knew Vinteuil's town in childhood, listens. " Suddenly for him and for the reader too, the little phrase of the sonata recurs—half heard, changed, but giving complete orientation, so that he is back in the country of his childhood with the knowledge that it belongs to the unknown [universe which the sonata describes]."

> The little phrase, *Forster says*, has a life of its own, unconnected with the lives of its auditors, as with the life of the man who composed it. It is almost an actor, but not quite, and that " not quite " means that its power has gone towards stitching Proust's book together from the inside, and towards the establishment of beauty and the ravishing of the reader's memory. There are times when the little phrase—from its gloomy inception, through the sonata, into the sextet—means everything to the reader. There are times when it means nothing and is forgotten, and this seems to me the function of rhythm in fiction; not to be there all the time like a pattern, but by its lovely waxing and waning to fill us with surprise and freshness and hope.

Rhythm, as Forster conceives it, is not at all, it will be seen, like the Wagnerian *leitmotif*, though it may be distantly related to it.† It does not announce characters, or situations, or anything at all. It has a life of its own; it is organic: this is the great advantage it has over pattern. It must not be allowed to harden into a symbol, Forster says. Though it should always be clearly recognizable, it should grow and change. It may be defined as " repetition plus variation ". It is particularly suited to contribute to the " successive unity " of a novel.

This rhythm, we remember, is analogous to the easy rhythm —the rhythm of a phrase—of the symphony. Can the greater

* Forster calls it a sextet in *Aspects of the Novel*, a septet in an essay, " The Raison d'Etre of Criticism in the Arts ", in *Two Cheers for Democracy*. It is a septet, though which it is matters little.

† Peter Burra, in an excellent essay on Forster's art, which is reprinted in the Everyman edition of *A Passage to India*, disagrees with this view. What Mr. Forster calls rhythm, Burra maintains, " might more aptly be termed *leit-motif* ".

" rhythm ", the rhythm of the symphony as a whole, be achieved in the novel? " Is there any effect in novels comparable to the effect of the Fifth Symphony as a whole, where, when the orchestra stops, we hear something that has never actually been played? The opening movement, the andante, and the trio-scherzo-trio-finale-trio-finale that composes the third block, all enter the mind at once, and extend one another into a common entity." In *Aspects of the Novel* Forster says that he cannot find in the novel any analogy to this great rhythm, though there is something like it in *War and Peace*, in which the great chords begin to sound, and every item, when we have finished reading, leads a larger existence than it did as we read.* He thinks, however, that such an analogy may be possible, since fiction is likely to find its nearest parallel in music.

> Music, though it does not employ human beings, though it is governed by intricate laws, nevertheless does offer in its final expression a type of beauty which fiction might achieve in its own way. Expansion. That is the idea the novelist must cling to. Not completion. Not rounding off but opening out. When the symphony is over we feel that the notes and tunes composing it have been liberated, they have found in the rhythm of the whole their individual freedom.

It may seem a far remove from the novel, an imaginative art analogous to music and to painting, to the biography,

* In *Aspects of the Novel* Forster says that *A la Recherche du Temps Perdu*, the conclusion of which had not been published when he wrote, " is chaotic, ill constructed, it has and will have no external shape; and yet it hangs together because it is stitched internally, because it contains rhythms "—of the easy kind, of course. He changed his mind about the structure of the book after he read its conclusion. *A la Recherche du Temps Perdu*, he says, " is superior [to *War and Peace*] as an artistic achievement; it is full of echoes, exquisite reminders, intelligent parallels, which delight the attentive reader, and at the end, and not until the end, he realizes that those echoes and parallels occur as it were inside a gigantic cathedral; that the book, which seemed as we read it so rambling, has an architectural unity and pre-ordained form " (*Two Cheers for Democracy*, p. 229).

In the Rede Lecture on Virginia Woolf (1941) Forster notes, apparently with approval, that *To the Lighthouse* has been called a novel in sonata form.

which must always be tied to the life of an individual. But in a man's life may not phrases and themes repeat themselves, with many variations, so that to the perceptive observer who sees the life in retrospect it may appear as a work of art? And may not the biographer stand in some sense to his subject as a creator? He must, in any case, recreate him and give him life within the pages of a book; and the fatal certainty of history, the inalterable past, may give to his biography (if he uses his opportunities to the full) the inevitability and permanence of art. For the biographer knows from the beginning the course of his subject's life, even better than the novelist knows beforehand the *dénouement* of his plot.

This is Lytton Strachey's view of biography. Biography begins for Strachey with a lively interest in people and an equally vital concern for art. Human beings, he says, " have a value which is independent of any temporal processes—which is eternal, and must be felt for its own sake "; and he believes that " it is perhaps as difficult to write a good life as to live one ". A good life can be written only if the biographer submits himself to a severe artistic discipline. Thus Strachey agrees with Fry and Forster that the artist must keep his eye upon the infinite variety of nature, and, at the same time, relate nature's variety to an intellectual scaffolding.

Form, Strachey believes, is built around the biographer's point of view and is made possible by omission, selection, and summary. It is, after all, as impossible for the biographer to give us the whole of a man's life as it is for the novelist to transcribe life literally in his pages. " Every art ", Strachey says, " is based upon a selection ": " omission is the beginning of all art ". He applauds Henri Beyle's method in the novel, which is, he says, " the classical method—the method of selection, of omission, of unification, with the object of creating a central impression of supreme reality ". Beyle was also extraordinarily good at making a summary, and the ability to do this is " perhaps the best test of a man's intelligence ". How much to leave out and to compress should be decided for the biographer partly by his purpose and partly by his subject; it is, Strachey says, " largely a question of scale "; and the aim of the biographer should be to exclude " everything that is redundant and nothing that is significant"—redundant and significant, that is to say, to his biography, which is controlled by his point of view. Under any circumstances, pointed brevity is much better than an "ill-digested" mass of material. Strachey's purpose in his own biographies, as he makes clear in the Preface to *Eminent Victorians*, is to create a work of art from materials drawn from the amorphous, two-volume, "Standard" biographies of the Victorians.

To create a work of art in biography or history (for Strachey believes that history too is an art, and he sees it going always hand in hand with biography) imagination is required, no less than in painting, music, and fiction. Speaking of a weakness in Hume's histories, Strachey says that "the virtues of a metaphysician are the vices of a historian. A generalized, colourless, unimaginative view of things is admirable when one is considering the law of causality, but one needs something else if one has to describe Queen Elizabeth." The historian and the biographer must, willy-nilly, reconstruct: their information is not abundant enough to enable them to do otherwise. They had better, Strachey believes, reconstruct in an imaginative way.

> We shall never know, *he says,* exactly what Henry the Second said—in some uncouth dialect of French or English—in his final exasperation against Thomas of Canterbury; but it was certainly something about "a set of fools and cowards", and "vengeance", and "an upstart clerk". Hume, however, preferred to describe the scene as follows: "The King himself being vehemently agitated, burst forth with an exclamation against his servants, whose want of zeal, he said, had so long left him exposed to the enterprises of that ungrateful and imperious prelate." Such phrasing, in conjunction with the Middle Ages, is comic. The more modern centuries seem to provide a more appropriate field for urbanity, aloofness and common sense.

And since the biographer must reconstruct, we may suppose Strachey to have reasoned, he is wisest to do so, so to speak, from the inner life outwards. When his knowledge is incomplete he is least likely to go wrong if he uses this method, for of all things men's souls change least from generation to generation, and through our knowledge of the inner life we may be as close, in some respects, to Henry II and Thomas of Canterbury as we are to our contemporaries. At any rate, this is the method that Strachey used in his biographies. Like Racine, whom he admired most, perhaps, of all the French writers, he " selected the things of the spirit for the material of [his] work ". He shared completely Fry and Forster's, and, as we will see, Virginia Woolf's, interest in the secret life and the subconscious. And, having declared biography to be an art, he tried to make it as real as fiction by going beyond the evidence, by standing on tip-toe to try to see behind the known facts. For each of us knows (as Forster has said) that there is something—a secret life—behind the life that reveals itself in action.

In the work of omission, selection, and imaginative reconstruction, style, Strachey believes, is the biographer's best instrument. " The style once fixed, everything else followed," he says, speaking of the composition of Gibbon's *Decline and Fall*. Style conditions the whole treatment of the material, the whole " scope and nature " of the work ; it determines what will be excluded and how much will be brought in. It may, like Sir Thomas Browne's style, be full of detail, " rich with the spoils of the real world " ; or, like Racine's, it may rigorously suppress detail and eschew the *mot rare*. Strachey admires both styles. Browne's effects, he says, are " curiously analogous " to the effects of the " magnificent brushwork " of Rubens or Velazquez. And as Roger Fry, we have seen, speaks of " the pressure of a massive and rich experience " which is felt behind the late works of Titian and Rembrandt, so Strachey says that Browne's art " matured with himself ", and that " a long and calm experience of life seems, indeed, to be the background from which his most amazing sentences start out into being ". Racine's style, so different, can none the less " conjure up out of a few expressions of the vaguest import a sense of complete and intimate reality ". When he is most himself, " he writes with a directness which is indeed naked, and his sentences, refined to the utmost point of significance, flash out like swords, stroke upon stroke, swift, certain, irresistible ".

These two styles, in other respects so dissimilar, have one quality in common which all good style must share. In both there is a close texture, a co-ordination of the parts, and the whole material is fused into organic life. Strachey's comments on style are not unlike Fry's description of significant form. And he dislikes " mere ornament " which exists independently of matter, as much as Fry dislikes ostentation of skill in realistic representation. He says that the first Earl of Lytton was endowed with " a fatal facility " as a writer, and (speaking of Carlyle) that " the truth is that it is almost as fatal to have too much genius as too little ". These statements correspond exactly to Fry's belief, which has been referred to previously, that facility in representation may be even more fatal than downright incapacity. Strachey prefers the *cliché* and a " touch of colloquialism " to obscurity and pompous rhetoric ; and even grammatical clumsiness, if the writer is sincere and has something to express, may be better, he thinks, than artificial correctness. But the qualities to be aimed at are " those fine qualities of strength and clarity which form alone can give ". And, apart from the work of great masters with the power of Browne and Racine, the style that Strachey admires most is perhaps one such as Diderot's in *Le Neveu de Rameau* : " The writing, with its ease, its vigour, its colour, and its rapidity, might almost be taken for what, in fact, it purports to be—conversation put into print, were it not for the magical perfection of its form. Never did a style combine more absolutely the movement of life with the serenity of art. Every sentence is exciting and every sentence is beautiful."

Strachey has much more to say about style than about the architecture of a book as a whole ; and this is not surprising, since the biographer finds the main outline of his book in his subject's life. For this reason the choice of a subject is of great importance ; Strachey tells us that his choice of subjects for *Eminent Victorians* was determined by " motives of convenience and of art ". Having chosen, it is the biographer's business " to lay bare the facts of the case, as he understands them ". " That is what I have aimed at ", Strachey says, " in [*Eminent Victorians*]—to lay bare the facts of some cases, as I understand them, dispassionately, impartially, and without ulterior intentions. To quote the words of a Master—'Je n'impose rien ; je ne propose rien : j'expose.' " But what the biographer sees in his subject's life, how he understands the case, will depend upon his point of view ; and a point of view he must have, he must " maintain his own freedom of spirit ", or he will be unable to order his material into a work of art, and his book will resemble " nothing so much as a . . . heap of sawdust ". The biographer's point of view, like the creative vision of the painter which Fry has described, brings order out of chaos. And it is expressed by style. This is why Strachey believes that the style once fixed all else follows, and that the form of the biography or history as a whole grows out of style.*

We see, then, that Strachey believes that a biography should have significant form, and that, to borrow Forster's phraseology, it should tend towards anonymity—that it should be detached and impartial, and stand up by itself. His ideal biographer, we may conjecture, would accomplish in his work something similar to Sir Thomas Browne's achievement in the last chapter of *Urn Burial.* " Browne never states in so many words ", Strachey says, " what his own feelings towards the universe actually are. He speaks of everything but that ; and yet, with triumphant art, he manages to convey into our minds an indelible impression of the vast and comprehensive grandeur of his soul." The deepest emotions exude, in fact, as Fry puts it, like a perfume from form. And if the biographer's emotions are not so profound and comprehensive as Browne's, or if his art does not give them the same scope for expression, yet his feelings towards the universe control his point of view, and the biography, as a whole, should express that.

Forster, we have seen, sees the novel unfolding in time as a successive unity. Strachey was obliged to look upon the biography in somewhat the same way, since it tells the story of a life, but his conception of the point of view and of the

* Of the composition of Gibbon's *Decline and Fall*, Strachey says : " By the penetrating influence of style—automatically, inevitably—lucidity, balance and precision were everywhere introduced ; and the miracle of order was established over the chaos of a thousand years " (*Biographical Essays*, p. 144).

pervasive influence of style led him to regard it, in some respects, as a rather more static whole than Forster's ideal novel. Virginia Woolf sees the novel as something rather like a picture. Literature, she wrote in 1925, is " now undoubtedly . . . under the dominion of painting ". And demonstrating, perhaps, that we sometimes discover in a novel what we are looking for, she finds in *A la Recherche du Temps Perdu* an affinity with painting, as Forster found an affinity with music. " Were all modern paintings to be destroyed," she says, " a critic of the twenty-fifth century would be able to deduce from the works of Proust alone the existence of Matisse, Cézanne, Derain, and Picasso ; he would be able to say with those books before him that painters of the highest originality and power must be covering canvas after canvas, squeezing tube after tube, in the room next door."

Virginia Woolf's comments on the novel begin with a protest against " materialism " akin to Fry and Bell's protest against over-indulgence in realistic representation in painting. In both her much-quoted essays " Modern Fiction " (1919) and *Mr. Bennett and Mrs. Brown* (1924), she criticizes the Edwardian novelists Wells, Bennett, and Galsworthy. All three of them, she says, " have laid an enormous stress upon the fabric of things ". They are concerned with the body rather than the spirit, and so they may be called " materialists ". She imagines them travelling in the same compartment from Richmond to Waterloo with a small, anxious, threadbare old lady, Mrs. Brown ; and she records, so to speak, their literary reactions. Wells, she says, would describe a Utopia " where these musty railway carriages and fusty old women do not exist ". Galsworthy, " burning with indignation, stuffed with information, arraigning civilization ", would expatiate upon the wrongs of our economy. He " would only see in Mrs. Brown a pot broken on the wheel and thrown into the corner ". Bennett would describe the railway carriage, the cushions and their buttons, the advertisements, Mrs. Brown's clothes—everything, in fact, but Mrs. Brown herself. The Edwardian's books are reports of other things. " They leave one with so strange a feeling of incompleteness and dissatisfaction. In order to complete them it seems necessary to do something—

to join a society, or, more desperately, to write a cheque." *

Virginia Woolf does not believe that realism is always bad, any more than Fry believes that realistic representation may not be used to subserve the aesthetic demands of the picture. Turgenev, she says, combines "the fact and the vision" in his novels. Defoe, professing to aim at truth of fact, achieves truth of insight. In *Robinson Crusoe* "by reiterating that nothing but a plain earthenware pot stands in the foreground, [he] persuades us to see remote islands and the solitudes of the human soul. By believing fixedly in the solidity of the pot and its earthiness, he has subdued every other element to his design; he has roped the whole universe into harmony." Like Chardin, he has embodied a spiritual experience in what appears at first sight to be only a work of realistic representation.

But the Edwardians, Virginia Woolf believes, have done nothing of the sort. Their vision is superficial; they have entirely neglected Mrs. Brown, who is "human nature", "the spirit we live by, life itself". A Russian novelist would do better: he would "pierce through the flesh" to reveal the soul. And even if we have not his vision, we all know Mrs. Brown. "She is just as visible to you who remain silent as to us who tell stories about her," Virginia Woolf told the Cambridge

* Often, in these two essays, it might be Fry speaking. Here is Fry, for example, on an Egyptian portrait head of the Saiti period:

"Its realism is of the external and descriptive kind. The artist relies on the sharp delineation of minute particulars rather than on the profound internal rhythms. . . . We note that anxious insistence on sharp details of surface, on wrinkles of the skin and isolating contours, which distinguish such a descriptive conception. These are the things which an artist whose sensibility has enabled him to penetrate below the surface takes as it were in his stride, but which the descriptive artist clings to with desperate tenacity, since they are the only facts really grasped by his superficial vision" (*Last Lectures*, p. 63).

And on J. S. Sargent's portrait of the Duke of Portland—a passage that Virginia Woolf quotes in *Roger Fry*:

"First the collie dog which the Duke caresses has one lock of very white hair; secondly the Duke's boots are so polished that they glitter; thirdly the Duke's collar is very large and very stiffly starched; fourthly the Duke was when he stood for his portrait sunburnt. After that we might come to the Duke himself."

"Mr. Sargent", Fry says, "is simply a précis writer of appearances" (*Roger Fry*, pp. 110–11).

audience to whom she read *Mr. Bennett and Mrs. Brown.* " In the course of your daily life this past week you have had far stranger and more interesting experiences than the one I have tried to describe. You have overheard scraps of talk that filled you with amazement. You have gone to bed at night bewildered by the complexity of your feelings. In one day thousands of ideas have coursed through your brains ; thousands of emotions have met, collided, and disappeared in astonishing disorder." All this, " life itself ", or rather, we should say, the inner life, is Mrs. Brown. The inner life is individual to each of us, yet common to us all. As Dostoevsky knew, Virginia Woolf says, " Whoever you are, you are the vessel of this perplexed liquid, this cloudy, yeasty, precious stuff, the soul. The soul is not restrained by barriers. It overflows, it floods, it mingles with the souls of others." We are reminded of Forster's remark that to be a person in Dostoevsky " is to join up with all the other people far back ", and that " one can apply to his characters the saying of St. Catherine of Siena that God is in the soul and the soul is in God as the sea is in the fish and the fish is in the sea ". But Virginia Woolf's conception is more personal, less intellectualized than Forster's : " Mrs. Brown and I were left alone together. She sat in her corner opposite, very clean, very small, rather queer, and suffering intensely. The impression she made was overwhelming. It came pouring out like a draught, like a smell of burning." Mrs. Brown, Virginia Woolf says, must be the novelist's subject—the twentieth-century novelist's subject, at any rate. He must determine " never, never to desert Mrs. Brown ". " ' The proper stuff of fiction ' ", she says, " does not exist "—and then, with characteristic inconsistency, she tells us what it is—" everything is the proper stuff of fiction, every feeling, every thought ; every quality of brain and spirit is drawn upon ; no perception comes amiss ".*

* Virginia Woolf undoubtedly owes a great deal to the Russian writers of the last century—to Dostoevsky, Tolstoi, Tchekov, and Turgenev. She says that the soul " is the chief character in Russian fiction " (*The Common Reader*, p. 225) ; and in her essay on " Modern Fiction " she says : " English fiction can hardly avoid some mention of the Russian influence, and if the Russians are mentioned one runs the risk of feeling that to

Virginia Woolf is as dissatisfied with the method of the Edwardians as with their material, with the form of their work as with its content— though the two, of course, cannot be strictly separated. Arnold Bennett, she says, is an excellent workman. " He can make a book so well constructed and solid in its craftmanship that it is difficult for the most exacting of critics to see through what chink or crevice decay can creep in. There is not so much as a draught between the frames of the windows, or a crack in the boards. And yet—if life should refuse to live there ? " She is protesting, as Fry and Forster protest, against an art which has, she believes, become dry and hard because it is too far removed from life. " Is life like this ? " she asks. " Must novels be like this ? "

> Look within and life, it seems, is very far from being " like this ". Examine for a moment an ordinary mind on an ordinary day. The mind receives a myriad of impressions—trivial, fantastic, evanescent, or engraved with the sharpness of steel. From all sides they come, an incessant shower of innumerable atoms ; and as they fall, as they shape themselves into the life of Monday or Tuesday, the accent falls differently from of old ; the moment of importance came not here but there ; so that, if a writer were a free man and not a slave, if he could write what he chose, not what he must, if he could base his work upon his own feeling and not upon convention, there would be no plot, no comedy, no tragedy, no love interest or catastrophe in the accepted style, and perhaps not a single button sewn on as the Bond Street tailors would have it. Life is not a series of gig lamps symmetrically arranged ; life is a luminous halo, a semi-transparent envelope surrounding us from the beginning of consciousness to the end. Is it not the task of the novelist to convey this varying, this unknown and uncircumscribed spirit, whatever aberration or complexity it may display, with as little mixture of the alien and external as possible ?

" Let us record the atoms as they fall upon the mind in the

write of any fiction save theirs is waste of time." In 1922 and 1923 she helped S. S. Koteliansky translate Dostoevsky's *Stavrogin's Confession*, A. B. Goldenveizer's *Talks with Tolstoi*, and *Tolstoi's Love Letters*. Strachey, as well as Forster, was equally an admirer of the Russians, especially of Dostoevsky. (See Strachey's essay " A Russian Humorist " in *Literary Essays*.)

order in which they fall," she continues, " let us trace the pattern, however disconnected and incoherent in appearance, which each sight or incident scores upon the consciousness." And, elsewhere, she objects to Percy Lubbock's conception of form, as he describes it in *The Craft of Fiction* ; " whenever Mr. Lubbock talks of form it is as if something were interposed between us and the book as we know it. We feel the presence of an alien substance which requires to be visualized imposing itself upon emotions which we feel naturally, and name simply, and range in final order by feeling their right relations to each other."

Yet Virginia Woolf believes, as the last sentence may indicate, that novels should have form, or perhaps we should say internal order, since she objects to the use of a word that may cause us to visualize the novel as a shape. She cannot herself avoid using it, however. " The thirty-two chapters of a novel ", she says, " . . . are an attempt to make something as formed and controlled as a building " ; Henry James's novels (which she regards more highly than Forster does) all have upon them " the final seal . . . of artistic form, which, as it imposes its stamp, sets apart the object thus consecrated and makes it no longer part of ourselves." She holds fully Fry and Forster's belief that a novel, like all works of art, should be self-contained, that it should come from the deepest part of its author's being, should be more real than life, and should at once surprise us and convince us that it is true. In fact, her aesthetics is more severe than Forster's (she says that his attitude in *Aspects of the Novel* is " unaesthetic ") ; and, at the same time, she is determined, as he is not, to reveal every nuance that she can explore of the inner life. In this task the old conventions of novel-writing, she believes, will not do. Devoted as she was both to life and art, her problem before the new discoveries of psychology and the sensitiveness of her own mind was precisely parallel to Cézanne's, as Fry describes it, before the " new revelations " of the Impressionist painters : " How, without missing the infinity of nature, the complexity and richness of its vibrations, how to build that solidly and articulately co-ordinated unity in which the spirit can rest satisfied."

The transformations which impressions undergo in becoming part of a novel are not easily traced, and can never be traced completely ; but Virginia Woolf gives us some hints of how the process took place in her mind. She saw and felt, apparently, with an intensity akin to the intensity of the painter's creative vision, as Fry has described it, which crystallizes things into a harmony.

> What is meant by reality ? *she asks.* It would seem to be something very erratic, very undependable—now to be found in a dusty road, now in a scrap of newspaper in the street, now a daffodil in the sun. It lights up a group in a room and stamps some casual saying. It overwhelms one walking home beneath the stars and makes the silent world more real than the world of speech—and then there it is again in an omnibus in the uproar of Piccadilly. Sometimes, too, it seems to dwell in shapes too far away for us to discern what their nature is. But whatever it touches it fixes and makes permanent. That is what remains over when the skin of the day has been cast into the hedge ; that is what is left of past time and of our loves and hates.*

The strange significance which attaches itself to certain moments of being—painters have known it too. Chardin, for example : " The way that people took their place in the space of the room had at moments some special meaning which he was quick to seize," Roger Fry says. Virginia Woolf gives us a more detailed account of one of these significant moments. She was looking out of her window, when,

> as so often happens in London, there was a complete lull and suspension of traffic. Nothing came down the street ; nobody passed. A single leaf detached itself from the plane tree at the end of the street, and in that pause and suspension fell. Somehow it was like a signal falling, a signal pointing to a force in things which one had overlooked. It seemed to point to a river, which flowed past, invisibly, round the corner, down the street, and took people and eddied them along. . . . Now it was bringing from one side of the street to the other diagonally a girl in patent leather boots, and then

* *A Room of One's Own*, pp. 165–6.

> a young man in a maroon overcoat ; it was also bringing a taxi-cab ; and it brought all three together at a point directly beneath my window ; where the taxi stopped ; and the girl and the young man stopped ; and they got into the taxi ; and then the cab glided off as if it were swept on by the current elsewhere.
>
> The sight was ordinary enough ; what was strange was the rhythmical order with which my imagination had invested it ; and the fact that the ordinary sight of two people getting into a cab had the power to communicate something of their own seeming satisfaction.*

One moment of this sort might do to make a painting. It takes many of them, and many less significant moments as well, to make a novel ; and they all must be combined and made to work together in a world of their own. This world takes shape in the subconscious, Virginia Woolf believes, while the writer is unaware that he is composing :

> Unconsciousness, which means presumably that the under-mind works at top speed while the upper-mind drowses, is a state we all know. We all have experience of the work done by unconsciousness in our own daily lives. You have had a crowded day, let us suppose, sightseeing in London. Could you say what you have seen and done when you came back ? Was it not all a blur, a confusion ? But after what seemed a rest, a chance to turn aside and look at something different, the sights and sounds and sayings that had been of most interest to you swam to the surface, apparently of their own accord ; and remained in memory ; what was unimportant sank into forgetfulness. So it is with the writer. After a hard day's work, trudging around, seeing all he can, feeling all he can, taking in the book of his mind innumerable notes, the writer becomes—if he can—unconscious. In fact, his under-mind works at top speed while his upper-mind drowses. Then, after a pause the veil lifts ; and there is the thing—the thing he wants to write about—simplified, composed. Do we strain Wordsworth's famous saying about emotion recollected in tranquillity when we infer that by tranquillity he meant that the writer needs to become unconscious before he can create ? †

* *A Room of One's Own*, pp. 144–5. † *The Moment*, pp. 109–10.

In the book that the writer creates each word should be matched as exactly as possible to his vision, to the thing that he sees after the veil lifts. To paraphrase a statement of Fry's on significant form, which has been quoted earlier, "[the words with] which the work is made [should be], as it were, penetrated and impregnated by an idea". And if the writer is successful there will be significant moments in his book, glimpses of reality, which are akin to, but transcend by far, their counterparts in life. Virginia Woolf imagines that she is reading the book of a hypothetical young woman novelist, and speaks, in *A Room of One's Own*, of the criterion by which it must be judged :

> . . . no abundance of sensation or fineness of perception would avail unless she could build up out of the fleeting and the personal the lasting edifice which remains unthrown. I had said that I would wait until she faced herself with "a situation". And I meant by that until she proved by summoning, beckoning and getting together that she was not a skimmer of surfaces merely, but had looked beneath into the depths. Now is the time, she would say to herself at a certain moment, when without doing anything violent I can show the meaning of all this. And she would begin—how unmistakable that quickening is!—beckoning and summoning, and there would rise up in memory, half forgotten, perhaps quite trivial things in other chapters dropped by the way. And she would make their presence felt while someone sewed or smoked a pipe as naturally as possible, and one would feel, as she went on writing, as if one had gone to the top of the world and seen it laid out, very majestically, beneath.

The unity of a novel, the co-ordinated unity in which the spirit can rest satisfied, is emotional. The novelist feels emotions naturally, names them simply, and, with the help of the subconscious, ranges them in final order by feeling their right relations to one another. This is what we mean, Virginia Woolf says, when we speak of form : "The 'book itself' is not form which you see, but emotion which you feel, and the more intense the writer's feeling the more exact without slip or chink its expression in words". We should not, she believes, ask the novelist first of all to tell us a story and give us a plot :

his book should be held together by a connexion of emotions, not of events. The novelist's business, in his own medium, is similar, it appears, to the painter's, who disengages the emotional elements inherent in natural form and arranges them in a system of his own to express his feeling and intuition. Like the painter, the novelist discovers emotional harmonies. Why these harmonies are significant we cannot say, but we know that they speak to something very deep within us. " Perhaps it is ", Virginia Woolf says, " . . . that Nature, in her most irrational mood, has traced in invisible ink on the walls of the mind a premonition which . . . great artists confirm ; a sketch which only needs to be held to the fire of genius to become visible. When one so exposes it and sees it come to life one exclaims in rapture, But this is what I have always felt and known and desired ! " " It looks as though ", as Roger Fry puts it, " art had got access to the substratum of all the emotional colours of life."

Virginia Woolf looked at the novel, then, in much the same way as Fry looked at painting, and as a result she was able to solve the major problem with which, as a writer, she was confronted. Her aesthetics is of the kind that is most valuable to an artist : it clears the way for her own work. Her criticism of Bennett, Galsworthy, and Wells must be regarded partly in this light, though it is cogent in other respects as well. The novel, as these three Edwardians practised it, was in need of revitalization, of an infusion of something new from life. It is quite true, of course, that Virginia Woolf's proposal to " record the atoms as they fall upon the mind in the order in which they fall ", to " trace the pattern, however disconnected and incoherent in appearance, which each sight or incident scores upon the conciousness ", is, taken literally, impossible. Wordsworth's proposal to write poetry in the everyday language of shepherds and farmers is equally impossible. Both Virginia Woolf and Wordsworth had to modify their theory in practice. But Wordsworth destroyed the stilted diction into which eighteenth-century poetry, as it moved away from life, had hardened ; and Virginia Woolf, who, like Wordsworth, wished to leaven the conventions of art with the stuff of life, conceived a form of novel which should be more organic than the

Edwardian novel. In practice, as we shall see, her conception of emotional form and of the power of the subconcious to select the significant from the insignificant, enabled her to transpose her impressions of life into highly disciplined aesthetic wholes.

Though Virginia Woolf's conception of the novel is close to Fry's conception of painting, it is not so close to his conception of fiction—as he expressed it before he translated Mauron's essay, at any rate. Fry's notion of " inevitable sequences " in the novel, of the novelist's use of the " inexorability of fate ", recalls Hardy's novels, though there is something like it in Forster's description of plot. As Forster points out, however, such sequences are more suitable to the drama than to the novel (it is no accident that Hardy's *Dynasts* is cast in dramatic form) ; and Forster has too much respect for the characters of a novel to believe that they should be controlled inexorably by the plot.

In fact, Virginia Woolf thinks that Forster assumes too easily that fiction " is more intimately and humbly attached to the service of human beings than the other arts " ; and much of her criticism of his attitude in *Aspects of the Novel* as " unaesthetic " is based on this objection. Actually, he is interested in different, less subjective aspects of life than she, and, partly because of this difference, more of the old apparatus of novel-writing suits him than suits her. So he comes in for some of the same criticism (though in milder form, since his sins are less) as the Edwardians. He is praised as well, however, particularly for his remarks on rhythm : here he is working out his own method, and, moreover, he is aware of a relationship between fiction and another art. It is true, of course, that, to use a dangerous word, Virginia Woolf's aesthetics is " purer " than Forster's. While she speaks of arranging emotions in their right relations, he sees the novel as a less manageable thing, composed of many disparate items which the novelist must combine, somehow, in whatever way may be best, into a work of art. " For me ", he says, " the whole intricate question of method resolves itself . . . into the power of the writer to bounce the reader into accepting what he says." With this warning, or proviso, he examines the devices, as he sees them, that novelists have used to help them " bounce " their readers—to help them only: their power to "bounce", he knows, is over and above any device they may use. His book is concerned mainly with an empirical examination of the novel, and for this reason it is of more value to students (it was given first as the Clark Lectures at Trinity College, Cambridge), and perhaps to fledgling novelists, than Virginia Woolf's essays. But her clear statement that emotions arranged in a system of their own are the essence of fiction is indisputable, and must always be the cynosure of novelists who are strong enough to find their own way.

Whatever their differences, Virginia Woolf and Forster agree that the novelist must neglect neither life nor art. This belief, as applied to the various arts, was a postulate of Bloomsbury aesthetics, and it no doubt had a good deal to do with Lytton Strachey's conception of biography. His conception is eminently sensible. A biography cannot, as Strachey knew, be purely empirical. The biographer cannot give us a copy of his subject's life, any more than Virginia Woolf could record all the impressions that she received; and even if he could do so, we would not find his book much to the point. Boswell's practice, for example, is not empirical, though it may at first give us the impression of being so. He does not collect incident for incident's sake: he collects it to illumine Johnson. His focus upon Johnson is too steady to allow him to indulge in mere elaboration of insignificant detail. The conversations that Boswell records are not transcriptions; they are much more to the point than transcriptions would be. He had to select and reconstruct; and he reconstructs Johnson's inner life too—from Johnson's prayers and meditations, from his fear of death, his desire for company, his superstitious acts, from hints dropped by the way in his conversation. If Boswell had not reconstructed much of Johnson's mind his book would not give us the satisfaction that it does. Of course, the biographer cannot—not even Boswell, who knew Johnson so well—get his subject's life completely right. He would have to have God's omniscience to do that. Nor can he avoid expressing a point of view, however much he might like to; it will creep in, even into the most colourless sentences. The biographer, as Strachey suggests, does better to recognize than ignore this truth, and to let his point of view organize his biography: this is, after all, an honest procedure.

The point of view of Victorian biographies is often laudatory: it is equally legitimate for the biographer to take the opposite point of view. But there is a point of view that, as it transcends both these, is more legitimate than either. It is not concerned first of all to praise or blame. It is impartial, except in so far as it is coloured, and indeed formed, by the biographer's widest view of life and the universe. Because it is more tolerant than the view of the conventional moralist, it admits more of life than he would welcome, and the biography that it controls gives us, as Boswell's *Life of Johnson* witnesses, a sense of both the infinite variety of life and the order of art. Such a biography may attain, moreover, a truth of insight that the professedly "scientific" biography cannot reach, and show us a reality that only art can present.

Infinite organic variety, order, truth of insight, reality—these are the things that Bloomsbury demands of art, the touchstones with which they try works of art of all kinds, from the biography to music, from painting to the novel. Variety and truth of insight may be related to the artist's sensibility, order and reality to his power to organize the materials he draws from life into aesthetic wholes. This power may be called intellectual, so long as it is realized that it is only akin to, not the same as, the power to construct logical systems in science or philosophy. The great strength of Bloomsbury's aesthetics is that it asserts that sensibility and intellect are equally necessary to the artist, that, as Virginia Woolf puts it, the artist must be androgynous, with the sensibility of a woman and the intellect of a man, and—this is an allied requirement so that sensibility and intellect may work freely together—with the prejudices of neither. The artist's business, Bloomsbury believes, is to use his intellect and sensibility to construct works that will satisfy us both for their aesthetic unity and for the vision of life which they give us. Beyond this, Bloomsbury has no demands to make of him, and no rules to offer. He must find his own way to express his vision, or intuition, of life, and in finding that he will find the form of his work. No one can tell him what form his work should take: his intuition demands its own form. This is another advantage of Bloomsbury's aesthetics, which complements their insistence upon both intellect and sensibility in art. They do not believe that form is an artificial thing which is imposed upon the content of the work, but that it is inseparable from the content, part and parcel of it. So their aesthetics cannot harden into a system of rules. They set a high ideal before the artist and tell him that he must be an individual if he is to achieve it.*

The essential part of Bloomsbury's aesthetics is empirical; it is based on a careful examination of works of art and of the individual's reaction to them. But in attempting to explain some of the phenomena that this examination reveals, especially the strange, apparently unanalysable sense of reality and significance which some works of art give us, Bloomsbury makes conjectures that cannot, in the present state of our knowledge, be proven or disproven. Such conjectures, of course, are perfectly legitimate; without them knowledge would stagnate. And in this case they are made concerning the nature of the subconscious, about which the psychologist is learning more and more and may one day be able to give the aesthetician the information he seeks. Meanwhile, mysti-

* Forster: "Form is not tradition. It alters from generation to generation. Artists always seek a new technique, and will continue to do so as long as their work excites them. But form of some kind is imperative" (*Two Cheers for Democracy*, p. 103).

Strachey: "The whole theory of 'rules' in literature—the whole conception that there were certain definite traditional forms in existence which were, absolutely and inevitably, the best—was shattered for ever [by the French Romantics]. The new doctrine was triumphantly vindicated—that the form of expression must depend ultimately, not upon tradition nor yet upon *a priori* reasonings, but simply and solely on the thing expressed" (*Landmarks in French Literature*, p. 127).

Virginia Woolf: "Any method is right, every method is right, that expresses what we wish to express, if we are writers; that brings us closer to the novelist's intention if we are readers" ("Modern Fiction", *The Common Reader*, p. 192).

Fry: "Every artist has to create his own method of expression in his medium, and there is no one way, right or wrong. But every way is right when it is expressive throughout of the idea in the artist's mind" (quoted by Virginia Woolf, *Roger Fry*, p. 250).

cism, as we have seen, will occasionally attend conjectures such as Bloomsbury makes. But in Bloomsbury's case it is a mysticism that postulates nothing, recognizes that our knowledge is incomplete, and asks only that the mystery be cleared up.* For example, though Forster, as we have seen, admires " prophecy " in fiction, though of all the aspects of the novel he discusses, it is the one that seems best to support his conjectures about the subconscious, yet, " always," he says, " at the back of my mind, there lurks a reservation about this prophetic stuff ". Mysticism, in Bloomsbury, is accompanied by a healthy scepticism. Moreover, the question whether Bloomsbury's conjectures about the subconscious are right or wrong has nothing at all to do with the validity of their aesthetics. Whatever the explanation of the feelings which we experience before works of art, the fact is that we experience them, and that is all that really matters to the aesthetician or to the artist.

Bloomsbury's aesthetics is concerned only to help the artist to create, and every one to enjoy, good works of art. It owes most to Roger Fry. He reiterated the half-forgotten truth that art is autonomous. He showed where art touches life and where it is separate from it. He declared that art complements science and is on a par with it ; and he demonstrated that art deals with the real experiences of life just as surely as science does. He made it clear that form and content are not separate in a work of art. And most important of all, perhaps, he pointed with a wand at pictures to explain what he meant. Yet, though he was mainly interested in painting, he did not forget the other arts, and he maintained that the ultimate principles of all art are the same. He was an empiricist who could interpret facts and who always welcomed new information. Thanks largely to him, Bloomsbury's aesthetics includes within its purview nearly all the arts, and has the virtues, not always found in combination, of coherency and open-mindedness.

* See p. 38.

PART II
VALUES

CHAPTER IV

E. M. FORSTER, LYTTON STRACHEY, VIRGINIA WOOLF

THE form of a writer's work depends upon his aesthetics and his attitude to life. Of these two controlling factors, the latter has the greater effect upon form. A writer may not consciously formulate a theory of aesthetics at all, and even if he does he is as likely as not to disobey his own rules. But his attitude to life tells upon everything he writes, and may even govern his aesthetics. We have looked at the aesthetics of E. M. Forster, Lytton Strachey, and Virginia Woolf—aesthetics which owe much to Roger Fry. We have seen something, as well, of the philosophy of the group to which they belonged—a philosophy which influenced all the members of the Bloomsbury Group, though none of them, it is likely, would agree entirely with it. In this chapter we will try to discover and understand as much as we may of the attitudes to life of Forster, Strachey, and Virginia Woolf. And then we will be ready to examine their novels and biographies.

" Attitude to life " is an unsatisfactory phrase. It is vague and it is clumsy. If we attempt to find a phrase that is less vague, however, we are likely to distort. The nearer we come to works of art, the less will precise terms serve us. One's attitude to life is a complex thing. It is made up of beliefs and ideals, of likes and dislikes, of emotions and the way one " feels " about things. It is controlled partly by the intellect, and partly by deep instinctive desires. Now it is guided by reason, and now it is pushed by some inexplicable emotional reaction that has its origin, it may be, deep in the subconscious. One's attitude to life determines the spiritual values that one puts on things : this is as nearly as it may be defined. We shall not, of course, be able to uncover much of the whole emotional and intellectual complex that is the attitude to life of Forster or Strachey or Virginia Woolf. The mind does not give up its secrets so easily. Furthermore, the mind changes, even from day to day, and we shall have to regard it, by and large, as static. We shall also have to pay more attention to intellectual concepts than to emotions, and even when we speak of emotions we shall have, perforce, to do so in intellectual terms. This is where criticism fails because it is not, and cannot be, an art ; it is intellectual, not emotional. But we will be able to find out some of the values that these three writers attach to things, some of the scaffolding, as it were, of their books. Our search will be concerned mainly with their shorter, more didactic writings, for in biographies and novels—it is a test of a work of art—beliefs and emotional attachments are likely to be consumed in the form of the whole.

A consideration of E. M. Forster reminds us at once that an attitude to life is likely to be neither simple nor logical. Forster's intellectual outlook on the world is grey ; his emotional response to life is bright. He agrees with Beethoven (if Helen Schlegel of *Howards End* has interpreted Beethoven's Fifth Symphony correctly)* that panic and emptiness always threaten the splendour of life, and periodically overwhelm it. Periods of civilization, when the human spirit is relatively free and is able to create, alternate with war and oppression, when force, violence, and stupidity are dominant. Force and violence, Forster says, are " the ultimate reality on this earth "; but they do not always get to the front ; and one of our jobs is to keep them in the background, " to prevent [force] from getting out of its box ", for as long as possible. Meanwhile we may create, and we may, if we will, enjoy life ; for Forster is a naturalist, a refined Rabelais, a less mystic and a cooler D. H. Lawrence.

Forster believes that the natural passions and emotions of the body are good, and that if man would enjoy them honestly and unashamedly the world would be a better place than it is. He is on the side of the Ancient Greeks, who admired a

* See p. 65.

beautiful naked body as well as a mature, well-developed mind. He accepts wholly both the physical and the spiritual life of man. We have already seen that he will have nothing to do with a theory of the novel which will not allow life, in all its fullness and richness, to come in, and that he criticizes Henry James's use of pattern on this score. His difference with James is more fundamental than a mere disagreement upon a principle of aesthetics. Forster cannot approve of James, because James, with an exquisite motion of rejection, cannot quite accept life. " Maimèd creatures can alone breathe in Henry James's pages," Forster says. " They are incapable of fun, of rapid motion, of carnality, and of nine-tenths of heroism. Their clothes will not take off. . . . Even their sensations are limited." In some respects Forster would no doubt prefer to James the Italian D'Annunzio, who, " if we ask him to sign a suburban gentleman's agreement . . . will impale us contemptuously upon the point of his pen as he did President Wilson ", and who, his biographer tells us, placed two signs outside his door : " Beware of the dog " and " Beware of the master ". The Italians find nothing funny or vulgar in such an inscription, Forster says ; " it is to them a cynical proclamation of virility, which she who ignores ignores at her peril ". Forster sees clearly that D'Annunzio has some characteristics that are unpleasant enough ; what he admires is D'Annunzio's vital responsiveness and his contempt for the conventions of suburbia. These qualities Forster believes to be found in Italy more often than in England.

Forster's short stories, which are frankly didactic in intent, are much occupied with Greek mythology. In one of them, " The Story of a Panic ", Pan visits and scatters in traditional fashion a group of tiresome, conventional people who are holidaying (they are from England) in the Italian countryside. They are all filled with a groundless terror, all, that is, but one of them, a boy who is young and stubborn enough to have so far escaped the clutches of convention and good form. He welcomes Pan, and is saved from the fate of his elders by his meeting with him. In another of the short stories, " The Curate's Friend ", a curate meets a faun while having tea outdoors with some friends on the Wiltshire Downs. Only the curate sees the faun, " for to see him there is required a certain quality, for which truthfulness is too cold a name and animal spirits too coarse a one ", and in spite of his association with the Church the curate has this quality and his friends have not. (Clergymen as a rule are not likely, Forster believes, to be on Pan's side ; they are more likely to be priests of convention. The clergyman in " The Story of a Panic " thought that Pan was the Devil.) The faun looks like a naked boy. He does not know what " tempt " means or what self-denial is. He encourages sexual passion, and he believes that people should swear when they are cross and laugh when they are happy. After the curate has met him his mind is cleared of cant and his religion of sham ; he is at one with nature and with the generous, contented people of his congregation. Pan represents for Forster an honest, natural acceptance of the body and of desire. He is the spirit of nature, or rather, of man in harmony with nature. He stands for the great truth that is learned by the hero of another short story, in which there are no fauns or pleasant countryside, but only an omnipotent, sterile machine—the truth that " Man is the measure. . . . Man's feet are the measure for distance, his hands are the measure for ownership, his body is the measure for all that is lovable and desirable and strong." Forster asks above all for spontaneity and vitality ; he hates the *ersatz*. He therefore trusts youth and love. And when he allows himself to dream he dreams of a magic island in which there is eternal youth and men go naked beneath the sun.*

The Pans of the short stories have a further significance. They personify the link which Forster feels to exist between men and the countryside—the countryside which has been man's home since the youth of our race and which he has made and moulded while countless, nameless generations have come and gone. Forster's feeling for nature is partly Wordsworthian and partly pagan, but the deities of his fields and

* The best of these dreams, *A Letter to Madan Blanchard* (reprinted in *Two Cheers for Democracy*), is inspired by a feeling similar to that which prompted Matthew Arnold to write " The Scholar Gipsy ". " The Point of It " (*Collected Short Stories*) and " Happiness ! " (*Abinger Harvest*) have the same affinity.

downs, the geniuses of his woods and trees, are the past generations who have lived and died there. The Wiltshire Downs have a peculiar significance for him, as they had for D. H. Lawrence, because of the memorials of ancient times that they contain. Wild, virgin scenery could not hold a meaning comparable to this. ". . . places: in them also I believe," Forster says in his preface to *Two Cheers for Democracy*. And the book concludes with some random notes on places near Abinger, Surrey. "I excite myself", he says, "by learning the names of the woods on the Ordnance Map, by hearing a wry-neck, and by seeing a swallow and a bat —all these pleasures early. Think I will learn the names of all the fields in the parish. Wish I had talked to old men." Here is one of the topographical notes:

> Sandy Field, between Deer leap and the Railway. Here, a few years ago, three black cinerary urns of the 1st century A.D. were found, the most perfect of which was given to the B.M. by Mrs. E., now herself dead. I saw it there, proffered by a polite colonel, and to-day went to the field. There is a pond, large but difficult to find, and no doubt of the Silent Pool type, for it lies under the down. This was crammed with carp, and when it was cleared out some of them stocked Paddington. Ernest R. told me all this. Up in Deer Leap is a tumulus, spiky with trees, and the field called "Great Slaughter Field" is on the other side. (Great Sloe Tree Field really). Peaceful feeling after turning out this tiny pocket of history. Pond lies on watershed and drains towards Mole.

Usually nature is friendly to man. In the desert, not far from Alexandria, she has given, Forster says, year after year, an "extraordinary show to a few Bedouins, has covered the Mareotic civilization with dust and raised flowers from its shards". Occasionally she is malevolent, as at Blind Oak Gate, near Abinger: "No peace here. Only a sense of something vaguely sinister, which would do harm if it could, but which cannot, this being Surrey; of something muffled up and recalcitrant; of something which rises upon its elbow when no one is present and looks down the converging paths." But when man and nature have lived together for long centuries, nature sustains and supports. Old Mr. Lucas, a character in Forster's short story " The Road from Colonus ", discovers this. Without dignity and without grace he was becoming senile ; he was travelling in Greece, but life was stale and flat. Then he came to a tiny inn beside which was an enormous hollow plane tree from whose " living trunk there gushed an impetuous spring ". An old woman sat spinning at the inn ; a small pig stood beside her. Mr. Lucas stepped inside the tree.

> Others had been before him—indeed he had a curious sense of companionship. Little votive offerings to the presiding Power were fastened on to the bark—tiny arms and legs and eyes in tin, grotesque models of the brain or the heart—all tokens of some recovery of strength or wisdom or love. There was no such thing as the solitude of nature, for the sorrows and joys of humanity had pressed even into the bosom of a tree.

He leant against the wood of the tree, closed his eyes, and lay motionless.

> . . . when he opened his eyes, something unimagined, indefinable, had passed over all things, and made them intelligible and good.
>
> There was meaning in the stoop of the old woman over her work, and in the quick motions of the little pig, and in her diminishing globe of wool. A young man came singing over the streams on a mule, and there was beauty in his pose and sincerity in his greeting. The sun made no accidental patterns upon the spreading roots of the trees, and there was intention in the nodding clumps of asphodel, and in the music of the water. To Mr. Lucas, who, in a brief space of time, had discovered not only Greece, but England and all the world and life, there seemed nothing ludicrous in the desire to hang within the tree another votive offering—a little model of an entire man.

He determined, against the wishes of his travelling companions, to stop for a night, or a week, at the tiny inn. As he fought to remain, " the issue assumed gigantic proportions. . . . The moment was so tremendous that he abandoned words and arguments as useless, and rested on the strength of his mighty unrevealed allies : silent men, murmuring water, and whispering trees."

The English countryside gives Forster a sense of companionship similar to that which Mr. Lucas felt in Greece. The old inhabitants who built Stonehenge, the Romans whose ashes have mingled with the soil, the Saxons who raised their earthworks on the downs, Mrs. E., Ernest R., the polite colonel, and, above all, the country-folk who from generation to generation have made and named the fields and woods, have watched the trees grow and know the secrets of their parish—they are all, in a sense, part of the earth with which they have lived ; their joys and sorrows have pressed into its bosom, like the votive offerings which hung within the tree in Greece. Forster has written two pageants of country life, one of them for the parish of Abinger, the other, *England's Pleasant Land*, for a Surrey District Preservation Society. " Our Pageant ", he says of *The Abinger Pageant*, " is not planned quite on ordinary pageant lines. It is rural rather than historical and tries to show the continuity of country life." And of *England's Pleasant Land* he says :

> The action covers a period of nearly one thousand years.
>
> The scene of the play is the English countryside, close to a village and to a manor house, which have grown up during the centuries.
>
> The play is not about any particular person. It is about the land, and the characters should be thought of as types who are connected in various ways with rural England. This will be brought out in the acting. For example, the same actor will play the Norman Knight at domesday, the Squire who encloses the common land in the eighteenth century, and the Squire who dies at the end of the nineteenth century. Similarly with the Squire's family, the villagers Jack and Jill, Mr. Bumble, the lady guests, etc. Their costumes may alter, but their characters will not change.

The countryside, Forster believes, may put a man in touch with his forbears, reminding him that he is one with them and, further, that life may go out from him to the unborn. We have seen, in the last chapter, that Forster thinks that the individual may reach out to his fellows through the subconscious, that he shares something in common with them there. The countryside is another and a more tangible link, which enables a man to feel the vast totality of livingness, which has been throughout the centuries, of his parish and his country.

Commercialism and industrialism, which threaten the countryside, may destroy in a moment all this distillation of the centuries. And though it is easily destroyed, it cannot be replaced.

> I was brought up as a boy in one of the home counties, *Forster says*, in a district which I still think the loveliest in England. There is nothing special about it—it is agricultural land, and could not be described in terms of beauty spots. It must always have looked much the same. I have kept in touch with it, going back to it as an abiding city and still visiting the house which was once my home, for it is occupied by friends. A farm is through the hedge, and when the farmer there was eight years old and I was nine, we used to jump up and down on his grandfather's straw ricks and spoil them. To-day he is a grandfather himself, so that I have the sense of five generations continuing in one place. Life went on there as usual until this spring.* Then someone who was applying for a permit to lay a water pipe was casually informed that it would not be granted since the whole area had been commandeered. Commandeered for what? Had not the war ended? Appropriate officials of the Ministry of Town and Country Planning now arrived from London and announced that a satellite town for 60,000 people is to be built. The people now living and working there are doomed; it is death in life for them and they move in a nightmare. The best agricultural land has been taken, they assert; the poor land down by the railway has been left; compensation is inadequate. Anyhow, the satellite town has finished them off as completely as it will obliterate the ancient and delicate scenery. Meteorite town would be a better name. It has fallen out of a blue sky.
>
> "Well," says the voice of planning and progress, "why this sentimentality? People must have houses." They must, and I think of working-class friends in north London who have to bring up four children in two rooms, and many are

* Written in 1946.

even worse off than that. But I cannot equate the problem. It is a collision of loyalties. I cannot free myself from the conviction that something irreplaceable has been destroyed, that a little piece of England has died as surely as if a bomb had hit it. I wonder what compensation there is in the world of the spirit, for the destruction of the life here, the life of tradition.

It is the spiritual damage that Forster deplores. The countryman, he believes, is brought up in an ancient tradition which enables him to see life whole. For him soul and body are one ; he expresses himself honestly and naturally ; he is in harmony with his surroundings ; his home and his fathers help him. But as the world shifts with ever increasing swiftness from an agricultural to an industrial life, more men are uprooted from the land, the harmony of their lives is disrupted, the " sane pastoral virtues " are destroyed—and replaced, all too often, Forster believes, by the ugliest characteristics of commercialism. As factories and satellite towns grow in the countryside, some men come to think of " nothing but money, money, money when [they look] at the trees and fields ". Of course, an individual of this sort may pay eloquent lip-service to the beauty of nature : it is the thing to do, and he is likely enough to upbraid the countryman for failing to appreciate his surroundings. He ladles out his emotions according to the requirements of " good form ", which he has learned at his Public School. Thanks to his training, his heart, Forster says, is " undeveloped ". He fears the spontaneous expression of honest emotions ; and he is contemptuous of intellect—adherence to convention has relieved him of the need to think or feel for himself. Success is his test for all things, and such beliefs as he has are supported by a comfortable Christianity, or by a conviction of self-righteousness, or both. In fact, he believes himself to have high spiritual aspirations, for he is, above all, badly muddled. He neither thinks nor feels clearly. And when he follows a wrong course of action he usually believes that he is right, for he has begun by confusing himself.

These are the endemic spiritual ills of our industrial age, Forster believes ; men who have broken with the past and turned away from nature, without finding anything as valuable to replace the orderly life they have left, are prone to them. These ills play their part in the recurrence of war and oppression, in the letting loose of force and violence upon the world. And they are caused, ultimately, by the application of science :

> We cannot reach social and political stability for the reason that we continue to make scientific discoveries and to apply them, and thus to destroy the arrangements which were based on more elementary discoveries. If Science would discover rather than apply—if, in other words, men were more interested in knowledge than in power—mankind would be in a far safer position, the stability statesmen talk about would be a possibility, there could be a new order based on vital harmony, and the earthly millennium might approach. But Science shows no signs of doing this : she gave us the internal combustion engine, and before we had digested and assimilated it with terrible pains into our social system, she harnessed the atom and destroyed any new order that seemed to be evolving. How can man get into harmony with his surroundings when he is constantly altering them ? The future of our race is, in this direction, more unpleasant than we care to admit, and it has sometimes seemed to me that its best chance lies through apathy, uninventiveness, and inertia.*

But man is inventive ; he does, under our present forms of government, at any rate, desire power more than knowledge : we live in the age of the internal combustion engine and the atom bomb ; and we must make the best of it. Furthermore, we cannot now get on without scientific planning. But we must see to it, Forster says, that the scientist plans for our bodies only, and not for our minds.†

* *Two Cheers for Democracy*, p. 100.

† Forster's view of the application of science is similar to Lowes Dickinson's. " The West ", Dickinson says, " has invented, if not science, the applied sciences ; and in so doing has made the externals of life, for the well-to-do at any rate, and perhaps also, when all is said, for the poor, immensely more comfortable than they have ever been before. It has made it possible for a much greater number of people to live on a given area ; but at the same time it has almost destroyed the beauty of life and the faculty of disinterested contemplation " (" An Essay on the Civilizations of India, China and Japan ", reprinted in *Letters from John Chinaman*, p. 70). Forster also shares Dickinson's love of Ancient Greece, his respect

For science can explain little of life and understand even less. There is an unseen, there is a spiritual life, there is "poetry, mystery, passion, ecstasy, music", and these things count: man cannot live by bread alone. Hence the importance of art, of personal relationships, and of the private life, in which, says Forster, "I believe".

In our private lives, Forster says, we should connect the seen and the unseen; we should, in other words, find our own souls. Thought and emotion, love and desire, truth and kindness, reason and sensibility—these must be bound together and from them our actions must spring if we, as individuals, are to be whole. And individuals we must be if our lives are to be valuable. We must think and feel for ourselves; we must not allow convention or good form or authority to come between us and our souls. We must face ourselves squarely and avoid muddle. Courage too is required. Without it we cannot stand out against convention and authority, we cannot even face ourselves, we cannot have a free mind. Moreover, freedom and knowledge will perish in the world if we do not stand up for them and testify. And without courage we cannot create while force grumbles and threatens from within its box, in which, at best, it is but insecurely shut.

Forster values friendship equally with a whole and healthy private life. Friendship too, he believes, is based on the unseen.

for personal affection, and his liberalism. (See pp. 12–13.) Both Forster and Dickinson value the body as well as the mind. And near the end of Dickinson's dialogue *After Two Thousand Years* (1930), Philalethes, a modern young man, suggests to Plato a theory of the subconscious similar to Forster's:

Ph. We are beginning to see that the consciousness of men, as most of us have it, is but a superficial appearance, that reaches down —though most of us are unaware of it—into a great common reservoir, where everything that has once been perceived or thought or dreamed, is somehow recorded. . . .

Pl. Let me understand you. You seem to suggest . . . that individual minds or souls are like points of rock emerging from the sea at different distances, and appearing like a swarm of tiny islands, though really they are connected below in a common reef, from which in fact they all arise.

Ph. Yes, something like that.

> One must be fond of people and trust them if one is not to make a mess of life, *he says*, and it is therefore essential that they should not let one down. They often do. The moral of which is that I must, myself, be as reliable as possible, and this I try to be. But reliability is not a matter of contract—that is the main difference between the world of personal relationships and the world of business relationships. It is a matter for the heart, which signs no documents. In other words, reliability is impossible unless there is a natural warmth.*

Forster's friends are of many different nationalities and colours. His essays and the dedications of his books give us a good list of them, for he likes to pay tribute to his friends and to acknowledge his debts. There is Syed Ross Masood, the Indian educationist, who " woke me up out of my suburban and academic life, showed me new horizons and a new civilization and helped me towards the understanding of a continent " ; and Charles Mauron, " the friend who, after Roger Fry, has helped me with pictures most ". There is C. P. Cavafy, the Alexandrian poet, and Forrest Reid, the Irish novelist ; Jack Sprott of the University of Nottingham, England, and Bill Roehrich of Lost Farm, Tyringham, Massachusetts, to both of whom Forster has dedicated *Two Cheers for Democracy.* There are also, of course, Lowes Dickinson, and Virginia Woolf, and other Cambridge and Bloomsbury friends ; and there are the nameless Indians and Egyptians and Americans met in chance encounters while travelling. These people, and others like them, make up Forster's " aristocracy "—" not an aristocracy of power, based upon rank and influence, but an aristocracy of the sensitive, the considerate and the plucky ". " Its members ", he says, " are to be found in all nations and classes, and all through the ages, and there is a secret understanding between them when they meet." " They are sensitive for others as well as for themselves, they are considerate without being fussy, their pluck is not swankiness but the power to endure, and they can take a joke." He would prefer, of course, that they enjoyed their bodies : " I do not feel that my aristocrats

* *Two Cheers for Democracy,* p. 78.

are a real aristocracy if they thwart their bodies, since bodies are the instruments through which we register and enjoy the world." But he respects a belief in asceticism if it is passionately or mystically held, and so, he says, sensitiveness, consideration for others, and pluck are enough for admission to his aristocracy. His aristocrats " want to create something or discover something, and do not see life in terms of power. . . . They found religions, great or small, or they produce literature and art, or they do disinterested scientific research, or they may be what is called ' ordinary people ', who are creative in their private lives, bring up their children decently, for instance, or help their neighbours." Forster believes that " they represent the true human tradition, the one permanent victory of our queer race over cruelty and chaos ".

With people of this sort about, Forster says, life cannot be dismissed as a failure. But the tragedy of life is that no way has been found to make the good qualities of friendship and the private life effective in public affairs. The news-vendor outside the Houses of Parliament can leave his papers with his cap beside them and be sure that any one who takes a paper will drop coppers in the cap. But the Members inside Parliament cannot trust one another as the news-vendor trusts the man on the street. " The more highly public life is organized the lower does its morality sink." Forster distrusts men when he views them collectively, but he has faith in the individual. So he believes that " the Saviour of the future —if he ever comes—will not preach a new Gospel. He will merely utilize my aristocracy, he will make effective the good will and the good temper which are already existing. . . . Not by becoming better, but by ordering and distributing his native goodness, will Man shut up Force into its box, and so gain time to explore the universe and to set his mark upon it worthily."

Meanwhile, and perhaps for always—for Forster has no sanguine hopes that the millennium will come—man must make the best of things as they are. In his private life, love, " the greatest of all things ", should prevail ; but since we cannot love what we do not know personally, tolerance, not love, is the virtue most required in public life. Tolerance is a lukewarm virtue ; its practice requires a nice balance. It means putting up with people and standing things, but not giving in or agreeing that things which we do not like are well as they are. For if we give in and agree in defiance of our better convictions, we lose our individuality and our freedom. It is tolerance that makes freedom possible in a heterogeneous world. Therefore, Forster values Laodiceanism and eclecticism, and he knows that truth may sometimes be found in paradox.* As we have seen, he is a naturalist, but he can respect asceticism ; again, he admires " prophecy " in the novel, but he is suspicious of it. He puts tolerance and lukewarmness into practice. And he supports Democracy because, imperfect as it is, it is the most tolerant form of government that has so far been evolved. It is sometimes oppressive enough, but " it does start from the assumption that the individual is important, and that all types are needed to make a civilization ". It allows criticism and permits people to express themselves creatively. It therefore gives Forster's aristocrats their best chance, and, above all, it gives artists more freedom than they would have elsewhere to produce good work. This is perhaps its major merit.

For society, Forster says, " can only represent a fragment of the human spirit ", and art gives man something of profound importance which he cannot find elsewhere. Art does not seek power ; it seeks only to understand, to increase our emotional and spiritual experience. In a world in which science progresses swiftly and disrupts society by the application of its discoveries, art shows us order which is to be found nowhere else, except perhaps in mystic experience, and which will endure, as it has in the past, when the rest of civilization decays. Therefore, and because art increases our knowledge, it has power to sustain and support.† It gives us in a greater degree, for it is more permanent and more orderly, something

* He has much in common with Samuel Butler here.

† Matthew Arnold is, of course, called to mind. See, for example, the sonnet " To a Friend " (" Who prop, thou ask'st, in these bad days, my mind ? "), and " Stanzas in Memory of the Author of ' Obermann ' ". Forster comments on " To a Friend " in " A Note on the Way ", reprinted in *Abinger Harvest*.

which is found also in the countryside, where life through long generations has evolved a certain order and completeness and the present inherits the wisdom of the past. Art is a surer medium of spiritual communication than the countryside. Based upon the unseen it reaches down into the subconscious and out to all ages. As public life favours the expression of the worst in man, of his desire for power, so art gives expression to the best in man, his desire to understand. It is the best testimony that man can give of his dignity. In the midst of chaos, Forster believes, it stands out against panic, emptiness and violence, and gives us cause to hope.

Forster's beliefs and values are clearly expressed in his essays, and are embodied in something like a mythology in his short stories and novels. He is, moreover, much concerned with contemporary affairs, and has a good deal to say about them. Lytton Strachey, in contrast, stands behind his essays and biographies, enigmatic and silent. He has less of the artist's inspiration than Forster. Therefore he is a biographer, as Gibbon, with whom he has a good deal in common, is an historian. But, though his works are slighter, he is as much an artist as Gibbon is ; and, inspiration aside, his art is purer than Forster's. He refuses to comment. He lets his beliefs mould his works, so that it is only from the biography or essay as a whole, or from hints dropped, as it were, inadvertently by the way, or from critical articles in which some terms of reference are demanded, that we can discover his values. In his works he turns his back steadfastly upon contemporary affairs, as though he fears that to look at them would threaten his detachment and prevent him from creating works of art, which, he agrees with Forster, are the highest product of civilization, and, of all the works of man, alone endure. And —perhaps it is another indication of his desire for detachment —he loves urbanity and cosmopolitanism as much as Forster loves spontaneity and the virtues of the countryman.

Strachey, indeed, desires detachment above all things.

> In what resides the most characteristic virtue of humanity ? *he asks in an essay on Hume.* In good works ? Possibly. In the creation of beautiful objects ? Perhaps. But some would look in a different direction, and find it in detachment.

> To all such David Hume must be a great saint in the calendar; for no mortal being was ever more completely divested of the trammels of the personal and the particular, none ever practised with a more consummate success the divine art of impartiality. And certainly to have no axe to grind is something very noble and very rare. It may be said to be the antithesis of the bestial. A series of creatures might be constructed, arranged according to their diminishing interest in the immediate environment, which would begin with the amoeba and end with the mathematician.

To be detached one must be intelligent and trust reason. Strachey admires Hume because he trusted reason in every department of his work and his life. Hume's *Treatise of Human Nature* " opened a new era in philosophy. The last vestiges of theological prepossessions—which were still faintly visible in Descartes and Locke—were discarded; and reason, in all her strength and all her purity, came into her own." Similarly, in his History of England, Hume made one of the first attempts " to apply intelligence to the events of the past ". His History was not warped, like Bossuet's, by theology nor, like Voltaire's, by a desire to discredit Christianity. " Hume had no . . . *arrière pensée*; he only wished to tell the truth as he saw it, with clarity and elegance." And the same calm intelligence governed his life. When he knew he was dying, " with ease, with gaiety, with the simplicity of perfect taste, he gently welcomed the inevitable ". His last, brief letter to an old friend, in which he described his fatal disease and bid farewell, " was the final expression of a supreme detachment ". Strachey, in his respect for reason and for detachment, looks with admiration towards the eighteenth century, the century of Hume and Gibbon, with its amazing self-sufficiency, its good manners and good taste, and its long " days of leisure and urbanity " in which " the rich fruit ripen[ed] slowly on the sun-warmed wall, and [came] inevitably to its delicious perfection ".*

In order to enjoy the detachment and to exercise the reason of a Hume or a Gibbon, two things, besides intelligence, are required: self-knowledge and a sense of humour. One must

* *Biographical Essays.*

neither deceive oneself nor take oneself too seriously. All was well with Gibbon and with his work, Strachey says, because " he understood something that, for his purposes, was more important even than the Roman Empire—himself. He knew his own nature, his powers, his limitations, his desires ; he was the master of an inward harmony." He had a sense of humour too, and he cleaved his way through the Decline and Fall of the Roman Empire with " a magisterial gaiety ". Strachey emphasizes Hume's humour and complete freedom from pretentiousness. Though he was idolized by French society during his sojourn in Paris, his manners remained unassuming. He returned to Edinburgh for the last years of his life ; and Strachey recounts " the well-known tale of the weighty philosopher getting stuck in the boggy ground at the base of the Castle rock, and calling on a passing old woman to help him out. She doubted whether any help should be given to the author of the Essay on Miracles." Hume at once complied with her request that he repeat the Lord's Prayer and the Belief. Again, " there is the vision of the mountainous metaphysician seated, amid a laughing party of young ladies, on a chair that was too weak for him, and suddenly subsiding to the ground ". And we have seen that Hume was gay even in the face of death. Strachey tried to carry the same qualities of self-possession, unpretentiousness, and gaiety into his own life. His " friends remember him as wonderfully and continuously gay ", John Russell says in an article in *Horizon* ; he " was a gay person who loved fun and nonsense ", says E. M. Forster. He found his saints in the eighteenth century, and he was equally attracted to France, where gaiety is reputed to be more common than in England, and where the language, Strachey says, " is the appointed vehicle of brilliant thought ".

By as much as Strachey admires the eighteenth century he dislikes the nineteenth. In the one, he believes, many of man's best qualities were dominant ; in the other they were submerged by their opposites. In contrast to Hume, and his gay, clear-sighted, unpretentious scepticism, is Dr. Thomas Arnold, who, as Strachey sees him, was solemn, pompous, priggish, and muddle-headed, and whose highest ambition was to write a History of Rome which should be, in his own words,

" the very reverse of Gibbon—in this respect, that whereas the whole spirit of his work, from its low morality, is hostile to religion, without speaking directly against it, so my greatest desire would be, in my History, by its high morals and its general tone, to be of use to the cause [of religion] without actually bringing it forward ". Arnold, in his little world at Rugby, Strachey intimates, regarded himself as Jehovah and his pupils as the Chosen People. And another Victorian, Gladstone, believed that he was chosen by God for a divine mission. In the life of his great opponent, Disraeli, " it is . . . difficult to find anything . . . which is not vanity ". The most gifted historian of the age, Carlyle, with his turgid sentences and his impassioned moral sense, which he could never keep out of his work, is entirely lacking in the " magisterial gaiety " of Gibbon. " If only ", Strachey says, " he could have enjoyed himself ! " These men did not know themselves ; they lacked detachment and a sense of the ridiculous. And Strachey believes that the Victorian Age as a whole was oppressively solemn ; it was an age of " self-complacency ", " self-contradiction ", and " barbarous prudery " ; it was " unaesthetic to its marrow-bones ". For artists, he says, " its incoherence, its pretentiousness, and its incurable lack of detachment will always outweigh its genuine qualities of solidity and force ".

Strachey's comments on the Victorian Age, if one did not go beneath them to discover the values upon which they are based or beyond them to the rest of his work, might lead one to believe that he is a cynical critic unwilling to express admiration. The truth is quite the reverse ; and it is somewhat unfortunate that his popular reputation rests almost entirely upon his Victorian biographies, though, as we will see in a later chapter, there is more than enough material in these works to discredit the facile belief that he is merely an iconoclast. The impression left by his literary and biographical essays, in which the range of his interests is better displayed, is of generosity and catholicity of taste. He appreciates both the restrained, matter-of-fact work of Beyle, who read the *Code Napoléon* each day to discipline his style, and the inspired imaginative flights of Blake ; the chiselled perfection of Chinese poetry and the realism, sobriety, and discomfort of Thomas Hardy's technically imperfect poems ; the grand, complex, undisciplined plays of the Elizabethans and the masterpieces, ordered by the three unities, of the French dramatists of the *Grand Siècle* ; and, as we have seen in the preceding chapter, the mystery and abundance of Sir Thomas Browne's style and the precision and clarity of Racine's. He agrees with Sainte-Beuve that the first duty of the critic is not to judge but to understand—which is not to say that the critic, having understood, should not judge—and he applies the principle to life as well as to literature. He treats with sympathy the lives of Mrs. Inchbald and Thomas Lovell Beddoes, and with understanding and respect the life, which many had condemned as a failure, of the first Earl of Lytton. Strachey's essays on Hume and Gibbon demonstrate a great capacity for admiration ; and he respects, if in a lesser degree, Boswell as well as Gibbon, Rousseau as well as Hume. The fact is that Strachey, far from being a cynic, admires genuine worth wherever he sees it. Furthermore, he commends Rousseau for his " instinctive, overmastering perception of the importance and the dignity of the individual soul " ; and he upholds Vauvenargues, another eighteenth-century man, who opposed La Rochefoucauld.

> The passionate heart of Vauvenargues, *Strachey says*, revolted against a portrait of humanity restricted and distorted to the extent of being (for all the sobriety of the presentment) really nothing more than a highly ingenious caricature. His mind, so sympathetic as to be often sentimental, so averse from paradox as to be sometimes platitudinous, opposed to La Rochefoucauld's paradoxical cynicism a profound belief in the simple goodness which resides in the emotions of men.

And Strachey tries to protect Vauvenargues from an English translation and commentary which did not do him justice.

Strachey's own heart was passionate, and as one would expect of an Apostle and a disciple of Moore, he valued honest emotion and affection. " A man's feelings are his very self," he says, " and it is around them that all that is noblest and profoundest in our [modern] literature seems naturally to centre." He honours Racine for his portrayal of passionate characters and his "supreme mastery" over the human heart. And he respects love, whether it is "'the tender eye-dawn of aurorean love' . . . the happy, sweet, almost childish passion of two young creatures" that the medieval "chante-fable" *Aucassin et Nicolete* shows us, or the terrible, complicated, fatal passion of Julie de Lespinasse, which Strachey describes in one of the best of his essays.*

Mademoiselle de Lespinasse was the *protégée* of Madame du Deffand; but she broke away from her patroness to found a salon of her own. Strachey's description of her salon may be in part a reflection of his own experiences in Bloomsbury, of the affection and friendship he found there: "Oh! It was a place worth visiting—the little salon in the rue Saint-Dominique. And, if one were privileged to go there often, one found there what one found nowhere else—a sense of freedom and intimacy which was the outcome of a real equality, a real understanding, a real friendship such as have existed, before or since, in few societies indeed." And Mademoiselle de Lespinasse, "inspiring and absorbing all, was the crowning wonder, the final delight. To watch the moving expressions of her face was to watch the conversation itself, transmuted to a living thing by the glow of an intense intelligence." Presently, a young Spanish nobleman, the Marquis de Mora, visited Paris. "He was handsome, clever, and *sensible*; he delighted the French *philosophes*, he fascinated the French ladies; among his conquests was Mademoiselle de Lespinasse. He departed, returned two years later, renewed acquaintance with Julie, and, this time, fell deeply in love." Strachey's evaluation of Mora is significant: "All that is known of him goes to show that he was a man of high worth, endowed with genuine talents, and capable of strong and profound emotions." And "to Julie, then and ever afterwards, he appeared to be a perfect being, a creature of almost super-human excellence. She returned his passion with all the force of her nature; her energies had suddenly carried her into a new and splendid universe; she loved him with the intensity of a woman who has lost her youth, and loves for the first time."

* *Biographical Essays*, pp. 153–64.

Mora determined upon marriage, "in spite of the disparity of age, of wealth, and of position". The only bar to their happiness was his ill-health, for he was beginning to display the symptoms of consumption. But at last, after four years of waiting and preparation, they were about to be married. Then, Mora suffered a violent attack of illness, and had to return to Spain. Mademoiselle de Lespinasse, in her anxiety and disappointment, met, at this juncture, the Comte de Guibert, whose book on military tactics had made him the fashion of the hour, who was young, brilliant, and "gallant in every sense of the word". Her fate was sealed. They soon became friends, and she "poured out to him the whole history of her agitations and her sorrows". He besieged her, and before long she began to feel a passion, born of the situation in which she found herself, which was to bind her inextricably to him. For, "by cruel irony, the one event which, in other circumstances, might have come as a release, proved, in Julie's case, nothing less than the final misfortune. Mora died, and his death took away from her for ever all hope of escape from an intolerable situation." The Comte de Guibert was not a man of Mora's calibre. "His unfaithfulness, and his marriage, were, after all, little more than incidents in her anguish; they were the symptoms of an incurable disease. They stimulated her to fresh efforts towards detachment, but it was in vain. She was a wild animal struggling in a net, involving herself, with every twist and every convulsion, more and more inextricably in the toils." Strachey traces the story with understanding to its ironic close, when, after the death of Julie de Lespinasse, the Comte de Guibert discovers that it was really Mora, and not himself, that she loved throughout.

Strachey respects Mademoiselle de Lespinasse and has nothing but sympathy for her because he sees that she was a woman of real worth, of strong intelligence and deep emotions, who was the victim of circumstances which she could not control. Like Mora, when she loved she loved wholly. "'Je n'aime rien de ce qui est à demi,' she wrote of herself, 'de ce qui est indécis, de ce qui n'est qu'un peu. Je n'entends pas la langue des gens du monde : ils s'amusent et ils bâillent ; ils ont des amis, et ils n'aiment rien. Tout cela me paraît déplorable.' " She saw clearly and did not deceive herself: " Her complete consciousness of the situation made her position more pitiable, but it did not help her to escape." Her story could be told as successfully as it is in Strachey's essay, only by a man who was himself capable of intense feeling.

Strachey's desire for detachment does not, by any means, cause him to repudiate emotion. He sees that the man who, in his search for detachment, denies his humanity, defeats his own purpose. La Rochefoucauld's detachment appears to be supreme. It places him, Strachey says, " either above or below humanity ". It is the contemptuous aloofness of aristocratic pride, as far as may be from the unassuming detachment of Hume; and one wonders if, after all, La Rochefoucauld knew himself. " ' Vanity of vanities, all is vanity ' is his perpetual text (but in a sense different from the Preacher's); and in the safe isolation of this *parti pris*, hedged round by his pride, nourished by his scorn, illuminated by his wit, La Rochefoucauld felt clearly enough how well he could dispense with everything besides—even, perhaps, with the truth itself." And Strachey distrusts equally another kind of detachment, which is the very opposite of La Rochefoucauld's—the detachment of the mystic. He comments on it in his essay on " The Poetry of Blake ":

> Besides its unreasonableness, there is an even more serious objection to Blake's mysticism—and indeed to all mysticism: its lack of humanity. The mystic's creed—even when arrayed in the wondrous and ecstatic beauty of Blake's verse—comes upon the ordinary man, in the rigidity of its uncompromising elevation, with a shock which is terrible, and almost cruel. The sacrifices which it demands are too vast, in spite of the divinity of what it has to offer. What shall it profit a man, one is tempted to exclaim, if he gain his own soul, and lose the whole world? The mystic ideal is the highest of all; but it has no breadth. The following lines express, with a simplicity and an intensity of inspiration which he never surpassed, Blake's conception of that ideal:
>
> And throughout all Eternity
> I forgive you, you forgive me.
> As our dear Redeemer said:
> " This the Wine, & this the Bread."

> It is easy to imagine the sort of comments to which Voltaire, for instance, with his "wracking wheel" of sarcasm and common-sense, would have subjected such lines as these. His criticism would have been irrelevant, because it would never have reached the heart of the matter at issue; it would have been based upon no true understanding of Blake's words. But that they do admit of a real, an unanswerable criticism, it is difficult to doubt. Charles Lamb, perhaps, might have made it; incidentally, indeed, he has. "Sun, and sky, and breeze, and solitary walks, and summer holidays, and the greenness of fields, and the delicious juices of meats and fishes, and society, and the cheerful glass, and candlelight, and fireside conversations, and innocent vanities, and jests, and *irony itself*"—do these things form no part of your Eternity?

Strachey desired neither the detachment of pride nor of mysticism, but the self-possession of an ideal eighteenth-century man, which should combine the common sense of Voltaire and the passion and sensibility of Rousseau. He wished to gain his own soul without repudiating the world, and to tread the middle path between cynicism and sentimentality. He valued self-possession the more because he had a passionate heart and a strong intellect: his intellect demanded detachment, his emotions reached out towards the world. Moreover, his case was complicated because he was at once strongly attracted and repulsed by sex. This unhealthy fascination is evident in *Elizabeth and Essex*; in his other books, though there are hints of it, he keeps it under control. Once more we see, as we saw in considering Forster, that a man's emotions may play at cross-purposes with his intellect. And it is so whether his emotions are what we are pleased to call "healthy" or not. Perhaps it is thus, if intellect and emotions are attuned, that the tension which is civilized life is produced. At any rate, Strachey was able, in most of his work, to keep a balance between reason and emotion because he loved the good qualities of humanity and had a profound respect for truth.

It does not follow that because Strachey often criticized humanity he did not also love it. The man who knows why he admires knows when to despise. And the testimony of Strachey's love is his profound interest in character, which served him, in his writing, in lieu of the artist's inspiration. The careful, detailed analysis of character which he carried on, under Moore's guidance, in the " Society " at Cambridge, was continued throughout his life and shapes his biographies. And he is interested in characters of all types, enamoured, as it were, with life's richness, and delighted by its idiosyncrasy. He is fascinated by Hume's imbecile expression, " so strangely out of keeping with mental agility " ; he enjoys Gibbon's absurd figure which reflected something, a little vanity, a little pomposity, in the inner man, which made him preposterous, and therefore human—" without that touch of nature he would have run the risk of being too much of a good thing ". He notes that the contradictions in Voltaire's nature—his egotism and his disinterestedness, his meanness and his generosity, his treacherousness and his humanity—were carried even into his physical constitution : " His health was so bad that he seemed to pass his whole life on the brink of the grave ; nevertheless his vitality has probably never been surpassed in the history of the world." He is pleased that Sir John Harington, an Elizabethan dandy with a tip-tilted nose, who wrote light verse and scurrilous epigrams—a ridiculous man—should have invented the water-closet. The rich variety of characters found in Strachey's essays and biographies, and the relish with which they are presented, almost entitle his work to stand, in this respect, beside the works of Chaucer, Shakespeare, Scott, and Dickens—the great portrayers of humanity. It is because one must use the word " relish ", rather than " gusto " or " zest ", in describing Strachey's presentment of character, however, that his gallery of portraits is kept out of this high rank. We are aware that the author stands above his characters, examining them ; his identity is not wholly consumed in the act of creation. Perhaps they analysed too much in the Society, or perhaps Strachey had to strive too hard for detachment, with the result that the strain is evident in his work.

In considering the patterns which are sometimes found in life, the congruity in incongruity and strange concatenations of events, Strachey was often led to reflect upon fate. What chance led Newman's father, still undecided between the two Universities on the " fatal morning " when the gig came round for his son, to turn the horse's head away from Cambridge and so plunge Newman into the midst of the Oxford Movement? By what good fortune did Voltaire, in spite of abominable health, in spite of his perpetual attempts to get leave to return to Paris (which, if they had succeeded, would have destroyed the greater part of his independence and influence), live to be eighty-four in the safe, grand isolation of Ferney, and to complete, after the age of sixty, almost all the work for which he is now remembered? The theme of fate plays an important part in Strachey's essays and biographies, and it is difficult to tell whether he himself believed at times in fate or whether he used the theme only for its artistic value. Certainly, it served him well in his art; and perhaps the historian and the biographer, looking, as they do, at the immutable past, tend to become fatalistic. But Strachey, with his faith in reason and intelligence and his belief in the value of detachment, is, clearly, not a fatalist, even though he occasionally toys with the idea of fate. In his work this theme personifies, as it were, "the mysterious and relentless powers of circumstance and character", which fascinated him.

Strachey was almost as interested in circumstance as in character: he had an eye for history as well as for human nature. "An international conference", he once said to André Maurois, "is simply so many men, each with his fixed character, his habits, his neuralgia, his good or bad digestion. The history of the conference, if it could be written, would be not only the analysis of the great confronted interests, but a picture of the mutual reactions of these temperaments on each other." * And Strachey is constantly aware not only of the effect of men upon history, but also of the effect of history upon men. When he writes of "Madame de Sévigné's Cousin" he gives us a sense of the steady, persistent metamorphosis of the age of Louis XIV into the eighteenth century by showing the effects of the change as they were registered upon his central character. His essays on the *philosophes* and their friends warn us of the approach of the French Revolution. And in an essay on

* In *The Economic Consequences of the Peace* and in some of the essays in *Essays in Biography*, Maynard Keynes looks at the 1919 Peace Conference at Versailles from this point of view.

Madame de Lieven he describes how this Russian noblewoman carried the proud traditions of an imperious aristocracy into the nineteenth century, was a force in international politics and the mistress of Princes—but, in the year 1837, " unable to resist any longer the permeations of the Time Spirit ", she fell, the victim of a sentimental passion, into the bourgeois arms of Monsieur Guizot, who was " the living epitome of all that was most middle-class ".

Strachey depended upon patient, conscientious research to help him reconstruct character and history and evaluate the effects of their interaction. He commends the method of the eminent French historians and critics of the second half of the nineteenth century, in whose work, he says, the romantic, personal element is carefully suppressed and " is replaced by an elaborate examination of detail, a careful, sober, unprejudiced reconstruction of past conditions, an infinitely conscientious endeavour to tell the truth and nothing but the truth ". His own method, though somewhat more imaginative in its reconstruction of the inner life of his subjects, is similar. His references and bibliographies, as well as his essays—some of which were by-products, so to speak, of his larger works—testify to the breadth and thoroughness of the reading he did in preparation for his biographies. And he believed, of course, that no relevant detail discovered in research should be suppressed—in short, that truth should be above all other considerations. He objected, for example, to the omission by Mrs. Paget Toynbee in her edition of Horace Walpole's *Letters* of a great many passages which, Mrs Toynbee said, were " quite unfit for publication ". And he repeated the objection as Paget Toynbee's supplementary volumes to the edition were published with similar omissions : " Surely, in a work of such serious intention and such monumental proportions the publication of the *whole* of the original material was not only justifiable, but demanded by the nature of the case." He had this to say about a translation by Miss S. G. Tallentyre of a selection from Voltaire's letters :

> There is a natural tendency—visible in England, perhaps, especially—towards the elegant embellishment of great men ; and

> Voltaire has not escaped the process. In Miss Tallentyre's translation, for instance, of a small selection from his letters, with an introduction and notes, Voltaire is presented to us as a kindly, gentle, respectable personage, a tolerant, broad-minded author, who ended his life as a country gentleman much interested in the drama and social reform. Such a picture would be merely ridiculous, if it were not calculated to mislead. The fact that Voltaire devoted his life to one of the noblest of causes must not blind us to another fact—that he was personally a very ugly customer. . . . The contradiction is strange ; but the world is full of strange contradictions ; and, on the whole, it is more interesting, and also wiser, to face them than to hush them up.*

This belief, founded upon a devotion to truth and to humanity, guided Strachey and informs his biographies.

But intellect, as Strachey would have admitted, is not the only instrument that may serve man in his search for truth ; and we may seek to understand life in ways quite other than through a patient, exacting examination of the lives of our predecessors. Virginia Woolf was as devoted as Strachey to truth, but her method of seeking it is different from his. The major part of her work does not depend on studious, bookish research ; she is well acquainted with the library, but she has little use in her novels for the facts that it offers her. So we may find as we read her books that there are tigers and elephants in South America, or that Scarborough is seven hundred miles from Cornwall ; her characters may feed wide-awake chickens by lantern-light, or cut roses, without surprise, in a Lincolnshire garden at Christmas ; and in one of her books a very minor character is now called Raymond Oliver, and again, without explanation, Sinclair. She would not have been concerned if these lapses had been pointed out to her : they do not, after all, injure her work. In her search for truth she goes straight past the commonplace facts of every day to something more elusive and more profound. " Truth is various ; truth comes to us in different disguises," she says, discussing Plato's Dialogues ; " it is not with the intellect alone that we perceive it."

* *Biographical Essays*, pp. 54–5.

The differences between Virginia Woolf and Strachey are indirectly defined in Virginia Woolf's first novel, *The Voyage Out*. This book, which was begun about 1907 and took seven years to write, reflects much of her experience during the early years of Bloomsbury. *Principia Ethica* is read, as we have seen,* by Helen Ambrose, one of the main characters ; and it is implicit in much of the novel, or at least, in much of the conversation of St. John Hirst and Terence Hewet, the two young men from Cambridge. " D'you think you *do* make enough allowance for feelings ? " Hewet asks Hirst. " Feelings ? " Hirst replies. " Aren't they just what we do allow for ? We put love up there, and all the rest somewhere down below." And he outlines a pyramid in the air with his hands. The difficulty, he says, is to find an appropriate object to love. Hirst and Hewet, Rachel Vinrace and Helen Ambrose, the four central characters of the novel, believe in the value of honest, frank conversation. Rachel is a young woman of twenty-four who has been so sheltered by her father and by the two maidenly aunts who brought her up in Richmond, that she knows nothing of the relations between the sexes. Helen Ambrose takes Rachel's education in hand during a holiday in South America : " Talk was the medicine [Helen] trusted to, talk about everything, talk that was free, unguarded, and as candid as a habit of talking with men made natural in her own case." Helen and Rachel, Hirst and Hewet depend upon conversation of this sort to strengthen their friendship ; and they believe that it is important that friends should know one another as thoroughly as possible. Behind the main action of the novel, Ridley Ambrose, Helen's husband, broods in his study over the poems of Pindar, which he is editing, as Leslie Stephen brooded, perhaps, in the mind of Virginia Woolf. Certainly Ambrose is composed of some of the characteristics of Stephen. He recites poetry aloud to himself ; he goes on long walks through the country ; he sometimes dramatizes himself and makes a great fuss over a slight annoyance ; he worries that his books may be ignored ; he occasionally makes audible, embarrassing remarks to himself about his guests in their presence—all traits that Leslie Stephen shared. And

* See p. 20.

there is a good deal of Lytton Strachey in St. John Hirst. We first see Hirst seated at ease in a hotel lounge, where, in the shade of a curtain, he appears to consist entirely of legs. His body is stooped, ugly, and very thin, but his intellect is majestic ; he is " strong, searching, unyielding in mind " ; and we are impressed throughout the book by his intellectual strength. He considers himself to be, moreover, a person of strong passions ; he believes that sympathy, understanding, and affection are the things that really matter ; but he does not, on the whole, get on well with women ; and he remarks that he abhors the female breast. He has a jaunty manner, but he proves himself, in fact, to have great powers of sympathy and affection when Rachel is taken mortally ill and these qualities are tested. When he sits in the hotel lounge he amuses himself by watching the people there ; he compares them to various animals, and he constructs little theories about them from their gestures and appearance. He is " indeed much given to the study of his kind ". He reads Gibbon with admiration and lends the *Decline and Fall of the Roman Empire* to Rachel to read as an essential part of her education. He believes that one can influence people " by one's point of view, books and so on " ; he sometimes thought, he told Helen, that " almost everything was due to education ".

Virginia Woolf herself is represented in *The Voyage Out*, or at least, her point of view is set forth, partly by Rachel and partly by Terence Hewet, to whom Rachel becomes engaged. Though Rachel differs a good deal from her creator in her upbringing and her interests, there is something in her of the shy, aloof young woman that Duncan Grant describes, who, during her first years in Bloomsbury, was " intensely receptive to any experience new to her ", and to whom her new existence had not yet become alive.* Terence Hewet is a novelist who wants to write a novel about Silence : " the things people don't say ". "But the difficulty ", he says, " is immense." And few people care for " the novel itself, the whole conception, the way one's seen the thing, felt about it, made it stand in relation to other things, not one in a million cares for that. And yet I sometimes wonder whether there's anything else

* See p. 7.

in the whole world worth doing. . . . other people are always wanting something they can't get. But there's an extraordinary satisfaction in writing, even in the attempt to write." He tells Rachel, who is an accomplished pianist, that novel-writing for him is much like piano-playing for her: "We want to find out what's behind things, don't we?" They are overlooking a town at dusk, and he waves towards the lights beneath them: "Look at the lights down there, scattered about anyhow. Things I feel come to me like lights. . . . I want to combine them. . . . Have you ever seen fireworks that make figures? . . . I want to make figures."

Rachel and Hewet disagree with Hirst, though their respect for his intellect is unbounded. But perhaps Hirst depends too much on intellect. "How are you going to judge people merely by their minds?" Rachel asks him. The intellect analyses; it separates things that are not separate; it tends to make things appear simpler than they are. "I'm not like Hirst," Hewet says. "I don't see circles of chalk between people's feet. I sometimes wish I did. It seems to me so tremendously complicated and confused. One can't come to any decision at all; one's less and less capable of making judgments. . . . And then one never knows what any one feels. We're all in the dark. We try to find out, but can you imagine anything more ludicrous than one person's opinion of another person? One goes along thinking one knows; but one really doesn't know." Such a view as this would make impossible, for the writer who held it, biography of the kind that Strachey wrote. The mysterious, relentless powers of circumstance and character no longer exist, or if they do exist they cannot be ascertained. The clearly defined pattern which may be seen when a life is viewed in retrospect, which may be grasped by the intellect and presented from this point of view or from that, is probably an illusion, a pattern imposed on events by the intellect itself for its own convenience and satisfaction. Some such conclusion as this must be drawn from Hewet's view of life, and there is no doubt that he expresses Virginia Woolf's own belief.

But it is not likely that Virginia Woolf reached this belief by criticizing Strachey's views. The difference between them is rather one of temperament, of upbringing and education, and of sex. While Strachey went up to Cambridge to study literature, history and philosophy, to become an Apostle, and to have, in fact, almost complete freedom, Virginia Woolf remained in her father's home. She could, it is true, read anything she liked in her father's library ; but her formal education in advanced subjects was somewhat similar to that of Rachel Vinrace as it is described in *The Voyage Out* : " Kindly doctors and gentle old professors had taught her the rudiments of about ten different branches of knowledge, but they would as soon have forced her to go through one piece of drudgery thoroughly as they would have told her that her hands were dirty." * No one, Virginia Woolf protests in a Feminist book, *A Room of One's Own*, expected much of women intellectually, and we have seen that Leslie Stephen " cared little enough for the higher education of women ".† The education that Virginia Woolf and Rachel Vinrace received, however, had, as Virginia Woolf points out, one great advantage : " it put no obstacle in the way of any real talent that the pupil might chance to have "—none, except, perhaps, the fear that women could not accomplish much intellectually or in art. But there were other obstacles—obstacles which were not directly related to education. Though Leslie Stephen was in the vanguard of Victorian thought, he had not, by any means, seriously questioned the middle-class domestic conventions of the nineteenth century. These conventions, of course, applied primarily and mainly to women ; and it must have been extraordinarily difficult for Stephen's daughters to live intellectually, so to speak, in an enlightened and advanced era, and to be, at the same time, surrounded by unreasoned and unreasonable social taboos and demands. In a paper read to The Women's Service League, Virginia Woolf speaks of the beginning of her literary career. She began as a book reviewer, but before she could review her first book, a novel by a famous man, she had to do battle, she says, with a phantom.

* Credit should be given here to Virginia Woolf's women teachers, especially to Miss Pater and to Miss Janet Case, who, no doubt, were not teachers of this sort.

† See p. 4.

> And the phantom was a woman, and when I came to know her better I called her after the heroine of a famous poem, The Angel in the House. It was she who used to come between me and my paper when I was writing reviews. It was she who bothered me and wasted my time and so tormented me that at last I killed her. . . . I will describe her as shortly as I can. She was intensely sympathetic. She was immensely charming. She was utterly unselfish. She excelled in the difficult arts of family life. She sacrificed herself daily. If there was chicken, she took the leg ; if there was a draught she sat in it—in short she was so constituted that she never had a mind or a wish of her own, but preferred to sympathize always with the minds and wishes of others. Above all—I need not say it—she was pure. Her purity was supposed to be her chief beauty—her blushes, her great grace. In those days—the last of Queen Victoria—every house had its Angel. And when I came to write I encountered her with the very first words. The shadow of her wings fell on my page ; I heard the rustling of her skirts in the room. Directly, that is to say, I took my pen in my hand to review that novel by a famous man, she slipped behind me and whispered : " My dear, you are a young woman. You are writing about a book that has been written by a man. Be sympathetic ; be tender ; flatter ; deceive ; use all the arts and wiles of our sex. Never let anybody guess that you have a mind of your own. Above all, be pure." And she made as if to guide my pen.

And when Virginia Woolf came to write novels there was another difficulty. She describes herself as a young writer " letting her imagination sweep unchecked round every rock and cranny of the world that lies submerged in the depths of our unconscious being ". Then she makes a discovery—but she is brought up short and roused from her dreams.

> She was indeed in a state of the most acute and difficult distress. . . . she had thought of something, something about the body, about the passions which it was unfitting for her as a woman to say. Men, her reason told her, would be shocked. The consciousness of what men will say of a woman who speaks the truth about her passions had roused her from her artist's state of unconsciousness. She could write no more. The trance was over. Her imagination could work no longer. This I believe to be a very common experience with women

writers—they are impeded by the extreme conventionality of the other sex. For though men sensibly allow themselves great freedom in these respects, I doubt that they realize or can control the extreme severity with which they condemn such freedom in women.

"These then", Virginia Woolf continues, "were two very genuine experiences of my own. These were two of the adventures of my professional life. The first—killing the Angel in the House—I think I solved. She died. But the second, telling the truth about my own experiences as a body, I do not think I solved. I doubt that any woman has solved it yet."

Virginia Woolf's Feminism, which is expressed in two argumentative books, *A Room of One's Own* and *Three Guineas*, and in several essays, is based upon an urgent desire that "the educated man's daughter" should have, as Virginia Woolf puts it, a room of her own, that she should have as much freedom as her brother to be an individual, an artist, and an intellectual. These controversial works are at once the result and the expression of Virginia Woolf's struggle to attain this freedom for herself. It is a tribute to her art, and to her practice of her belief that there should be no bias or advocacy in creative writing, that Feminism, in any militant or controversial sense, is entirely excluded from her novels—which is not to say, of course, that her novels are not written from a feminine point of view.

And it is not surprising that Virginia Woolf, coming as she did to the freedom of Bloomsbury from a conventional upper-middle-class Victorian home, should have been, during the first few years in Bloomsbury, shy, aloof, and "intensely receptive" of new experiences. She needed to re-orient herself in her new life; and her re-orientation had to be emotional rather than intellectual. Her intellectual life had always been relatively free; it was mainly her emotions that convention had cramped. And to her, both as an individual and as an artist, emotions were as important as intellect was to Strachey. The age was changing. The change in Virginia Woolf's life was only a symptom, accentuated and accelerated, of the general shift. Virginia Woolf's and Strachey's reactions to the change were characteristic of each of them. Strachey analysed intellectually some of the protagonists of the old order, and stated, in effect, that their values might be replaced by something better. Virginia Woolf sought in her new life an emotional order which could be expressed in works of art. " Well, I'll sit down and think about it," St. John Hirst says in *The Voyage Out*. " One really ought to. If . . . people would only think about things, the world would be a far better place for us all to live in." This is Strachey's attitude. " We are sharply cut off from our predecessors," says Virginia Woolf. " A shift in the scale—the war, the sudden slip of masses held in position for ages—has shaken the fabric from top to bottom, alienated us from the past and made us perhaps too vividly conscious of the present. Every day we find ourselves doing, saying, or thinking things that would have been impossible to our fathers." We have to depend, she concludes, on our senses and emotions, " whose testimony is trustworthy, rather than on [our] intellects whose message is obscure ".

Certainly the testimony that Virginia Woolf's senses brought her was not obscure. She loved to wander about London, submitting herself to impressions. Here, in the great city, was life itself ; there was more to be learned from walking down Oxford Street or lingering in the Strand than from reading all day in the British Museum. The reports came quickly, from all sides, and they were not second-hand. The eye brought the first and the most vivid messages. " Let us dally ", she says in an essay called " Street Haunting : A London Adventure "—" Let us dally a little longer, be content still with surfaces only—the glossy brilliance of the motor omnibuses ; the carnal splendour of the butchers' shops with their yellow flanks and purple steaks ; the blue and red bunches of flowers burning so bravely through the plate glass of the florists' windows." " For the eye ", she says, " has this strange property : it rests only on beauty ; like a butterfly it seeks colour and basks in warmth." But all Virginia Woolf's senses were active, abnormally active, in as much as few of us indeed see and hear and feel with such splendid intensity. In a quiet room in Kensington or Bloomsbury, especially when dusk or fog seemed to exclude the rest of the world, she would be aware of the sound of traffic, the pulse of London, throbbing in the streets. And here is her transcription of the sensations caused by a Mozart quartet for strings—the players are about to begin, the bows descend—

> Flourish, spring, burgeon, burst! The pear tree on the top of the mountain. Fountains jet; drops descend. But the waters of the Rhone flow swift and deep, race under the arches, and sweep the trailing water leaves, washing shadows over the silver fish, the spotted fish rushed down by the swift waters, now swept into an eddy where—it's difficult this—conglomeration of fish all in a pool; leaping, splashing, scraping sharp fins; and such a boil of current that the yellow pebbles are churned round and round, round and round—free now, rushing downwards, or even somehow ascending in exquisite spirals into the air; curled like thin shavings from under a plane; up and up. . . . How lovely goodness is in those who, stepping lightly, go smiling through the world! Also in jolly old fishwives, squatted under arches, obscene old women, how deeply they laugh and shake and rollick, when they walk, from side to side, hum, hah! *

She was responsive, as well, to the animal sensations of the body. She had been motoring one evening through Sussex, absorbing the beauty around her and reflecting upon it. "And then the body who had been silent up to now began its song, almost at first as low as the rush of the wheels: 'Eggs and bacon; toast and tea; fire and a bath; fire and a bath; jugged hare,' it went on, 'and red currant jelly; a glass of wine; with coffee to follow, with coffee to follow—and then to bed; and then to bed.' . . . And the rest of the journey was performed in the delicious society of my own body." She is at home with Spenser. *The Faery Queen*, she says, brings into play one layer of the mind after another. "The desire of the eye, the desire of the body, desires for rhythm, movement, the desire for adventure—each is gratified. And this gratification depends upon the poet's own mobility. He is alive in all his parts. He scarcely seems to prefer one to another. We are reminded of the old myth of the body which has many organs, and the lesser and the obscure are as important as the

* "The String Quartet", *A Haunted House*, p. 25.

kingly and important." In *Flush*, a biography of Elizabeth Barrett Browning's dog, Virginia Woolf's love of describing sensations is given free play. She imaginatively enters Flush's mind as he races across the Berkshire fields, or walks for the first time in London, or in Florence. And she enjoys herself immensely, as this mock-epic simile, describing Flush's first entry into Elizabeth Barrett's bedroom, testifies :

> Only a scholar who has descended step by step into a mausoleum and there finds himself in a crypt, crusted with fungus, slimy with mould, exuding sour smells of decay and antiquity, while half-obliterated marble busts gleam in mid-air and all is dimly seen by the light of the small swing lamp which he holds, and dips and turns, glancing now here, now there—only the sensations of such an explorer into the buried vaults of a ruined city can compare with the riot of emotions that flooded Flush's nerves as he stood for the first time in an invalid's bedroom, in Wimpole street, and smelt eau-de-Cologne.

But beneath the joy and beauty of life, Virginia Woolf felt, lay ugliness and horror. She was, at different moments, as intensely aware of the one as of the other. Behind the West End of London, she knew, was the East End, with its poor and its slums, its grimy factories and its slimy docks. Illness or accident might at any time strike and kill, or worse, cause the pleasures of the body to be replaced by agony and pain. Flush was pitched into a sack, was taken to Whitechapel and chained in a dark and horrid place by men who would cut his head and paws off and send them to his mistress if she did not ransom him in time. " When one gave up seeing the beauty that clothed things, this was the skeleton beneath," Helen Ambrose thought in *The Voyage Out* as she drove east along the Embankment to board the ship for South America. And the theme of beauty with horror ever close beside is pursued to the end of the novel. At the comfortable hotel in South America, amidst leisurely holiday-makers, Rachel Vinrace looks out from a window upon the wrong side of hotel life, and sees two large women plucking the yellow bodies of hens on blood-smeared trays, while a wizened old woman chases a chicken, catches it, and slices off its head. The

Amazon is rich with gorgeous tropical beauty, but it was there, in all probability, that Rachel caught the fever which kills her just after she has become engaged to Terence Hewet—at the moment when life seems most beautiful she is taken ill. When Hewet kisses her while she is delirious, she sees an old woman slicing a man's head off with a knife. And in an essay entitled "Three Pictures", which seems to be based on a personal experience, Virginia Woolf illustrates again the beauty and the tragedy of life. At the turn of the road in a village she saw a fine young sailor, just back from China, with a bundle in one arm, and his young wife, who was soon going to bear him their first child, on the other. "Everything was right and good and as it should be, one felt about that picture. There was something wholesome and satisfactory in the sight of such happiness; life seemed sweeter and more enviable than before." Virginia Woolf thought of the happy sailor and his wife at odd moments during that day and the next; the picture of them floated in her eyes, "making most things appear much brighter, warmer, and simpler than usual; and making some things appear foolish; and some things wrong and some things right, and more full of meaning than before". Then, in the middle of the night, a loud cry, made by a woman's voice, "made by some extremity of feeling almost sexless, almost expressionless", rang through the village. "It was as if human nature had cried out against some iniquity, some inexpressible horror." Dead silence followed. "One lay in the dark listening intently. It had been merely a voice. There was nothing to connect it with. No picture of any sort came to intrepret it, to make it intelligible to the mind. But as the dark arose at last all one saw was an obscure human form, almost without shape, raising a gigantic arm in vain against some overwhelming iniquity." Daylight returned, and the weather was fine, and the countryside beautiful. "All was as quiet, as safe could be. Yet, one kept thinking, a cry had rent it; all this beauty had been an accomplice that night; had consented; to remain calm, to be still beautiful; at any moment it might be sundered again." To cheer herself, Virginia Woolf thought of the sailor and his wife; she lingered over every detail of his homecoming, until the happiness of that picture suffused things once more, and even the village churchyard, with the grave-digger throwing up shovelfuls of yellow earth while his children played nearby and his wife brought out his tea, appeared cheerful and good. But the grave was for the young sailor—" 'He died two nights ago, of some foreign fever. Didn't you hear his wife? She rushed into the road and cried out. . . . Here, Tommy, you're all covered with earth!' " "What a picture it made!" Virginia Woolf says. It is worth recalling that Thoby Stephen, handsome and vital, died in his youth while enjoying a holiday with his brother and sisters in Greece.

What, then, is the truth about life? Is its beauty real? or its horror? Or is there something behind them both, more real than either? And how is one to find out? Virginia Woolf uses the painter's tools of disinterested vision and contemplation in her search for reality, and she begins by looking at solid objects. "Even the grown man keeps something of his unbiological, disinterested vision with regard to a few things," Roger Fry says. "He still looks at flowers, and does not merely see them. He also keeps objects which have some marked peculiarity of appearance that catches his eye." * Virginia Woolf has written a short story about a young man who gave up a political career to collect broken bits of china, lumps of glass, and stones.† He put his first two finds, a bright, star-shaped piece of china and a dull, smooth lump of glass, upon his mantelpiece. "The contrast between the china so vivid and alert, and the glass so mute and contemplative, fascinated him, and wondering and amazed he asked himself how the two came to exist in the same world, let alone to stand upon the same narrow strip of marble in the same room. The question remained unanswered." He later found a remarkable piece of iron which had come from outer space—"And yet the meteorite stood upon the same ledge with the lump of glass and the star-shaped china". The secret of the universe may indeed be held even in small, inanimate things. "What is the significance of anything as an end in itself?" Clive Bell asks. "What is that which is left when we have stripped a thing of all its associations, of all its significance as a means? What is left to provoke our emotion? What but

* *Vision and Design*, p. 31. † "Solid Objects", *A Haunted House*, pp. 69–76.

that which philosophers used to call 'the thing in itself' and now call 'ultimate reality'? Shall I be altogether fantastic in suggesting, what some of the profoundest thinkers have believed, that the significance of the thing in itself is the significance of Reality?" * In another short story Virginia Woolf describes herself contemplating a mark on the wall (which turned out to be a snail), gathering her thoughts around it. "Indeed, now that I have fixed my eyes upon [the mark]," she says, "I feel that I have grasped a plank in the sea; I feel a satisfying sense of reality which at once turns the two Archbishops and the Lord High Chancellor [she had been thinking of Whitaker's Table of Precedency] to the shadows of shades. Here is something definite, something real. Thus, waking from a midnight dream of horror, one hastily turns on the light and lies quiescent, worshipping the chest of drawers, worshipping solidity, worshipping reality, worshipping the impersonal world which is a proof of some existence other than ours." The impersonal world contains, besides inanimate things, snails and insects and flowers and trees. Sometimes Virginia Woolf, with wonderful sympathy, imagines herself, as it were, inside it:

> I like to think of the tree itself: first the close dry sensation of being wood; then the grinding of the storm; then the slow, delicious ooze of sap. I like to think of it, too, on winter's nights standing in the empty field with all leaves close-furled, nothing tender exposed to the iron bullets of the moon, a naked mast upon an earth that goes tumbling, tumbling, all night long. The song of birds must sound very loud and strange in June; and how cold the feet of insects must feel upon it, as they make laborious progresses up the creases of the bark, or sun themselves upon the thin green awning of the leaves, and look straight in front of them with diamond-cut red eyes.†

So for Rachel Vinrace one day, "Flowers and even pebbles in the earth had their own life and disposition, and brought back the feelings of a child to whom they were companions." ‡

* *Art*, pp. 53–4. † "The Mark on the Wall", *A Haunted House*, pp. 35–43.
‡ Cf. Wordsworth's "There was a Boy", "Nutting", and the "Ode: Intimations of Immortality from Recollections of Early Childhood".

Virginia Woolf searched for reality more often, however, in her own sensations, which, as we have seen, she trusted. She describes something of this search, the beginning of the process by which it was carried on, perhaps, in a short sketch called " Monday or Tuesday " :

> Desiring truth, awaiting it, laboriously distilling a few words, for ever desiring—(a cry starts to the left, another to the right. Wheels strike divergently. Omnibuses conglomerate in conflict)—for ever desiring—(the clock asseverates with twelve distinct strokes that it is midday ; light sheds gold scales ; children swarm)—for ever desiring truth. Red is the dome ; coins hang on the trees ; smoke trails from the chimneys ; bark, shout, cry " Iron for sale "—and truth ?

Besides submitting herself to the sounds and sights of London, she watched people and tried, with the same sympathy and insight that enabled her to imagine what it would be like to be a tree, to enter into their lives. " The fascination of the London street ", she says, " is that no two people are ever alike ; each seems bound on some private affair of his own." She tried to follow them, in imagination, and to discover what their affairs were ; she would build stories about them to explain their idiosyncrasies—though she was aware that her stories were almost certainly wrong. She had a sharp eye for hints of dress, expression, and action that reveal character ; and she was sensitive to the signs, often so slight that they have to be felt rather than seen, of the emotions of others. " It is always an adventure ", she says, " to enter a new room ; for the lives and characters of its owners have distilled their atmosphere into it, and directly we enter it we breast some new wave of emotion." Coming home from that walk which is recorded in " Street Haunting ", she thought of the people she had seen : " one could tell oneself the story of the dwarf, of the blind men, of the party in the Mayfair mansion, of the quarrel in the stationer's shop. Into each of these lives one could penetrate a little way, far enough to give oneself the illusion that one is not tethered to a single mind, but can put on briefly for a few minutes the bodies and minds of others. One could become a washerwoman, a publican, a street singer.

And what greater delight and wonder can there be than to leave the straight lines of personality and deviate into those footpaths that lead beneath brambles and thick tree trunks into the heart of the forest where live those wild beasts, our fellow men?" But if our fellows are wild beasts in so far as it is very hard to come near enough to them to enter their minds, they are not so, Virginia Woolf believes, in other respects. She loves human nature, and she believes that, when we come to know it, we find it more beautiful than we could have imagined. "Wherever I go, mysterious figures," she says in a short story, "I see you, turning the corner, mothers and sons; you, you, you. I hasten, I follow. This, I fancy, must be the sea. Grey is the landscape; dim as ashes; the water murmurs and moves. If I fall on my knees, if I go through the ritual, the ancient antics, it's you, unknown figures, you I adore; if I open my arms, it's you I embrace, you I draw to me—adorable world!"

At home after a walk through the streets, after the noise and colour and thronging humanity, Virginia Woolf wanted to reflect alone. So after reading the Elizabethans and enjoying the extravagant rhetoric and pageantry of their plays, the mind, she says, as if tired with company, "steals off to muse in solitude; to think, not to act; to comment, not to share; to explore its own darkness, not the bright-lit-up surfaces of others. It turns to Donne, to Montaigne, to Sir Thomas Browne, to the keepers of the keys of solitude." She wished no longer to receive sensations or to try to find her way into the lives of others, but to muse upon the sensations she had gathered and to study her own mind. "I want to think quietly, calmly, spaciously," she says in "The Mark on the Wall", "never to be interrupted, never to have to rise from my chair, to slip easily from one thing to another, without any sense of hostility, or obstacle. I want to sink deeper and deeper, away from the surface, with its hard separate facts." * So one could discover what living is like, could hold out before the mind, as it were, the various sights and sounds, the memories and anticipations that are aroused, the emotions, thoughts, conversation, and imaginings, other people and one's reactions

* Cf. p. 88.

to them, the movements and feelings of the body—all the things that make a moment. One could find out how the mind works : how one's several selves carry on an internal dialogue ; how thought and emotion meet and merge and affect one another ; how numerous the layers of consciousness are, so that one may, at the same time, take notes at a meeting in Bloomsbury with one part of the mind and look at flowers at Kew with another, or, standing on the kerb, see the policeman beckon, hear the traffic, see the colour in the shop windows, move with the crowd across the road, while the dialogue goes on, perhaps, about something far away and long ago. And when one sank, sitting in one's chair after a walk, deeper and deeper through the layers of the mind, one might, for a moment, as the scenes of the day arranged themselves, glimpse reality.

Reality, whatever it is, Virginia Woolf believed, is outside the limitations of time and space that we humans must endure ; or, to put it in another way, reality holds both space and time in their entirety, not just the little portion of them that an individual holds in the tiny thimble of his mind. She illustrates this truth very early in her first novel—and she will repeat the illustration again and again in later books. As the ship carrying Rachel Vinrace and the Ambroses to South America sails out into the Atlantic, Virginia Woolf pauses to describe England, which has been left behind. It is October, and the weather is fine and warm. " Great tracts of earth lay now beneath the autumn sun, and the whole of England, from the bald moors to the Cornish rocks, was lit up from dawn to sunset, and showed in stretches of yellow, green, and purple." We are meant to see England in its entirety, as though we soared high above it and yet could distinguish every detail. We are shown the roofs of the great towns, thousands of small gardens with old ladies snipping the flowers, "innumerable parties of picnickers ", lovers, sick people and old people, men with cigars and women with grey hairs, long-tailed birds crossing from wood to wood. " But while all this went on by land, very few people thought about the sea. . . . For all they imagined, the ships when they vanished on the sky-line dissolved, like snow in water. The grown-up view, indeed, was not much clearer than the view of the little creatures in bathing drawers who were trotting into the foam all along the coasts of England, and scooping up buckets full of water." The passengers on the ship were almost equally unaware of England. " When the ship was out of sight of land, it became plain that the people of England were completely mute. The disease attacked other parts of the earth ; Europe shrank, Asia shrank, Africa and America shrank, until it seemed doubtful whether the ship would ever run against any of those wrinkled little rocks again." But England is there, Europe is there, Asia, Africa, and America are there ; and if we could see the whole of reality, and were not bound to one little body and mind, we would see them all, with the old ladies snipping flowers in the garden, and the long-tailed birds, and the seas between the continents, and the ships upon the seas. Almost immediately after the passage in *The Voyage Out* describing the mutual isolation of England and the ship, Virginia Woolf shows us Rachel Vinrace reflecting, in a dreamy state, upon the incompleteness of human relations :

> Reality dwelling in what one saw and felt, but did not talk about, one could accept a system in which things went round and round quite satisfactorily to other people, without often troubling to think about it, except as something superficially strange. . . . Inextricably mixed in dreamy confusion, her mind seemed to enter into communion, to be delightfully expanded and combined with the spirit of the whitish boards on deck, with the spirit of the sea, with the spirit of Beethoven Op. 112, even with the spirit of poor William Cowper there at Olney. Like a ball of thistledown it kissed the sea, rose, kissed it again, and thus rising and kissing passed finally out of sight.

And later, during a discussion with Richard Dalloway, a fellow passenger, Rachel finds it impossible to express what she feels to be the truth—or even to seize the truth firmly : " She was haunted by absurd jumbled ideas—how, if one went back far enough, everything perhaps was intelligible ; everything was in common ; for the mammoths who pastured in the fields of Richmond High Street had turned into paving stones and boxes full of ribbon, and her aunts." Reality includes the whole of time, as well as all space, and we can grasp but fragments of it. Virginia Woolf discovered through her senses, so to speak, the truth that Kant found intellectually : that space and time are human concepts, that we look, to use Kant's illustration, through spectacles that cause us to organize our experience in terms of time and space—terms which are purely relative to ourselves. This view of reality accounts, in part, for the ever-recurring image of the sea in Virginia Woolf's books. The sea laps all the shores of the world ; it has been and will be, so it seems to us mortals, through all time. The waves disturb its depths no more than the years ripple the surface of eternity.

To understand, to reach out towards reality and seek unity with it, one must, therefore, escape as far as possible from the narrow chamber of one's own mind. There are several ways in which escape may be sought. One may contemplate inanimate objects, or imagine oneself into the impersonal world of nature. One may drink in, as Virginia Woolf did, the outside world, and see, perhaps, in an apparently casual collocation of things in a street or in the countryside, a hint of a world more permanent than the world of every day.* Then, as one reflects upon what one has seen, and heard, and felt, one sinks away from the hard, separate facts of the surface ; the divisions of the mind, divisions of time and space that are demanded by the active life, are broken down ; the past merges with the present, and the present expands to include the past, so that one is no longer walking down Oxford Street merely, or sitting in a chair contemplating a mark on the wall, but one may, at moments, see the whole of London, and of England, and the whole of one's life, spread out before one. And as one sinks even farther, one reaches that deep, unconscious sea, which is far away from the surface personality and is shared by the living, the dead, and the unborn ; one sinks from one's individual wave into the depths.

This sort of reflection requires solitude, yet it is a highly impersonal and unegoistical state : its detachment is that of the mystic, whose body is solitary while his mind seeks union with that which is outside himself. But Virginia Woolf, of course, was no recluse, or rather, she was a recluse only at

* See pp. 87–8. Cf. *To The Lighthouse*, pp. 198–9.

intervals. She loved both company and solitude, just as she loved to wander through the streets and then to sit alone in her room. And though she wished to find union with a reality infinitely greater than her ego, she knew that one's soul must possess itself and be free before it can expand and communicate.* Nevertheless, the need to possess oneself and the desire for union, as well as the need for solitude and the love of company, play against one another and create tension. Hence Virginia Woolf's insistence upon the value of good manners—really a demand for civilized freedom—which is to be found throughout her books and is related to her dislike of convention.

Manners should not be confused with convention, though they often are. In fact the two are completely opposed. Convention disregards the individual ; good manners are based upon respect and consideration for him. Victorian convention had put up the barriers that Virginia Woolf had to break in order to be herself. It had insisted that the educated man's daughter should be The Angel in the House ; it had set up for her false ideals of " purity ", had dominated her and cut her off from much that is valuable in life. If good manners and not convention had been uppermost in the Victorian Age, women would have been able to associate freely with men and would have been allowed to control their own lives : they would have been treated, in short, as individuals and equals. Perhaps it was a fear that men would try to dominate her, that they would act in the conventional way, that caused Virginia Woolf to be rather aloof and fierce in her manner towards them during her first years in Bloomsbury.† Convention, moreover, is often dishonest ; and Virginia Woolf demanded honesty in manners, as in all else. Convention conceals ; it pretends to be what it is not, deceives itself, and becomes pompous and pretentious ; it imagines that it admires and respects women ; it prefers to be " improved " and elevated rather than look at truth. Furthermore, it cramps and squashes men into different classes, separating them from one another (as it separates men from women), yet encouraging them to try to climb into a higher class ; and so it stimulates

* This truth is illustrated in Rachel's development in *The Voyage Out.*

jealousy, possessiveness, pugnacity, greed, and the desire for power.

As we should expect, Virginia Woolf distrusts man's desire for power as much as Forster does ; and she believes, moreover, that an active life, to the extent that it cuts a man off from contemplation, prevents him from understanding. Her position in this respect is indirectly stated in an essay on Montaigne.

> The laws are mere conventions, utterly unable to keep touch with the vast variety and turmoil of human impulses, *she says, interpreting Montaigne* ; habits and customs are a convenience devised for the support of timid natures who dare not allow their souls free play. But we, who have a private life and hold it infinitely the dearest of our possessions, suspect nothing so much as an attitude. Directly we begin to protest, to attitudinize, to lay down laws, we perish. We are living for others, not for ourselves. We must respect those who sacrifice themselves in the public service, load them with honours, and pity them for allowing, as they must, the inevitable compromise ; but for ourselves let us fly fame, honour, and all offices that put us under an obligation to others.*

There can be no doubt that Virginia Woolf agrees with Montaigne. She knows that some must lead active lives for the good of society, but she believes the active life is inferior to the private, contemplative life. And she respects an active life only if it is disinterested and guided by tolerance and a love of truth rather than by a desire for power. Disinterestedness, tolerance, integrity, and courage (without which the first three are impossible) are the virtues she most admires. Disinterestedness and integrity enable one to seek truth ; tolerance allows each to seek it in his own way. In *Three Guineas* she envisions an ideal college for women which is founded on these virtues. This college is experimental and adventurous ; it has no chapels and no traditions ; it teaches only the humane arts—" not the arts of dominating other people ; not the arts of ruling, of killing, of acquiring land and capital ". There are no barriers of wealth or class or ceremony, no degrees and no distinctions ; competition is abolished, and " all the different

* *Common Reader,* I, p. 90.

degrees and kinds of mind, body and soul merit " co-operate. The student is able to discuss her art with people who do not think of examinations or degrees, or of honour or profit, but of the art itself. And in Virginia Woolf's second novel, *Night and Day*, she shows us an active life that she admires. Mary Datchet, one of the characters, is the secretary of a society working for women's suffrage. She is in love with Ralph Denham and wishes to marry him ; but just before Denham proposes to her she realizes that she cannot marry him, for she sees that he is in love with another woman. " The truth seemed to support her ; it struck her, even as she looked at his face, that the light of truth was shining far away beyond him ; the light of truth, she seemed to frame the words . . ., shines on a world not to be shaken by our personal calamities." She renounces Denham, resigns her job with the suffrage society, and devotes herself to the furtherance of larger schemes for the benefit of man. " She saw to the remote spaces behind the strife of the foreground, enabled now to gaze there, since she had renounced her own demands, privileged to see the larger view, to share the vast desires and sufferings of the mass of mankind." We are made to admire Mary Datchet's courage, integrity, and disinterestedness ; we are shown that she both possesses herself and merges her ego with a greater reality. She is saved by her devotion to truth ; but we feel none the less that her life is tragic, that she has had to accept something of lesser value than she might have had. " Having lost what is best," she tells herself, " I do not mean to pretend that any other view does instead."

Virginia Woolf desired friendship and communion with others, then, so long as her integrity and freedom as an individual were respected. And she did not wish to suffer Mary Datchet's isolation from love. Indeed, entirely apart from her personal feelings, apart from her natural liking for people and her interest, as a novelist, in them, her conception of life made love and a knowledge of others necessary. When she sought to enter the minds of others, when she wished to clasp humanity to her, she was trying, once more, to escape from the limitations of individuality. " This, I fancy, must be the sea," she says, speaking of humanity, in a passage that has already been quoted. She wished to enter it, to drench herself in the reality that is to be found, not in an individual mind, but in the mind, conceived as an entity, of mankind. She protests again and again against the individual's loneliness, against the barriers that lie between people and isolate them one from another. " Would there ever be a time when the world was one and indivisible ? " Rachel Vinrace asks herself as she watches Terence Hewet reading. " Even with Terence himself—how far apart they could be, how little she knew what was passing in his brain now ! " Later she says to him : " I hate these divisions. . . . One person all in the dark about another person." Immediately she becomes contemplative, and Hewet, in his turn, feels that she is cut off from him. And the difficulty of communicating, the difficulty of knowing even those closest to us, is a major theme in *Night and Day.* The great value of free and sincere conversation, of friendship, and of love, Virginia Woolf believed, is that these things break through, momentarily at least, the barriers between individuals. When Ralph Denham offered Katharine Hilbery, the heroine of *Night and Day*, a pact meant to assure absolute sincerity and freedom in friendship, she saw his offer as a chance to step from darkness into light.* Rachel and Hewet depended upon conversation to break down the barriers between them ; and as their minds came into closer contact they felt a new sense of reality. When they talked, " with every word the mist which had enveloped them, making them seem unreal to each other, . . . melted a little further, and their contact became more and more natural. Up through the sultry southern landscape they saw the world they knew appear clearer and more vividly than it had ever appeared before." Helen Ambrose and St. John Hirst had a similar experience after a conversation during which they had come to know and to like one another better. But love has even a greater power than conversation to increase one's understanding and so to heighten one's sense of reality. After Hewet became engaged to Rachel, it appeared to him that the world was different than before —" it had, perhaps, more solidity, more coherence, more importance, greater depth. Why, even the earth sometimes

* p. 34.

seemed to him very deep ; not carved into hills and cities and fields, but heaped in great masses." He saw, in fact, with an artist's vision. Katharine Hilbery and Ralph Denham fell in love too and became engaged. On the night of their engagement it seemed to Katharine " that the immense riddle was answered ; the problem had been solved ; she held in her hands for one brief moment the globe which we spend our lives in trying to shape, round, whole, and entire from the confusion of chaos ". Denham, for his part, " had a vision of an orderly world ". And, to turn from fiction to real life, let us look at Virginia Woolf's account of Roger and Helen Fry's honeymoon : " The honeymoon was spent . . . abroad, and it was a time for both of them of ' perfect happiness '. Happiness is a difficult emotion to convey in letters written from a hotel bedroom with bags to be packed or unpacked, with clothes and paint-boxes littering the floor, and often ' not a scrap of paper left to write upon '. Yet it was conveyed, and there it still is—a sense that everything had fallen into place and all the odds and ends of existence had come together to make a whole, a centre of peace and satisfaction." Love and companionship may rivet together the fragments of the world and give us a view of reality, Virginia Woolf believed, before, perhaps, horror and madness break in and the reign of chaos is restored.

For Virginia Woolf did not believe that in this life we may escape wholly from loneliness and horror to gain a clear and constant vision of reality. " Our penitence deserves a glimpse only ; our toil respite only," she says in *To the Lighthouse*. But, if we are artists, we may fix for ever the glimpses we are given as we walk in the street or through the countryside, as we contemplate the impersonal world or muse upon our experiences and sink into the subconscious, as we love and talk and enjoy the companionship of others. She believed, as she has told us in a passage quoted in Chapter II, that " it is [the writer's] business to find [reality] and collect it and communicate it to the rest of us ". It was because writing gave her an opportunity to fix her experiences in a work of art—a reality immune from the accidents and exigencies of time and space—that she enjoyed writing so thoroughly and agreed with

Hewet that there was perhaps nothing else in the world so worth while. When others read her books they would feel as she felt, they would see for a moment the reality she had seen. Though Roger Fry is dead and Helen Fry died after spending much of her life in an asylum for the insane, the happiness they knew on their honeymoon, " a sense that everything had fallen into place ", is still to be found in their letters. When Rachel Vinrace read Gibbon she felt that his words drove " roads back to the very beginning of the world . . . and by passing down them all knowledge would be hers, and the book of the world turned back to the very first page ". At another time she played Bach in the hotel lounge in South America. Her audience " sat very still as if they saw a building with spaces and columns succeeding each other rising in the empty space. Then they began to see themselves and their lives, and the whole of human life advancing very nobly under the direction of music." Art increases our understanding by expressing truth that can scarcely be communicated in any other way. We escape, when we submit ourselves to art, from the bounds of personality, because the artist has given his experience " its grouping and standing in the universal " and has submerged his ego in the formal, impersonal world of art.

But the final surrender of personality, the final submersion of the ego, is made only at death. " Extinction ! " Virginia Woolf says as she imagines herself flying towards death with a pilot who resembles Charon ; " The word is consummation." Death is cruel—so it appears, at least, to the living—but if it increases, at times, the horror of life, it also releases us from life's horror. And were it not for death, we would not see beauty so intensely : because we know we must die, we value life's beauty more highly. In death, beauty and horror merge at last—it is a comment upon them both. The barriers of life are finally broken, and the individual wave becomes once more a part of the sea. In *The Years*, Virginia Woolf's last novel but one, Delia Pargiter has a " moment of understanding " as she stands beside her mother's open grave and watches the earth drop on the coffin : " She was possessed by a sense of something everlasting ; of life mixing with death, of death becoming life. For as she looked she heard the sparrows chirp quicker and quicker ; she heard wheels in the distance sound louder and louder ; life came closer and closer." Again and again the characters in Virginia Woolf's novels have a new sense of reality when death strikes ; and we, the readers, are made to feel that death is a significant part of life, that life is rightly bound inextricably to it. Death ends Rachel Vinrace's education in *The Voyage Out*. She moves closer and closer to reality throughout the book—as she receives her first kiss from Richard Dalloway and discusses the relations between the sexes with Helen Ambrose, as she talks to St. John Hirst and Terence Hewet, as she falls in love with Hewet and is engaged to him. Finally, she becomes ill ; time and space are utterly confused in her delirium ; and she dies. Hewet sits beside her bed during the last moments of her life, and his mind becomes almost indistinguishable from hers :

> An immense feeling of peace came over Terence, so that he had no wish to move or to speak. The terrible torture and unreality of the last days were over, and he had come out now into perfect certainty and peace. His mind began to work naturally again and with great ease. The longer he sat there the more profoundly was he conscious of the peace invading every corner of his soul. Once he held his breath and listened acutely ; she was still breathing ; he went on thinking for some time ; they seemed to be thinking together ; he seemed to be Rachel as well as himself ; and then he listened again ; no, she had ceased to breathe. So much the better—this was death. It was nothing ; it was to cease to breathe. It was happiness, it was perfect happiness. They had now what they had always wanted to have, the union which had been impossible while they lived. Unconscious whether he thought the words or spoke them aloud, he said, " No two people have ever been so happy as we have been. No one has ever loved as we have loved."
>
> It seemed to him that their complete union and happiness filled the room with rings eddying more and more widely. He had no wish in the world left unfulfilled. They possessed what could never be taken from them.

It is only when Hewet has ceased to think with Rachel, when he has been recalled, by the entry of others, to the world of time and space and to his position in it, that he feels that death is cruel.

Virginia Woolf's quest for reality, like Rachel's, ended in death—death which she sought herself. In 1941, when it was evident even to those whose senses were far less active than hers that horror had broken through the beauty of life and was dominant, when she feared that she was about to suffer another attack of mental illness, she entered a stream to join for ever the sea of reality, to be

> Rolled round in earth's diurnal course,
> With rocks, and stones, and trees.

It will be seen that Virginia Woolf's conception of reality and Forster's feeling for the countryside have something in common. Of course, there are differences too. Though Virginia Woolf believed that she sometimes saw glimpses of reality in the countryside, she did not often, on the whole, look for it there. She was a city-dweller, while Forster, by preference, at least, is a countryman. His feeling for the countryside has been developed by living there and knowing it intimately from childhood. Virginia Woolf looked at the countryside with an artist's vision, and the significance that she sometimes found as she looked is a part only of a larger mystic conception—a mystic conception which is much more comprehensive than Forster's feeling for the countryside, though his feeling too is tinged with mysticism. Moreover, the impersonal world of nature is the most significant part of the countryside for Virginia Woolf; for Forster, the personality of nature, which has been derived from past generations, is the important thing. But Forster sees the countryside, in a sense, as a sea, comparable to the subconscious mind of the race, and this accords with Virginia Woolf's view of reality.

But, we may ask—and should ask—is there any validity in such views as these? What is reality?—is there, in truth, something more permanent behind the world of appearances? And as for the countryside, is it, in fact, as Forster believes it to be?

It is clear at once that there is much less mysticism in Forster's view of the countryside than in Virginia Woolf's conception of reality. Reduced to its simplest intellectual terms, Forster's belief is that the countryside is preferable to the city —that it is man's home as the city cannot be—and, further, that an agricultural environment is better for man's character than an industrial-commercial environment, as we know the latter environment to-day, at any rate. It is not that Forster has any naïve belief in a Golden Age. " Our freedom is really menaced to-day ", he says, " because a million years ago Man was born in chains." Man " has been a coward for centuries, afraid of the universe outside him and of the herd wherein he took refuge ".* Forster believes, however, that there is a good deal of innate goodness, besides cowardice, in man, and that, through long centuries, there has been evolved in the country-side an orderly way of life that gives a fuller expression to man's capabilities than cities allow to most of their inhabitants. He does not believe that an agricultural life is the highest life attainable. He admires much more the lives of the artist, the intellectual, and, perhaps, the mystic. To decide upon the validity of his view of average country and city life, an immense amount of sociological data would be required, and even then the decision made would almost inevitably depend mainly upon what one valued in life. And such a decision would be, for the most part, beside the point. Forster tells us that the application of new scientific discoveries is disrupting society and causing widespread uneasiness, that, in fact, our knowledge of science is far in advance of our knowledge of how to live. These are truths that are indisputable.

But Forster's view of the countryside cannot be wholly explained in intellectual terms. If it could it would not serve him so well in his art—and we will see that it is just here that it serves him best. His attachment to the countryside is emotional ; it is an affair of the heart, which, as he has told us, signs no documents. The intellect may sign the documents or refuse to sign them—it makes no difference to the heart. And besides Forster's love of the countryside, inextricably combined with it, is the mystic feeling that we have examined, the feeling that the joys and sorrows of humanity have pressed themselves into the bosom of nature, so that one is not

* *Two Cheers for Democracy*, p. 21.

alone in the countryside, but may feel the presence of one's ancestors.

Similarly, Virginia Woolf's conception of reality involves much more than a realization of the truth that an individual mind can experience only a fragment of time and space. She contemplated the universe with the artist's disinterested vision, a vision which, as Roger Fry has shown us, is not concerned with action or the consequences of action, with power or with the practical affairs of life, but is concerned only with understanding. She stripped from the outside world the veil that the active life imposes. And, above all, she shows us in her books, as fully as she can, what her experience of living was. Her *experience of living* : what living was like as she experienced it—not her *experience of life*, which, in popular usage, at any rate, means something quite different, something which is usually given as a guide to action. And here, finally, is the validity of the emotions and mystic intuitions that Virginia Woolf presents in her novels : these emotions and intuitions are valid because Virginia Woolf experienced them : this is the truth upon which her novels are based. She does not say to us : " Here is universal truth. Act accordingly." She says, rather : " This is what I have experienced. This is true so far as I am concerned, so far as my experience reaches. Understanding, not action, is required." Forster's feeling for the countryside is equally valid because it is a part of his experience. Unlike Virginia Woolf, however, he does at times wish his novels to prompt us to action. In so far as this is true, he is not as pure an artist as Virginia Woolf. And to the extent that he is concerned to prompt action in affairs that are contemporary and ephemeral, his art may be expected to be less enduring than hers. His didacticism, however, deals much more with man's character, which, of course, is universal to all ages, than with problems which may prove to be peculiar to the twentieth century. And he too is more concerned in his novels with understanding than with action.

There are two distinct ways in which the novelist, the poet, the biographer, or the playwright may teach. He may try to guide our actions directly. " Let us alter our iniquitous social system," Bernard Shaw says to us in *Widower's Houses* and in

Mrs. Warren's Profession. "Let us rid ourselves of prudery," Forster says in *A Room with a View.* Virginia Woolf has no immediate message of this kind. She does not set out to teach; but her novels do teach, none the less. Perhaps they teach more effectively than *Widower's Houses* or *Mrs. Warren's Profession* or *A Room with a View.* For we cannot be given new understanding without, in some way, being changed. But if we are told to act—Do we always obey? ". . . beauty teaches, . . . beauty is a disciplinarian," Virginia Woolf says in an essay on Conrad. ". . . read Conrad, . . . and he must be lost indeed to the meaning of words who does not hear in that rather stiff and sombre music, with its reserve, its pride, its vast and implacable integrity, how it is better to be good than bad, how loyalty is good and honesty and courage, though ostensibly Conrad is concerned merely to show us the beauty of a night at sea." And similarly, when we read Virginia Woolf we learn that courage is good, that tolerance and disinterestedness and honesty are good, that truth is the most important thing of all. The author has no designs upon us; she does not *tell* us these things: she *shows* them to us; and our understanding is increased. It is probable that this sort of teaching is always more effective than the first kind. Of course, plays or novels directed against a particular evil may, occasionally, effect an immediate social improvement. Galsworthy's *Justice* and *Escape* were effective in this way: they brought about a certain amount of prison reform. But as conditions change, whether or not the change is helped by the novel or play, the work of art that is directed towards a specific problem loses its force: it is no longer valid. *Widower's Houses* and *Mrs. Warren's Profession* are scarcely heard of to-day; *A Room with a View* has already dated. The social system has altered—and there are new iniquities to be attacked; prudery of the conventional Victorian sort that *A Room with a View* criticizes is no longer quite so widespread as it was. If *A Room with a View* endures, its endurance will be due to qualities other than the social conscience which it displays. Books that are works of art endure; social tracts are ephemeral. So it is possible that Virginia Woolf's novels, which set out to be nothing but works of art, may teach the world more than those plays of Shaw's which set out, as most of his plays do, to teach. The derisive term " ivory tower of art " should be carefully used. It may be useful if it is intended to mean, when used critically, that an artist should not allow his work to become dry and hard by busying himself with artificial problems unrelated to life. But if it means that the artist should concern himself in his art with affairs which are contemporary and ephemeral, that he should produce social tracts rather than works of art, it is clearly false. For the good of mankind it is necessary that some among us should contemplate rather than act. The numbers who do so are pitifully small. We do not ask the " pure " scientist to stop his apparently useless activity, to come down out of his ivory tower of science and become an engineer. We have learned that, though he contemplates merely for the sake of discovering truth, merely for the sake of contemplation, his discoveries are likely to be useful after all. Others may apply them. If we accorded the artist the same respect we give the scientist, our knowledge of how to live might not be so far behind our knowledge of science. The artist's discoveries are made in the unseen world of the spirit and can only be applied there. Their value is, therefore, not so apparent to our practical world. But by helping us to understand, the artist, who does not act himself, may help us to act rightly and wisely. And good actions, in a world in which science has given us the means to destroy civilization, have become a matter, not simply of morality, but of life or death for mankind.

Lytton Strachey combines didacticism and art to a very high degree. He wishes to teach ; but his desire to create works of art is equally strong ; and he knows that the artist teaches best by being faithful to art. Biography serves Strachey well, for it is by nature a didactic art. It is based inevitably upon man's character, and is therefore concerned with morality ; but the biographer is protected, if he keeps his focus upon his subject, from attributing undue importance to ephemeral things. He must often consider affairs contemporary to his subject's life, but he should consider them only in so far as they affect or display his subject's character. Strachey was admirably equipped as a biographer. From his undergraduate days, at least, character and art were his major interests. He valued both reason and emotion. He did not allow himself to become involved in contemporary affairs. And he had no philosophy which might cause him to judge his subjects, or distort his account of them, according to a preconceived view of the universe. He was an individual who stood by himself, unsupported except by his own reason and intuition. But he had, as we have seen, a well-defined set of humanistic values ; and he kept these values so constantly before him that they lend symmetry and coherence to his biographies. For it is only the biography as a whole that expresses Strachey's values ; he does not intrude them upon the reader. His teaching does not injure his art ; he does not wish to guide our actions, but to increase our understanding through the study of character.

The most cogent criticism of Strachey's method is the criticism Virginia Woolf seems to make in *The Voyage Out* : that the pattern which Strachey sees when he views a life may be imposed unwittingly by Strachey himself and have no real existence. But this is a criticism that may be applied to all biography that is worth reading ; it is, in fact, a criticism of all knowledge. For in order to understand at all the mind must impose patterns ; it must create order from the chaos of experience. The danger is manifest : the mind may be wrong : there may be no pattern at all. We should be aware of the danger, but to be aware is enough. We must then continue to seek the pattern which seems best to accord with truth. And, of course, Virginia Woolf too looked for a pattern in life, though she did not seek it in the same way as Strachey. She organized her experience ; and when her sensations were ranged in a fitting order, when they had fallen into place, she believed that she saw reality.

Indeed, in spite of obvious differences, Virginia Woolf and Strachey have a great deal in common. Each desired affection and comradeship. They were also affectionate themselves, yet both of them valued and practiced detachment. Virginia Woolf, though her sensations and emotions were so vivid, though she sought union whilst Strachey sought detachment, was the more aloof of the two. She did not have to discipline herself so strongly as Strachey did ; she had to overcome man-made barriers in order to be detached ; Strachey had to overcome himself. Yet, there were spiritual adjustments at least as profound as Strachey's for her to make. And though at first intellect seems to predominate in Strachey and emotions in Virginia Woolf, one wonders, after one has considered them together, how much value there is in these distinctions. The mind, after all, is organic : for convenience of discussion it is useful to divide intellect from emotion, but the division should not be pushed too far. Virginia Woolf wished to leaven intellect with feeling ; Strachey wished to control feeling with intellect. He uses the intellect to analyse character ; she uses it to analyse the mind and its experience. Intellect assists Virginia Woolf in organizing her experience into works of art ; it organizes Strachey's values in his biographies ; yet the ultimate unity of both Strachey's biographies and Virginia Woolf's novels is emotional.

Virginia Woolf, Strachey, and Forster share the same first principles, the same ultimate values. All three respect both reason and sensibility. They all value self-possession, self-knowledge, and humour ; they dislike pomposity, pretension, and muddle. They agree that man is the measure ; and they are much occupied with the question, What is a good man? They have no false optimism—Strachey is perhaps the most optimistic of the three—but they believe that man may improve himself if he makes a determined effort to understand. They want every one to be whole, to be an individual who expresses his natural emotions and affections and values friendship. They admire honesty, tolerance, disinterestedness, and courage ; they respect truth above all. They desire understanding rather than power, and they seek it in contemplation and in art. Art, they believe, is indispensable because it is an enduring expression of man's spiritual life.

PART III

COMPOSITION

CHAPTER V

E. M. FORSTER

AFTER history, after philosophy and aesthetics, after values, we come, finally, to the work of art, to Strachey's biographies and to Virginia Woolf's and Forster's novels. We have seen something of the milieu from which these works grew, of the theories and principles that were intended to rule at their creation, of the thoughts and emotions which may be expected to inform them. We have tried to see, as well as we might, some of the essential, but elusive, spiritual material from which these three authors built their books, and the master plans at which they glanced, when they had time, as they worked. We will now have done with aesthetic theories ; we will search no longer for the spiritual provenance of these works : we will look at the works themselves, paying special attention to their structure, to the way in which Forster, Strachey, and Virginia Woolf have used their materials. We will remember, however, that " structure ", though it includes " shape " in its meaning, is not synonymous with " shape ", that shape and material, form and content, are, in fact, inseparable in any work, whether it be a book or a building. With this truth in mind, we will examine first the novels of Forster.

But when we try to see, to examine, and to discuss the structure of a novel, as we would discuss, for example, the architecture of a cathedral, we are immediately confronted with a problem that is not easily solved. This problem is well defined by Percy Lubbock in the first sentences of *The Craft of Fiction* :

> To grasp the shadowy and fantasmal form of a book, to hold it fast, to turn it over and survey it at leisure—that is the effort of a critic of books, and it is perpetually defeated. Nothing, no power, will keep a book steady and motionless

> before us, so that we may have time to examine its shape and design. As quickly as we read, it melts and shifts in the memory ; even at the moment when the last page is turned, a great part of the book, its finer detail, is already vague and doubtful. A little later, after a few days or months, how much is really left of it? . . . Nobody would venture to criticize a building, a statue, a picture, with nothing before him but the memory of a single glimpse caught in passing ; yet the critic of literature, on the whole, has to found his opinion upon little more.
>
> . . . Since we can never speak of a book with our eye on the object, never handle a book—the real book, which is to the volume as the symphony to the score—our phrases find nothing to check them, immediately and unmistakably, while they are formed. . . . The form of a novel—and how often a critic uses that expression . . .—is something that none of us, perhaps, has ever really contemplated.

Among the books which we have to discuss, this statement is particularly true of Forster's novels, because their structure depends so much upon story, plot, and " rhythms " of the kind which Forster describes in *Aspects of the Novel.* Strachey's biographies, however different they may be from one another in other respects, all have one obvious affinity in form and content : each describes a life, or lives. Virginia Woolf's novels are impregnated with space, as Forster's, with the exception of *A Passage to India*, are not ; and they are usually held much more clearly within a frame than is the case with Forster's novels. To read a novel of Virginia Woolf's, if one may generalize, is, as it were, to watch a painter at work. The painting is created as we watch and as time passes, but the whole of the canvas is there from the beginning. But to read a novel of Forster's is like listening to a symphony. The novel expands ; what we have read indeed melts into the past ; for new vistas are continually opening before us. Yet the slightest hints are often of importance to the plot, and the quietest phrases may develop into " rhythms ".

In this chapter, therefore, an attempt will be made to abstract the essential material from each of Forster's novels, so that we may, if possible, keep the novel steady and motionless before us while we discuss its structure. When, in the following chapters, we discuss Strachey's biographies and Virginia Woolf's novels, we will rely upon our memory of those books.

The disadvantage of the method that is to be pursued in this chapter is its length. The structure of a novel of Forster's cannot be resumed in a paragraph or two. An advantage may be gained, however, when we begin to discuss the novel. It will then be fresh in our minds, and the names of characters will recall not only their characteristics but their actions ; a reference to an incident will recall both the incident and its situation in the novel. The discussion of the structure of the novel may then be conducted with the barest explanations, and this is a real advantage in considering the intricate design of a novel of Forster's. The reader who has read Forster's novels recently may prefer to go directly to the discussion which follows the summary of each novel.

Forster's novels are five in number. The first four, *Where Angels Fear to Tread*, *The Longest Journey*, *A Room with a View*, and *Howards End*, were published from 1905 to 1910 ; the fifth, *A Passage to India*, appeared in 1924. The absence of other novels from Forster's pen is strange and has been lamented by reviewers and critics with a persistence that must long since have grown monotonous to Forster's ears. Here is a writer who, at the age of thirty-one, had produced four excellent novels and seemed to be at the beginning of a prolific career ; but in the forty-four years that have followed he has given us only one more novel. He must expect a clamour from his audience ! He has not, however, been completely silent ; essays and critical articles have appeared, broadcasts have been given, and most of these productions have been collected and published in *Abinger Harvest* and in *Two Cheers for Democracy*. Forster's short stories, some of which were written before his first novel, and all of which were written before the First World War, have also been published in a collected edition. *The Hill of Devi*, an account of his experiences in the Indian state of Dewas Senior, came out in 1953. But with the exception of a fine biography of Lowes Dickinson, there has been no major work since 1924.

Where Angels Fear to Tread is a remarkably sure and successful book for a first novel. No doubt Forster had gained some valuable experience, before writing it, from his first short stories ; and he had executed a considerable part of the draft of an earlier novel, which has not been published.* His success in *Where Angels Fear to Tread* is due mainly to the fact that he does not strain his powers. He does not try to do anything in this book that he cannot accomplish with apparent ease. Like all Forster's novels, *Where Angels Fear to Tread* describes a clash, in this case a clash between the English town of Sawston, a "joyless straggling" sample of suburbia, the product of a new and shallow society, and the old walled Italian city of Monteriano, where beauty, cruelty, charm, vulgarity, and mystery are inextricably mixed, but where a joyful, native vigour, rooted in the past, is a dominant trait. It is not a case of black against white, of right against wrong. These terms are too cold, too far removed from flesh and blood, to describe the struggle that takes place in Forster's book. Forster loves Monteriano, but he shows us its shortcomings. It can be cruel and thoughtless ; it is lazy and dirty ; its women are given little more freedom than slaves. He dislikes Sawston, and he shows us few of its merits. It treats its women as equals : that is as much as Forster says for it ; for its cleanliness and industry become almost a reproach through association with a prim moral sense ; and Sawston is capable of cruelties that are cold and calculated, not thoughtless or warm-blooded. Forster is not as fair to suburban society in *Where Angels Fear to Tread* as he is in later novels ; but he is just fair enough, in showing the weaknesses of Monteriano, to make the clash real without pausing to weigh one side against the other. As a result, his story moves swiftly ; it is lean—scarcely 50,000 words in length ; and we are carried so skilfully through a melodramatic plot that we feel the novel to be inevitable, in spite of numerous incidents which would be improbable enough in any other context. The clash, in its bare outlines, is between hypocrisy and sincerity, between a society that represses its impulses and one that expresses them as naturally as it breathes or eats.

* Rose Macaulay, *E.M.F.*, pp. 26–7.

The novel begins at Charing Cross Station, where a family party is seeing Lilia Herriton, a young widow, off to Italy. With a few careful, economical strokes, the situation, from which the rest of the novel develops, is described. Lilia is neither intelligent nor mature, but she has not lost the faculty of enjoyment, and she expresses herself freely enough to annoy the Herritons, who are from Sawston. She leans from her carriage to laugh brainlessly, so the Herritons think, at the farewell party, which appears to her rather ridiculous. It consists of her brother- and sister-in-law, Philip and Harriet Herriton, Mrs. Herriton herself, and Lilia's little daughter, Irma. Much overshadowed by the Herritons is Lilia's mother, Mrs. Theobald, who has come from Yorkshire, squired by Mr. Kingcroft, a shy, good-natured young man, to say good-bye to her only daughter. We learn, as we accompany the Herritons and Irma back to Sawston for tea, after they have seen Lilia safely off, that Mr. Kingcroft is an admirer of Lilia's. Lilia is attractive to men, and susceptible enough to them, but so far Mrs. Herriton has kept the widow's admirers at a distance. She has indeed dominated Lilia ever since her marriage and made her conform to Sawston standards. There were difficulties when Irma was born : Mrs. Theobald tried to interfere : but she was defeated. " That curious duel which is fought over every baby was fought and decided early. Irma belonged to her father's family, not to her mother's." When Lilia's husband died, the struggle began again. " Lilia tried to assert herself, and said that she should go to take care of Mrs. Theobald. It required all Mrs. Herriton's kindness to prevent her. A house was finally taken for her at Sawston, and there for three years she lived with Irma, continually subject to the refining influences of her late husband's family." But she was troublesome. She coasted down the High Street on a bicycle one Sunday evening and fell off at the turn by the church. She nearly became engaged to Mr. Kingcroft during a visit to Yorkshire. Her influence upon Irma was not good. So, thanks to the inspiration of her brother-in-law, Philip, she was persuaded to travel in Italy, accompanied by the sober, charming Caroline Abbott, who lives two turnings away.

Peace is restored in the Herriton household, and Irma's training is resumed. But the calm is shattered three months later when it is learned in Sawston that Lilia has become engaged to an Italian in Monteriano. The sober Miss Abbott had failed in her duties. Philip is dispatched to Monteriano at once to retrieve the situation. The peas which Mrs. Herriton was planting when the news of the disaster came are left uncovered, and are eaten by sparrows. This accident and a quarrel with the cook and the housemaid are the most significant outward signs of disturbance at Sawston. And Mrs. Herriton is more upset by her neglect of the peas than by any other event of the troublesome day.

Mrs. Herriton is one of those characters—we will meet them often in Forster's novels—who embodies much more than her own individuality. If she does not reach back to the universal, she reaches back to Sawston : she epitomizes the Sawstonian traits that Forster most dislikes and that are in the clearest opposition to Monteriano. She does not go to Monteriano herself, but she sends her minions—Caroline Abbott, Philip, and, eventually and finally, Harriet. She provokes the clash at Monteriano, and is present there as a force of which Caroline, Philip, and Harriet are constantly aware. She has made Lilia part of Sawston for a time, and means not to lose her ; she has controlled Philip ; she has made Harriet, who is dull and unintelligent, into a humourless prig, endued with a cold but fierce religion. Philip and Caroline will escape from her ; they will be saved by Monteriano ; but their time is not yet.

They meet now at the Monteriano station, Philip having completed his trip from England. The station is eight miles from the town, a topographical detail which Forster uses to great advantage. Monteriano is not to be seen from the railway. As we journey uphill towards it in a horse-drawn carriage, we feel that it is a city of the past, far removed from twentieth-century civilization, self-contained on its own hill, compact within its own walls—as remote as may be from the straggling suburban villas of Sawston. The eight-mile drive is important to the mechanics of the plot too. Now it gives Philip and Caroline time to talk before they meet Lilia ; later two carriages will collide, with fatal results, on their way from Monteriano to the station.

Philip and Caroline are each in a difficult position. Caroline has disappointed the trust that Mrs. Herriton put in her. She seems at first inclined to defend the engagement, but she is in a bad state of nerves, and she satisfies neither Philip nor herself. Philip is embarrassed because he has travelled before in Italy, has become enamoured with the country, and has ever since been its ambassador. His love of Italy caused him to encourage Lilia's travels enthusiastically, though Sawstonian motives first prompted him to suggest them. And his attachment to Italy is largely sentimental and theoretical. In theory he loves outraging English conventions, though he gave Lilia a very severe talking to when she fell off her bicycle on the High Street. Now his theories and his attachment are put to a rigorous test. " For three years he had sung the praises of the Italians, but he had never contemplated having one as a relative." And he is in Monteriano, on his mother's orders, to stop Lilia's match. When he learns from Caroline that Lilia's fiancé is a dentist's son, he is given a severe jolt. He shudders with disgust and pain, not for Lilia, but for himself. " A dentist ! A dentist at Monteriano. A dentist in Fairyland ! False teeth and laughing gas and the tilting chair at a place which knew the Etruscan League, and the Pax Romana, and Alaric himself, and the Countess Matilda, and the Middle Ages, all fighting and holiness, and the Renaissance, all fighting and beauty ! " So, Forster tells us, Philip loses some of his spurious, sentimental feeling for Italy. It is the first step towards his salvation ; the real Monteriano is already freeing him from the impediments of Sawston. He has, moreover, one advantage from the first : he appreciates beauty. On the journey from the station to Monteriano, " the carriage entered a little wood, which lay brown and sombre across the cultivated hill ", and which was filled with a profusion of violets. " Philip paid no attention at the time : he was thinking what to say next. But his eyes had registered the beauty, and next March he did not forget that the road to Monteriano must traverse innumerable flowers."

At Monteriano he offers Lilia's lover a thousand lire if the engagement is broken ; but he learns that the couple were married as soon as they heard he was coming. There is nothing for him to do but to return to Sawston ; and Caroline Abbott, whose nerves have remained unsettled, returns with him.

Lilia's marriage turns out badly enough. Her husband, Gino Carella, is, on the whole, an amiable youth ; a strong and intelligent woman might make something of him as a husband ; but Lilia is neither strong nor intelligent. She goes under to him as she went under to Mrs. Herriton. Though she supports him, for he has no money and sees no need to work, he soon forces her to obey Italian conventions strictly, forbidding her to go out by herself. Since she has no friends at Monteriano, she is, in fact, imprisoned in her home with her servant Perfetta, a deaf and queer widowed cousin of Gino's. She is hedged in even more securely by convention at Monteriano than she had been at Sawston. Meanwhile, Gino enjoys the free and equal society of his fellows at the *caffé* ; and Lilia discovers, before long, that he is unfaithful to her. She suffers intensely. The Herritons have ceased all communication with her, but she writes to Irma of her unhappiness in a letter which Mrs. Herriton intercepts. Gino appears to the Herritons, of course, to be a brute and a cad ; but the fault is as much Lilia's as his. He and Lilia come from two utterly different societies ; they never succeed in bridging the gulf that lies between Monteriano and Sawston. Gino is little more than a boy ; Lilia is ten years and more his senior ; but she brings him no strength of character ; she is cowardly. She dies, mercifully, as she gives birth to Gino's first child, a son.

Gino embodies Monteriano as Mrs. Herriton embodies Sawston. He is handsome and athletic, charming and graceful. He is " strong not only in body, and sincere as the day ". He knows how to enjoy himself thoroughly. Beyond this we are told little of him, except to be shown that he is not very clean, that he is untidy, that he looks awkward and absurd when he tries, for Philip's benefit, to dress in English fashion, and that he cares little for work. Moreover, he was tempted by Philip's offer of a thousand lire, and he might have accepted it if he and Lilia had not already been married. Yet Gino makes an irresistible impression upon the reader, a much stronger impression than any one else in the novel, though none of the characters is weakly drawn. He draws his force from the city of Monteriano ; he represents it so effectively that its walls and towers, its sunlight and its filth, its charming inhabitants and its vulgar opera house are almost a part of his character. Monteriano, past and present, works through him ; it is this that explains his strength ; and we are not surprised to find that he is vividly aware, as he plays with his son, that physical and spiritual life may stream out of him for ever. Mrs. Herriton epitomizes Sawston, but the town itself is not described : without Mrs. Herriton it would not exist. Gino, on the other hand, would not exist were it not for Monteriano. This device, the reverse and obverse of the same method, used in establishing the fundamental antithesis of the novel, weights the aesthetic balance, as it were, decisively against Sawston, and convinces us that Monteriano, in spite of its careless indolence, is much stronger than Sawston. For on one side is a woman, and perhaps her daughter ; on the other is a proud and ancient city. It is not simply a piece of aesthetic juggling—if this is ever possible, it is not done here. Forster believes that Gino stands squarely within his race and draws vitality from it, but that Mrs. Herriton is a new and shallow offshoot of her race, with only the sucker's spurious luxuriance.

When the news of Lilia's death reaches Sawston, the Herritons decide, or rather, Mrs. Herriton decides for them, that Irma, who has not been told of her mother's second marriage, will be told only that Lilia is dead, and that no one will be told of her Italian son. They decide to live a lie ; and they suffer for their falseness. Spiritual degeneration always attacks Forster's characters when they are dishonest ; it is a swift and inevitable retribution in his novels for deceit. His belief in the consequences of dishonesty is partly Freudian and partly mystic—a combination which his conception of the subconscious makes possible.* And the subconscious is closely related, in Forster's view, with race. The Herritons' lie seems to him to be of the worst possible kind : they have tried to prevent Irma from knowing that

* See Chapter III.

she has a brother: they have meddled with the sacred, racial laws of consanguinity. Mrs. Herriton, as the representative of Sawston, is scarcely capable of degeneration, but her hollowness becomes more evident in this section of the book—a section which might be entitled "muddle". Harriet is neither fine nor intelligent enough to suffer deeply for the lie, but even she becomes more peevish than usual; her conscience begins to bother her, and she worries about the Italian child's religious education. She is packed off to the Tirol, lest she cause trouble. The degeneration is most evident in Philip. He seeks ungenerous motives in sincere actions of others; he begins to enjoy his mother's diplomacy and to be amused by her insincerity; he is sinking wearily, and becoming, without protest, a spiritual part of Sawston. But the sincerity of youth, and of the South, destroys the lie. To Gino, who respects family relationships, it seems quite natural, no doubt, that his son should correspond with Irma. At any rate, Irma receives two picture postcards, which elude Mrs. Herriton, from her "lital brother" at Monteriano. In spite of a promise given to Mrs. Herriton, she is unable to keep the secret; she speaks proudly of her brother at school; and Sawston knows the truth.

Caroline Abbott, though she had no part in the Herritons' lie, was also somewhat involved in muddle. She confided to Philip, before Irma's indiscretion, that she had encouraged the match between Lilia and Gino. She had seen, when Lilia fell in love, that Lilia had an opportunity, perhaps for the first and only time, to do something real. She had intended to support Lilia against Sawston and to stay with her in Monteriano, for a time, after her marriage. But when a telegram had come from Mrs. Herriton, demanding an explanation, she had consented to Lilia's suggestion that they answer with a lie—"Lilia engaged to Italian nobility". "That was wrong," she tells Philip. "Lilia there was more cowardly than I was. We should have told the truth. It lost me my nerve, at all events." She had intended to tell Philip the truth when she met him at the Monteriano station, but because she and Lilia had started with a lie she could not. She was frightened, and returned with Philip to Sawston.

When Caroline hears of Lilia's baby, she determines to act.

On finding that Mrs. Herriton desires only that the baby be forgotten, she decides to go to Monteriano to try to adopt it. She feels responsible for the Italian child because she believes that it has come into the world through her negligence ; she has accepted Sawston's view of Gino, and thinks that the impulse on which she acted in Monteriano was wrong. But Mrs. Herriton, though she cares little for the welfare of the baby, cannot allow Caroline to act more generously towards it than she. What would Sawston say ? It would be an intolerable situation if Caroline brought the child up at the Herritons' very gates. So Mrs. Herriton quickly develops a fond and generous interest in Irma's little brother. She underlines—for her own purposes, of course—Irma's longing for him. She says that she will act impulsively and bring the child to Irma. Her hypocrisy is displayed—never more clearly ; and Forster contrasts it, without over-emphasis, to Gino's sincerity and frankness. For Gino refuses, very politely, an initial offer, made in a letter from Mrs. Herriton's solicitors, to adopt his son ; and he regrets that his picture postcards (which Mrs. Herriton believes him to have sent with the blackest intentions) have been found obnoxious. The upshot of the matter is that Philip is dispatched once more to Italy —this time to bargain for Gino's son ; Harriet is beckoned from the Tirol to join him and to see that he does not fail ; and at Monteriano they meet the meddlesome Caroline Abbott.

The stage is set for the conclusion of the drama, which is led to a climax in a series of brilliant scenes.

The first of these scenes takes place in the vulgar, healthy, ebullient atmosphere of the Monteriano opera house. Philip is hailed by Gino, pulled exuberantly from the stalls into Gino's box, and introduced to Gino's friends as a long absent brother, while an indignant Harriet leaves the theatre, and obliges Caroline Abbott to follow her out. The second scene is at Gino's house the following morning. Caroline Abbott has come to persuade Gino to give up his son. But when she sees the baby with its father, she renounces her mission. " The comfortable sense of virtue left her. She was in the presence of something greater than right or wrong." She washes the baby for Gino—a scene ordinary enough, but it reaches back to the universal. The washing is a ritual, a pledge between Gino and Caroline, a tribute, on her part, to the mysterious bond of parenthood. Philip enters to see Caroline holding the naked baby in her lap, Gino kneeling beside her chair.

At noon Philip and Caroline meet in the church of Santa Deodata, where Caroline has gone humbly—she had intended the baby to be Low Church—to pray. She tells Philip that she has changed sides, and she urges him to come down himself on one side or the other. For Philip, realizing that he is his mother's tool, has taken no decisions for himself ; he poses as the tolerant, amused onlooker ; he is unconcerned whether his mission succeeds or fails, but he means to come out of it honourably. " That's not doing anything ! " Caroline warns him. " You would be doing something if you kidnapped the baby, or if you went straight away. But that ! To fail honourably ! To come out of things as well as you can ! Is that all you are after ? " " It's not enough to see clearly," she says ; " I'm muddle-headed and stupid, and not worth a quarter of you, but I have tried to do what seemed right at the time." It is true that we will be judged by our intentions, not by our accomplishments. " But we must intend to accomplish—not sit intending on a chair." " I wish something would happen to you, my dear friend," she tells Philip as the scene ends ; " I wish something would happen to you." It is not by chance that this scene takes place in a church, for it expresses much of Forster's religion. And in the light of subsequent events, Caroline's remarks have the force of prophecy. After lunch Philip reassures her that " nothing hangs " on his bargaining with Gino. " Every little trifle, for some reason," she replies, " does seem incalculably important to-day, and when you say of a thing that ' nothing hangs on it ', it sounds like blasphemy. There's never any knowing—(how am I to put it ?)—which of our actions, which of our idlenesses won't have things hanging on it for ever." She urges him to bundle Harriet into a carriage and drive her straight away from Monteriano.

Of course, Philip fails to obtain the baby from Gino. The three English visitors prepare to depart from Monteriano in the evening, and they order two carriages to take them to the station. It is raining, it is very dark, when evening comes. Gino had forecast rain two days before, and since morning—Philip had noticed it as he entered Santa Deodata's—one could feel a pleasant suggestion of rain in the air. Caroline leaves first, for her driver wishes to go slowly on the descent to the station. Philip is delayed because Harriet has mysteriously disappeared. A note comes to him, carried by the local idiot, ordering him to pick her up outside the city gate. When he does so he finds that she has the baby. As they descend through silent rain and darkness, Philip reflects upon the events of their visit. He remembers having seen the baby sprawled naked on Caroline's knee, Gino kneeling nearby. He is filled with sorrow " and with the expectation of sorrow to come ". " It was as if they were travelling with the whole world's sorrow, as if all the mystery, all the persistency of woe were gathered to a single fount." The baby is crying very hard but silently, Philip sees as he strikes matches and looks in its face. (That is the time, Gino once told Caroline Abbott, to be frightened—when the baby is crying but making no noise.) The carriage careens swiftly and recklessly down towards the station ; it enters the wood where Philip had seen violets in spring ; and there it strikes Caroline Abbott's carriage and overturns. Philip's elbow is broken ; the baby is killed ; and Harriet screams that she kidnapped it.

Then, at last, Philip faces himself squarely and decides to act. " Round the Italian baby who had died in the mud there centred deep passions and high hopes. People have been wicked or wrong in the matter ; no one save himself had been trivial. . . . If one chose, one might consider the catastrophe composite or the work of fate. But Philip did not so choose. It was his own fault, due to acknowledged weakness in his own character. Therefore he, and no one else, must take the news of it to Gino." He goes to Gino ; he admits his fault—that he has been cowardly and idle ; and he suffers. For Gino grasps him by the broken elbow and tortures him fiendishly. His life is saved only by the arrival of Caroline Abbott. When the danger has passed, when Philip has revived from a swoon, he sees Caroline with Gino's head upon her breast. She appears to Philip as a goddess. "Her hands were folded round the sufferer, stroking him lightly, for even a goddess can do no more than that." The sight made Philip happy; "he was assured that there was greatness in the world. There came to him an earnest desire to be good through the example of this good woman. He would try henceforward to be worthy of the things she had revealed. Quietly, without hysterical prayers or banging of drums, he underwent conversion. He was saved."

Gino's rage having passed, he becomes Philip's firm and intimate friend. And as the train carrying Harriet, Caroline, and Philip leaves Italy, Caroline confides to Philip that she is in love with Gino. But Gino, like Philip, looked upon her as a goddess, so there was no affair. Harriet is ill, and hopelessly muddled about her part in the tragedy. She will soon recover, physically, at least, for she is already speaking of "the mysterious frustration of one's attempts to make things better". Caroline and Philip are returning to Sawston, but they are no longer part of it. They have been saved by their contact with Monteriano.

Where Angels Fear to Tread, like all Forster's novels, is two things at once: a moral treatise and a work of art. Art and morals are more successfully combined in this book, however, than in any other of Forster's first four novels, partly because the moral discussion is not as fully developed as in his later books, but also because it is made, with a remarkable degree of success, to serve a structural purpose. The data needed to establish the antithesis in the moral dialogue is almost all given by the time Forster brings Caroline, Philip, and Harriet together at Monteriano; it serves the aesthetic, as well as the moral, purpose of making the clash between Sawston and Monteriano real; and all this first part of the book is preparation for the great scenes which follow and which justify the novel aesthetically. The moral theme is dominant in only one of these scenes: the scene between Philip and Caroline in Santa Deodata's, in which the moral dialogue is resolved. And here it is not intrusive; it is in keeping with the religious atmosphere of the scene; and the mood of the scene as a whole is beautifully harmonized with the scenes that surround it. Moreover, Caroline's moralizing is made to serve as prophecy which directs the future course of the novel. In fact, art and ethics reinforce one another in *Where Angels Fear to Tread*, as even the effect upon the ear of the names " Sawston " and " Monteriano " testifies. " Sawston " is harsh, ungracious, and ugly ; it falls like a lump from the tongue. " Monteriano " is graceful, musical, and light.

The action which culminates in the death of the baby would be improbable in life, but it is not improbable in the novel because Forster prepares us so well for it. We have seen that Caroline mentions kidnapping in Santa Deodata's ; that she advises Philip that there is never any telling which of our actions, or idlenesses, will not have things hanging on it for ever ; that she warns him to take Harriet away. Given these warnings, given Philip's vacillation, given Harriet's cold fanaticism, the kidnapping, when it occurs, is readily accepted. And the accident which kills the baby is the final chord in an ominous theme of which Caroline's cautious driver, Harriet's disappearance, the idiot, the silent rain and darkness, Philip's sorrowful premonitions, the baby's quiet, uncanny crying, and the reckless career of the carriage are part. In this atmosphere of horror Philip's sadness is but increased by his recollection of the beautiful scene at Gino's house when the baby lay on Caroline's knee. The rain, which at noon had been a pleasant suggestion, is now, as it were, a universal manifestation of grief, the great counterpart of the baby's silent tears. All that was good, or that might have been good, has become evil ; all the persistency of woe is gathered to a single fount. As a final irony, the accident occurs in the wood where Philip had once seen violets growing in rich and beautiful profusion. We should not be too concerned with the probability of the situation. Its justification is aesthetic, not logical ; Forster creates beauty as he describes the fatal drive.

The justification of the four great scenes that take place in Monteriano in the second half of the book is also aesthetic. These scenes are admirably related and contrasted to one another within the larger proportions of the style of the book. The comedy and joyful good-fellowship of the opera is followed by the calm, religious beauty of the scene at Gino's house as

Caroline Abbott washes the baby. The religious mood is intensified and becomes more introspective at Santa Deodata's, where Philip's soul is examined. Finally, Philip, tortured by Gino, suffers, and expiates his sin. The other scenes are irresistibly recalled, and become almost a part of this last, lurid scene ; for the religious theme comes to its fruition as Philip's soul is saved ; Philip's torturer is the brother who pulled him into a box at the opera ; and Caroline Abbott holds Gino's head on her breast in the same Madonna-like way that she held his child. The scenes are inextricably linked together, and yet, how different they are in mood and in tempo. Forster's style in this novel is swift and lean ; and, as nearly always in Forster's works, it is perfectly simple and straightforward, almost colloquial. So, when he slows the tempo for a moment and allows himself some decoration, as he does in describing Caroline's ministrations to the baby, the scene he depicts stands out from the fabric of his work, and is fixed indelibly in the reader's memory :

> He put a chair for her on the loggia, which faced westward, and was still pleasant and cool. There she sat, with twenty miles of view behind her, and he placed the dripping baby on her knee. It shone now with health and beauty ; it seemed to reflect light, like a copper vessel. Just such a baby Bellini sets languid on his mother's lap, or Signorelli flings wriggling on pavements of marble, or Lorenzo di Credi, more reverent but less divine, lays carefully among flowers, with his head upon a wisp of golden straw. For a time Gino contemplated them standing. Then, to get a better view, he knelt by the side of the chair, with his hands clasped before him.
>
> So they were when Philip entered, and saw, to all intents and purposes, the Virgin and Child, with Donor.*

Preceded by the ebullient gaiety of the opera, followed, that very night, by melodrama and torture, this scene stands apart, secure in its own peaceful beauty. It is recalled by Philip before the accident ; it is echoed as Philip watches Caroline comfort Gino ; it becomes, in its way, one of those " rhythms " which, Forster says, stitch a novel together from the inside.

* pp. 156–7.

Besides these large, scenic relationships, besides this example of rhythm, there are many other significant relations in the novel. Forster's choice and disposition of his characters is excellent. Mrs. Herriton and Gino are opposite poles, fixed points of reference between which the other characters move. Lilia is dominated by each of them in turn. She bears two children, neither of which is really hers ; for one belongs to Sawston, the other to Monteriano. But in her ability to enjoy herself sincerely, Lilia, in spite of her weakness, is a part of Monteriano even while she is in Sawston. Her opposite, Harriet, whose will is as strong as Lilia's is weak, is part of Sawston even in Monteriano. Lilia is packed off to Italy ; Harriet to the Tirol—places suitable, respectively, to the temperament of each. With the exception of Gino, who becomes more mature in the book, these four characters do not change. Caroline and Philip, of course, do change ; and their spiritual history binds the novel together and gives us a sense of the passage of time. It is the story, in so far as the story can be separated from the plot, of the novel. After an initial promise of better things, shown by Philip's love of beauty and of Italy and by Caroline's short-lived enthusiasm for Lilia's marriage to Gino, they both sink on returning from Monteriano to Sawston. They are eventually saved, Caroline first and Philip later, because they face themselves squarely, because they act on their convictions, and because they respect Gino's parenthood. They do not rush in, as Harriet does, where angels fear to tread. Caroline, from the beginning, is on a considerably higher level than Philip—perhaps that is why he comes to regard her as a goddess. And both of them are brought to salvation through the influence of Monteriano. It is therefore right that Philip should become Gino's intimate friend and that Caroline should love Gino and tell Philip of it. Within this triad, as it were, there is another pleasing relationship : both Philip and Gino regard Caroline as a goddess. The balance of the different elements of the novel, one feels, is complete. Not until his fifth novel, *A Passage to India*, does Forster attain again such harmony.

But Forster is not satisfied with balance only. " Expansion.

That is the idea the novelist must cling to. Not completion. Not rounding off but opening out," he has told us at the conclusion of *Aspects of the Novel.** Expansion is the idea he clings to in his second novel, *The Longest Journey*, in which a young man, Rickie Elliot, slowly discovers the history of his dead mother, sinks spiritually and then rises, and finally gains a vicarious posterity through his half-brother, his mother's son. Three themes that we have met in *Where Angels Fear to Tread* are much more fully developed : that to lie is to risk spiritual ruin ; that an action, or idleness, may have things hanging on it for ever ; and that there is a true, and sacred, racial strain whose survival is necessary, and perhaps inevitable. All Forster's love of the English countryside and its past is called upon ; the novel looks back to the prehistoric dawn of Stonehenge, and forward, down the stream of time, through the arches of the years. The title is from Shelley's " Epipsychidion ", and refers to marriage—to those

> Who travel to their home among the dead
> By the broad highway of the world, and so
> With one chained friend, perhaps a jealous foe,
> The dreariest and the longest journey go.†

The title should not be taken as Forster's comment upon marriage. It is a comment upon Rickie's marriage only. Shelley's lines, which are quoted in the novel, sum up, both emotionally and intellectually, much of Rickie's life. And Rickie suffers illusions about a woman that are similar, perhaps, to the illusions with which Shelley glorifies the lady to whom " Epipsychidion " is addressed.

The novel begins at Cambridge, where Rickie is " idling in the parsley meadows, and weaving perishable garlands out of flowers " in the Apostolic, Grecian atmosphere, sublime with the radiance of youth, that Forster, Lowes Dickinson, and Roger Fry also knew. Rickie, who is in his final year in

* Above, p. 76.

† In quoting these lines in the novel, Forster substitutes " sad friend " for " chained friend ", a reading which is to be found in one of Shelley's studies for the poem.

Classics, has made no decisions about his future. His parents are both dead. He is not brilliant, but he is gifted with imagination and with a vein of fantasy that has a Grecian turn. He thinks he would like to write, and he has produced a few short stories that are similar to Forster's own stories. He is exceedingly generous—perhaps too generous, too kind, and too pliable. He is lame as a result of an hereditary weakness passed on by his father. His father was a shallow, cowardly man with a hard veneer of culture and a pronounced sadistic streak. He gave his son no cause to love him. Rickie's mother, who was mistreated by his father and left for a time to bring up Rickie alone, had a beautiful voice and came from country stock. Rickie adores her memory.

There are possibilities both for good and for evil in Rickie; and he early takes the wrong turning. He becomes engaged to a woman who, as Stewart Ansell, Rickie's philosophic friend, has warned Rickie, does not exist, but is only a product of Rickie's diseased imagination. The woman, Agnes Pembroke, entered Rickie's rooms in the first scene of the novel to find herself in the midst of a philosophic discussion on the nature of reality; and Ansell refused to acknowledge her presence. Later he told Rickie that she had no real existence. Rickie's illusions about Agnes were increased when he saw her in the strong arms of her first fiancé, Gerald Dawes. Gerald had bullied Rickie at school, and was still a bully at heart; but he was an athlete, as handsome as Agnes herself; and Rickie, who admires bodily perfection, saw them as a pair of Athenian lovers, surrounded by a divine, golden aura. Gerald was killed shortly afterwards on a football field; and in time, thanks largely to Agnes's planning, Rickie finds himself engaged to the woman whom he regards as little less than a goddess. Ansell, who is the prophet in this novel, foresees an "appalling catastrophe", but is unable to bring Rickie to his senses. Agnes lives with her brother Herbert at Sawston, the same Sawston, spiritually, at least, that Forster describes in *Where Angels Fear to Tread.*

Soon after the engagement Rickie takes Agnes to visit his father's sister, Mrs. Failing, at her estate of Cadover in Wiltshire. Mrs. Failing has inherited the physical and spiritual infirmities of the Elliots. She too is lame ; and inside she is hollow. She is cynical ; she enjoys causing others discomfort. Her husband is dead, and she has no family ; but a youth, Stephen Wonham, has an anomalous position in her household. Stephen's physique is splendid ; he radiates vitality. His moral code is that one should follow one's inclinations and enjoy oneself so long as no one else is harmed. His only intellectual interest is manifested by his reading of cheap agnostic literature, which he thumbs in his desire to disprove the teachings of Christianity. The only picture in his room is the Demeter of Cnidus, goddess of fruitfulness and agriculture. Stephen is the son of his race as surely as Gino Carella is the true descendant of his. He is as much a part of the ancient countryside in which he lives as Mrs. Failing is inimical to it. But Rickie, who lacks experience of life and is not without a certain prudish conventionality, does not appreciate Stephen's qualities ; he regards Stephen as an uncouth and vulgar rustic. It is a very severe shock to Rickie, therefore, when Mrs. Failing, in a fit of annoyance, reveals that Stephen is Rickie's illegitimate half-brother. She refuses to tell Rickie more, and he assumes that Stephen is an Elliot. Rickie is now presented with what in this novel is called a " symbolic moment ", one of those moments upon which things hang for ever, and which, " if a man accepts, he has accepted life ". But if the moment is rejected, it passes : " the symbol is never offered again ". Stephen is unaware of his relationship with Rickie—Shall Rickie tell him of it or not ? Rickie is conscious of the importance of the moment. If he were left alone he would tell Stephen, in spite of his distaste for him, which has increased now that he associates Stephen with Mr. Elliot. But he allows Agnes, who speaks of scandal, to dissuade him ; and Stephen remains in ignorance.

Rickie's sin, it will be seen, is exactly the same as the sin the Herritons committed when they tried to prevent Irma from knowing of the existence of her Italian brother. It is a sin not only against blood relationship but also against the sacred racial strain ; and Forster's attitude towards such a sin is as grim and uncompromising as any Puritan creed. Rickie's punishment begins at once and is described at length in the central section of the book—a section entitled " Sawston ". He is unable to sell his short stories. He marries Agnes and becomes the assistant of her brother Herbert, who is a Master and Head of a House in Sawston's flourishing Public School. The School is a barbarous, inhuman machine which throws small boys together before they are old enough to understand one another and tries to prevent them from being individuals. It is implicitly contrasted to Cambridge. And its representative in the novel is Herbert Pembroke, the School's finest organizer. Forster's study of Pembroke is an analysis of muddle. Herbert is contemptuous of the intellect, though his own intellect is not weak. He is untouched by beauty. He is a priest of convention ; and he has one test for all things —success. " It never took him long to get muddled, or to reverse cause and effect." Rickie, slowly but inevitably, becomes this man's spiritual compatriot. His marriage is a failure. Agnes is a Sawstonian with little character of her own. She is selfish and somewhat sadistic ; and Rickie is too weak, and too late in discovering the real Agnes, to make a better woman of her. Stephen had once shocked Rickie by remarking that when he had a girl he would keep her in line ; but if Rickie had kept Agnes in line it would have been better for them both. As it is, they degenerate together. To add to Rickie's sorrow, Agnes bears him a daughter more deformed than he. The baby soon dies, but Rickie has learnt that no child must ever be born to him again. " He perceived more clearly the cruelty of Nature, to whom our refinement and piety are but as bubbles, hurrying downwards on the turbid waters. They break, and the stream continues." Rickie is not fully aware of his degeneration ; and he believes that Stephen is inherently bad, that Stephen has inherited the Elliot's spiritual infirmity. But Stephen, Rickie reflected, would have children : " He, not Rickie, would contribute to the stream ; he, through his remote posterity, might be mingled with the unknown sea ". After these reflections Rickie lay down to sleep, and in the night he heard his mother crying. " She was crying quite distinctly in the darkened room. He whispered, ' Never mind, my darling, never mind ', and a voice echoed, ' Never mind—come away—let them die out

—let them die out.' He lit a candle, and the room was empty. Then, hurrying to the window, he saw above mean houses the frosty glories of Orion."

This long, dreary, Sawstonian episode in Rickie's life is brought to an end by a train of events which Agnes sets in motion. Stephen, rather drunk, had one day read an impolite poem about Mrs. Failing while he and Rickie rode over Salisbury Plain ; and Rickie, indignant at what he regarded as Stephen's coarse ingratitude, had spoken of the incident to Agnes. In the hopes of gaining Cadover as an inheritance for herself and Rickie, Agnes, without Rickie's knowledge, now repeats Rickie's words in a letter to Mrs. Failing, and causes Stephen to be turned out. The situation has the whole force of this section of the novel behind it ; it is the final comment on the relations between Agnes and Rickie, on the one hand, and Stephen, on the other. When Mrs. Failing dismisses Stephen, she gives him documents that reveal his birth to him ; and after breaking some windows at Cadover in a drunken carouse with village friends, he hastens to Sawston to give Rickie the news. Agnes sends Stephen off, but not before he has spoken to Ansell, who, though he has kept away from Rickie since Rickie's marriage, has not forgotten him, and is in Sawston to observe Rickie, in case he can be helped. It is perhaps a symbolic moment for Ansell ; at any rate it is the moment for which he has been waiting ; and he acts vigorously. In an improbable scene he denounces Rickie and Agnes and reveals the truth before the assembled students of Herbert's House. The truth is a revelation to Rickie, as well as to the students, for he learns that he and Stephen had the same mother, not the same father. Mrs. Elliot, we learn from an episode that is now inserted in the novel, had left her husband for a Wiltshire farmer, a man who was worthy of her. But in Stockholm, whence he had taken her to await a divorce, he was drowned while swimming. She returned to her husband, who was glad to have her back and to hush the matter up. Stephen was born abroad and was raised at Cadover, near his father's home.

After the shock of Ansell's revelation, Rickie's spiritual cure is begun. He is at first inclined to renounce his love of his mother, to renounce life itself in his disappointment with the dead woman he has idolized. But Ansell, who now visits Rickie daily, prevents him from doing so. He takes Rickie, as Rickie puts it, on a journey, new even to Ansell himself, " behind right and wrong, to a place where only one thing matters—that the Beloved should rise from the dead ". So when Stephen returns to Sawston some days later, drunk and prepared to smash up Rickie's home, Rickie's hatred of him has turned to love ; he welcomes Stephen as a brother, and puts him to bed. " On the banks of the grey torrent of life, love is the only flower. A little way up the stream and a little way down had Rickie glanced, and he knew that she whom he loved had risen from the dead, and might rise again. ' Come away—let them die out—let them die out.' Surely that dream was a vision ! To-night also he hurried to the window—to remember, with a smile, that Orion is not among the stars of June."

Stephen, sober and contrite, takes over Rickie's treatment the following morning. He shows Rickie a more immediate truth than Ansell's philosophy had revealed : that Rickie has neither hated nor loved Stephen for his own sake, that he has not regarded Stephen as a man in his own right, but has associated him first with a hated father and next with a beloved mother. He asks Rickie to come with him away from Sawston, and Rickie responds to the appeal, and leaves Agnes, because Stephen's voice is the voice of their mother. " Habits and sex ", Forster comments, " may change with the new generation, features may alter with the play of a private passion, but a voice is apart from these. It lies nearer to the racial essence and perhaps to the divine ; it can, at all events, overleap one grave."

Rickie goes to live with Stewart Ansell's family. He is at peace with himself, and begins to write once more. Stephen is working on a farm. They go together one day to Wiltshire, Rickie to stay the night at Cadover on his aunt's invitation, Stephen to stop in the village. Rickie allows Stephen to accompany him only after making him promise that he will not get drunk. The novel is drawing to its close, and its last pages are filled with incidents that stand for more than themselves, that are attended by infinity. Stephen and Rickie drive from Salisbury in a trap, over the downs to Cadover. Night is gathering. Stephen speaks of his desire to marry. They come to a ford, and Stephen, in excellent spirits, leaps out to wade and to show Rickie a trick. He crumples some paper into a ball, and sets it alight.

> The paper caught fire from the match, and spread into a rose of flame. " Now gently with me," said Stephen, and they laid it flower-like on the stream. Gravel and tremulous weeds leapt into sight, and then the flower sailed into deep water, and up leapt the two arches of a bridge. " It'll strike ! " they cried ; " no it won't ; it's chosen the left ", and one arch became a fairy tunnel, dropping diamonds. Then it vanished for Rickie ; but Stephen, who knelt in the water, declared that it was still afloat, far through the arch, burning as if it would burn for ever.*

The flame has become the racial essence, the spirit of life, which Stephen, not Rickie, will transmit. But Rickie has helped Stephen to launch it on the stream.

At Cadover Mrs. Failing advises Rickie to return to Agnes. " . . . beware of the earth," she tells him. " We are conventional people, and conventions—if you will but see it—are majestic in their way, and will claim us in the end. We do not live for great passions or for great memories or for anything great." Rickie pities her, and believes that he knows better. She leaves him. He sits alone, musing upon her words and upon the incident at the ford, drinking coffee from an expensive china cup, playing with a piece of chalk that Stephen had hurled through Mrs. Failing's windows when she turned him out of Cadover. The chalk slips from his fingers and breaks the cup. The incident is an indication that Mrs. Failing is right, and that the solid race that springs from the chalk downs, Stephen's stock, will smash the Elliots, who, within their hard veneer of culture, are hollow.

Rickie goes to the village to find that Stephen is with friends at the inn, and is drunk. He cries bitterly at the door that Stephen has broken his word ; he then walks away. Convention has taken hold of Rickie again, and he has lost faith

* p. 302.

in Stephen. " The shoulders of Orion rose . . . over the topmost boughs of the elm. From the bridge the whole constellation was visible and Rickie said, ' May God receive me and pardon me for trusting the earth.' " He is ready to return to Agnes. He thinks sadly of the flame upon the water. " That mystic rose and the face it illumined meant nothing. The stream—he was above it now—meant nothing, though it burst from the pure turf and ran for ever to the sea. The bather, the shoulders of Orion—they all meant nothing, and were going nowhere. The whole affair was a ridiculous dream." He comes to a level-crossing, and there, in the light from a train, he sees Stephen, who has followed him from the inn, lying drunk across the rails. " Wearily he did a man's duty." He saved Stephen's life, but could not save himself. " The train went over his knees. He died up in Cadover, whispering, ' You have been right ', to Mrs. Failing."

In the last chapter of the novel we learn that Rickie gains some posthumous fame from his short stories, which are built round a Nature theme, and from a novel which he wrote while staying with the Ansells. Stephen has married, and lives on his own farm in Wiltshire. In the final scene he takes his young daughter out to spend a night with him on the downs. He reflects upon the strangeness of life and wonders why he is here. " He was alive and had created life. By whose authority ? Though he could not phrase it, he believed that he guided the future of our race, and that, century after century, his thoughts and his passions would triumph in England." Rickie had died saving his life—but what could he do for Rickie ? " One thing remained that a man of his sort might do. He bent down reverently and saluted the child ; to whom he had given the name of their mother."

On a first reading *The Longest Journey* may appear to be an unsatisfactory and disjointed novel. It is shaped by beliefs and emotional attachments which the author holds strongly, but which are likely to be strange enough to the reader. Past and present are mingled, and Forster interpolates episodes at his pleasure. There are several sudden deaths, and any number of improbable incidents. The novel moves more slowly and is much more diffuse than *Where Angels Fear to Tread*, so that those small but significant touches which Forster uses to prepare the reader may be lost. A few beautiful " rhythms " in the book are evident at once. Running water recurs again and again as a rhythm, and is associated with the stream of life. Rickie hears his mother's voice in a dream, calling " Come away . . ." He hears it again when he recalls the dream, and again when Stephen asks him to leave Sawston. Orion is subtly related to Rickie's mother, to the stream of life, and to muddle, without being identified with any of these things. It retains a curiously suggestive power of its own. And the level-crossing is used as a rhythm which recurs persistently. In the first scene at Cadover Mrs. Failing watches the smoke from a train. The train is carrying Rickie and Agnes to Cadover, and we learn later that it killed a child on the crossing at the Roman road. The child's play-fellow was pulled off the line in time. The accident is mentioned several times ; other children have been killed at the crossing ; and Stephen tells Mrs. Failing angrily that she should bridge it. Rickie pauses at the crossing, notes that it is dangerous, and thinks of the dead child. Again, he and Agnes stand there and hear the rumble of an approaching train. This is the crossing, of course, where Rickie is killed. In the last chapter of the book, we learn that it has been bridged. But these rhythms are not enough by themselves to bind the book into a satisfying whole. Flashes of beauty, searching analysis of character, fine descriptions of Wiltshire, are to be found in the novel ; but it may appear, at first, to be shapeless.

The Longest Journey, however, deserves a second reading. There are numerous events in it that take on a new significance when the whole course of the novel is known ; for it is a novel that expands, and that reveals the past, and the significance of the past, as it moves forward. In the first chapter, for example, we are told that there is a picture of Stockholm in Rickie's rooms at Cambridge. There is also a picture of his mother. Both pictures come to Sawston when Rickie marries, but neither we nor Rickie know that there is a relation between them, or that Stockholm has a peculiar significance. It is not until the third, and concluding, Part of the book, after Ansell has revealed Stephen's parentage, that we learn, in an interpolated episode, that Mrs. Elliot fled to Stockholm with Stephen's father. Nor do we know before Ansell's revelation, that Stephen is Mrs. Elliot's son. It is only when this knowledge is given us that the irony of Rickie's position becomes clear. Believing Stephen to be an Elliot, Rickie, when he and Agnes visit Cadover, unwittingly sides with his father's family, which he hates, against his mother, whom he continues to adore. When he rejects the symbolic moment, he enters a conspiracy with Mrs. Failing and Agnes against Stephen. The irony is repeated in the last scenes of the novel when Rickie and Stephen go to Cadover. Mrs. Failing's warning to Rickie to beware of the earth seems to be substantiated by the events which follow. But the Elliot blood in Rickie is ultimately responsible for his death. And Mrs. Failing's cynical sadism, manifested by her neglect of the dangerous crossing which Stephen had urged her to bridge, is a direct cause of Rickie's death. Mrs. Failing is the physical and spiritual representative of the Elliot family. Yet Rickie dies at Cadover, whispering, "You have been right", to Mrs. Failing.

Rickie's prudish conventionality and his proneness to illusion also play their part in his death; and they are related to the theme of reality and unreality which is introduced in the first scene by a philosophic discussion at Cambridge and which runs through the novel. Rickie's prudishness prevents him from seeing Stephen's good qualities when he and Stephen first meet. It leads him to speak to Agnes of Stephen's drunken disrespect for Mrs. Failing. It causes his disgust and his lack of faith in Stephen when he finds Stephen drunk at the village inn. In each case prudery comes between Rickie and reality with disastrous results: the symbolic moment is rejected; Stephen is turned out of Cadover; and, finally, Rickie is killed at the level-crossing. Rickie's illusions play a similar rôle in the novel. He glorifies Agnes Pembroke, is unable to see the real woman, and so is led into a disastrous marriage. He adores an unreal image of his mother, an image so coloured by Sawston's conception of ideal womanhood that he is ready to renounce life itself when he finds that the real woman had an illegitimate child. He begins to build similar illusions around Stephen, with the result that his new-found strength is shattered when he finds Stephen drunk. Ansell early warns Rickie of the dangers of a diseased imagination. He keeps away from Rickie while Rickie is surrounded by conventions, lost in a cloud of unreality at Sawston. Stephen, of course, is at Cadover during this period. When Rickie returns to reality, he returns to Ansell and to Stephen. Ansell, Stephen, Stephen's mother and father, and Mr. Failing, Mrs. Failing's deceased husband—another character who comes out of the past to play a part in the novel—are real people whose minds are clear and who can break through conventions ; Agnes, Mrs. Failing, Herbert Pembroke, Rickie's father, and Gerald Dawes are unreal ; Rickie hovers between the two camps.

There are numerous relations between these characters. The three Elliots—Rickie, his father, and Mrs. Failing—all, of course, suffer from lameness. Mr. Elliot, Agnes, Mrs. Failing, and Gerald Dawes are linked together by the trait of sadism, which, in varying degrees, they all display. Agnes, Gerald, and Stephen are all handsome. Their fine bodies are inevitably contrasted with the deformed bodies of the Elliots. Stephen and Gerald, in particular, have splendid athletic physiques. Stephen reminds Agnes so vividly of Gerald, on one occasion, that she leaves the room sobbing. Rickie is also reminded of Gerald by Stephen ; he thinks, when he sees Stephen at Cadover, that Stephen shares Gerald's brutality, Gerald's " peevish insistence on the pound of flesh ". But this is exactly where Rickie is wrong, and his mistake underlines the difference between Stephen and Gerald. Stephen may strike out at his enemies, but his moral code insists that no pleasure of his shall cause pain to others, and much of Mrs. Failing's annoyance with him is caused by his insistence that the people on her estate should be better treated. Stephen and Ansell see more clearly than any of the other characters. Ansell, a philosopher, has found reality through the mind. Stephen has found it instinctively, through the body. " If you ask me what the Spirit of Life is, or to what it is attached," Ansell says, " I can't tell you. I only tell you, watch for it. Myself I've found it in books. Some people find it out of doors or in each other. Never mind. It's the same spirit, and I trust myself to know it anywhere, and to use it rightly." He recognizes the Spirit of Life in Stephen when he meets him.* Both Stephen and Ansell act vigorously on their convictions—they do not sit intending in a chair. " When the moment comes [to help Rickie] ", Ansell had said, " I shall hit out like any ploughboy." He does so, and with Stephen destroys Agnes's and Rickie's lie. When Ansell and Stephen first met, Ansell watched Stephen smoke, and Stephen " gave the idea of an animal with just enough soul to contemplate its own bliss ". But in spite of Ansell's superior intellect, Stephen has knowledge to which Ansell has not attained. " The conviction grew [on Ansell] that [Stephen] had been back somewhere—back to some table of the gods, spread in a field where there is no noise, and that he belonged for ever to the guests with whom he had eaten." It will be remembered that Stephen had a picture of the Demeter of Cnidus in his room. One day in the British Museum, Ansell " left the Parthenon to pass by the monuments of our more reticent beliefs—the temple of the Ephesian Artemis, the statue of the Cnidian Demeter. Honest, he knew that here were powers he could not cope with, nor, as yet, understand." After he has met Stephen he is able to understand better these goddesses of agriculture and fertility, and to take Rickie on that journey " behind right and wrong, to a place where only one thing matters—that the Beloved should rise from the dead ". Ansell was reading a book of essays by Mr. Failing when he met Stephen. Some of the traits of Ansell and of Stephen had been combined in Mr. Failing. He was a philosopher who had tried to put socialism into practice at Cadover. Like Stephen, he had been concerned for the welfare of his workers. He had shown Stephen the trick of floating a flame down a stream. Ansell approves Mr. Failing's distinction between vulgarity (concealing something) and coarseness (revealing something). Like Ansell, Mr. Failing hated vulgarity and respected coarseness. Mr. Failing stands, as it

* Cf. Forster's remark that there is a secret understanding between his " aristocrats " when they meet (see p. 110 above).

were, behind Ansell and Stephen as yet another link between them. In the last chapter of the novel we learn that Ansell is at Stephen's farm in Wiltshire.

Stephen, clearly, is much more than a strong, honest, unspoiled countryman. As Mrs. Herriton embodies Sawston and Gino embodies Monteriano, Stephen embodies the strain that Forster hopes will survive in England ; he is, in Forster's view, the true breed of Englishman. But it is more difficult to represent a race than a town, and Stephen does not succeed as consistently as Mrs. Herriton or Gino. He functions on two different levels, as a man, and as the representative of a race ; and there are moments when he convinces on neither level. As a symbol of the vital racial spirit he must smash the windows of convention and of smug and hollow pride at Sawston and at Cadover. But the Stephen who smashes Rickie's furniture at night is not the same man as the Stephen who is heartily ashamed the next morning and wishes to pay for the damage to the last penny. It is true that he is drunk at night and sober in the morning ; but this is hardly enough to explain the change. The truth is that he is a representative of his race at night and a man in the morning. When, however, the man expands to include the race, as Stephen does when he floats the lighted paper under the bridge, all is well, and he becomes a character of incalculable force.

Life and death, the past, the present, and the future, are integral parts of the plan of this novel ; Forster looks both up and down the stream of life. The episodes which are drawn from the past, the characters who come out of the past and into the present to influence the future, are not thrown in at haphazard. The stream of life flows on ; the past is part of the present ; the present merges into the future. The two most important episodes that are drawn from the past are inserted, respectively, near the beginning and near the end of the book. Each has the effect of a strange, almost foreign, tune which suddenly flowers surprisingly in a symphony, but whose presence, we realize as we listen, has not been unsuspected, for there have been hints of it in the harmony of the dominant theme. Something is wanted to explain Rickie's lameness and his shy, uncertain, generous, imaginative nature. Something much greater than an affair of Mr. Elliot's is needed to explain Stephen. As the death of Gino's baby ended the theme of the drive in *Where Angels Fear to Tread*, each of these episodes is ended with a sudden death—the first with Mrs. Elliot's death, the second with the death of Stephen's father. The two episodes complement one another ; the second completes the first ; even though, in keeping with the development of the novel, the episode which came first in time comes second in the book. Death is almost a rhythm in *The Longest Journey*, a rhythm which emphasizes Stephen's survival. The sudden deaths, like a progression of great chords, culminate in the death of Rickie. Surrounded by all this death, it is marvellous, it seems the work of fate, that Stephen should survive. His theme, as it were, expands, and continues after the novel has ended.

The question remains whether Forster might not have gained if he had taken the reader more fully into his confidence. Forster thinks not. His answer is given in *Aspects of the Novel* in a passage which has already been quoted. " Over [the plot of a novel], as it unfolds," Forster says, " will hover the memory of the reader . . . and will constantly rearrange and reconsider, seeing new clues, new chains of cause and effect, and the final sense (if the plot has been a fine one) will not be of clues or chains, but of something aesthetically compact, something which might have been shown by the novelist straight away, only if he had shown it straight away it would never have become beautiful." Perhaps, in *The Longest Journey*, Forster over-estimates his readers' memory.

There is little mystery in Forster's next novel, *A Room with a View*. It is not necessary to look very far beneath the surface for the meaning of this book, and its structure is much simpler than the structure of *The Longest Journey*. *A Room with a View* is the only novel of Forster's in which the story, a narrative of events arranged according to their sequence in time, is a dominant aspect. A draft of the first half of this novel was written as early as 1903 ; Forster completed the book in 1907 ; * he perhaps found that it gave him a necessary period

* Macaulay, p. 78.

of relaxation after writing *The Longest Journey* and before undertaking *Howards End*. *A Room with a View* may also be regarded as an exercise in style. Forster's style, athletic and economical in *Where Angels Fear to Tread*, becomes heavier in *The Longest Journey*. It embraces more ; it is at times weighted with half-formulated suggestions ; it looks back at moments to a romantic style ; and again it looks forward, a short space, to the style of D. H. Lawrence. Here, for example, is a passage which describes, from Rickie's point of view, Rickie's ride with Stephen on Salisbury Plain :

> In Cadover, the perilous house, Agnes had already parted from Mrs. Failing. His thoughts returned to her. Was she, the soul of truth, in safety? Was her purity vexed by the lies and selfishness? Would she elude the caprice which had, he vaguely knew, caused suffering before? Ah, the frailty of joy! Ah, the myriads of longings that pass without fruition, and the turf grows over them! Better men, women as noble—they had died up here and their dust had been mingled, but only their dust. Those are morbid thoughts, but who dare contradict them? There is much good luck in the world, but it is luck. We are none of us safe. We are children, playing or quarrelling on the line, and some of us have Rickie's temperament, or his experiences, and admit it.
>
> So he mused, that anxious little speck, and all the land seemed to comment on his fears and on his love.
>
> Their path lay upward, over a great bald skull, half grass, half stubble. It seemed each moment there would be a splendid view. The view never came, for none of the inclines were sharp enough, and they moved over the skull for many minutes, scarcely shifting a landmark or altering the blue fringe of the distance. The spire of Salisbury did alter, but very slightly, rising and falling like the mercury in a thermometer. At the most it would be half hidden ; at the least the tip would show behind the swelling barrier of the earth. They passed two elder-trees—a great event. The bare patch, said Stephen, was owing to the gallows. Rickie nodded. He had lost all sense of incident. In this great solitude—more solitary than any Alpine range—he and Agnes were floating alone and for ever, between the shapeless earth and the shapeless clouds. An immense silence seemed to move towards them. A lark stopped singing, and they were glad of it. They were

approaching the Throne of God. The silence touched them ; the earth and all danger dissolved, but ere they quite vanished Rickie heard himself saying, " Is it exactly what we intended ? "

" Yes," said a man's voice ; " it's the old plan." *

It would not be fair to judge Forster's style in *The Longest Journey* from the first paragraph of this quotation. Much of this paragraph is a transcription of Rickie's thoughts at a time when his illusions concerning Agnes are at their height. But the paragraph would be impossible in *Where Angels Fear to Tread* ; and the passage as a whole illustrates tendencies that are by no means latent in *The Longest Journey.* In *A Room with a View* Forster turns his back on these tendencies. His penchant for finding the supernatural in the natural is not entirely suppressed—nor will it be suppressed in future novels ; but those qualities of lightness, clarity, strength, and grace, which characterize Forster's writing at its best, are evident throughout *A Room with a View.*

A Room with a View is a love story, the story of the courtship and marriage of Lucy Honeychurch. She is courted not only by two young men, but also by the forces of good and evil —for even in this book, the lightest of Forster's novels, good and evil are present. Lucy is visiting Florence with Charlotte Bartlett, an older cousin who acts as Lucy's chaperon. They have just arrived at the Pension Bertolini, and they are disappointed because they have been given rooms with no view. Another guest, Mr. Emerson, overhears their complaints, and offers to exchange rooms with them : he and his son, he says, have rooms with a view, which they would be glad to let the ladies have. Mr. Emerson is a kindly old philosopher who has never been able to understand the need for conventions. " He is kind to people because he loves them ; and they find him out, and are offended, or frightened." Miss Bartlett is both offended and frightened. Who is this ill-bred old man ? He has not been formally introduced. She must put Lucy under no obligation to him or to his son. All the tact of Mr. Beebe, a clergyman who, after his holiday in Italy, is. to become vicar of Summer Street, the English parish in which Lucy lives, is required to persuade Charlotte to accept

* pp. 127–8.

the offer. She accepts it rudely and peevishly. She is a representative of convention and muddle. Many of the qualities she lacks are to be found in Mr. Beebe. He has a sense of humour ; he enjoys giving happiness to others ; he is tolerant, sympathetic, and charitable. He appreciates Mr. Emerson's qualities, even though Mr. Emerson opposes the teachings of the Church and disbelieves in personal immortality. Mr. Beebe is sharply contrasted with another representative of the Church, Mr. Eager. Mr. Eager is hypocritical, uncharitable, and snobbish. He is bitterly opposed to Mr. Emerson, though Mr. Emerson tries to be friendly to him. From opposite camps, across muddle and over conventions, Lucy and Mr. Emerson's son, George, smile at one another.

Lucy is one of Forster's most delightful characters. She stands for nothing but herself ; and she is created with wonderful sympathy and understanding. Her character develops in the novel. She plays Beethoven with passion and originality at the Pension Bertolini ; Mr. Beebe remarks that if ever she takes to live as she plays it will be very exciting for every one. She has a splendid soul : the question is whether she will find it and learn to express it in life as she does in music, or whether muddle and convention will obscure it from the world and from herself. Italy begins to reveal her soul to her ; and she becomes somewhat involved with George Emerson, though not because of Charlotte's peevish agreement to the exchange of rooms. Lucy witnesses a murder as she walks alone one evening in the Piazza Signoria ; she faints ; she opens her eyes to find herself in George's arms. This experience and the walk back to the pension afterwards means a good deal both to Lucy and to George. Lucy finds, the next day, that she sees more clearly and is more honest. When Mr. Eager maligns the Emersons, she calls him to account : it is the first time that she has been so daring. A few days later a number of the English guests at the Bertolini go for a drive, and stop for a ramble on the slopes of Fiesole. Lucy, searching for Mr. Beebe, tumbles down upon a terrace to find George Emerson standing, amidst a profusion of violets, before an immense view. " For a moment he contemplated her, as one who had fallen out of heaven." Then he stepped quickly forward and kissed her. A voice called Lucy's name, and Miss Bartlett "stood brown against the view".

Charlotte Bartlett does her duty as a chaperon. She speaks severely to George; she takes Lucy off at once to Rome; and has Lucy promise, lest blame be attached to the chaperon, to say nothing of the incident to Mrs. Honeychurch. Lucy, who has been accustomed to keep nothing from her mother, finds the concealment troublesome. And she learns that one concealment leads to another.

The scene now changes to the fashionable country parish of Summer Hill, and to the Honeychurch's home, Windy Corner, which overlooks a beautiful view of the Sussex Weald. Lucy has returned to Windy Corner, where she lives with her mother and her brother, Freddy. The Honeychurch household is a delightful creation, as delightful as Lucy herself. It is as healthy and honest as the Pembroke household, in *The Longest Journey*, is disordered and muddled.

Lucy becomes engaged, after much hesitation, to Cecil Vyse, whom she met in Rome. Cecil, Forster says, is medieval. He resembles a Gothic statue of a fastidious saint. "Well educated, well endowed, and not deficient physically, he remained in the grip of a certain devil whom the modern world knows as self-consciousness, and whom the medieval, with dimmer vision, worshipped as asceticism. A Gothic statue implies celibacy, just as a Greek statue implies fruition. . . ." Cecil wishes to protect Lucy and to treat her chivalrously; the only relationship he conceives is feudal. But Lucy yearns for companionship and equality with the man she loves. Cecil is cultured, but he appreciates art for its snob value rather than for itself. And, though he can discuss books and pictures, he knows nothing of human relationships. He has a malicious sense of humour; he enjoys thwarting people. He brings the Emersons to Summer Hill, arranging the lease of a house in the village for them, because he believes that Summer Hill will find them unsuitable, and he expects to enjoy the ensuing discomfort. He is unaware that Lucy has met the Emersons in Florence. Lucy connects Cecil with a drawing-room which has no view, just as she remembers George Emerson standing before a large view. She herself is associated in the book and in Cecil's mind with a view. Windy Corner has a fine view, but Lucy, after her engagement to Cecil, is gradually cut off from it.

George Emerson is Cecil's opposite. He lacks Cecil's polish, but he is kind and affectionate. Throughout much of the novel he is unhappy and perplexed. He has seen his father's kindness rebuffed too often to have much faith in the world, and only his love for Lucy relieves his depression. He believes that love and youth " matter intellectually ". He has learned his values from his father ; and he wants men and women to be equals. " The Garden of Eden ", George's father maintains, ". . . is really yet to come. We shall enter it when we no longer despise our bodies." George has none of Cecil's asceticism. He expressed his love for Lucy frankly and spontaneously by kissing her. Cecil is engaged to Lucy for some time before he asks her, stiffly and formally, if he may kiss her. They are both embarrassed, and the kiss is a conspicuous failure. " Passion ", Forster comments, " should believe itself irresistible. It should forget civility and consideration and all the other curses of a refined nature. Above all, it should never ask for leave when there is a right of way. Why could he not do as any labourer or navvy—nay, as any young man behind the counter would have done ? "

Cecil's inadequate kiss took place in a pine wood beside a small pool, " The Sacred Lake ", where Lucy, as she confided to Cecil, used to go bathing until Charlotte Bartlett found her out and caused a row. Shortly after the Emersons arrive in Summer Hill, Freddy takes George Emerson and Mr. Beebe to bathe in The Sacred Lake. They enjoy themselves immensely. After bathing, they are romping about without costumes, playing football with one another's clothes, when they are interrupted by Mrs. Honeychurch, Lucy, and Cecil, who happen to be walking through the wood. Cecil, chivalrous as usual, tries to protect the ladies, and to lead them away from the shocking sight. George, who has managed to find a pair of trousers, and regards himself as dressed, calls happily to Lucy across the errant clothes, the conventions of the world, which, for a moment, are scattered.

The next week-end Freddy invites George to Windy Corner

for tennis. Cecil is disagreeable and refuses to play. He sits criticizing a cheap novel while George and Lucy enjoy the movement and competition of the game. Once more he unwittingly brings George and Lucy together, and not only in the game of tennis. For the novel is by one of the guests of the Pension Bertolini, Miss Lavish, who was on Fiesole when Lucy was kissed by George, and who has used the incident, of which she has learned from a dishonest Charlotte Bartlett, in her novel. After the game is over, Cecil reads aloud Miss Lavish's description of the kiss, and the past is vividly recalled to Lucy and George. Left alone with Lucy for a moment, George kisses her again.

Lucy is badly muddled. For some time she has deceived herself and others. Her dishonesty began, in fact, when she allowed Charlotte Bartlett to pledge her to secrecy and to hustle her off to. Rome after George's first kiss. Lucy has had bad dreams : her subconscious has rebelled against the muddle. She loves George, but she will not admit her love even to herself; she cloaks her desire and attributes it to " nerves ". She has refused to look inwards and to face herself. Now, after George has kissed her a second time, she prepares to stifle love, " the most real thing ", Forster says, " that we shall ever meet ". " The contest lay not between love and duty. Perhaps there never is such a contest. It lay between the real and the pretended, and Lucy's first aim was to defeat herself." She is soon equipped with the armour of falsehood, which " is subtly wrought out of darkness and hides a man not only from others, but from his own soul ". She dismisses George from Windy Corner, though not before he has declared his love and pointed out some of Cecil's faults. Perhaps George enables her to see somewhat more clearly, as he did after the murder in the Piazza Signoria. At any rate, she overhears Cecil, soon after George has left, peevishly refusing to oblige Freddy by making a fourth at tennis. The scales fall from her eyes, and she sees that Cecil is intolerable. She breaks her engagement with him the same evening, assuring him, or rather, reassuring herself, that she loves no one else. Cecil admires her as never before : he is an ascetic at heart, and renunciation pleases him. Mr. Beebe, too, is pleased when he learns that the engagement has been broken. But because she has deceived herself and lied to George and to Cecil, Lucy joins " the vast armies of the benighted ". " The night received her, as it had received Miss Bartlett thirty years before."

There follows in Lucy's life a period similar to the Sawstonian episode in Rickie Elliot's, or to the period in Philip Herriton's life when he helped his mother live a lie. Lucy has disordered " the very instruments of life ", and it is impossible for her to be honest. She moves away, spiritually, from her mother and Freddy ; her home no longer exists for her. As Rickie Elliot became Herbert Pembroke's compatriot, so Lucy becomes Charlotte Bartlett's peer. She prepares to leave Windy Corner physically, as well as spiritually, and to travel in Greece with two elderly, maidenly ladies that she met at the Pension Bertolini. Charlotte and Mr. Beebe encourage the trip ; Charlotte, because she wishes, apparently, to see Lucy far away from George Emerson ; Mr. Beebe, because he shares a belief of St. Paul's. " His belief in celibacy, so reticent, so carefully concealed beneath his tolerance and culture, now came to the surface and expanded like some delicate flower. 'They that marry do well, but they that refrain do better.' So ran his belief, and he never heard that an engagement was broken off but with a slight feeling of pleasure. In the case of Lucy, the feeling was intensified through dislike of Cecil ; and he was willing to go further—to place her out of danger until she could confirm her resolution of virginity."

Lucy is rescued by Mr. Emerson, the old philosopher who presents Forster's point of view (when Forster does not present it himself) in this novel. During a conversation that takes place, significantly, in Mr. Beebe's study, in the presence of theological volumes that line the wall, Mr. Emerson discovers that Lucy is badly muddled. Muddle, he tells her, is the worst thing in the world—worse than Death or Fate ; and he obliges her to admit that she loves George. He shows her, moreover, " the holiness of direct desire " ; he robs the body of its taint. He quotes Samuel Butler : " ' Life ', wrote a friend of mine, ' is a public performance on the violin, in which you must learn the instrument as you go along.' I think he puts it well. Man has to pick up the use of his functions as he goes along—especially the function of Love." Love, Mr. Emerson says, is of the body ; " Not the body, but of the body. Ah ! the misery that would be saved if we confessed that ! Ah, for a little directness to liberate the soul ! Your soul, dear Lucy ! " As he spoke Lucy felt that " the darkness was withdrawn, veil after veil, and she saw to the bottom of her soul ". " He gave her a sense of deities reconciled, a feeling that, in gaining the man she loved, she would gain something for the whole world." Having brought her over to his side, he tells her that " we fight for more than Love or Pleasure : there is Truth. Truth counts, Truth does count ".

The novel ends where it began, at the Pension Bertolini, where Lucy and George are spending their honeymoon. As they look one evening from the window of the room that Mr. Emerson once gave up so that Lucy might have a view, they reflect upon the events that have recently passed. Cecil Vyse had improved immensely after Lucy broke her engagement with him ; but since he has heard of her marriage the good has been undone. He has, moreover, become cynical about women. Lucy's family, confused by her sudden about-face, and disgusted at her past hypocrisy, are estranged from her. They are influenced by Mr. Beebe, who will never forgive Lucy ; though only he himself knows the real reason for his disappointment in her. But Charlotte Bartlett, Lucy and George decide on reviewing her actions, arranged that Lucy should meet Mr. Emerson alone in Mr. Beebe's study. Apparently she wished, far down in her mind, that Lucy and George should be together, though she fought them on the surface. When Forster's characters are muddled, their conscious and subconscious minds work at cross-purposes ; and in this particular case the subconscious is triumphant.

" Youth enwrapped [Lucy and George]," we are told in the last paragraph of the novel ; " the song of Phaethon announced passion requited, love attained. But they were conscious of a love more mysterious than this. The song died away ; they heard the river, bearing down the snows of winter into the Mediterranean." Like Stephen Wonham, Lucy and George are part of the stream of life ; and the rôles they have to play transcend the individual.

Charlotte Bartlett's unexpected action in helping to bring George and Lucy together is the final touch that puts Charlotte and Mr. Beebe in complete balance with each other. Charlotte is peevish, muddled, joyless, graceless, and intolerant. She excels at getting her own way through appearing to be completely unselfish. Until the very end she is preëminent as the chaperon who keeps Lucy and George apart, who, representing convention, stands directly between Lucy and the view which George could reveal. She champions Lucy's proposed trip to Greece, and wins Mr. Beebe's support for it. Mr. Beebe is cultured, tolerant, sympathetic, cheerful, and kindly disposed towards youth. "It was one of Mr. Beebe's chief pleasures to provide people with happy memories." Apparently he sees clearly. He persuaded Charlotte, the stern chaperon, to accept Mr. Emerson's offer of the rooms with a view. Yet Mr. Beebe's carefully concealed belief in celibacy causes him to try to win Lucy for the ranks of virginity, and to despise her for loving George. While Charlotte, muddled and scarcely knowing what she does, helps Lucy to declare her love. Charlotte and Mr. Beebe very neatly change positions. It is a fine example of Forster's use of irony.

Mr. Beebe, with his warm and kindly culture, is linked with Cecil Vyse, whose culture is a veneer, and who enjoys thwarting people. So different in other respects, these two both derive pleasure from renunciation. Both of them are shocked and disappointed when Lucy marries ; and their characters suffer as a result. Cecil becomes cynical about women ; Mr. Beebe will have no more to do with Lucy, and helps to turn her family against her.

Mr. Beebe also changes places with Mr. Emerson, or rather, Lucy finds Mr. Emerson to be what she had thought Mr. Beebe was. At the Pension Bertolini Mr. Beebe already assumes, in the eyes of Lucy, Charlotte, and Mr. Beebe himself, the rôle of Lucy's spiritual adviser. Mr. Emerson appears to them to be a queer, misguided, atheistical philosopher, whom it is better to avoid. But when Lucy falls into muddle, it is Mr. Beebe who would keep her in the armies of darkness, and it is Mr. Emerson who, in Mr. Beebe's study, rescues her and shows her her own soul and the importance of truth. He is able to do this because he recognizes, as Mr. Beebe does not, that love, though it is of the body, is holy. He is more truly religious than the clergyman, and a much sounder spiritual doctor.

Several themes run through the novel and help to bind it together. The theme of a view, like the theme of reality in *The Longest Journey*, with which theme it has much in common, is introduced on the first page and gathers significance as the novel develops. The medieval theme is introduced by Mr. Eager as he lectures to tourists in Santa Croce, and is associated first with Cecil and then with Mr. Beebe. Lucy often feels when she sees George that they are looking at one another across something. This half-conscious feeling is the only indication she has, throughout most of the book, of the conventions and muddle that lie between them. Lucy's playing is used as a theme which expresses her spiritual condition. As she falls into muddle, her playing degenerates. Places and incidents—George's and Cecil's kisses, The Sacred Lake, the room with a view at the Pension Bertolini—are used to relate scenes and to give the novel shape. But there are no rhythms in the book—none, at least, with the suggestive power and independence of Orion or of the level-crossing in *The Longest Journey*. Violets recur, but they express little, and are quite mechanically and inextricably associated with the Emersons. The nearest approach to a rhythm are the Italians, three in number—a vendor of photographs and two cab-drivers—who sympathize with Lucy or help her against the forces of convention.

The reader is carried on in *A Room with a View*, not by the plot, but by an interest in Lucy, and by Forster's pleasing style. For the style of the book, in spite of the serious matters that are dealt with, is consistently light. It is completely different in mood from the style of *The Longest Journey*, and is best illustrated, perhaps, in the bathing scene. Mrs. Honeychurch is speaking to Freddy, who is hiding in some bracken :

> " Dear, no doubt you're right as usual, but you are in no position to argue. Come, Lucy." They turned. " Oh, look —don't look ! Oh, poor Mr. Beebe ! How unfortunate again—"

For Mr. Beebe was just crawling out of the pond, on whose surface garments of an intimate nature did float; while George, the world-weary George, shouted to Freddy that he had hooked a fish.

" And me, I've swallowed one," answered he of the bracken. " I've swallowed a polly-wog. It wriggleth in my tummy. I shall die—Emerson, you beast, you've got on my bags."

" Hush, dears," said Mrs. Honeychurch, who found it impossible to remain shocked. " And do be sure you dry yourselves thoroughly first. All these colds come of not drying thoroughly."

" Mother, do come away," said Lucy. " Oh, for goodness' sake, do come."

" Hullo ! " cried George, so that again the ladies stopped.

He regarded himself as dressed. Barefoot, barechested, radiant and personable against the shadowy woods, he called :

" Hullo, Miss Honeychurch ! Hullo ! "

" Bow, Lucy ; better bow. Whoever is it ? I shall bow."

Miss Honeychurch bowed.

That evening and all that night the water ran away. On the morrow the pool had shrunk to its old size and lost its glory. It had been a call to the blood and to the relaxed will, a passing benediction whose influence did not pass, a holiness, a spell, a momentary chalice for youth.

There is a scene in *The Longest Journey* whose import is similar to this. A soldier joins Stephen and Rickie during their ride on Salisbury Plain. Stephen and the soldier become drunk, and Rickie, disgusted, returns to Cadover, leaving them to ride on without him. They quarrel, and Stephen throws the soldier from his horse into the mud. He rides off victoriously, shouting for joy ; he gallops into Salisbury scattering the people ; he rides into a stable, grasps a beam to pull himself up out of the saddle, swings from the beam and kicks at the other customers. Later he rides back to Cadover, wrestles with a shepherd on the way, bathes in his room, and climbs through a skylight to lie naked on the roof. Stephen felt a call to the blood as surely as Freddy, George, and Mr. Beebe did. He went back, back, back through the ages, behind all conventions ; he fought ; he shed his clothes. Freddy, George, and Mr. Beebe

* pp. 162–3.

shed their clothes and forget conventions for a moment ; but they merely swim and romp together. The difference is a measure of the difference between the moods of the two novels, moods which are reflected, respectively, in the sprightly style of the bathing scene, and in the style, mysteriously weighted with supernatural, Druidical suggestions, of Stephen's drunken escapade.

In *Howards End* Forster's philosophy, if not his art, reaches maturity. It would no longer be possible for him to write a swift, dramatic novel such as *Where Angels Fear to Tread.* For though he still sees a clash in life and still wishes to describe it, the clash is no longer so clearly defined. It embraces more ; it has endless ramifications. And to define it is not enough. Something must be done to bring the opposing sides closer together. In fact, the clash must be prevented if possible. *Howards End* asks, How are we to be saved in this industrial-commercial age ? How is force to be kept in its box ? How are panic and emptiness to be kept from overwhelming the world ? And the answer is given : " Only connect." Only connect the mind and the body ; only connect the seen and the unseen ; only connect the outer and the inner life. Tolerance is taught. For the first time in Forster's novels compromise is allowed ; an " aristocrat ", one in whom the Spirit of Life clearly resides, marries a Sawstonian, and the marriage is a success. *Howards End* was written but a few short years before the First World War, and Forster has the international situation much in mind. The South is put aside : there are matters of more immediate import in the North. Two of the major characters in the novel, Margaret and Helen Schlegel, are of German and English descent. Their father came to England when he saw that clouds of materialism were obscuring the spiritual life in Germany. He defined Germany's weakness to a German nephew : " You use the intellect, but you no longer care about it. That I call stupidity. You only care about the things that you can use, and therefore arrange them in the following order : Money, supremely useful ; intellect, rather useful ; imagination, of no use at all." Forster sees the same tendencies in England. He wishes to analyse them and to suggest remedies. Nor does he neglect his art. The structure of *Howards End*, in spite of weaknesses, shows a considerable advance over the previous novels. *Howards End* is not as harmonious as *Where Angels Fear to Tread*, but it is greater, and it is made of better materials. Once more Forster tries, not unsuccessfully, to extend his powers. He considers carefully both sociology and art. The two often reinforce one another in *Howards End.* Occasionally they clash.

As the novel begins Helen Schlegel is visiting the Wilcoxes at their home of Howards End in Hertfordshire. Howards End is an old farmhouse, but it is not far from suburbia. London can be seen approaching like a red rust across the meadows, threatening the house and the wych-elm that stands beside it, threatening the farm that is just through the hedge from Howards End. We are no longer in Wiltshire, deep in the country, deep in the past ; we are in the twentieth century, on the fringe of London, where the battle between country and town is being fought. And part of the force that builds London is at Howards End. Mr. Wilcox is a successful business-man ; his two sons, Charles and Paul, are following in his footsteps. The Wilcoxes drive swift motor-cars ; they have their hands on the ropes of affairs. They have gained their success by looking outwards ; they have not had time to look at their own souls. They represent the outer life, the life of " telegrams and anger ". They are not a part of the country, though they live at Howards End. Howards End belongs to Mrs. Wilcox, a different kind of person. The house has come down to her through her family, farming people. When she married Mr. Wilcox, all that was left of the farm was the meadow near the house. The rest had been sold ; even the meadow was mortgaged ; the house was falling into disrepair. Mr. Wilcox saved Howards End. He built a garage where the pony's paddock used to be ; he covered an old beam in the sitting-room with match-board ; he repaired the house and made it a home for his family. The Wilcox children are his, rather than his wife's. Even the daughter, Evie, is spiritually a Wilcox. All the Wilcoxes have hay-fever when the meadow is being cut ; but Mrs. Wilcox trails through the meadow in a long dress, holding wisps of hay in her hands, communing with the earth. She has mysterious, intuitive knowledge. "One knew that she worshipped the past, and that the instinctive wisdom the past can alone bestow had descended upon her—that wisdom to which we give the clumsy name of aristocracy. High born she might not be. But assuredly she cared about her ancestors, and let them help her." She can reconcile differences without effort. She knows things that no one else in the novel, least of all her own family, can fathom. Spiritually Margaret and Helen Schlegel, two independent young women, are more akin to her than are the Wilcoxes. They know that there is an unseen, though they have discovered it intellectually, through books and art and conversation, not instinctively, as Mrs. Wilcox has. They believe that personal relations are supreme, and that any human being is nearer to the unseen than any organization. Their response to all that they encounter in life is sincere and vital. They are the representatives of the inner life. They live in London at Wickham Place with their sixteen-year-old brother, Tibby, comfortably supported by the income from money bequeathed them by their mother. Tibby has a minor rôle in the novel. He is intelligent and cultured, but cold. Margaret and Helen, not Tibby, are the Schlegels in whom Forster is interested. The Schlegels, the Wilcoxes, and Mrs. Wilcox and Howards End (Mrs. Wilcox is almost a part of her house) are the main elements in the novel. They are brought together for a short time by Helen Schlegel's visit to Howards End.

Helen is enormously impressed by the Wilcoxes during her visit. (She and Margaret had met them while on vacation in Germany.) They seem so sure, so self-possessed; their knowledge of the world is so wide and so practical; their energy is fascinating. They tell her that her talk of Equality and of votes for women is nonsense; that Socialism is nonsense; that art and literature, except when conducive to strengthening the character, are nonsense. For a time Helen is glad to have her beliefs contradicted by these strong men, whose knowledge of life is not academic. Helen is less responsible than her sister Margaret, the elder of the two. She is kissed one night by Paul, the younger Wilcox son, who tells her that he loves her. It is a tremendous experience for Helen, and she writes to

Margaret to give her the news that she and Paul are in love. But the next morning Helen's faith in the Wilcoxes is shattered. Paul, she sees, is badly frightened. He was somewhat foolish the night before ; he has to make his way in the world—he is going to Nigeria to work in an overseas part of his father's business—and he cannot afford to become involved with Helen. " When I saw all the others so placid," Helen told Margaret later, " and Paul mad with terror in case I said the wrong thing, I felt for a moment that the whole Wilcox family was a fraud, just a wall of newspapers and motor-cars and golf-clubs, and that if it fell I should find nothing behind it but panic and emptiness." She relieves Paul's fears when she is able to speak to him alone, and sends a telegram to Margaret telling her that the affair is ended.

But before Margaret receives the telegram, an aunt of the Schlegels, Aunt Juley, who is visiting at Wickham Place, has left for Howards End to be near Helen at this crisis in her life. Margaret herself is unable to go because Tibby has a severe attack of the Wilcox complaint, hay-fever. Under the circumstances, Aunt Juley is not a good emissary. She of course does not know that the affair is over. And she is not very intelligent ; she is conventional ; she is easily muddled. She causes little harm in the novel—partly because she has a minor rôle, and partly because she is kind-hearted and genuinely loves Helen and Margaret. She is the only character in Forster's novels who is muddled and conventional, yet likeable. At Howards End she mistakes the elder brother, Charles, for Paul. When Charles learns from her of Paul's indiscretion, he is furious ; and Helen's brief contact with the Wilcoxes ends in anger and tears.

Some time later the Schlegels, with Aunt Juley, a German cousin Fräulein Mosebach, and her young man Herr Liesecke, attend a performance of Beethoven's Fifth Symphony at the Queen's Hall. The performance, or rather, Helen's interpretation of the symphony, is a key to the novel. We have already seen that Helen's interpretation accords with Forster's view of life, which is that panic and emptiness always threaten the splendour of life and periodically overwhelm it ; that periods of civilization and freedom alternate with war and oppression ;

that force is, at best, insecurely shut within its box. The message of the symphony is quietly pointed by the presence of Aunt Juley and the German couple. Fräulein Mosebach remembers all the time that Beethoven is "echt Deutsch". Aunt Juley, who is "British to the backbone", praises the last number on the program, Elgar's "Pomp and Circumstance", and insists that the Germans should hear "what *we* are doing in music". But the Germans leave before this great composition is played. The full emotional impact of the third and fourth movements of the Fifth Symphony is felt by Helen and reinforces the experience she has had at Howards End. "[The third movement] started with a goblin walking quietly over the universe, from end to end. Others followed him. They were not aggressive creatures; it was that that made them so terrible to Helen. They merely observed in passing that there was no such thing as splendour or heroism in the world. . . . Helen could not contradict them, for, once at all events, she had felt the same, and had seen the reliable walls of youth collapse. Panic and emptiness! Panic and emptiness! The goblins were right." But the goblins are contradicted in the symphony. They are scattered; there *is* heroism and glory and splendour. "Gusts of splendour, gods and demigods contending with vast swords, colour and fragrance broadcast on the field of battle, magnificent victory, magnificent death! Oh, it all burst before the girl, and she even stretched out her gloved hands as if it was tangible. Any fate was titanic; any contest desirable; conqueror and conquered would alike be applauded by the angels of the utmost stars." Then the goblins return. And at the end of the symphony they are scattered again. Helen leaves the hall. Music can tell her no more. She applies to her own life the view of the universe that Beethoven has given. "The music had summed up to her all that had happened or could happen in her career." And, as the future will prove, she is literally right. Helen is vividly aware of the goblin footfalls, of the panic and emptiness in life. But she has her moment of heroism in the novel, and after a time of panic and emptiness, she is, finally, triumphant. The last two movements of the Fifth Symphony describe almost exactly the vicissitudes of her life. We are not given Margaret's impressions of the symphony, except to be shown that she enjoyed it and that she disagrees with Helen's view. Margaret can only see the music. Her view, it is certain, is less subjective than Helen's. The meaning of the symphony, if she believed it to be true, would be applied more universally by her than by Helen ; she would apply it to the whole of life, not primarily to her own life. And throughout the novel, Margaret, who acts, as it were, for Forster, tries, within her own small sphere of influence, to keep force in its box.

A goblin footfall follows the Schlegels home from the Queen's Hall. The symphony begins to expand at once into the lives of the characters of the novel ; the cogency of Beethoven's message begins to be demonstrated. When Helen left the hall, preoccupied with the symphony, she absent-mindedly took with her an umbrella belonging to a young man, a stranger, who had been talking to Margaret. The young man is Leonard Bast, a clerk who stands " at the extreme verge of gentility ". Though the umbrella is old and shabby, it means a good deal to him ; for it is a symbol of respectability, and he cannot well afford another. He fears that it has been stolen, that the Schlegels have played the confidence trick on him. He is too poor to be able to afford to trust people ; and Margaret has a glimpse of squalor as she sees his suspicion. She takes him to Wickham Place after the concert to claim his property, but he refuses to stay to tea. He is shy of the Schlegels, and embarrassed because his umbrella is so shabby. The incident impressed Margaret and Helen. " It remained as a goblin footfall, as a hint that all is not for the best in the best of all possible worlds, and that beneath these superstructures of wealth and art there wanders an ill-fed boy, who has recovered his umbrella indeed, but who has left no address behind him, and no name."

The next day the Wilcoxes re-enter the Schlegels' lives. They have taken up a flat in the ornate block opposite Wickham Place ; for Charles is being married, and it is convenient for them to be in London until after the wedding. Mrs. Wilcox calls on the Schlegels and is snubbed by Margaret ; but she protests against the snub and wins Margaret to her. They soon become friends. Mrs. Wilcox is not a success with

Margaret's intellectual friends ; she is not intellectual, or alert, or a good conversationalist. Yet, she gives Margaret the idea of greatness. " Margaret, zigzagging with her friends over Thought and Art, was conscious of a personality that transcended their own and dwarfed their activities." Mrs. Wilcox is impressed by Margaret's ability to discuss life wisely, but she suggests that Margaret has gained her knowledge from books and lacks experience. She is disturbed when she learns that the Schlegels will have to leave Wickham Place when their lease expires in two or three years. The house will then be pulled down to make way for more flats, and this seems horrible to Mrs. Wilcox. Howards End, she says, was nearly pulled down once, and it would have killed her. Suddenly, she invites Margaret to come with her to see Howards End, now, this very day. Margaret first refuses, then accepts : Mrs. Wilcox's invitation seems strangely important. But at King's Cross they meet Mr. Wilcox and Evie, who have just returned unexpectedly from Yorkshire. The expedition to Howards End is cancelled.

Margaret does not see Mrs. Wilcox alive again. Mrs. Wilcox has not been well in London ; she falls seriously ill, dies, and is buried near Howards End. Her funeral is described. Margaret attends it ; and countrymen are present—gravediggers and a woodcutter and Mrs. Wilcox's neighbours—besides the Wilcoxes. The woodcutter leaves last, furtively taking for his sweetheart a chrysanthemum from Mrs. Wilcox's grave —a chrysanthemum that Margaret sent. Then, we are shown the grave alone, with clouds and a night sky above it, the church beside it, and, towards morning, frost upon it. Mrs. Wilcox is at one with the earth.

At Howards End the next day her family receives a rude shock. Mrs. Wilcox has requested, in a note sent on from the nursing home where she died, that Howards End be given to Margaret Schlegel. After a family consultation, the Wilcoxes decide to ignore the request. Forster's comments on their decision are a measure of his tolerance in this novel :

> Ought the Wilcoxes to have offered their home to Margaret ? I think not. The appeal was too flimsy. It was not legal ;

> it had been written in illness, and under the spell of a sudden friendship ; it was contrary to the dead woman's intentions in the past, contrary to her very nature, so far as that nature was understood by them. To them Howards End was a house : they could not know that to her it had been a spirit, for which she sought a spiritual heir. And—pushing one step farther into these mists—may they not have decided even better than they supposed ? Is it credible that the possessions of the spirit can be bequeathed at all ? Has the soul offspring ? A wych-elm tree, a vine, a wisp of hay with dew on it—can passion for such things be transmitted when there is no bond of blood ? No ; the Wilcoxes are not to be blamed. The problem is too terrific, and they could not even perceive a problem. No ; it is natural and fitting that after due debate they should tear the note up and throw it on to their dining-room fire. The practical moralist may acquit them absolutely. He who strives to look deeper may acquit them—almost. For one hard fact remains. They did neglect a personal appeal. The woman who had died did say to them, " Do this ", and they answered, " We will not." *

There is a tone of generosity in this passage that is not to be found in those uncompromising novels, *The Longest Journey* and *Where Angels Fear to Tread.* And Margaret, oblivious, of course, of Mrs. Wilcox's request, is equally generous to the Wilcoxes. At first impact they had made a favourable impression upon Helen—an impression which quickly evaporated. Margaret's respect for them grows more slowly and is more enduring. " They were not ' her sort ', they were often suspicious and stupid, and deficient where she excelled ; but collision with them stimulated her, and she felt an interest that verged into liking, even for Charles. She desired to protect them, and often felt that they could protect her, excelling where she was deficient." They had grit. They knew how to control the practical affairs of life ; their hands were on all the ropes. " How dare Schlegels despise Wilcoxes, when it takes all sorts to make a world ? " The outer life of " telegrams and anger " that the Wilcoxes led, Margaret recognized, is a real force. " Don't brood too much ", she wrote to Helen, who was visiting in Germany, " on the superiority of the unseen

* p. 104.

to the seen. It's true, but to brood on it is medieval. Our business is not to contrast the two, but to reconcile them."

Two years after Mrs. Wilcox's death the Schlegels are beginning to look for a new home. London continues to be built and pulled down and rebuilt ; the Schlegels' lease of Wickham Place is about to expire. For the first time Margaret begins to understand something of Mrs. Wilcox's respect for a home ; she learns that a house may be a spirit, rich with the precious distillation of the years. At this juncture Leonard Bast comes once more to Wickham Place. His wife, a slatternly woman, calls first. She has found Margaret's card in one of Leonard's books. Leonard has been away overnight, and Mrs. Bast has come to ask for her husband. Once more the Schlegels hear a goblin footfall ; once more they have a glimpse of squalor ; they realize more fully the value of their money. The next day Leonard appears to apologize for his wife's call. This time he stays to talk, and he interests the Schlegels. " One guessed him as the third generation, grandson to the shepherd or ploughboy whom civilization had sucked into the town ; as one of the thousands who have lost the life of the body and failed to reach the life of the spirit. Hints of robustness survived in him, more than a hint of primitive good looks. . . ." He wishes to be cultured ; he seeks beauty in the Queen's Hall and in books ; he feels inferior to the Schlegels, but wants to talk to them to display his intellectual attainments. Margaret, to whom the impending loss of Wickham Place has given a new insight into the life of London, reflects as she watches him that culture had worked in her own case ; " but during the last few weeks she had doubted whether it humanized the majority, so wide and so widening is the gulf that stretches between the natural and the philosophic man, so many the good chaps who are wrecked in trying to cross it ". Leonard respects culture because of its social value ; he respects books because he hopes to gain culture from them ; his love of beauty is largely sentimental. But Margaret and Helen discover that there is something real in Leonard, nevertheless. On that night he had not come home to his wife, he had walked out of London into the country. He had been reading Jefferies and Borrow and Stevenson, and he wanted to see for himself what they described ; he wanted to return to the Earth. So he left his office, took the Underground to Wimbledon, and then began to walk. " He had visited the county of Surrey when darkness covered its amenities, and its cosy villas had re-entered ancient night. Every twelve hours this miracle happens, but he had troubled to go and see for himself. Within his cramped little mind dwelt something that was greater than Jefferies' books —the spirit that led Jefferies to write them ; and his dawn, though revealing nothing but monotones, was part of the eternal sunrise that shows George Borrow Stonehenge." Moreover, he tells Helen and Margaret honestly that the dawn was not wonderful when it came. It was grey, and he was cold and tired. The expedition, on the whole, was not enjoyable. " It was more a case ", Leonard says, " of sticking to it."

At a meeting of an informal discussion club, which takes place immediately after Leonard's call, Margaret and Helen speak of Leonard. What can be done for him ? What should be done for him ? After the meeting, while walking on the Chelsea Embankment, they meet Mr. Wilcox. He has grown even more opulent ; he is particularly well satisfied with himself ; he feels that he would like to protect Margaret and Helen ; he is ready to speak patronizingly of their discussion club. They tell him of Leonard Bast ; and he advises them, confidentially, that the company for which Leonard works, Porphyrion Fire Insurance, is about to smash. Leonard had better find another job while there is yet time. The subject is changed, and Margaret learns that Howards End has been let. It would not " do " for the Wilcoxes, spend as much money on it as they might. Mr. Wilcox has taken a house in London, in Ducie Street, and another, Oniton Grange, in Shropshire. Margaret is saddened by the news. She knew of Mrs. Wilcox's love for Howards End, and she had not imagined that Mrs. Wilcox's family would leave the house. Every one, she reflects, is moving ; and Mr. Wilcox has forgotten his wife.

Margaret and Helen invite Leonard to tea at once to give him Mr. Wilcox's warning. But Leonard is shy and nervous and suspicious. The ladies want to know too much about his affairs. Moreover, the Schlegels are Romance to Leonard ; they represent the world of leisured ease and culture that he dreams of attaining ; and he does not wish to mix his dreams with the drab monotony of his life at the Porphyrion Insurance Company. The tea ends in a vulgar row, a row which Mr. Wilcox witnesses, for he and his daughter, Evie, come unexpectedly to call. The Schlegels regard Leonard as an individual with rights equal to theirs. Mr. Wilcox regards him as a certain " type ", a member of a lower class, which one must keep at a distance. He feels more than ever that the Schlegels need some one to protect them.

From this moment begins Mr. Wilcox's courtship of Margaret—surely one of the strangest courtships in fiction. Mr. Wilcox uses devious methods in his courting : he does not go straight up to his lady and announce his love. Evie, then the house in Ducie Street, are used as cat's paws. Evie invites Margaret to lunch at Simpson's restaurant—and Mr. Wilcox is there. Mr. Wilcox writes Margaret, while she is visiting Aunt Juley at Swanage, that he will lease the Ducie Street house to the Schlegels if they wish, but Margaret must come *at once*—he underlines the words—to go over the house with him. Margaret goes, and finds that Mr. Wilcox has summoned her, not to lease a house, but to make a proposal of marriage to her. Margaret's actions, if more honourable, are even stranger than Mr. Wilcox's. On the way to London, in discussing Mr. Wilcox's proposal with Helen, and before her marriage (for she accepts the proposal), she justifies the Wilcoxes' existence. She proves to her own satisfaction (clearly she has had doubts about the matter) that Wilcoxes and their life of telegrams and anger are necessary to the world—as we know it, at any rate. " If Wilcoxes hadn't worked and died in England for thousands of years," she tells Helen during a picnic with Aunt Juley in the Purbeck Hills, " you and I couldn't sit here without having our throats cut. There would be no trains, no ships to carry us literary people about in, no fields even. Just savagery. No—perhaps not even that. Without their spirit life might never have moved out of protoplasm." The Wilcoxes have made civilization possible. They guarantee the Schlegel's income—Margaret does not forget that she lives on the proceeds from investments. " More and more ", she says to Helen, " do I refuse to draw my income and sneer at those who guarantee it." And Mr. Wilcox, though he lacks fine feelings and deep insight, had saved Howards End when it was about to be pulled down, Margaret reflects. This is an unusual way to fall in love, yet Forster assures us that Margaret loves Mr. Wilcox. He tells us, indeed, that Margaret finds that Mr. Wilcox's self-confidence and optimism stimulates her and banishes morbidity. But Margaret has never been morbid, and her most pronounced characteristic, Forster has told us in the early pages of *Howards End*, is " a profound vivacity, a continual and sincere response to all that she encountered in her path through life ". " It is impossible ", says Forster, commenting on Margaret's relationship with Mr. Wilcox, " to see modern life steadily and see it whole, and she had chosen to see it whole. Mr. Wilcox saw steadily. He never bothered over the mysterious or the private. . . . Some day—in the millenium—there may be no need for his type. At present, homage is due to it from those who think themselves superior, and who possibly are." Forster pays his homage by marrying Margaret to Mr. Wilcox. Helen is horrified and hysterical when she learns that Margaret intends to accept the proposal. She is incoherent, and she speaks of panic and emptiness. Between them, the Schlegel sisters represent two sides of Forster. Forster's intellect accepts Mr. Wilcox ; his emotions revolt against the acceptance. Helen warns Margaret that she can never like Mr. Wilcox.

Henry—Forster tells us that we must now call Mr. Wilcox Henry—proves during his engagement to be as indirect as a lover as he was as a suitor. He is ashamed of his love.

> Outwardly he was cheerful, reliable, and brave ; but within, all had reverted to chaos, ruled, so far as it was ruled at all, by an incomplete asceticism. Whether as a boy, husband, or widower, he had always the sneaking belief that bodily passion is bad, a belief that is desirable only when held passionately. Religion had confirmed him. The words that were read aloud on Sunday to him and to other respectable men were the words that had once kindled the souls of St. Catherine and St. Francis into a white-hot hatred of the carnal. He could not be as the saints and love the Infinite with a seraphic ardour, but he could be a little ashamed of loving a wife.*

* p. 197.

The first kiss he gives Margaret is brutally lacking in tenderness, and takes her utterly unprepared. Afterwards, Henry hurries away—he was seeing her to Aunt Juley's door. But Margaret, though she herself has learned only to desire honestly, understands his weakness, and intends to help him. " Margaret greeted her lord with peculiar tenderness on the morrow. Mature as he was, she might yet be able to help him to the building of the rainbow bridge that should connect the prose in us with the passion. Without it we are meaningless fragments, half monks, half beasts, unconnected arches that have never joined into a man. With it love is born, and alights on the highest curve, glowing against the grey, sober against the fire." But Henry, in spite of his inadequacy, is well contented with himself. His plans are maturing splendidly—there is only one slight annoyance : his tenant at Howards End has to go abroad, and wishes to sublet. Mr. Wilcox does not intend to allow him this privilege. Preoccupied with his own affairs, he is not pleased when Leonard Bast's affairs are mentioned by Margaret and Helen. Helen has had a letter from Leonard to tell her he has taken the Schlegels' advice, left Porphyrion Insurance, and gone to another job—at a reduced salary. Mr. Wilcox remarks absently that the Porphyrion is a good business ; its affairs have recently been put in order. He is unable to see that any one is responsible for Leonard's unfortunate loss of money.

Soon afterwards there occurs the first of a series of incidents that seems to draw Margaret to Howards End, or to indicate that Mrs. Wilcox's wish, that Howards End be given to Margaret, is to be fulfilled. Mr. Wilcox and Margaret motor to Hertfordshire to see Howards End, which is vacant, now that the tenant has gone abroad. It is raining, and Margaret stands on the porch of the house while Henry goes to get the keys from the farm through the hedge. But the house, Margaret finds, is unlocked, and she enters, clutching in her hands weeds that she has plucked from the porch. It is the first time she has seen Howards End. " Penned in by the desolate weather, she recaptured the sense of space which the motor had tried to rob from her. She remembered again that ten square miles are not ten times as wonderful as one square mile, that a thousand square miles are not practically the same as heaven. The phantom of bigness, which London encourages, was laid for ever when she paced from the hall at Howards End to its kitchen and heard the rains run this way and that where the watershed of the roof divided them." Then she finds that there is some one else in the house. An old woman, Miss Avery from the farm, who has mysterious connexions with the past, and who knew Howards End before there were Wilcoxes there, comes down the stairs and says, "Oh! Well, I took you for Ruth Wilcox." Margaret, she says, has Mrs. Wilcox's way of walking. And of course, though Miss Avery does not say so, Margaret has a bunch of weeds in her hand, as Mrs. Wilcox, when she walked in the meadow at Howards End, had been wont to carry a wisp of hay. Back at Wickham Place that night, Margaret finds that Howards End continues to have a strong influence upon her. The sense of flux, which had been given her by motor-cars and by London, and which had haunted her that year as she looked for a house, left her for a time.

> She forgot the luggage and the motor-cars, and the hurrying men who know so much and connect so little. She recaptured the sense of space, which is the basis of all earthly beauty, and, starting from Howards End, she attempted to realize England. She failed—visions do not come when we try, though they may come through trying. But an unexpected love of the island awoke in her, connecting on this side with the joys of the flesh, on that with the inconceivable. Helen and her father had known this love, poor Leonard Bast was groping after it, but it had been hidden from Margaret until this afternoon. It had certainly come through the house and old Miss Avery. Through them: the notion of "through" persisted; her mind trembled towards a conclusion which only the unwise have put into words. Then, veering back into warmth, it dwelt on ruddy bricks, flowering plum-trees, and all the tangible joys of spring.*

Margaret demonstrates her affection for the countryside on a trip to Oniton Grange, Mr. Wilcox's house in Shropshire, which she visits next. Evie Wilcox is to be married at Oniton

* p. 216.

Grange (her wedding takes place before Margaret's), and the wedding party travels from London in all the luxury that wealth can provide. A trio of motor-cars meets their train at Shrewsbury ; and on the way to Oniton one of them runs over a country girl's cat. Two chauffeurs and one of the men from the party are left to deal with the girl, and the ladies are hurried on in the third car, driven by Charles Wilcox. Margaret asks Charles to stop ; she wishes to go back to the girl. Charles refuses, and Margaret leaps from the moving car, falling on her knees, and cutting her hands. " No doubt she had disgraced herself. But she felt their whole journey from London had been unreal. They had no part with the earth and its emotions. They were dust, and a stink, and cosmopolitan chatter, and the girl whose cat had been killed had lived more deeply than they." That evening Margaret walks alone in the grounds of the Grange. Nearby are a village, its church, and the ruins of a castle. She stoops down at times as she walks, and strokes the turf. And she startles Charles, who is nearby in the gathering dusk, by announcing : " I love this place. I love Shropshire. I hate London. I am glad that this will be my home." Margaret has learned a good deal in recent months of the power of home, and she is determined " to create new sanctities among these hills ".

Evie's wedding is as luxurious as the journey to Oniton promised it would be. Margaret is not allowed to walk to the church ; she must ride, though the church is only around the corner. Mr. Wilcox is apologetic ; he intimates that Mrs. Wilcox had wanted to walk to Charles's wedding, but it could not be allowed ; convention forbids. After the last guests have gone, Henry and Margaret are left alone amidst the débris that the wedding has left behind. Tables on the lawns are still crowded with rich food, half-eaten, rich wine that the guests could not finish. Then, in the midst of this luxurious profusion, Helen appears with Mr. and Mrs. Bast. Leonard has lost his new job—the firm has reduced staff—and he is nearly destitute. Helen holds Mr. Wilcox morally responsible ; she has come to confront him with the Basts. Margaret tries to reconcile the two sides, to connect, to help them to reach an agreement. Mrs. Bast, who has become rather tipsy from the wine the wedding-guests left, addresses Henry affectionately. It soon appears that some years ago, during Henry's first marriage, she had been his mistress. Margaret forgives Henry—the tragedy is Mrs. Wilcox's, not hers—and to protect him she dismisses the Basts. Helen spends the night with them at the hotel in the village. To her it appears that Mr. Wilcox has ruined Leonard in two ways: through Leonard's wife, and through the bad financial advice that caused Leonard to lose his job. The next day Margaret leaves Oniton Grange with Henry. She never sees it again, though she had resolved to create new sanctities there, for Henry soon lets it, without consulting her.

Margaret marries Henry and lives at Ducie Street. Plans are drawn for a new home in the country. Helen has gone to Europe. She tried first to settle five thousand pounds on Leonard Bast, but he refused the money. Tibby is at Oxford. Wickham Place has been pulled down, and the Schlegels' furniture has been stored at Howards End, which is still vacant. Then Margaret learns from the Charles Wilcoxes, who live near Howards End, that Miss Avery has begun to unpack the Schlegels' possessions. Margaret goes up to Howards End to see for herself. She feels again the influence of the countryside. She calls first, in search of Miss Avery, at the farm near Howards End. "In these English farms," she reflects, "if anywhere, one might see life steadily and see it whole, group in one vision its transitoriness and its eternal youth, connect—connect without bitterness until all men are brothers." At Howards End Margaret finds that Miss Avery has set out most of the Schlegels' furniture, their books, their father's sword, with wonderful care and tact. The house, Miss Avery says, has been empty long enough. Margaret tries to set her right. She and her husband, she explains, are not going to live at Howards End; they have decided to build a new house in Sussex. "You think you won't come back to live here, Mrs. Wilcox, but you will," Miss Avery replies. "In a couple of weeks", she tells Margaret later in their conversation, "I'll see your lights shining through the hedge of an evening. Have you ordered in coals?" Margaret intends to have the furniture removed to London, but before she can do so Aunt Juley falls seriously ill, and Margaret has to go to her at Swanage.

Helen, who has been mysterious and distant in her relations with Margaret since the affair at Oniton, is recalled from the Continent. She becomes even more mysterious. Aunt Juley is out of danger by the time Helen reaches London, so Helen decides not to come to Swanage. Margaret begins to fear that Helen may have gone mad through brooding on the Wilcoxes. She has given only a banker's address in London, and she refuses to meet Margaret and Tibby. She does, however, want some of her books. This request enables Mr. Wilcox, who acts with business-like precision when Margaret consults him, to lay a trap for Helen. He has Margaret write Helen telling her to go to Howards End for the books, and he arranges that he and a doctor shall take her by surprise while she is there. Margaret joins the expedition—though Henry wishes to leave her at Charles's house—and discovers the reason for Helen's secrecy. Helen is with child. Margaret manages, with difficulty, to persuade Henry and the doctor to leave ; and she finds herself alone with Helen in Howards End amidst their own furniture.

The relations between Margaret and Helen are difficult at first. Their affection for one another is unchanged, but there is something between them that is hard to overcome. Then a common interest in the books and chairs and carpets that surround them and awaken memories of the past brings them together. " Explanations and appeals had failed ; they had tried for a common meeting-ground, and had only made each other unhappy. And all the time their salvation was lying round them—the past sanctifying the present ; the present with wild heart-throb, declaring that there would after all be a future, with laughter and the voices of children. Helen, still smiling, came up to her sister. She said, ' It is always Meg.' They looked into each other's eyes. The inner life had paid." And Howards End has come alive again. Tom, the boy from the farm, sent by Miss Avery, comes to the door with milk. Helen suggests that she and Margaret spend the night there before she returns to Germany ; and Margaret goes to ask Henry's leave.

Henry's leave is not given. He will not have Helen in his house. He had a mistress while he was married to Mrs. Wilcox. Helen, unmarried, has had a lover; and Henry, though he has been forgiven by Margaret, will not forgive Helen. Margaret shows remarkable forbearance as she tries to persuade him to grant Helen's request. She does not wish to break with Henry; the scene, as it were, sums up her relationship with him. It is only when she sees clearly that she cannot reconcile him to Helen, and that he will certainly refuse Helen's request, that she speaks out and tries to show him himself. But it is useless. Henry cannot connect. He can see no relationship between himself and Helen; he cannot see that he has no right to criticize her. He is hopelessly muddled; and he accuses Margaret of blackmail when she mentions Mrs. Bast and speaks of his betrayal of Mrs. Wilcox. Margaret leaves to stay the night with Helen at Howards End without his permission.

The connexion between Helen and Henry is closer than Margaret knew; for Leonard Bast is the father of Helen's unborn child. That night at Oniton, after Leonard had been dismissed and Helen had found that Mr. Wilcox had ruined him in two ways, she had given herself to him—given herself with her own will, and almost against Leonard's. "Helen loved the absolute. Leonard had been ruined absolutely, and had appeared to her as a man apart, isolated from the world." Moreover, Helen tells Margaret, the affair with Leonard may have grown from the kiss, so full of meaning for Helen, that Paul Wilcox gave her. "Both times", she says, "it was loneliness, and the night, and panic afterwards."

We are now given an opportunity to contrast Leonard with Mr. Wilcox, for Leonard's history subsequent to his visit to Oniton is recounted. The contrast is implicit—Forster draws no comparisons—but it is plain for all to see. Leonard remains as poor as Mr. Wilcox is affluent. None the less he refuses Helen's gift of five thousand pounds. He is eaten with remorse: it does not occur to him to blame Helen, or any one but himself, for the night at Oniton. He feels a new tenderness for his wife. "There is nothing to choose between us, after all," he thinks. Unlike Mr. Wilcox, he is able to connect. And he is not muddled. " He never confused the past. He remained alive, and blessed are those who live, if it is only to a sense of sinfulness. The anodyne of muddledom, by which most men blur and blend their mistakes, never passed Leonard's lips." Leonard, it is clear, is much more fit than Mr. Wilcox to inherit the future.

Leonard decides to seek Margaret out. He wishes to confess, to discuss the past, and to have news of Helen. After much searching, he discovers that Margaret lives at Ducie Street ; and on the day he calls there he finds she has gone to Howards End. He too goes to Howards End, arriving on the morning after Helen and Margaret have spent the night. As Leonard approaches, the theme of goblins stalking over the universe, a theme that has grown from Beethoven's Fifth Symphony, is introduced again. Charles Wilcox is at Howards End when Leonard arrives. Charles has come to turn Helen and Margaret out ; and he has learned that Leonard was Helen's lover. When Leonard comes up the walk Charles collars him. He intends to beat Leonard " within an inch of his life "; he seizes the Schlegels' sword for the purpose, and strikes Leonard a blow with the flat of it. But Leonard, who has not been well, dies from heart disease.

Charles is tried for manslaughter. " It was against all reason that he should be punished, but the law, being made in his image, sentenced him to three years' imprisonment. Then Henry's fortress gave way. He could bear no one but his wife, he shambled up to Margaret afterwards and asked her to do what she could with him. She did what seemed easiest—she took him down to recruit at Howards End." So Miss Avery's prophecy is fulfilled, and Margaret makes a home for both Henry and Helen at Howards End.

The last scene of the novel takes place at Howards End fourteen months later. Tom's father is cutting the meadow, and Tom takes Helen's baby, a boy, to play in the hay. Helen and Margaret are sitting outside overlooking the meadow. Helen smells a bunch of hay, whilst Margaret comments that the hay will sweeten to-morrow. Inside Howards End the Wilcox family are closeted in a dark and airless room—for they are still susceptible to hay-fever—to discuss the money and property settlements that Mr. Wilcox intends to make. Once more, as at the beginning of the novel, Wilcoxes and Schlegels are together at Howards End. The division between them, however, is not now so strongly pronounced as it was. At least, Margaret has reconciled Helen and Henry, who have come to like one another. Both Helen and Henry have changed. Helen is contented and no longer worries as she used to; while Henry has begun to worry, to look clearly at the past, and to criticize himself for the first time. As a result, he is badly shaken, and has lost his old self-confidence. Margaret too has changed—or perhaps she has only developed. She is less talkative than she used to be—Mrs. Wilcox would no longer remark that Margaret seems to have gained her knowledge of life from books. Margaret has turned more and more from words and books to things and to the unseen. She has made a home for Helen and Henry and straightened out their tangled lives. And the unseen has helped her. ". . . things that I can't phrase have helped me," she says. She feels the power of the countryside, and of Mrs. Wilcox, and of Howards End. "The meadow was being recut, the great red poppies were reopening in the garden. July would follow with the little red poppies among the wheat, August with the cutting of the wheat. These little events would become part of her year after year." "I feel that you and I and Henry", she had told Helen during their first night at Howards End, "are only fragments of [Mrs. Wilcox's] mind. She knows everything. She is everything. She is the house, and the tree that leans over it. . . . She knew about realities." And Margaret tells Helen in this final scene that "very early in the morning in the garden I feel that our house is the future as well as the past".

Mrs. Wilcox's wish concerning Howards End is to be fulfilled, at any rate. Margaret is summoned to the Wilcox meeting, and in her presence Henry announces to his family, whom he has treated generously, that he will leave Howards End to Margaret. "Margaret did not answer. There was something uncanny in her triumph. She, who had never expected to conquer anyone, had charged straight through these Wilcoxes and broken up their lives." Then Margaret learns, for the first time, that Mrs. Wilcox intended her to have Howards End. " Margaret was silent. Something shook her life in its inmost recesses, and she shivered." Margaret herself means to bequeath Howards End to Leonard Bast's and Helen's son. The future heir enters Howards End with his mother and Tom as the novel ends ; and Helen cries, " The field's cut ! the big meadow ! We've seen to the very end, and it'll be such a crop of hay as never ! "

Forster's choice of characters in *Howards End* is governed mainly by sociological considerations : he chooses characters who will best allow him to present and study middle-class English life, as he sees it, in the first decade of the twentieth century. And the disposition of these characters in the novel is arranged by Forster with excellent art. Mr. Wilcox is the successful, practical, wealthy business-man. He and his sons are materialists ; they lead the outer life ; they despise anything that is not a material good or that cannot be used as a means to material wealth. They are immensely confident ; for it is much easier to deal with the seen than with the unseen ; and so long as the Wilcoxes and their sort do not question the premises upon which their lives are based, they will swagger through the world, believing their success in business to be the measure of their worth. It is only when Henry begins, at the end of the novel, to consider the inner life that his self-confidence is shaken. At the other end of the middle-class ladder is Leonard Bast, who works for men like the Wilcoxes, and is as poor as they are wealthy, as hesitant as they are confident. Leonard is groping towards culture, towards some of the accoutrements, at least, of the inner life ; but his groping is prompted largely by Wilcox motives : he sees culture as a means that will help him to climb up the middle-class ladder. He has, however, a rudimentary inner life of his own. Leonard is dependent upon the Wilcoxes' whims ; he is a means which their kind employs when he can be of use. But not even the Wilcoxes are the final masters of the outer life. There are forces greater than they, forces which are international and which spring both from materialism and from a perversion of the inner life. These forces are represented in *Howards End* by the Schlegels' patriotic German cousin, Fräulein Mosebach, and by Aunt Juley, who is " British to the backbone ". Aunt Juley and Fräulein Mosebach, so innocuous and yet so sinister, vie with one another in extolling the unparalleled virtues of their respective countries. Between the German and the English patriots, between Leonard Bast and the Wilcoxes, and intensely themselves, are Helen and Margaret Schlegel, who lead a cultured, leisurely life, and are concerned with intrinsic, spiritual goods. Responsive to all that they encounter, they are in an excellent position either to crusade for what they believe to be the right, or to attempt, through compromise, to reconcile the opposing camps that surround them. Helen chooses the first way, Margaret the second. Their respective characters and their different reactions to the Wilcoxes determine the choice of each. Helen is at first greatly impressed by the Wilcoxes because they are so sure of their own position and pursue their ends so successfully. Then she sees through them, and despises them completely. Margaret, who saw them more clearly from the beginning, realizes that they are admirably suited to provide the material basis of our civilization. But like eunuchs, they are suited for their task at their own expense, and she pities them. Within the Wilcox family, but scarcely part of it, more akin, in fact, to the Schlegels, is Mrs. Wilcox. And within the Schlegel family, but more akin to the Wilcoxes, is Tibby. It is not that Tibby is superficially like the Wilcoxes. No more is Mrs. Wilcox superficially like the Schlegels. The balance is more subtle and effective. Tibby is cultured ; he knows and respects art as much as the Wilcoxes, in their ignorance, despise it. He dislikes the Wilcoxes. But he is cold and unsympathetic. " His was the Leisure ", Forster tells us, " without sympathy—an attitude as fatal as the strenuous : a little cold culture may be raised on it, but no art." Mrs. Wilcox, though she is not cultured, has an inner life that is even more profound than the Schlegels'. She knows the countryside and its past, and draws spiritual sustenance from the earth, from her home, and from her ancestors. Leonard Bast, whose grandfather came to London from a farm, and who desires at times to return to the earth, is dimly related, through the countryside, to Mrs. Wilcox. Moreover, both Leonard and Mrs. Wilcox are injured by Mr. Wilcox's affair with the woman who becomes Leonard's wife. Leonard dies at Howards End, where, we are told, Mrs. Wilcox wished to die—but Henry sent her to a nursing home instead. And Leonard's son inherits Mrs. Wilcox's beloved house. Mrs. Wilcox is so closely associated with Howards End that she lives on in it after her death : the influence that Howards End exercises is her influence. And Margaret, as she becomes less talkative, as she turns from books and comes to understand the countryside and the power of home, as she gains profounder knowledge and learns how to reconcile differences more easily, becomes Mrs. Wilcox in personality as well as in name, and is as closely associated with Howards End. Howards End itself is almost a character in the novel. It is made from Forster's deepest feelings for the countryside. In it is concentrated, as it were, all the precious distillation of years of country life ; those who know and understand Howards End are enabled to see life whole and to reconcile its differences. Howards End is the centre around which the action of the novel moves and where the central characters find peace at last. It illustrates the message of the novel : " Only connect ".

To this extent at least Forster's sociological investigation and his art reinforce one another. But there are also points at which they clash ; and the most serious of these clashes occurs in a part of the novel that is of crucial importance to the whole : Henry and Margaret's courtship and marriage. It is necessary to Forster's sociological thesis that the Wilcoxes and the Schlegels be reconciled in some degree. It is necessary to his plot that Margaret inherit Howards End. The obvious solution is to marry Henry and Margaret. In theory this solution might work well enough, but as Forster employs it, it is arbitrary and unconvincing. The trouble is that Forster, though he tries his best to understand Henry, to be fair to him, and to sympathize with him, dislikes Henry thoroughly. Forster's intellect tells him that Henry is needed in our modern world and that he is to be pitied. But Forster's heart will not sign the documents ; and in novel-writing the heart is often a better guide than the intellect. At any rate, it is fatal for an author to go against his emotions. The result in this case, as we have seen, is that Margaret is made to fall in love with Henry for sociological and theoretical reasons, rather than for personal, human emotions. Violence is done to her ; the reader is disturbed ; and Forster's own conscience is not good. We do not ask why Margaret married this man ; we feel that she emphatically would not have married him. And when Forster tells us that as Margaret walked at Oniton " on her lover's arm, she felt that she was having her share [of happiness] ", it is impossible to believe him. After Margaret's marriage the plot of *Howards End* ceases to convince, and all the supernatural mechanism that Forster may employ will not restore the reader's faith in it. We know that Miss Avery's prophecies will be fulfilled and that Margaret will come to live at Howards End. But we are not convinced that it is inevitable that she should live there. All that remains is a detached interest to see how Forster will work the mechanism.

Fortunately, there is much more than plot in *Howards End.* Again, as in *A Room with a View*, several themes run through the novel. The flux and fret of London and of twentieth-century civilization are continually contrasted to the permanence and peace of the countryside. Different aspects of the inner and the outer life—money, material and spiritual goods, death, imagination and the vulgar admiration for that which is big—are considered and reconsidered and contrasted with one another. The question whether or not it is possible with any steadiness to see life whole is put again and again ; and the message " Only connect " is repeated in answer. One of the finest and most comprehensive rhythms that Forster employs is found in *Howards End.* It involves hay. It is introduced at the very beginning of the novel in a letter from Helen to Margaret in which Helen mentions Tibby's hay-fever, says that the Wilcoxes suffer from the same malady, and then describes Mrs. Wilcox trailing over the grass and smelling bunches of hay. It reappears again and again, never in quite the same form, but always clearly recognizable. At times it is a woman walking alone, communing with the earth, carrying hay or weeds or flowers in her hands. Again it is hay-fever, and again merely the image of a wisp of hay which is used to describe Mrs. Wilcox in London—" she was a wisp of hay, a flower "—and which enters Margaret's mind as she thinks of Leonard Bast lying dead in the garden at Howards End—" death a wisp of hay, a flower, a tower ". It expands, as it were, from the meadow at Howards End to mark the division between the Wilcoxes and Tibby (who all suffer from hay-fever), on the one hand, and Mrs. Wilcox, the Schlegels, and Leonard Bast (who all love the countryside and are not at odds with hay), on the other. It relates Margaret inextricably with Mrs. Wilcox ; and it connects, through the image of the wisp of hay, Mrs. Wilcox, Leonard, and death. In the last chapter of the novel the hay rhythm is associated with Helen, whose letter introduced it in the first chapter, and with her son, who is to inherit Howards End. The novel concludes with Helen's announcement that the meadow has been cut—" such a crop of hay as never ".*

But there is an even greater rhythm than this in *Howards End*, a rhythm which cannot be tagged with a name such as " hay " or " the level-crossing " or " Orion ", but which comes from the very structure of the book, and is comparable, to return to Forster's definition in *Aspects of the Novel*, not to the " diddidy dum " with which Beethoven's Fifth Symphony begins, but to the much greater " rhythm " of the symphony as a whole, which is due mainly to the relation between its movements. In fact, this rhythm in *Howards End* is intimately related to Beethoven's Fifth Symphony : Helen's interpretation of the last two movements of the Fifth Symphony is a *précis* of it. Goblins walk over the universe, it will be remembered, and observe that there is no such thing as splendour or heroism. Then the world is filled with panic and emptiness. The goblins are scattered, to be replaced by glory, heroism, and splendour. The goblins return, and again panic and emptiness are supreme. At the end of the symphony Beethoven builds up the ramparts of the world and brings back " the gusts of splendour, the heroism, the youth, the magnificence of life and death ". But he has stated clearly that the goblins are there and that panic and emptiness may at any time overwhelm the splendour of life. This rhythm

* E. K. Brown discusses this rhythm at some length in his *Rhythm in the Novel*, pp. 46–51.

is magnified and repeated both in Helen's life and in the development of the novel as a whole.

Helen knows a brief period of splendour at the beginning of the novel as she admires the Wilcoxes and is made supremely happy by Paul's kiss. ". . . her life was to bring nothing more intense than the embrace of this boy who played no part in it," Forster tells us. Then, on the morning after the kiss, Helen feels that the Wilcoxes, whom she had admired so recently, are a fraud, that there is nothing behind their motor-cars and golf-clubs but panic and emptiness. Helen's next moment of splendour and glory occurs when she confronts Mr. Wilcox with the Basts and gives herself to Leonard afterwards. Her action is analogous to her feelings during one of the magnificent, heroic passages in the symphony: "Any fate was titanic; any contest desirable; conqueror and conquered would alike be applauded by the angels of the utmost stars." And she conceives a child who is worthy to inherit the future. There follows again a period of panic and emptiness while she flees to the Continent and isolates herself from Margaret. Finally, at Howards End, happiness returns, and the magnificence of life and death is again apparent to Helen. As we have seen, Helen's affair with Paul is clearly related in the novel, by Helen herself, both to the Fifth Symphony and to her night with Leonard. Her sexual relation with Leonard is made an integral part of the rhythm which her life follows. This relation is almost as important to the plan of the novel as Margaret's marriage with Mr. Wilcox; and, judged by its improbability in life, it would appear to be harder to achieve. Yet Helen's impulsive action is beautifully harmonized with her character and with the events of her life—it is a necessary part of the novel—while Margaret's marriage is a discord: Forster's emotions guide him throughout when he deals with Helen and Leonard; they are suppressed when he deals with Margaret's relationship with Mr. Wilcox.

Enveloping this rhythm which occurs in Helen's life is a rhythm, corresponding to it, which comes from the larger proportions of the structure of *Howards End*. Helen has identified the Wilcoxes with panic and emptiness, and Forster shows us throughout the novel that she is right. The Wilcoxes are competent enough when they are concerned with the outer life, where force counts; but their souls are hopelessly muddled; and they are afraid of personal relations. ". . . they avoided the personal note in life. All Wilcoxes did. It did not seem to them of supreme importance. Or it may be as Helen supposed: they realized its importance, but were afraid of it. Panic and emptiness, could one glance behind." On the day after Mr. Wilcox's first kiss, which was so inconsiderate and ashamed, Margaret "looked deeply into [his] black, bright eyes. What was behind their competent stare? She knew, but was not disquieted." Leonard Bast is associated with the goblins of the symphony. The *leitmotif* of the goblin footfall announces his approach or is heard at his departure, as that mysterious, minor, Wagnerian *leitmotif* is heard in *The Flying Dutchman* whenever the Dutchman is near, or even when he enters the thoughts of others. The goblins "were not aggressive creatures. . . . They merely observed in passing that there was no such thing as splendour or heroism in the world." They are succeeded by panic and emptiness whose presence they proclaim. Leonard, who is certainly not an aggressive creature, reminds the Schlegels that there is panic and emptiness in the world. If his employers and masters, the Wilcoxes, had even a touch of heroism, his plight would not be as it is. And each time that Leonard appears in the novel, he is followed immediately by the Wilcoxes, or is closely associated with them. He comes to Wickham Place with Helen from the Queen's Hall, and the next day the Wilcoxes appear in the block of flats opposite Wickham Place. He returns more than two years later, and the same evening the Schlegels meet Mr. Wilcox, whom they have not seen since Mrs. Wilcox's death. Leonard comes to tea at Wickham Place, and before he leaves Mr. Wilcox and Evie call unexpectedly. The panic and emptiness whose existence he mutely proclaims costs him his job; and Helen brings him to Oniton to confront Mr. Wilcox. Finally, he comes to Howards End and finds Charles Wilcox there before him. Ironically, Charles, who has not a touch of heroism in him, strikes Leonard with the flat of the Schlegels' father's sword—the sword of a man who was a true hero, who fought for the Fatherland before he left it, " who beat the Austrians, and the Danes, and the French, and who beat the Germans that were inside himself". Leonard simply collapses and quietly dies when Charles strikes him : he was not an aggressive creature. The Schlegels are the heroes, or rather the heroines, in the novel. They disperse panic and emptiness. Helen is impulsively and inconsistently heroic : Margaret is the real heroine. " Go on and marry him," Helen says to Margaret when she sees that Margaret is not to be deterred from marrying Henry. " I think you're splendid ; and if anyone can pull it off, you will." She says Margaret is a heroine. " You mean to keep proportion, and that's heroic, it's Greek, and I don't see why it shouldn't succeed with you. Go on and fight with him and help him." In the final scene at Howards End Helen repeats that Margaret is heroic. And indeed, Margaret has charged straight through the Wilcoxes and broken up their lives. She has built up the ramparts of life. But panic and emptiness still threaten, even though they are shut within their box for a time. The Wilcoxes are meeting within Howards End, and if Henry has changed, Paul is as much a Wilcox as ever. He is sulky, and shows flashes of an ugly temper.

No doubt, Forster intended Margaret's marriage to be justified as an heroic action within this rhythm, as Helen's relation with Leonard is justified by the rhythm which her life describes. But the large, structural rhythm in which Margaret has a part is too great to be associated intimately enough with her to make her marriage convincing ; and Margaret is, moreover, claimed by the plot as well ; while Helen is claimed only by her rhythm, though her son is part of the plot. Margaret's character and the great structural rhythm of the novel convince us that Margaret is heroic, but her heroism does not convince us that her marriage is real.

The effect of the structural rhythm of *Howards End* is indescribable ; it is indeed comparable to the effect of a great symphony. The rhythm is so successful because it externalizes Forster's deepest emotions, his intuitions about life, and his philosophy. It is organic ; not a pattern which is imposed upon the material of the novel. Its message is remarkably cogent to-day. Since Forster wrote there have been two World

Wars, and during the intervals of peace that have followed each, force has growled and rumbled from within its box, threatening momentarily to overwhelm the world again. This aspect of Forster's view of life appears now to be inevitable. But it was not inevitable in the years 1908 to 1910, when *Howards End* was written. That was a comparatively halcyon time; and though force was beginning to threaten from its box, most men looked forward to peace, not to war, to construction, not to destruction, to the continued steady advance of civilization, not to a return towards barbarism. *Howards End* is a striking example of a work of art in which the artist's intuition foreshadows the future.

Perhaps because Forster is deeply concerned with wider problems in *Howards End*, he expresses the beauty of rural life more finely than ever before. He sees the countryside in a wider context; he stands farther from it than he stood while writing *The Longest Journey*; and as a result there are flashes of clearer beauty in his treatment of it than anything he achieved in that novel. The incident of the woodcutter, Mrs. Wilcox's grave, and Margaret's chrysanthemum is an example. Again, as Leonard lay dead in the garden at Howards End, Margaret "moved through the sunlit garden, gathering narcissi, crimson-eyed and white. There was nothing else to be done; the time for telegrams and anger was over, and it seemed wisest that the hands of Leonard should be folded on his breast and be filled with flowers." And these are not mere patches of beauty inserted for their own sake to stand isolated in the fabric of the novel. The first incident relates Margaret, while she is still a Londoner, with Mrs. Wilcox and the countryside. The second relates Margaret, Leonard, and Mrs. Wilcox, and is a part of the hay rhythm.

The style of the novel is equally good. Here is a passage which describes Margaret communing with the earth at Oniton. It is evening, and Charles Wilcox watches her.

> As he sat thinking, one of the ladies left the terrace and walked into the meadow; he recognized her as Margaret by the white bandage that gleamed on her arm, and put out his cigar, lest the gleam should betray him. She climbed up the mound in zigzags, and at times stooped down, as if she was

stroking the turf. It sounds absolutely incredible, but for a moment Charles thought that she was in love with him, and had come out to tempt him. Charles believed in temptresses, who are indeed the strong man's necessary complement, and having no sense of humour, he could not purge himself of the thought by a smile. Margaret, who was engaged to his father, and his sister's wedding-guest, kept on her way without noticing him, and he admitted that he had wronged her on this point. But what was she doing ? Why was she stumbling about amongst the rubble and catching her dress in brambles and burrs ? As she edged round the keep, she must have got to windward and smelt his cigar-smoke, for she exclaimed, " Hullo ! Who's that ? "

Charles made no answer.

" Saxon or Kelt ? " she continued, laughing in the darkness. " But it doesn't matter. Whichever you are, you will have to listen to me. I love this place. I love Shropshire. I hate London. I am glad that this will be my home. Ah, dear "—she was now moving back towards the house—" what a comfort to have arrived ! "

" That woman means mischief," thought Charles, and compressed his lips. In a few minutes he followed her indoors, as the ground was getting damp. Mists were rising from the river, and presently it became invisible, though it whispered more loudly. There had been a heavy downpour in the Welsh hills.*

The supernatural is at hand in this passage. The darkness, the hay rhythm, Margaret's remarks and their effect upon Charles combine so that Margaret becomes, not an individual woman, but the eternal woman who loves the earth and communes with it from generation to generation. But Forster's expression is completely simple. There is no search for words. Margaret's bandage " gleamed " on her arm ; and " gleam " is used in the same sentence to describe Charles's cigar. There are two *clichés*—" absolutely incredible ", and " in a few minutes ". The sentences are uninvolved. The complicated effect of the passage is achieved with complete lucidity and ease.

A Passage to India, written fourteen years after *Howards End*,

* pp. 228–9.

is perhaps Forster's last word as a novelist. It has something in common with works which other artists have produced towards the end of their careers, with Ibsen's *Master Builder*, Shaw's *Apple Cart* (after which Shaw should have stopped writing plays, for he has nothing further to say in them), Shakespeare's *Tempest*, Turner's last paintings, and Virginia Woolf's *Between the Acts*. In *A Passage to India* the intuitions, thoughts, and emotions that are the stuff of Forster's novels are merged with the universal. The panic and emptiness that is loosed is not human ; it has little to do with the Wilcoxes or their kind—though there are several characters in *A Passage to India* who are as spiritually blind as the Wilcoxes. It is evil itself, and it comes from without the universe. " Before time, it was before space also. Something snub-nosed, incapable of generosity—the undying worm itself." It causes a sincere and previously clear-thinking girl, Adela Quested, to fall into muddle through no fault of her own. It so infects Mrs. Moore, a woman with intuitive powers similar to, though more universal than, Mrs. Wilcox's, a woman who had once believed that God is love and omnipresent—so infects her that she comes " to that state where the horror of the universe and its smallness are both visible at the same time ", and leaves India, cynical, irritable, and selfish, to die on the voyage home. The source of evil in the novel are caves in the ancient Marabar Hills, hills which rise like fists and fingers twenty miles to the south of the Indian city of Chandrapore, and " are older than anything in the world. . . . If flesh of the sun's flesh is to be touched anywhere, it is here, among the incredible antiquity of these hills." The universe, and beyond the universe, infinite realms of space and time, are woven, as it were, into the novel. " Outside the arch ", Mrs. Moore is aware, " there seemed always an arch, beyond the remotest echo a silence." Adela Quested and Ronny Heaslop, Mrs. Moore's son by her first marriage, drive through the Indian night in a motor-car, " And the night that encircled them, absolute as it seemed, was itself only a spurious unity, being modified by the gleams of day that leaked up round the edges of the earth, and by the stars."

The world and the present are not, of course, absent from

the novel. *A Passage to India*, in this respect, is the product of two visits to India, made by Forster in 1912–13 and 1921.* The differences between India and Anglo-India are the basis of the clash that takes place in the novel ; and the psychology of each side is analysed with Forster's usual penetration. How might their differences be reconciled ? The answer, given by Dr. Aziz, the leading character among the Indians in the novel, is not unlike the message of *Howards End*. " Kindness, more kindness, and even after that more kindness. I assure you it is the only hope," Aziz tells his English friend, Fielding. But this answer is not repeatedly reiterated, as " Only connect " is reiterated in *Howards End* ; it is by no means intended as an answer to all India's difficulties. Those difficulties are more internal than external ; they are between Hindu and Moslem, and between the various sects and divisions within these races, as well as between English and Indian. No simple solution, perhaps no solution at all, is to be found for India's problems. In fact, *A Passage to India* is the only novel of Forster's that has no specific message. It only presents a view of India and, through that view, a view of life.

The vast Sub-Continent with its innumerable divisions, its multitudinous masses of humanity, and its mystics who search for unity amidst the muddle, or beyond the muddle, that surrounds them, is made part of the book, with the purpose, not so much to present a social document as to consider the problem, a problem of art as well as religion, of the Many and the One. Mr. Turton, the Collector and chief English official in the city of Chandrapore, in order to please Adela Quested and Mrs. Moore, who are newly arrived from England and wish to meet Indians, invites a number of the more prominent natives of his district to a party at the English club. Some of the Indians view the invitation with distrust ; but the Nawab Bahadur, a mild, dignified, kindly old gentleman whose opinion carries great weight, speaks in favour of it.

He had spoken in the little room near the Courts where the pleaders waited for clients ; clients, waiting for pleaders, sat in the dust outside. These had not received a card from

* These visits are described, chiefly by Forster's letters, in *The Hill of Devi*.

> Mr. Turton. And there were circles even beyond these—people who wore nothing but a loin-cloth, people who wore not even that, and spent their lives in knocking two sticks together before a scarlet doll—humanity grading and drifting beyond the educated vision, until no earthly invitation can embrace it.
>
> All invitations must proceed from heaven perhaps ; perhaps it is futile for men to initiate their own unity, they do but widen the gulfs between them by the attempt. So at all events thought old Mr. Graysford and young Mr. Sorley, the devoted missionaries who lived out beyond the slaughter-houses, always travelled third on the railways, and never came up to the club. In our Father's house are many mansions, they taught, and there alone will the incompatible multitudes of mankind be welcomed and soothed. Not one shall be turned away by the servants on that verandah, be he black or white ; not one shall be kept standing who approaches with a loving heart. And why should the divine hospitality cease here ? Consider, with all reverence, the monkeys. May there not be a mansion for the monkeys also ? Old Mr. Graysford said No, but young Mr. Sorley, who was advanced, said Yes ; he saw no reason why monkeys should not have their collateral share of bliss, and he had sympathetic discussions about them with his Hindu friends. And the jackals ? Jackals were indeed less to Mr. Sorley's mind, but he admitted that the mercy of God, being infinite, may well embrace all mammals. And the wasps ? He became uneasy during the descent to wasps, and was apt to change the conversation. And oranges, cactuses, crystals, and mud ? and the bacteria inside Mr. Sorley ? No, no, this is going too far. We must exclude someone from our gathering, or we shall be left with nothing.*

But the Hindus, not Mr. Sorley, have the final word in the novel ; and Mrs. Moore finds Christianity to be inadequate. Hindu philosophy, India itself, appears to Forster to reduce Mr. Sorley's doctrines to absurdity.

Forster's presentation in this novel is without insistence or didacticism or argument. Partly for this reason, he comments less than in previous novels. Also, the structure of *A Passage to India* is surer than the structure of any other of Forster's novels, with the exception of the much slighter *Where Angels Fear to*

* p. 28.

Tread ; and the style is more mature, more confident, and stronger than ever before. It is not necessary for the commentator to step forward or to point out the way. The novel is divided into three parts, " Mosque ", " Caves ", and " Temple ", which, as Forster tells us in a note to the Everyman edition, " also represent the three seasons of the Cold Weather, the Hot Weather, and the Rains, which divide the Indian year ".

After a description of Chandrapore with its civil station that stands on a rise above the town, and a brief reference to the Marabar Hills, which contain " the extraordinary caves ", and whose " fists and fingers " may be seen on the southern horizon, the action of the novel begins. Dr. Aziz has come to dine with his kinsman Hamidullah. Mr. Mahmoud Ali is another guest. These three are educated Mohammedans ; Aziz is an assistant to the Civil Surgeon, Major Callendar ; Hamidullah and Mahmoud Ali are lawyers. The lawyers are discussing whether or not it is possible to be friends with an Englishman—a question which is given a good deal of attention in the novel. Mahmoud Ali thinks not. He has recently been insulted in Court, and not for the first time, by the City Magistrate, Ronny Heaslop. Hamidullah, a tolerant man who has studied at Cambridge, and who remembers friends in England, says that it is possible in England, but impossible in India. The English have no chance in India. " They come out intending to be gentlemen, and are told it will not do." " They all become exactly the same, not worse, not better. I give any Englishman two years, be he Turton or Burton. It is only the difference of a letter. And I give any Englishwoman six months. All are exactly alike." Aziz would rather forget Englishmen and be jolly with his friends, but his dinner is interrupted by a message from the Civil Surgeon, who wishes to see Aziz at his bungalow.

By the time Aziz arrives there, Major Callendar has left to see to the case for which he had called Aziz. He has left no message. His wife and another Englishwoman take the tonga Aziz has hired and drive to the club in it without asking leave or offering thanks. Hurt, and disappointed that his evening has been spoiled for nothing, Aziz enters a mosque ; and there he finds an Englishwoman—Mrs. Moore. At first he is angry; he has recently been insulted by Englishwomen; and he came to the mosque to be far from the English and to muse upon his own country, Islam. But Mrs. Moore is polite, and more than that, kind; she has left her shoes at the door of the mosque as one should; she has come from the English club to visit the mosque. She says, "God is here." Soon she and Aziz are friends, and Aziz tells her his wrongs. She talks frankly to him and treats him as an equal. He bursts out impulsively, "You understand me, you know what others feel. Oh, if others resembled you!" She is rather surprised, and replies that she does not think she understands people well; she only knows whether she likes or dislikes them. "Then you are an Oriental," Aziz tells her. And he escorts her back to the club.

Later that evening Mrs. Moore, Adela Quested, and Ronny Heaslop leave the club to return to Ronny's bungalow. "Mrs. Moore, whom the club had stupefied, woke up outside. She watched the moon, whose radiance stained with primrose the purple of the surrounding sky. In England the moon had seemed dead and alien; here she was caught in the shawl of night together with earth and all the other stars. A sudden sense of unity, of kinship with the heavenly bodies, passed into the old woman and out, like water through a tank, leaving a strange freshness behind." Mrs. Moore, who has come only recently from England, is already beginning to feel the influence of India—of the real India, not of Anglo-India—and to find herself closely attuned to it. In the mosque where she had talked to Aziz there was "an ablution tank of fresh clear water, which was always in motion, being indeed part of a conduit that supplied the city". And Mrs. Moore sees the mosque at the turn of the road just after she has this sense of unity. At the bungalow, she prepares for bed.

> Going to hang up her cloak she found that the tip of the peg was occupied by a small wasp. She had known this wasp or his relatives by day; they were not as English wasps, but had long yellow legs which hung down behind when they flew. Perhaps he mistook the peg for a branch—no Indian animal has any sense of an interior. Bats, rats, birds, insects

> will as soon nest inside a house as out; it is to them a normal growth of the eternal jungle, which alternately produces houses trees, houses trees. There he clung, asleep, while jackals in the plain bayed their desires and mingled with the percussion of drums.
>
> "Pretty dear," said Mrs. Moore to the wasp. He did not wake, but her voice floated out, to swell the night's uneasiness.*

The passage, already quoted, concerning Mr. Sorley's theological difficulties, follows almost immediately; and Mrs. Moore, who accepts the wasp, is tacitly contrasted to Mr. Sorley, who rejects it.

The party at the club to which Mr. Turton invites prominent natives follows soon afterwards. Mr. Turton, with Anglo-Indian wit, calls it a "Bridge Party", a party to bridge the gulf between East and West. Normally, Indians are not allowed at the club even as guests; but the Collector has arranged the party after hearing Adela Quested remark that she would like to see "the real India". Adela has come to India with Mrs. Moore to visit Ronny Heaslop, who wishes to marry her. She wants to see what effect India has had upon him before she makes her decision. She is, Mrs. Moore thinks, a queer, cautious girl. She lacks physical charm; but she is sincere and honest, and always says exactly what is in her mind. "If one isn't absolutely honest what is the use of existing?" she asks Mrs. Moore. And she lives this belief out in the novel. She is very fond of Mrs. Moore. She genuinely wishes to know Indians and to be friends with them; she dislikes Anglo-India's attitude towards natives. She is exceedingly fair-minded and has an abundance of good will and common sense. In fact, her fault, or rather, her deficiency, is perhaps that she is too sensible and too dry. Cyril Fielding, the English Principal of the Government College at Chandrapore, who has as much good will towards Indians as she, finds something theoretical in her criticism of English manners at the Bridge Party. She wishes to meet Indians because they are Indians, rather than because they are individuals. There is a certain lack of vitality in Adela Quested which corresponds

* pp. 25–6.

with her lack of physical charm, and which bars her, in spite of a fair and logical mind, from deep understanding.

Her suitor, Ronny Heaslop, is not unlike her; but his experiences have been different. He too lacks physical charm. He has a red nose (his distinguishing feature so far as the Indians who know him are concerned); and he is rude to natives. Like Adela, Forster tells us, he has an abundance of common sense and good will; but the only link he can understand with Indians is the official; and his superiors have taught him to distrust all Indians. To him, all Indians appear alike, as all English appear alike to most Indians. When Mrs. Moore describes Aziz, without mentioning Aziz's race, Ronny is unable to conceive that the doctor of whom she speaks is Indian: it does not occur to him to regard natives as individuals with whom one might have friendly, human relations. Ronny is the Public School product with an undeveloped heart, and his Public School training has been continued and intensified in Anglo-India. There is no privacy in Anglo-India. Consequently, convention has great force there. Ronny had been interested in the arts in England, and had played the viola. But Anglo-India's "ignorance of the arts was notable, and they lost no opportunity of proclaiming it to one another; it was the Public School attitude, flourishing more vigorously than it can yet hope to do in England. If Indians were shop, the Arts were bad form, and Ronny had repressed his mother when she inquired after his viola; a viola was almost a demerit, and certainly not the sort of instrument one mentioned in public." Anglo-India has a difficult job to do. Ronny is the City Magistrate at Chandrapore. "Every day he worked hard in the court trying to decide which of two untrue accounts was the less untrue, trying to dispense justice fearlessly, to protect the weak against the less weak, the incoherent against the plausible, surrounded by lies and flattery." Ronny's case is, outwardly, a good case. But it has one fatal weakness. Ronny is self-satisfied and complacent even in the midst of India. His heart is undeveloped. "One touch of regret—not the canny substitute but the true regret from the heart—would have made him a different man, and the British Empire a different institution."

In these circumstances, it is not to be expected that the Bridge Party will be a success. The Indians remain on one side of the club garden ; most of the English remain on the other. The Collector is officially jovial. Mrs. Moore and Adela talk to the Indian ladies and make a good impression, though they find it almost impossible to get beyond mere civilities. Fielding is the only Englishman who remains on the Indian side while refreshments are served. Aziz stays away from the party, though he was invited. He has a game of polo with an English subaltern whom he chances to meet at the Maidan. The exhilaration of the game draws them together, and they part with a good opinion of one another. Then Aziz meets Dr. Panna Lal, an elderly and timid Hindu colleague from the hospital. Aziz had agreed to go to the party with Dr. Lal in Lal's new tum-tum, but at the last moment he had changed his mind without letting Lal know. Lal had counted on Aziz to manage his horse ; and in Aziz's absence the horse had taken Lal into some hollyhocks at the club. Nervous and humiliated, Lal upbraids Aziz and refuses to accept his apologies. Then, in a scene reminiscent of Stephen Wonham's wild ride into Salisbury, Aziz gallops his pony past Lal's tum-tum, causing Lal's horse to bolt.

But the Bridge Party has one good, or desired, effect. Fielding invites Adela Quested and Mrs. Moore to the Government College for tea in order to meet Professor Godbole, an elderly Hindu who will sing Indian music for them. And because Adela mentions that Mrs. Moore has met and likes Aziz, Aziz is invited too.

From this tea at the College springs all the subsequent action of the first two Parts of the novel. Fielding and Aziz meet for the first time, and find at once that they like one another. Aziz impulsively invites Mrs. Moore and Adela to come with him to visit the Marabar Caves. It is Aziz's afternoon. He feels that he is among friends, and among English friends at that. Professor Godbole, a charming, enigmatic old gentleman, remains politely and quietly in the background. " He wore a turban that looked like pale purple macaroni, coat, waistcoat, dhoti, socks with clocks. The clocks matched the turban, and his whole appearance suggested harmony—as if he had reconciled the products of East and West, mental as well as physical, and could never be discomposed." He contrasts finely with Aziz, who is pushed here and there by the surface currents of his emotions. Godbole is a Brahman ; Aziz a Mohammedan. When Adela seeks information about the caves, she turns to the Brahman, who seems to know about them. But he very politely and charmingly tells her nothing. Aziz realizes that Godbole is keeping something back ; he fences with the Brahman, but learns nothing. " The comparatively simple mind of the Mohammedan was encountering Ancient Night." Then Ronny comes to call for Adela, and spoils the pleasant afternoon. He is annoyed because Fielding has taken Mrs. Moore on a tour of the College, and Adela, uninterested in the tour, has been left alone to talk and smoke with two Indians. Aziz is upset because he has been the centre of attention, and now he is rudely ignored by Ronny. His nerves are on edge, and he is impertinent to Ronny and greasily confidential to Adela, in spite of himself. When Fielding returns, Ronny scolds him for leaving Adela alone with Aziz and Godbole. " Could one have been so petty on a Scotch moor or an Italian alp ? Fielding wondered afterwards. There seemed no reserve of tranquillity to draw upon in India. Either none, or else tranquillity swallowed up everything, as it appeared to do for Professor Godbole. Here was Aziz all shoddy and odious, Mrs. Moore and Miss Quested both silly, and he himself and Heaslop both decorous on the surface, but detestable really, and detesting each other." Then Professor Godbole, as it were, composes the scene that Ronny has disturbed. Adela regrets, as she takes her leave, that she did not hear the Professor sing. He replies that he may sing now, and he does. The song baffles the western ear and seems unintelligible, though the servants nearby listen in wonder. " The sounds continued and ceased after a few moments as casually as they had begun—apparently half through a bar, and upon the subdominant." The singer, Godbole explains, is a milk-maiden, who appeals to Shri Krishna, Lord of the Universe, to come to her. But the god does not come. Mrs. Moore hopes he comes in another song—but no, Godbole says, " He neglects to come ". " Ronny's steps had died away, and there was a moment of absolute silence. No ripple disturbed the water, no leaf stirred ".

That evening Adela tells Ronny that she will not marry him. She had, indeed, inadvertently announced to the company at Fielding's tea that she did not intend to stay in India ; and Aziz had referred to her remark before Ronny ; but Ronny had paid no attention to him. He is badly hurt and disappointed when he hears the news from Adela and learns that Aziz knew of it before he did ; but he takes it well and behaves decently. " He felt angry and bruised ; he was too proud to tempt her back ; but he did not consider that she had behaved badly, because where his compatriots were concerned he had a generous mind." He and Adela are at the Maidan, and the Nawab Bahadur, the old gentleman who had used his influence to persuade Indians to attend the Bridge Party, approaches and asks Ronny and Adela to come for a ride in his new car. As they set off he refers humorously to Dr. Panna Lal's accident which damaged the hollyhocks at the club. He intends to take them down the Gangavati road, but he falls asleep beside his Eurasian chauffeur almost as soon as the drive begins. Ronny instructs the chauffeur to take the Marabar road instead, since the Gangavati road is under repair. As they drive through the darkness, a jolt causes Adela's hand to touch Ronny's, " and one of the thrills so frequent in the animal kingdom passed between them, and announced that all their difficulties were only a lovers' quarrel ". Then, just after they have crossed a bridge over a nullah, there is an accident ; the car swerves out of control and comes to a stop at the edge of an embankment. But no one has been hurt. Only Adela has seen the cause of the accident : an animal with a hairy back, she says, rushed out of the night and struck the side of the car. The Nawab Bahadur's fear is disproportionate, and appears to Ronny ridiculous, though typically Indian. No doubt the animal came up out of the nullah and was dazzled by the headlights. Ronny and Adela, united once more, go back along the road with an electric torch to look for tracks ; but the road is used too much for any single animal's tracks to be distinguished. Only the marks of the car, which indicate that it was indeed struck by some external force, are legible in the dust. The Nawab Bahadur says that the accident would not have occurred if they had taken the Gangavati road, and he begins to blame his chauffeur. But Ronny explains to him how they have come to be on the Marabar road. Another car approaches, and is stopped by Ronny. It is driven by Miss Derek, an enthusiastic, hard, unlovely, and untrustworthy young woman, of the same type as Miss Lavish, the novelist in *A Room with a View* who described George and Lucy's kiss in her book. Miss Derek is the companion of a Maharani ; she is on holiday at Chandrapore ; she is driving the Maharajah's car ; and she has taken both the car and the holiday without the Maharajah's permission. She drives Adela, Ronny, and the Nawab Bahadur back to Chandrapore ; the Nawab's Eurasian chauffeur is left with the damaged car. By the time Ronny and Adela reach Ronny's bungalow, they are engaged ; and Ronny announces the engagement to his mother. It is Mrs. Moore who first expresses in the novel the notion that the animal on the Marabar road may have been a ghost. When she heard of the accident, " Mrs. Moore shivered : 'A ghost!' But the idea of a ghost scarcely passed her lips. The young people did not take it up, being occupied with their own outlooks, and deprived of support it perished, or was reabsorbed into the part of the mind that seldom speaks." Down in Chandrapore the Nawab Bahadur tells his friends of the accident. " Nine years previously, when first he had had a car, he had driven it over a drunken man and killed him, and the man had been waiting for him ever since. The Nawab Bahadur was innocent before God and the Law, he had paid double the compensation necessary ; but it was no use, the man continued to wait in an unspeakable form, close to the scene of his death. None of the English people knew of this, nor did the chauffeur ; it was a racial secret communicable more by blood than speech."

Part One, " Mosque ", ends with the approach of the Hot Weather, and with a pact of friendship between Aziz and Fielding. Aziz shows Fielding a photograph of his deceased wife—a great compliment, because Aziz believes in the purdah. He tells Fielding that he has three children ; and he regrets that Fielding, who is unmarried, will leave no children behind him. Fielding replies that he would far rather leave a thought than a child. " A hard-bitten, good-tempered, intelligent fellow, on the verge of middle age ", Fielding is indeed rather coldly intellectual, for all his desire to be friends with Indians. He is sane, experienced, and clear-sighted. " Experience can do much, and all that he had learnt in England and Europe was an assistance to him, and helped him towards clarity ; but clarity prevented him from experiencing something else." " I believe in teaching people to be individuals," he tells Aziz, " and to understand other individuals. It's the only thing I do believe in." Aziz, so sensitive, emotional, and impulsive, complements Fielding. Though he voyages on the shifting tides of emotion, " he was safe really—as safe as the shore-dweller who can only understand stability and supposes that every ship must be wrecked, and he had sensations the shore-dweller cannot know ". Aziz is highly conscious of beauty, though his bungalow is untidy and infested with flies. He recites poetry to his friends, and even the roughest and least educated of them listens with pleasure and without shame— " literature had not been divorced from their civilization ", as it has been divorced from Anglo-India. Aziz himself writes poetry. " He possessed a soul that could suffer but not stifle, and led a steady life beneath his mutability."

The ancient Marabar Hills and the caves they contain are described at the beginning of Part Two, " Caves ". " There is something unspeakable in these [hills]. They are like nothing else in the world, and a glimpse of them makes the breath catch." Inside the hills are innumerable caves, some of them with man-made entrances, others " never unsealed since the arrival of the gods ". Within the caves there is nothing but darkness, and, as the visitor sees when he strikes a match, marvellously polished walls.

Aziz has almost forgotten his offer to take Adela Quested and Mrs. Moore to the caves. For him, it was the expression of a wish rather than an invitation ; he did not consider it beforehand nor intend it seriously. But he learns, through a servant from the club, that Miss Quested remembers his invitation ; and this report causes him to fear that she may be deeply offended if he neglects it. So he decides to see the matter through. All who were present at Fielding's tea—Adela, Mrs. Moore, Professor Godbole, and Fielding himself—shall come. They will travel to Marabar by train, and Aziz has hired an elephant to meet them there. He has catered carefully for Hindu, Mohammedan, and Christian. When Mrs. Moore and Adela reach the Chandrapore station just before dawn, they find the platform swarming with servants and crowded with provisions. But in spite of Aziz's preparations the expedition begins inauspiciously. Fielding and Godbole miss the train. Godbole miscalculated the length of a prayer, delayed Fielding, and the two of them are held up at the gates of the level-crossing. Aziz can only call agonizingly to Fielding as the train leaves the station. He had counted on Fielding to help him manage the expedition. And Adela and Mrs. Moore are to discover that Professor Godbole might have been even more helpful than Fielding in the Marabar Hills.

Since Adela and Mrs. Moore heard Professor Godbole sing, a fortnight ago, their lives have been dull. Mrs. Moore has been apathetic ; her health is rather low ; and apathy, perhaps illness, is invading her soul as well as her body. " She felt increasingly (vision or nightmare ?) that, though people are important, the relations between them are not, and that in particular too much fuss has been made over marriage ; centuries of carnal embracement, yet man is no nearer to understanding man. And to-day she felt this with such force that it seemed itself a relationship, itself a person who was trying to take hold of her hand." The train proceeds towards the Marabar Hills. Adela is much occupied with her marriage plans. She reflects upon the drive and the accident on the Marabar road which brought her and Ronny together. She remarks to Mrs. Moore that their train must be near the scene of the accident now. The train crosses a nullah, and the wheels go " pomper, pomper, pomper " over the bridge. It crosses a second nullah, and a third. " Perhaps this is mine," Adela says ; " anyhow, the road runs parallel with the railway ". And the sound of the train, " pomper, pomper ", accompanies her words and her thoughts.

When the train reaches Marabar, there is little colour and

no vitality in the early morning scene that awaits the travellers. And as the elephant carries them towards the hills, " a new quality occurred, a spiritual silence which invaded more senses than the ear. Life went on as usual, but had no consequences, that is to say, sounds did not echo or thoughts develop. Everything seemed cut off at its root, and therefore infected with illusion." Mrs. Moore and Adela realize that Aziz is out of his depth. " His ignorance became evident, and was really rather a drawback. In spite of his gay, confident talk, he had no notion how to treat this particular aspect of India ; he was lost in it without Professor Godbole, like themselves." But Aziz himself is contented and happy because he has been allowed to show courtesy to the English ladies. Hospitality is very important to him. He asks Mrs. Moore if she remembers their mosque. " ' I do. I do,' she said, suddenly vital and young." Adela speaks of her marriage plans and of her future life in India, as she had spoken at Fielding's tea of her intention to leave India. And then the first cave is visited.

In it Mrs. Moore has a horrible experience. The cave is dark and crowded with servants and with villagers who have curiously followed the party. Mrs. Moore is parted from Aziz and Adela ; she nearly faints ; she struggles for air, " and some vile naked thing struck her face and settled on her mouth like a pad ". She hits her head, strikes out wildly, and with difficulty regains the entrance. Besides the crush and the stench, there was a terrifying echo in the cave. " ' Boum ' is the sound as far as the human alphabet can express it, or ' bou-oum ', or ' ou-boum '—utterly dull. Hope, politeness, the blowing of a nose, the squeal of a boot, all produce ' boum '. Even the striking of a match starts a little worm coiling, which is too small to complete a circle, but is eternally watchful." Mrs. Moore watches the people come out of the cave. " As each person emerged she looked for a villain, but none was there, and she realized that she had been among the mildest individuals, whose only desire was to honour her, and that the naked pad was a poor little baby, astride its mother's hip." She conceals from Aziz her dislike of the cave, in order not to disappoint him, but excuses herself from climbing higher to visit others. They exchange kind words of friendship—the last words expressing interest and affection that Mrs. Moore is to speak—and she suggests to him that he allow fewer people to come with him to the higher caves. Anxious to obey, he allows only a guide to accompany him and Adela as they set off. Mrs. Moore begins a letter to her two children in England, Stella and Ralph, while she waits ; but she gets no further than the salutation. She begins to reflect upon her experience in the cave.

> The more she thought over it, the more disagreeable and frightening it became. She minded it much more now than at the time. The crush and the smells she could forget, but the echo began in some indescribable way to undermine her hold on life. Coming at a moment when she chanced to be fatigued, it had managed to murmur : " Pathos, piety, courage—they exist, but are identical, and so is filth. Everything exists, nothing has value." If one had spoken vileness in that place, or quoted lofty poetry, the comment would have been the same—" ou-boum ". If one had spoken with the tongues of angels and pleaded for all the unhappiness and misunderstanding in the world, past, present, and to come ; for all the misery men must undergo whatever their opinion and position, and however much they dodge or bluff—it would amount to the same, the serpent would descend and return to the ceiling. Devils are of the north, and poems can be written about them, but no one could romanticize the Marabar, because it robbed infinity and eternity of their vastness, the only quality that accommodates them to mankind.
>
> She tried to go on with her letter. . . . But suddenly, at the edge of her mind, religion appeared, poor little talkative Christianity, and she knew that all its divine words from " Let there be Light " to " It is finished " only amounted to " boum ". Then she was terrified over an area larger than usual ; the universe, never comprehensible to her intellect, offered no repose to her soul ; the mood of the last two months took definite form at last, and she realized that she didn't want to write to her children, didn't want to communicate with any one, not even with God. . . . She sat motionless with horror. . . . For a time she thought : " I am going to be ill ", to comfort herself, then she surrendered to the vision. She lost all interest, even in Aziz, and the affectionate and

> sincere words that she had spoken to him seemed no longer hers but the air's.*

As old Mr. Lucas, in Forster's short story " The Road from Colonus ", finds the meaning of life within a hollow tree in Greece, so Mrs. Moore finds life's nullity in the Marabar cave.†

As Adela climbs up to a large group of caves with Aziz and the guide, she continues to think of her forthcoming marriage. Suddenly, she asks herself if she and Ronny love one another. " The rock [over which she was climbing] was nicked by a double row of footholds, and somehow the question was suggested by them. Where had she seen the footholds before? Oh, yes, they were the pattern traced in the dust by the Nawab Bahadur's car." No ; she and Ronny, Adela realizes, do not love one another. " There was esteem and animal contact at dusk, but the emotion that links them was absent." Should they marry without love ? She is inclined to think so ; love is not everything. She asks Aziz if he is married. Yes ? then how many wives has he ? The question shocks Aziz, and he dives into a cave to recover his composure. Adela, unaware that she has upset him, goes into another cave. Aziz comes out and finds the guide alone. A motor-car is coming across the plain. Aziz looks for Adela to give her the news. She has gone into a cave, the guide tells him. But there are any number of caves, all exactly alike—" It seemed their original spawning place ". Aziz, badly frightened, hunts feverishly and wildly for Adela. Then he sees her, far down a gully that leads from the mouths of the caves. She is speaking to another lady, and Aziz supposes that she ran down when she saw the car approaching. He is so relieved that he does not think her conduct odd. He finds her field-glasses at the mouth of a cave, their shoulder-strap broken, and he puts them in his pocket as he descends. He is overjoyed, when he reaches his little camp, to find Fielding with Mrs. Moore. Miss Derek has kindly driven Fielding out in the Maharajah's car. But where is Miss Derek ? and where is Adela ? Miss Derek's chauffeur soon arrives to announce that Miss Derek has driven Miss Quested back to Chandrapore. Aziz makes light of Adela's departure, but Fielding is troubled by it. As they

* pp. 128–9. † See p. 104.

return to the Marabar station, Fielding notes that the gully which begins at the mouths of the caves that Aziz visited with Adela, continues " as a nullah across the plain, the water draining off this way towards the Ganges ". Chandrapore is situated on the Ganges.

At the Chandrapore station Aziz is placed under arrest. He is charged with insulting Miss Quested in a Marabar Cave. The circumstantial evidence against him is strong. Adela reached Miss Derek in a terrible state. She had got among cactuses as she ran down the gully, and had hundreds of their spines in her flesh. She believed that she had struck her attacker with her field-glasses, that he had pulled at them, and that she had escaped him only when the strap broke. She could not bear Miss Derek's Indian chauffeur near her—it was that which first caused Miss Derek to suspect that Miss Quested had been attacked. Adela lies ill at the bungalow of the Superintendent of Police, whose wife is caring for her. " She was ", as even Fielding, Aziz's friend, reflects, " such a dry, sensible girl, and quite without malice : the last person in Chandrapore wrongfully to accuse an Indian." Aziz is confused as to what happened at the caves. The guide is not to be found. Indeed, Aziz had been so angry with him for losing sight of Adela that he had frightened the fellow off. Adela's field-glasses, with the shoulder-strap broken, were found in Aziz's pocket when he was arrested. But Fielding is certain that Aziz is innocent, and he works with Aziz's friends to clear his name.

Anglo-India is thoroughly aroused. Aziz's friends are equally stirred. Reason is thrown to the winds by both sides, and only Fielding keeps proportion. " He felt that a mass of madness had arisen and tried to overwhelm them all ; it had to be shoved back into its pit somehow, and he didn't know how to do it, because he did not understand madness : he had always gone about sensibly and quietly until a difficulty came right." Evil has indeed escaped from the caves in the Marabar Hills, as a conversation which Fielding has with Professor Godbole emphasizes. Fielding asks Godbole if Aziz is innocent or guilty. Godbole replies that the evil action in the Marabar Hills was performed by them all—by Aziz, by the guide, by Fielding, by Godbole, by Godbole's students, by Miss Quested herself.

"When evil occurs it expresses the whole of the universe. Similarly when good occurs." Fielding objects that this is to preach that evil and good are the same. "Oh no, excuse me. . . . Good and evil are different, as their names imply. But, in my own humble opinion, they are both of them aspects of my Lord. He is present in the one, absent in the other, and the difference between presence and absence is great, as great as my feeble mind can grasp. Yet absence implies presence, absence is not non-existence, and we are therefore entitled to repeat: 'Come, come, come, come.'" He abruptly changes the subject to discuss the antiquities in the Marabar Hills, of which he evidently has considerable knowledge. Before Fielding can talk to Godbole again, Godbole has slipped off to take a job in his native state of Mau. Fielding enrages the English at Chandrapore by insisting on using reason and searching for facts in Aziz's case. He resigns from the club (he has little choice but to do so), and before he leaves he is insulted both by the Collector and by the subaltern who had played polo with Aziz. The subaltern is on leave at Chandrapore; he does not realize that the unknown native with whom he played was Aziz. He still insists that that native was "all right". ". . . the evil was propagating in every direction, it seemed to have an existence of its own, apart from anything that was done or said by individuals. . . ."

While she was ill, Adela, as a result of her experience in the caves, hated any one to touch her. She suffered physically from sunstroke and from the cactus spines; mentally from her experience and from the Marabar echo. Like Fielding, she tried to use reason. "Adela was always trying to 'think the incident out', always reminding herself that no harm had been done." But the echo would return to her mind, destroy her logic, and cause her, for a time, to hate Aziz. Afterwards she would feel guilty. "She felt that it was her crime, until the intellect, reawakening, pointed out to her that she was inaccurate here, and set her again upon her sterile round." She believed that all would be well if she could see Mrs. Moore. But the old lady did not come to see her.

> And consequently the echo flourished, raging up and down like a nerve in the faculty of her hearing, and the noise in

> the cave, so unimportant intellectually, was prolonged over the surface of her life. She had struck the polished wall—for no reason—and before the comment had died away, he followed her, and the climax was the falling of her field glasses. The sound had spouted after her when she escaped, and was going on still like a river that gradually floods the plain. Only Mrs. Moore could drive it back to its source and seal the broken reservoir. Evil was loose . . . she could even hear it entering the lives of others. . . .*

After her physical recovery, Adela continues to abhor bodily contact with others. When Ronny calls for her to take her to his bungalow again, she refuses his arm. Though she has sympathy for Ronny and wonders how she can repay him for what he has suffered on her account, she feels about personal relationships rather as Mrs. Moore felt as the train from Chandrapore carried Aziz's party towards the Marabar Hills. " My dear, how can I repay you ? " Adela asks Ronny. " How can one repay when one has nothing to give ? What is the use of personal relationships when everyone brings less and less to them ? I feel we ought all to go back into the desert for centuries and try and get good." When they reach Ronny's bungalow, Mrs. Moore shows no pleasure at seeing Adela again and scarcely greets her. She has been sunk in apathy and cynicism, and has shown no interest in anything, since her experience in the Marabar Hills. " Her Christian tenderness had gone, or had developed into a hardness, a just irritation against the human race." Above all, she wishes not to be bothered by others. Adela takes her hand. " It withdrew, and she felt that just as others repelled her, so did she repel Mrs. Moore." Mrs. Moore shows interest only when Adela mentions the echo that she continues to hear. Adela asks her what the echo is. " If you don't know, you don't know," Mrs. Moore says ; " I can't tell you." Yet, Adela is comforted by Mrs. Moore's presence, and feels that the old lady is good and helps to cure her echo. Adela speaks Aziz's name and asks herself for the first time if she has made a mistake. The sound of that name, which every one at the civil station avoided mentioning—for it had become synonymous with the

* p. 168.

power of evil—" now rang out like the first note of a new symphony". At once the echo recedes from Adela's mind. She tells Ronny that Aziz is innocent: Mrs. Moore has said so. Ronny insists that Mrs. Moore has said nothing of the sort, and to prove his point he asks his mother if she has mentioned the prisoner. "I never said his name," Mrs. Moore replies; but she soon adds, indifferently, "Of course he is innocent." It is perhaps a truth that is communicable, like the story of the ghost on the Marabar road, more by blood than by speech, or that must be understood, if at all, by the subconscious mind. Mrs. Moore's mind "seemed to move towards them from a great distance and out of darkness". Her remarks that follow are bitter and cynical, but Adela insists that she sends the echo away, that she is good, and does nothing but good. Ronny's logic, however, demonstrates that his mother's defence of Aziz is feeble—in fact, no defence at all. Shortly afterwards Mrs. Moore crosses India to take ship for England at Bombay. She refuses to have anything to do with Ronny's "ludicrous law courts". "I will not be dragged in at all," she says.

Nevertheless, Mrs. Moore does play a part in Aziz's trial. It is her influence, not Ronny's law, or Fielding's reasonable search for facts, or Adela's attempts at logic, that determines the verdict. No new evidence is brought forward at the trial. We learn that the Marabar Caves are Jain. The nullah which begins at the group of caves concerned is mentioned again. The Superintendent of Police, in his case for the prosecution, speaks of Mrs. Moore—and causes pandemonium to break loose. Mahmoud Ali, assisting in Aziz's defence, screams that Mrs. Moore has been smuggled out of India by the English because she would have proven Aziz innocent. He creates such a tumult that Mrs. Moore's name is taken up by the audience; it spreads outside the court-room to the crowd in the streets; and there it is Indianized into Esmiss Esmoor and repeated over and over again in a rhythmical chant. Ronny is disturbed. He explains that before his mother sailed she had taken to talk in her sleep about the Marabar, and must have been overheard by the servants. "It was revolting to hear his mother travestied into Esmiss Esmoor, a Hindu goddess."

Adela, though the echo in her mind had been particularly disturbing immediately before the trial, is now healthier and more natural than usual. When the chanting stops, she is called to the witness stand ; and for the first time she is able to see clearly the events that took place in the Marabar Hills. Reaching down into the subconscious, she reconstructs them with detached and lucid vision of the same sort which Roger Fry says is necessary to the artist, and which is unassociated with action.

> A new and unknown sensation protected her, like magnificent armour. She didn't think what had happened, or even remember in the ordinary way of memory, but she returned to the Marabar Hills, and spoke from them across a sort of darkness to [the Superintendent of Police]. The fatal day recurred, in every detail, but now she was of it and not of it at the same time, and this double relation gave it indescribable splendour. Why had she thought the expedition "dull"? Now the sun rose again, the elephant waited, the pale masses of the rock flowed round her and presented the first cave ; she entered, and a match was reflected in the polished walls—all beautiful and significant, though she had been blind to it at the time.*

She sees clearly that Aziz did not follow her into the cave where she had believed she was attacked ; and because she is honest she withdraws the charge.

The half-suppressed emotions of the Indians are released ; the court-room empties ; and there is rejoicing in the streets. In the press Adela is flung against Fielding. There is danger of a riot ; Fielding is the only Englishman who is safe amongst the Indians ; he takes Adela, who cannot expect the other English to befriend her now, to the safety of the Government College. There she remains until she leaves for England, for Ronny's love is dead, and no one will receive her at the civil station. Thus these two, Adela and Fielding, so similar in spite of differences of age and sex and experience, are brought together and left to discuss the events they have just experienced.

So far as the events are concerned, their discussion is not

* p. 197.

enlightening. Like all who discuss, perhaps, they use the tools of logic ; and these tools do not suit the case. The incident in the cave and the unexpected course of the trial must be explicable by reason if Adela and Fielding are to understand them. In consequence, of course, they do not understand. Adela, so much more intimately involved in the affair than Fielding, realizes their failure as Fielding does not. Her misfortunes began, she tells him, about the time of the tea-party at the College. " I enjoyed the singing . . . but just about then a sort of sadness began that I couldn't detect at the time . . . no, nothing as solid as sadness : living at half pressure expresses it best. Half pressure." Her life did not return to normal until the trial, when the echo which had tormented her ever since her experience in the cave finally left her. But what was the echo ? what happened in the cave ? " I am up against something, and so are you. Mrs. Moore —she did know," Adela tells Fielding. Mrs. Moore is dead. She died, in the heat of May, soon after leaving India ; and her body " was lowered into yet another India—the Indian Ocean ". Ronny received the news just after the trial in a cable from Aden. As Adela remarks, Mrs. Moore was dead when her name was chanted outside the court-room. Before long two tombs reputed to contain her remains appear at Chandrapore ; there are signs of the beginning of a cult amongst the natives. " [Adela] was at the end of her spiritual tether, and so was [Fielding]. Were there worlds beyond which they could never touch, or did all that is possible enter their consciousness ? They could not tell. They only realized that their outlook was more or less similar, and found in this a satisfaction. Perhaps life is a mystery, not a muddle ; they could not tell. Perhaps the hundred Indias which fuss and squabble so tiresomely are one, and the universe they mirror is one. They had not the apparatus for judging." Both of them are unreligious. They can glimpse only occasional hints of the supernatural, and these they tend to discount. Associated with their lack of religion, perhaps the cause of it, is a dry lack of emotional vitality. They come to respect and like one another. " A friendliness, as of dwarfs shaking hands, was in the air." They can achieve no more. The puzzling echo dies out softly, the echo of an echo, in Fielding's mind : " ' In the old eighteenth century, when cruelty and injustice raged [in India], an invisible power repaired their ravages. Everything echoes now ; there's no stopping the echo. The original sound may be harmless, but the echo is always evil.' This reflection about an echo lay at the verge of Fielding's mind. He could never develop it. It belonged to the universe that he had missed or rejected." The echo, in dying, becomes a part of the social fabric of India.

The first Part of *A Passage to India* ended with a pact of friendship between Fielding and Aziz. As Part Two ends there is coolness between them. Aziz is disappointed that Fielding took Adela to the Government College instead of coming with him in a victorious passage through the city. Fielding uses Mrs. Moore's name, which Aziz reveres, to dissuade Aziz from claiming damages from Adela—Aziz's claim would have ruined her financially. Then Aziz hears rumours that Adela has been Fielding's mistress. Fielding is returning to England for a short time on official business. Aziz suspects he is returning to marry Miss Quested for her money, and he soon comes to believe his suspicions. He is entirely wrong as to the facts of the case, of course, but he is right in one respect : Fielding's affinity with Adela, his cold logical mind, would prevent him and Aziz from remaining close friends for long, in any case. Forster underlines this truth, as it were, by Aziz's suspicion of Fielding's relations with Adela. Moreover, differences of race and culture make friendship between Fielding and Aziz difficult. " Tangles . . . interrupted their intercourse. A pause in the wrong place, an intonation misunderstood, and a whole conversation went awry." And Aziz, since his disastrous expedition to the Marabar Hills, has become harder and less friendly in his attitude towards the English. He is beginning to see " the vague and bulky figure of a motherland " ; and he decides to leave British India to take service in a Hindu state.

The main action of *A Passage to India* ends in this second Part, " Caves ". The evil which came from the Marabar Caves has run its course. The characters of the novel are dispersed. Ronny is sent to a new post. Professor Godbole left soon after the Marabar incident for his native state of Mau. Aziz is to take service in a Hindu state, which proves, we learn in Part Three, to be Mau. Mrs. Moore, Adela, and Fielding each sail from India in Part Two and bring the reader progressively nearer to England. Before the trial, when the action of the novel is approaching a crisis, we see Mrs. Moore across India to Bombay, and with her watch the last ramparts of India melt " into the haze of a tropic sea " as her ship sails. Adela, who sails before the coolness develops between Aziz and Fielding, continues, as it were, Mrs. Moore's voyage. We see her through the Indian Ocean and the Red Sea to Port Said and Egypt. Finally, in the last chapter of " Caves ", Fielding's voyage is taken up at Egypt. He crosses the Mediterranean to Venice, and sees once more the beauty of form, " the harmony between the works of man and the earth that upholds them ", which he had nearly forgotten amidst the muddle of India. He continues northward by train, and sees again " the buttercups and daisies of June ". Plot and story are virtually ended in Part Two ; but Part Three, " Temple ", is nevertheless the necessary and organic conclusion of the novel.

" Temple " takes place at Mau during the Rains, and in the midst of a muddle that is as different as may be from the harmony of Venice. Professor Godbole is involved in the greatest religious festival of the year, the Krishna Festival, during which the birth of the Lord of the Universe is re-enacted, and a model of the village of Gokul, in which He was born, is taken in a torchlight procession to the great tank at Mau on the evening after the Birth. In the palace at Mau, amidst drums and cymbals, *papier mâché* and electric lights, religious chanting and the music from a Europeanized band, the Birth is awaited. Professor Godbole, who leads a choir at the ceremony, attempts to find unity, to connect, connect, and connect until the whole universe is one.

> Godbole consulted the music-book, said a word to the drummer, who broke rhythm, made a thick little blur of sound, and produced a new rhythm. This was more exciting, the inner images it evoked more definite, and the singers' expressions became fatuous and languid. They loved all men, the

whole universe, and scraps of their past, tiny splinters of detail, emerged for a moment to melt into the universal warmth. Thus Godbole, though she was not important to him, remembered an old woman he had met in Chandrapore days. Chance brought her into his mind while it was in this heated state, he did not select her, she happened to occur among the throng of soliciting images, a tiny splinter, and he impelled her by his spiritual force to that place where completeness can be found. Completeness, not reconstruction. His senses grew thinner, he remembered a wasp seen he forgot where, perhaps on a stone. He loved the wasp equally, he impelled it likewise, he was imitating God. And the stone where the wasp clung—could he . . . no, he could not, he had been wrong to attempt the stone, logic and conscious effort had seduced, he came back to the strip of red carpet and discovered that he was dancing upon it.

At midnight the Lord is born.

. . . the clock struck midnight, and simultaneously the rending note of the conch broke forth, followed by the trumpeting of elephants ; all who had packets of powder threw them at the altar, and in the rosy dust and incense, and clanging and shouts, Infinite Love took upon itself the form of SHRI KRISHNA, and saved the world. All sorrow was annihilated, not only for Indians, but for foreigners, birds, caves, railways, and the stars ; all became joy, all laughter ; there had never been disease nor doubt, misunderstanding, cruelty, fear.

As Godbole leaves the ceremony in the morning, he reflects upon his spiritual experiences.

He had, with increasing vividness, again seen Mrs. Moore, and round her faintly clinging forms of trouble. He was a Brahman, she Christian, but it made no difference, it made no difference whether she was a trick of his memory or a telepathic appeal. It was his duty, as it was his desire, to place himself in the position of the God and to love her, and to place himself in her position and to say to the God : " Come, come, come, come." This was all he could do. How inadequate ! But each according to his own capacities, and he knew that his own were small. " One old Englishwoman and one little,

little wasp," he thought, as he stepped out of the temple into the grey of a pouring wet morning, " It does not seem much, still it is more than I am myself." *

Aziz is also at Mau ; he is one of the Rajah's doctors. And Fielding, as Aziz learns from Godbole, has just arrived at Mau with his wife and her brother (for Fielding indeed married in England) on an official visit as an education officer. Godbole is delighted at Fielding's visit, though his religious duties allow him to give Fielding very little of his time. Since Aziz is Mohammedan, he has, of course, no part in the Krishna Festival ; but he does not intend to see Fielding. They meet by chance, however, at a Mohammedan shrine. Fielding and his brother-in-law enter the shrine, only to be chased out at once, to Aziz's amusement, by bees which have nested there. Fielding's brother-in-law is stung ; and the incident brings Aziz and Fielding together long enough for Aziz to find that Fielding has married Mrs. Moore's daughter Stella, not Miss Quested, and for Fielding to discover Aziz's foolish mistake. Aziz is shaken for a moment when he hears Mrs. Moore's name, but he parts from Fielding, telling him that he wishes no one who is English to be his friend.

The same evening Aziz takes an embrocation to the European Guest House for Ralph Moore's stings. He finds Ralph alone, Stella and Fielding having gone to the tank to watch the torchlight procession from the water. He is at first gruff and even cruel to Ralph ; but Ralph's voice, his remarks, and his appearance recall Mrs. Moore ; the noise of the religious festival, which can be heard, has a beneficent effect ; and Aziz's feelings towards Ralph become kindly. Ralph detects the change at once, to Aziz's surprise. Can Ralph always tell whether a stranger is his friend ? Aziz asks. Ralph says he can. " Then you are an Oriental," Aziz tells him—and with a little shudder remembers that he spoke the same words to Mrs. Moore in the Mosque at Chandrapore. Ralph is indeed Mrs. Moore's son ; and in gratitude to her Aziz takes Ralph to the tank and rows him out on it to watch the Hindu procession. Ralph seems to have a strange affinity with the Hindus. He directs Aziz to row near the goal of the pro-

* pp. 249–54.

cession. And in the darkness, amidst the religious fervour of the Hindus, amidst rain and thunder and the beating of drums, Aziz's boat collides with Fielding's, the two boats strike the model of the village of Gokul, and Stella and Fielding, Aziz and Ralph, are thrown together into the shallow waters of the tank.

The accident restores friendship between Aziz and Fielding. Indeed, the Hindu festival and Mrs. Moore's influence have smoothed away the differences between all the characters of the novel. Ronny and Fielding, now connected by Fielding's marriage to Ronny's half-sister, have agreed to forget old grievances and to become friends. Ronny writes Fielding that he wishes to make peace with Adela too. Aziz realizes for the first time how well Adela behaved towards him. He writes her to thank her and to tell her that he will henceforth connect her " with the name that is very sacred in my mind, namely, Mrs. Moore ". As force was shut within its box at the conclusion of *Howards End*, so there is a moment of peace and unity, in which love is supreme, as *A Passage to India* concludes. But force still threatened in *Howards End* ; and it is made clear in *A Passage to India* that the divisions of life will return. India is still divided from Anglo-India, Hindu from Moslem, Brahman from Untouchable. If love is supreme at the moment, there is still evil in the universe.

Fielding and Aziz are aware that they will not meet again after Fielding leaves Mau. Aziz has thrown in his lot with India ; Fielding has joined forces with Anglo-India ; each has hardened since Chandrapore. And the difference between their characters, the difference between emotion and intellect, remains. Meanwhile they are granted a moment of companionship. They go for a last ride together the day before Fielding's visit ends. Fielding speaks of his wife. " She has ideas I don't share—indeed, when I'm away from her I think them ridiculous. When I'm with her, I suppose because I'm fond of her, I feel different, I feel half dead and half blind. My wife's after something. You and I and Miss Quested are, roughly speaking, not after anything. We jog on as decently as we can, you a little in front—a laudable little party. But my wife is not with us." Mau calmed her, he says—both she and Ralph suffer from restlessness. " She found something soothing, some solution of her queer troubles here." " Why do my wife and her brother like Hinduism," he asks, " though they take no interest in its forms ? They won't talk to me about this. They know I think a certain side of their lives is a mistake, and are shy." Then the conversation turns to politics. The English must clear out of India, Aziz says. Fielding retorts that Indians need English help. The English must leave, Aziz insists ; and they will be made to go if they do not leave of their own accord. " Until England is in difficulties we keep silent, but in the next European war—aha, aha ! Then is our time." And after the English are gone, he says, riding his horse against Fielding's, " you and I shall be friends ".

> " Why can't we be friends now ? " said the other, holding him affectionately. " It's what I want. It's what you want."
> But the horses didn't want it—they swerved apart ; the earth didn't want it, sending up rocks through which riders must pass single file ; the temples, the tank, the jail, the palace, the birds, the carrion, the Guest House, that came into view as they issued from the gap and saw Mau beneath : they didn't want it, they said in their hundred voices : " No, not yet ", and the sky said : " No, not there." *

The relations in *A Passage to India* are so numerous as to appear inexhaustible. It is more organic than any other of Forster's novels ; it combines to a very high degree the infinite variety of life and the peculiar significance of art. There is nothing in it that one would wish to change, or that one feels could be other than it is. In common with *The Longest Journey* and *Howards End*, it expands as it progresses ; but it does so, through scenes that are inevitably related to one another, with a sureness that is unknown in those novels. One feels that they have been built, however skilfully ; but that *A Passage to India* has grown into its own beautiful proportions.

The novel grows from the discussion at Hamidullah's as to whether it is possible to be friends with an Englishman. This theme, of course, is carried throughout the novel—though it

* p. 282.

is not the theme of the novel—by the relations between Aziz and Fielding. The discussion at Hamidullah's is pointed and illuminated by the Bridge Party, and at the Bridge Party Fielding's tea is arranged. From Fielding's tea grows the Marabar expedition and Fielding's friendship with Aziz. There are hints at the tea of impending evil—Adela's inadvertent and untimely announcement that she intends to return to England ; Godbole's reticence about the Marabar Caves ; the disturbance that Ronny causes ; Godbole's strange song, in which the Lord of the Universe neglects to come. And Godbole, whose whole appearance is compact of harmony and tranquillity, composes the ruffled scene at the tea with the Hindu song, as Hinduism and Mrs. Moore's influence—the two are scarcely distinguishable in this respect—later create harmony between the characters of the novel.

The misfortunes in the novel grow from a trivial and ludicrous incident : Dr. Panna Lal's accident, in his new tum-tum, which damages the hollyhocks at the club. The Nawab Bahadur mentions Lal's misfortune as he and Adela and Ronny set off, a few hours after Fielding's tea, for their drive in the Nawab's new car. They drive towards the portentous Marabar Hills, and immediately after crossing a nullah they have the mysterious accident which is related by numerous bonds to the subsequent incident in the Marabar Caves. When Aziz's party is bound for the Marabar Hills, Adela recalls the Nawab's accident, and the train crosses several nullahs, with the result that we have an uneasy intuition of impending evil—an intuition that is reinforced by the preceding description of the hills and by Mrs. Moore's ominous feeling that personal relations are void. Adela's illusion of love for Ronny begins during the drive with the Nawab Bahadur and ends at the Marabar Caves. The footholds in the rock near the fatal cave recall the wheel marks of the Nawab's car as they were seen in the dust after the accident. Miss Derek drives Adela to Chandrapore both from the caves and from the scene of the Nawab's accident, having arrived unexpectedly on each occasion. As the novel unfolds, the nullah near which the Nawab's accident occurred is linked, with almost geographical accuracy, with the very source of evil in the Marabar Hills—the " original spawning place " of the caves—and provides, as it were, a channel through which evil flows towards Chandrapore.

Evil is externalized in the novel by the Marabar echo, the prelude to which—" pomper, pomper, pomper "—is heard as the train crosses the first nullah on the way to Marabar, and which runs from the caves into the lives of Indians and English alike at Chandrapore. It is Forster's finest rhythm, and it is completely organic ; there is not a hint of device in it. The echo, which sounds " bou-oum, ou-boum " in the caves, reverberates through the second Part of the novel, " Caves ", like an ominous, clearly enunciated symphonic theme, like the " diddidy dum "—too innocuous a description of that great phrase !—which reverberates through the first movement of Beethoven's Fifth Symphony.

The novel, to the accompaniment of Mrs. Moore's spiritual development, moves steadily from Christian and Moslem to Hindu. Mrs. Moore comes to India a Christian, believing that God is love, and that he is omnipresent. In the mosque, where she meets Aziz, ninety-nine names of God are inscribed on a frieze. " God is here," Mrs. Moore says. And his presence, for He *is* there, is indicated in the novel by the ablution tank of fresh, clear water, always in motion, and by Mrs. Moore's sudden sense of unity with the heavenly bodies. But both Mohammedanism and Christianity are found to be inadequate by Mrs. Moore. The echo in the Marabar cave destroys her experience in the mosque (the recollection of which made her vital and young for a moment just before she entered the cave) and overwhelms " poor little talkative Christianity ". Adela, usually unreligious, turns to Christianity in search of help after her experience in the caves. But Christianity is inefficacious. After praying before her trial, she finds that the echo in her mind has intensified. Fielding, we have seen, could not deal with the echo because it belonged to the universe that he had missed or rejected. " And the mosque missed it too. Like himself, those shallow arcades provided but a limited asylum. 'There is no God but God' doesn't carry us far through the complexities of matter and spirit ; it is only a game with words, really, a religious pun, not a religious truth." At Mau the Islamic creed, " There is no God but God ", " melts in the mild airs . . . ; it belongs to pilgrimages and universities, not to feudalism and agriculture". Christianity and Mohammedanism both exclude much of the universe from their purview, so it seems to Forster, and, in particular, neither accounts satisfactorily for evil nor makes due allowance for it. They are both helpless before the Marabar Caves ; and Mrs. Moore discovers there that God is not omnipresent, though she was right to think, as we learn later, that He is love. Only Godbole, the old Hindu professor, who explains to Fielding that evil is present when God is absent, and that both good and evil are aspects of God, understands the caves from the first ; and only Hinduism, a pantheistic religion which accepts everything in the universe, from modern machinery to the farthest stars, from good to evil, makes adequate allowance for the Marabar echo. Neither Christianity nor Mohammedanism can deal with it. Logic, law-courts, and reason are helpless before it : it is as useless to attempt to control it with this apparatus as to search in the dark with an electric torch for the tracks of a ghost. The echo is finally overcome by Mrs. Moore's influence, because she accepts and understands it, and is herself truly religious and good. This is the main theme of the novel, or rather, the outer garments of the main theme. It has an astonishing force (which, of course, cannot be appreciated when it is removed from its context) because it expresses Forster's deep intuition that the negation of love and personal relations, which for him is the essence of evil, cannot be overcome by reason alone, by Christianity, or by any religion that does not embrace the whole of life, but must be fought by the human spirit in co-operation with the life-giving forces of nature. Krishna, whose Festival, with the help of Mrs. Moore's influence, brings about the final concord in the novel, is a god of agriculture who embodies the reproductive powers of nature. Held by a pantheistic religion to be Lord of the Universe, he is a greater personification of the forces which the Demeter of Cnidus and the Ephesian Artemis also represent. It is emphasized in the novel that Krishna is love. And, as always in Forster's books, true religion is closely associated with the subconscious mind.

Mrs. Moore, adept in personal relations, completely ignores

the inhuman barriers which separate India from Anglo-India, and overcomes, as well, differences of race and culture, to recognize Aziz's goodness at once and to learn more of him during their brief meeting in the mosque than Fielding learns throughout his friendship with Aziz. The echo, which affects her more profoundly than Adela, causes her to lose faith in personal relationships ; but she is the only character in the novel, with the exception of Godbole, who recognizes clearly that the echo is evil. In spite of the effect of the echo upon her, she remains able to judge between good and evil. She criticizes herself for rejecting personal relationships, saying that she is bad and detestable ; and she knows that Aziz is innocent. Her spirit conquers finally, though she is cynical, selfish, and indifferent to others from the time she hears the echo until she leaves Chandrapore to travel across India to Bombay. Then her interest in India revives—a hint, recorded by her conscious mind, of her future triumph. The battle with evil is fought in her subconscious mind—where, Forster believes, we near the gates of the divine—and is unaffected by her death. While she is alive, she communicates to Adela through the subconscious the truth that Aziz is innocent ; and her posthumous influence at the trial enables Adela to reach down into the subconscious and to reconstruct clearly the events leading up to the incident in the cave. Finally, Mrs. Moore herself is drawn up out of Professor Godbole's subconscious to be associated with Krishna ; and her influence, combined with the influence of the Krishna Festival, establishes good relations between the characters of the novel. It is in this last Part of the novel that the full extent of Mrs. Moore's triumph becomes apparent.

Throughout the novel Mrs. Moore comes to understand India more and more, and is brought into closer and closer accord with it. " Mrs. Moore had always inclined to resignation. As soon as she landed in India, it seemed to her good, and when she saw the water flowing through the mosque tank, or the Ganges, or the moon, caught in the shawl of night with all the other stars, it seemed a beautiful goal and an easy one. To be one with the universe ! " At the mosque she understands and likes Aziz, and he calls her an Oriental. She accepts the wasp, which the missionaries reject. She senses the Indians' secret, " communicable more by blood than by speech ", of the ghost on the Marabar road. She understands the echo in the caves ; and, like Godbole, she knows that active intervention in Aziz's case will do no good. Both she and Godbole withdraw from Chandrapore before the trial. As she crosses India she is associated with the landscapes which she passes and which arouse her from the lethargy in which she had been sunk since visiting the caves. At Bombay she longs to see more of India and to stop in the huge city to disentangle " the hundred Indias that passed each other in its streets ". Soon after her ship leaves Bombay, her body is lowered " into yet another India—the Indian Ocean ". The caves she visited are associated with the Jains, a Hindu sect which exalts its saints above the lesser gods. She is exalted into Esmiss Esmoor, a Hindu goddess, to whom shrines are built. In becoming one with the universe she attains the Hindu pantheist's ideal. And when she appears in Godbole's mind during the Krishna Festival, when Godbole accepts the wasp as she accepted it, she is conclusively associated with Hinduism, or rather, with the aspects of Hinduism that Forster admires; for, as Forster says, Hinduism is riven into innumerable sects.

Like Mrs. Wilcox of *Howards End*, Mrs. Moore belongs much more to the supernatural than to humanity. Neither her character nor her appearance are described : we know her by her effect upon others and by their impressions of her, which are usually completely general, though often very strong. Aziz is puzzled as to why he has so much respect and love for her. " What did this eternal goodness of Mrs. Moore's amount to? To nothing, if brought to the test of thought. She had not borne witness in his favour, nor visited him in the prison, yet she had stolen to the depths of his heart, and he always adored her." She is akin to Godbole, who is trusted by all his friends, though they know not why. Both she and Godbole are old, and the wisdom and mystery of age surrounds them. From her first appearance in the mosque, Mrs. Moore is associated with religion ; and her interest in religion is continued in Stella and Ralph, who are, as it were, an extension of her personality. She is the most successful creation among those characters of Forster's who expand to embrace the universal. And Aziz is perhaps Forster's most successful purely human character. The penetration and sympathy which enabled Forster to create Gino Carella and Leonard Bast is here at its height, and the result is a sensitive, emotional Indian doctor who is astonishingly convincing. Forster's character-drawing is completely successful in *A Passage to India* because he does not try to mix the human and the supernatural in one character, as he did in creating Stephen Wonham and in transforming Margaret Schlegel into Mrs. Wilcox.

The large divisions of the structure of *A Passage to India*, " Mosque ", " Caves ", " Temple ", accord with the spiritual development of the novel, which moves from the peaceful seclusion of theism, which is found to be unreal, to the undeniable reality of evil, and, finally, to the synthesis which Hindu pantheism achieves. The Hindu ceremony in the last Part of the book opposes evil as the Rains drench out the terrible heat and drought of the Hot Weather. After her experience in the cave, as we have seen, Mrs. Moore reflected that " If one had spoken with the tongues of angels and pleaded for all the unhappiness and misunderstanding in the world, past, present, and to come ; for all the misery men must undergo whatever their opinion and position, and however much they dodge or bluff ", only the echo would reply, " the serpent would descend and return to the ceiling ". At the birth of Krishna in the temple, " All sorrow was annihilated, not only for Indians, but for foreigners, birds, caves, railways, and the stars ; all became joy, all laughter ; there had never been disease nor doubt, misunderstanding, cruelty, fear ". In the caves love is denied and life is declared to be sterile ; in the temple love is born and life confirmed. Aziz wishes sadly that Mrs. Moore could have seen the Rains, the best season of the Indian year. " Now is the time when all things are happy, young and old," he says. But of course, Mrs. Moore is present, though Aziz does not know it, in the Krishna Festival. And the Rains accord with that ceremony, as the Hot Weather accords with evil, and the Cold Weather with the seclusion of the mosque. These three divisions of the

Indian year enclose the novel, and compress its action, though perhaps several years elapse between Fielding's departure from Chandrapore and his visit to Mau, into a cycle, satisfying and complete, of the seasons. This arrangement, moreover, is attuned to the pantheistic theme of the novel.

Forster's style reaches its apogee of strength and brilliance in *A Passage to India.* The ease and lucidity of *Howards End* are retained, but new realms are triumphantly entered, new effects of imagery and rhythm achieved. The description of the Marabar Caves is richer than anything that is to be found in the previous novels. When a match is struck near the polished walls of a cave, " The two flames approach and strive to unite, but cannot, because one of them breathes air, the other stone. A mirror inlaid with lovely colours divides the lovers, delicate stars of pink and grey interpose, exquisite nebulae, shadings fainter than the tail of a comet or the midday moon, all the evanescent life of the granite, only here visible. Fists and fingers thrust above the advancing soil—here at last is their skin, finer than any covering acquired by the animals, smoother than windless water, more voluptuous than love." The description of Mrs. Moore's trip across India, and of her regret at leaving the country, is resplendent with Indian names ringing : " She would never visit Asirgarh or the other untouched places ; neither Delhi nor Agra nor the Rajputana cities nor Kashmir, nor the obscurer marvels that had sometimes shone through men's speech : the bilingual rock of Girnar, the statue of Shri Belgola, the ruins of Mandu and Hampi, temples of Khajraha, gardens of Shalimar." The style is as sure when the whimsical, wise simplicity of Godbole's speech is undertaken ; or when the punkah wallah, who continues to work the fan after Aziz's trial has ended and the court-room has emptied, is described in one of the most beautiful prose rhythms in the novel : " . . . before long no one remained on the scene of the fantasy but the beautiful naked god. Unaware that anything unusual had occurred, he continued to pull the cord of his punkah, to gaze at the empty dais and the overturned special chairs, and rhythmically to agitate the clouds of descending dust." Forster's style will do anything for him in this novel. After all this brilliance, it draws the book to its satisfying close in the sustained, translucent beauty of " Temple ".

If *A Passage to India* is Forster's last novel, neither we nor Forster need be disappointed. It is a worthy valediction.

CHAPTER VI

LYTTON STRACHEY

LYTTON STRACHEY came to fame, almost to notoriety, when *Eminent Victorians* was published in 1918. Many of the generation who fought the First World War welcomed the book : it was time to criticize the preceding age : the War seemed an inheritance from it.* But there were others, most of them of an older generation, who looked back to the Victorian Age as a time of peace and strength and leisure, which might never be regained. To them, *Eminent Victorians* seemed to profane the shrine of the temple. In the furore caused by its publication, the merits of the book as a work of art, which are real, tended to be overlooked. *Queen Victoria* followed *Eminent Victorians* in 1921. *Elizabeth and Essex* appeared in 1928. In 1932, at the age of fifty-one, Strachey died. He seemed to have burst upon the world unannounced in 1918 ; but of course, this was not the case. On the one hand, Froude's *Carlyle*, Samuel Butler's *The Way of All Flesh*, and Gosse's *Father and Son* had helped prepare the way for *Eminent Victorians* ; on the other, Strachey had served a long literary apprenticeship. In 1912 he published *Landmarks in French Literature*, a beautifully written, brief, but authoritative survey of French Literature from the Middle Ages to the late nineteenth century. He was the dramatic critic for *The Spectator* from 1907 to 1909.† And during the fifteen years immediately preceding the publication of *Eminent Victorians*, Strachey wrote a large number of essays and reviews for leading literary magazines. He continued to write essays until his death ; and many of his essays, from first to last, are essays in biography. In fact, whether Strachey is discussing an edition of Horace Walpole's letters or reviewing

* See Dobrée, " Lytton Strachey ", *The Post Victorians*, p. 577.

† Boas, *English*, VIII, Spring 1950, p. 8.

the works of Thomas Lovell Beddoes, he turns to biography at the first opportunity.

" Madame du Deffand ", which first appeared in the *Edinburgh Review* of January 1913, is one of the best of Strachey's biographical essays that preceded *Eminent Victorians*.* It is in a sense a companion piece to an essay written in 1906, " Mademoiselle de Lespinasse ", at which we have looked in a previous chapter. But while " Mademoiselle de Lespinasse " is simply a story, passionately felt and beautifully told without pause or apparent forethought, " Madame du Deffand " is detached and intricate, and assumes some of the formal characteristics of Strachey's biographies.

" Madame du Deffand " was written, ostensibly, as a review of Mrs. Paget Toynbee's edition of Madame du Deffand's letters to Horace Walpole ; and Madame du Deffand's affection for Walpole, " a singular adventure of the heart " which she experienced in old age, is the culminating point of the essay, the goal, which Strachey adumbrates in the first pages, towards which the essay moves, recreating, as it does so, much of Madame du Deffand's life. In the first sentences of the essay Strachey recounts an anecdote which he uses to put the episode he is about to describe in its historical setting. When Napoleon set off on his Russian campaign, he took with him in his carriage, to read on the way, the proof sheets of the first French edition of Madame du Deffand's correspondence with Walpole. Soon afterwards the correspondence was published. " The sensation in Paris was immense; the excitement of the Russian campaign itself was half forgotten; and for some time the blind old inhabitant of the Convent of Saint-Joseph held her own as a subject of conversation with the burning of Moscow and the passage of Berezina."

" The letters ", Strachey says, " were hardly more than thirty years old " ; the people of whom they spoke had not yet vanished from living memory—but what a gulf was fixed between " the eager readers of the First Empire " and the departed world of the old regime ! And how much farther is not that world from us ? " Since [the First Empire] a

* *Biographical Essays*, pp. 165–86.

century has passed ; the gulf has widened ; and the vision which these curious letters show us to-day seems hardly less remote—from some points of view, indeed, even more—than that which is revealed to us in the Memoirs of Cellini or the correspondence of Cicero."

But, Strachey emphasizes, human nature has not changed. " The soul of man is not subject to the rumour of periods ; and these [letters], impregnated though they be with the abolished life of the eighteenth century, can never be out of date." By this means, and with the help of a certain over-emphasis—is the eighteenth century indeed " hardly less remote " than the Renaissance or Ancient Rome? did the publication of the letters in fact cause the Russian campaign to be " half-forgotten " ?—Strachey casts his scene and his characters far in the distant past. Though his characters are human, and demand a human interest—they once lived, certainly : even in the days of the First Empire they could still arouse an eager, gossipy talk—they will move like marionettes to a pre-ordained goal. Madame du Deffand will inevitably become " the blind old inhabitant of the Convent of Saint Joseph ". And she will have, before she dies, " a singular adventure of the heart " with Horace Walpole, an adventure in which our interest has already been awakened.

Expansion, it is evident, is not the aim of Strachey's essays ; nor is it, as we will see, the aim of his biographies. He often, as in this essay, clearly marks off the limits of his composition in advance ; and within those limits he packs a great amount of anecdotic, allusive material, all of it economical, significant, and essential to his plan. Madame du Deffand, he says, was " perhaps the most typical representative " of the intellectual and aristocratic society which " reached its most concentrated and characteristic form about the year 1750 in the drawing-rooms of Paris. She was supremely a woman of her age ; but it is important to notice that her age was the first, and not the second, half of the eighteenth century ; it was the age of the Regent Orleans, Fontenelle, and the young Voltaire ; not that of Rousseau, the ' Encyclopaedia ', and the Patriarch of Ferney." Her quarrel with Mademoiselle de Lespinasse, with whom the Encyclopaedists were allied, " was itself far more a symptom of a deeply rooted spiritual antipathy than a mere vulgar struggle for influence between two rival *salonnières* ". Madame du Deffand, during the period of her life upon which Strachey focuses, was a survival from a past age. " For a fortnight (so she confessed to Walpole) she was actually the Regent's mistress ; and a fortnight, in those days, was a considerable time." She was delighted by Turgot's dismissal from office—" that fatal act, which made the French Revolution inevitable ". She detested the enthusiasm, the fine sentiment, the emotional ardours which were becoming the fashion in the second half of her century, and which disturbed the amenities of the society she knew. In that society, " each individual was expected to practise, and did in fact practise to a consummate degree, those difficult arts which make the wheels of human intercourse run smoothly ". The life she knew in the first half of the century is described and summed up in a metaphor : " The graceful, easy motions of that gay company were those of dancers balanced on skates, gliding, twirling, interlacing, over the thinnest ice." But the ice endured, though gaiety departed. The members of the company " refused to grow old ; they almost refused to die ". Time himself was polite to them ; and they lived on into the second half of the eighteenth century. Madame du Deffand's salon was sometimes visited in those later years by the sons of influential English parents.

> The English cub, fresh from Eton, was introduced by his tutor into the red and yellow drawing-room, where the great circle of a dozen or more elderly important persons, glittering in jewels and orders, pompous in powder and rouge, ranged in rigid order round the fireplace, followed with the precision of a perfect orchestra the leading word or smile or nod of an ancient Sibyl, who seemed to survey the company with her eyes shut, from a vast chair by the wall. It is easy to imagine the scene, in all its terrifying politeness.

The motions of the marionettes, the stubborn adherents of a moribund tradition, could not be more precise.

" The last phase of a doomed society ", mirrored in Madame du Deffand's letters to Walpole, is traced in some detail in the essay ; and then, as though to emphasize the stagnation of Madame du Deffand's salon, Voltaire is introduced. "Voltaire, alone of his generation, had thrown himself into the very vanguard of thought; to Madame du Deffand progress had no meaning, and thought itself was hardly more than an unpleasant necessity." Voltaire, as it were, is the outer world moving on; he is even the leader of the outer world; and his introduction into the essay gives us a vivid sense of time hurrying by and leaving the salon in the Convent of Saint Joseph untouched. He and Madame du Deffand corresponded, though they distrusted each other profoundly. Madame du Deffand kept Voltaire in touch with an influential circle in Paris; and she was not unaware of the glory of corresponding with Voltaire. "The result was a marvellous display of epistolary art," Strachey says; and he describes their letters and their relationship in a simile and an unforgettable metaphor. "They were on their best behaviour—exquisitely courteous and yet punctiliously at ease, like dancers in a minuet." Voltaire cajoles; he mingles flattery with reflection. Madame du Deffand purrs, "Monsieur de Voltaire". "Sometimes one just catches the glimpse of a claw beneath the soft pad, a grimace under the smile of elegance; and one remembers with a shock that, after all, one is reading the correspondence of a monkey and a cat."

Finally, after Madame du Deffand's ennui, cynicism, and distaste for life in the second half of the eighteenth century have been illustrated and underlined, her "singular adventure of the heart" with Horace Walpole is described in the last pages of the essay. It was an adventure entirely out of keeping with the rest of her life. She met Walpole when she was nearly seventy, and she was captivated by him.

> . . . she suddenly found that, so far from her life being over, she was embarked for good and all upon her greatest adventure. What she experienced at that moment was something like a religious conversion. Her past fell away from her a dead thing; she was overwhelmed by an ineffable vision; she, who had wandered for so many years in the ways of worldly indifference, was uplifted all at once on to a strange summit, and pierced with the intensest pangs of an unknown devotion.

The ennui, the stagnation, the distaste for life were ended;

she had at last found some one who pleased her. But "it was the final irony of her fate that this very fact should have been the last drop that caused the cup of her unhappiness to overflow". For Walpole did not reciprocate her passion, nor did he treat it with gentleness or respect. He liked her, and he was flattered by her letters, but no more than that. He feared ridicule; he corresponded with her only on condition that their letters be written in the tone of the most ordinary friendship. And when she became too affectionate, he stormed, and threatened that he would write no more. "After seven years of struggle, Madame du Deffand's indomitable spirit was broken; henceforward she would hope for nothing; she would gratefully accept the few crumbs that might be thrown her; and for the rest she resigned herself to her fate." Life became bitter and painful and even more filled with ennui. She gradually sank into extreme old age; and on her deathbed she dictated a last letter to Walpole.

So Madame du Deffand's story ends. "Perhaps the most typical representative" of the cultured, decorous society of the first half of the eighteenth century, a mistress of the amenities of human intercourse, who had opposed so long and so tenaciously the enthusiasms of the new generation, herself fell victim in her old age to an unreciprocated romantic passion and was overwhelmed by it. The irony could not be more complete. Strachey presents it quietly, without emphasis; and he concludes with a comment that is intentionally ambiguous.

> When one reflects upon her extraordinary tragedy, when one attempts to gauge the significance of her character and of her life, it is difficult to know whether to pity most, to admire, or to fear. Certainly there is something at once pitiable and magnificent in such an unflinching perception of the futilities of living, such an uncompromising refusal to be content with anything save the one thing that it is impossible to have. But there is something alarming too; was she perhaps right after all?

The tone of the essay, from the first anecdote to this final comment, is the friendly, easy tone of the after-dinner *raconteur*, who speaks from a comfortable chair, over a glass of wine perhaps, to an intelligent audience whom he knows and respects. Nothing is insisted upon ; everything is savoured. Strachey is at home and at ease in eighteenth-century France. The style is that of a highly polished conversation. The pace is leisurely, in spite of the mass of information that is given in a matter of eight thousand words. " Madame du Deffand " has in a high degree the merits of compactness and apparent informality that the essay form demands.

The discipline of essay-writing undoubtedly taught Strachey a good deal, and helped him to achieve in the four biographies in *Eminent Victorians* that " becoming brevity " which he recommends in his preface to the book. The longest of these biographies, " Cardinal Manning ", is of no more than 35,000 words ; " The End of General Gordon " is five thousand words shorter than " Manning " : " Florence Nightingale " is scarcely 20,000 words in length ; and " Dr Arnold ", at about 10,000 words, is only slightly longer than " Madame du Deffand ". None the less, the art of the miniature, which is practised in " Madame du Deffand ", is discarded in *Eminent Victorians.* The Victorian Age does not serve as *décor* in any of these biographies, as eighteenth-century France, seen, as it were, through the wrong end of an opera-glass, serves as *décor* for " Madame du Deffand ". Each biography is certainly surrounded by the Victorian Age, but only a portion of the Age, the portion which directly concerns the subject of the biography, is examined. The brevity of " Dr. Arnold ", for example, is achieved by keeping the scene at Rugby School, and fastening upon Arnold's career there. In " Madame du Deffand " Strachey works, as it were, in towards his subject from the framework of the eighteenth century ; in *Eminent Victorians* he works out from his subjects to the surrounding Age. As a result the central figures in *Eminent Victorians* are life-size ; they are realized in a way that Madame du Deffand is not. And whether, like Florence Nightingale, they control their own destinies with an iron will, or like General Gordon, are propelled by fate to an inevitable goal, they are not marionettes ; for they are intensely human.

" Cardinal Manning " is the fullest study in *Eminent Victorians* of the interaction of a man and an aspect of the

Victorian Age. It is a piece of detective work, a reconstruction of how, in Strachey's opinion, Manning's character and the circumstances in which he found himself—in particular, his association with the Oxford Movement—combined to raise him to the eminence he attained. As the pieces of the puzzle are fitted together, the man and his life emerge, and the structure of the biography grows.

The deductions that Strachey makes, and his consequent view of Manning, have, of course, been bitterly disputed. We are not concerned here with that dispute, nor with the disputes which Strachey's other biographies have aroused, but only with the structure of the biographies and with their artistic validity. Some points related to the dispute, however, which have to do with the art of biography, should be considered.

The figures in *Eminent Victorians* emerge with extraordinary clarity and force—if this were not the case the book would not have stirred the wrath of its opponents as it has. And they would not so emerge if Strachey were lying to us in the slightest degree—if in other words, he were presenting a view which he himself did not hold and hold strongly. Furthermore, the characters are created to a remarkable extent from their own words, taken from their books, their letters, their diaries, and their recorded conversation. A large part of *Eminent Victorians*, including nearly all of the most damaging evidence—and by no means all the evidence presented in the book is damaging—is in inverted commas. Strachey's view of Manning, for example, may be wrong—it is, in fact, certain to be wrong in some respects, since Strachey is no more omniscient than any other biographer—but it is an honest view, based upon a faithful examination of the evidence. Each person who studies that evidence anew will inevitably interpret it differently, and we can look for no final settlement of the matter, no absolutely correct and infallible picture of Manning. All that can be asked of any biographer is that he study the evidence carefully and present a view that is honest, intelligible, and convincing. The biographer may, however, put a good deal more of the evidence in our hands than Strachey does in *Eminent Victorians*. If he does so he gives us more opportunity to form our own opinion; he puts, as it were, some of the burdens of the biographer on us; though the picture of the man which emerges is, on the whole, the biographer's, since he has selected, arranged, and controlled the biography according to his view of his subject. The problem, which is one of scale, is a difficult one. The logical extreme on the one hand would be to give the reader all the evidence—to publish the sources instead of a biography; on the other the extreme would be to give a brief statement, a testimonial, in fact, of the biographer's estimate of the subject. In the first case we would not have to rely on the biographer at all; in the second we would have to rely on him entirely; in both cases biography would disappear. Strachey, who had a logical mind, but who respected biography to the highest degree, wished in theory to push the two extremes as far as possible within the limits of biography. "A biography should either be as long as Boswell's or as short as Aubrey's," he says in an essay on Aubrey, written in 1923. "The method of enormous and elaborate accretion which produced the *Life of Johnson* is excellent, no doubt; but, failing that, let us have no half-measures; let us have the pure essentials—a vivid image, on a page or two, without explanations, transitions, commentaries, or padding."

In his own biographies, of course, Strachey did not carry his theory this far; but, though modified in practice, it is behind the short biographies in *Eminent Victorians* and the long biography of Queen Victoria. And some of Strachey's biographical essays give us the "pure essentials" of the man on a page or two. Strachey realized, in any case, that the biographer cannot have it both ways. The sharp, incisive picture given in "Manning" is not to be achieved by "the method of enormous and elaborate accretion"; and by its very nature it cannot have the depth and completeness of *Johnson* or *Queen Victoria*. No more are André Rouveyre's caricatures meant to compete or compare with Rembrandt's portraits. But Art has room for both Rouveyre and Rembrandt, and would be the poorer if either were sacrificed. We must leave it at that, and allow the biographer to choose both the scale that accords with his view of his subject, and the treatment to which he believes the subject will respond. For the rest, let us trust the reader, and not imagine that irreparable damage will be done even if he is given a view which appears to us to be distorted.

In the discussion of the structure of Strachey's biographies which follows, it will be necessary to speak as though Strachey's view of his subjects is correct. " In Strachey's opinion " or " Strachey believes " cannot be repeated as each new point is taken up. But the views of the Victorians and Elizabethans in the biographies are, of course, Strachey's, and, in the well-worn words of innumerable editors, are not necessarily endorsed.

Even more clearly than in " Madame du Deffand ", Strachey marks out the limits of " Manning " in advance. The brief introduction is a summary of the biography. Manning's character is introduced when we are told that he was " distinguished less for saintliness and learning than for practical ability ". The historical and moral purposes of the biography are defined. It will consider " the light which his career throws upon the spirit of his age, and the psychological problems suggested by his inner history ". As the culminating point of " Madame du Deffand ", her " singular adventure of the heart ", is mentioned near the beginning of the essay, so we are given a vision, on the first page of the biography, of the goal of " Manning "—Manning late in life, the Archbishop of Westminster. " The tall gaunt figure," Strachey says, " with the face of smiling asceticism, the robes, and the biretta, as it passed in triumph from High Mass at the Oratory to philanthropic gatherings at Exeter Hall, from Strike Committees at the Docks to Mayfair drawing-rooms where fashionable ladies knelt to the Prince of the Church, certainly bore witness to a singular condition of affairs." And the questions which the biography is intended to answer are put :

> What had happened? Had a dominating character imposed itself upon a hostile environment? Or was the nineteenth century, after all, not so hostile? Was there something in it, scientific and progressive as it was, which went out to welcome the representative of ancient traditions and uncompromising faith? Had it, perhaps, a place in its heart for such as Manning—a soft place, one might almost say? Or, on the other hand, was it he who had been supple and

> yielding? he who had won by art what he would never have won by force, and who had managed, so to speak, to be one of the leaders of the procession less through merit than through a superior faculty for gliding adroitly to the front rank? And, in any case, by what odd chances, what shifts and struggles, what combinations of circumstance and character, had this old man come to be where he was?

The architect, as it were, has drawn marks upon the turf and said, "Here the building shall rise." He has flourished the ground plan before us, and, with a few waves of his hand, has indicated the proportions of the structure. The method has two advantages. It clearly defines the limits of the biography. And it lends artistic certainty and assurance to the whole structure. As we read the biography, the hints that have been given so briefly in the introduction are fulfilled, and we feel that all is in its place and as it should be. This is the very reverse of Forster's method in the novel. There is no expansion: everything is contained within the system that is defined in the introduction. There are no surprises: everything comes about as it has been foretold.

Although the biography is about Manning, Manning's character is only a part of the puzzle—how did this old man come to be where he was?—that Strachey sets out to solve. Strachey is interested in the interaction of character and circumstance. He therefore defines Manning's character in the first chapter of the biography, a chapter which, in spite of its position and the material of which it is made, is really comparable to the "Character" which concludes the Johnsonian biography. It takes us swiftly, in five pages, through Manning's childhood, Harrow, Oxford, the failure of his political hopes, his taking of Orders in the Established Church, his marriage, and the death of his wife; and so it serves the chronological development, the story, of the biography. But these external circumstances are carefully chosen and arranged to present Strachey's view of the inner man. The events chosen from Manning's childhood illustrate his fear of divine punishment and his interest in theology—the latter displayed by his early reading and acceptance of Paley's *Evidences*. His undergraduate years at Oxford are made to demonstrate his pride and his ambitious desire for worldly fame. His astuteness, his determination, his lack of scruples when his own interests are involved, are stressed throughout the chapter. And the whole of Manning's future career is foreshadowed in the description of his youthful escapade at Harrow, when he was seen, by a master who was riding by, in a field that was out of bounds. The master tied his horse to a gate and gave chase. " The astute youth outran the master, fetched a circle, reached the gate, jumped on to the horse's back and rode off. For this he was properly chastised ; but of what use was chastisement ? No whipping, however severe, could have eradicated from little Henry's mind a quality at least as firmly planted in it as his fear of Hell and his belief in the arguments of Paley."

The essential subject of this chapter is indeed that which is mentioned in its opening sentence : " Undoubtedly, what is most obviously striking in the history of Manning's career is the persistent strength of his innate characteristics." Manning's character is so definitively established that the rest of his career seems to depend only upon the circumstances which he may encounter. But, as though to show us that there will be a further development, Strachey adds a final touch at the conclusion of the chapter. When Manning's wife died prematurely, he was for a time inconsolable. " How could he have guessed that one day he would come to number that loss among 'God's special mercies'? Yet so it was to be." Strachey is harsh to the Archbishop of the Church of Rome who tried to erase his wife from his memory, and who was not displeased when he heard that her grave was falling into ruin. But he is completely sympathetic to the younger Manning who mourned his wife's death. " . . . when the grave was yet fresh, the young Rector would sit beside it, day after day, writing his sermons." The suggestive power which this sentence has in its context, and its simplicity, its sympathy and restraint, recall Wordsworth's line describing the grief of the old shepherd Michael, who, after the departure and failure of Luke, his only son, continued to build the sheep-fold he and Luke had begun together, but many a day " never lifted up a single stone ". Nevertheless, in spite of this final touch, there is something fearful in the irrevocable way in which Manning's character is established so early. Indeed, the fearfulness is only increased by the picture of the young Rector beside the new grave, and the vision of the callous Archbishop that Manning is to become.

In the rest of the biography, so far as the large proportions of the structure are concerned, two things are done. The way in which Manning's character combined with circumstances to take him to the highest English office of the Church of Rome is investigated. And Manning's life and character are contrasted with Newman's.

The outer factors in Manning's rise, as Strachey presents them, were the Oxford Movement, the Gorham Case (which demonstrated to Manning that the Established Church and its faith were ultimately controlled by an Act of Parliament), and a liaison between Manning and Monsignor Talbot, the private secretary to Pope Pius IX. Strachey also conjectures that Manning may have been assured, during an interview that he had with the Pope, that he would be well treated if he came over to Rome. Manning's inner history during his conversion to Rome is traced, largely from entries in his diary. All the different traits of his character, as Strachey has established them, are brought into play. His theological principles, his temperament, and his pride all attracted him to the Oxford Movement. The Movement " imputed an extraordinary, a transcendent merit to the profession which Manning himself pursued ". Manning's fear of divine punishment caused him to weigh carefully and painfully the relative merits, as he saw them, of the Church of England and the Church of Rome. The Gorham Case, which was a blow both to his pride and to his belief in the Established Church, finally decided him to go over to Rome. And, Strachey suggests, worldly ambition may have played a part in his decision, if the Pope had indeed promised him preferment in the Catholic Church. In any case, Manning's astuteness, determination, and eye to the main chance, combined with his liaison with Monsignor Talbot, led, within fourteen years of his conversion, to his appointment as Archbishop of Westminster by the direct Act of Pius IX, in spite of the strong opposition of English Catholics.

Newman's career parallels Manning's in the biography without distracting our attention from Manning. In fact, it tends to emphasize Manning's career, in somewhat the same way as the sudden deaths in Forster's *Longest Journey* emphasize Stephen Wonham's survival. Newman is as attractive to Strachey as Manning is unattractive. "He was a child of the Romantic Revival, a creature of emotion and of memory, a dreamer whose secret spirit dwelt apart in delectable mountains, an artist whose subtle senses caught, like a shower in the sunshine, the impalpable rainbow of the immaterial world. In other times, under other skies, his days would have been more fortunate." Newman was as disinterested and unworldly as Manning was worldly and ambitious ; and although Strachey believes that the energy Newman expended on theology was misused, Strachey is true to Apostolic and Bloomsbury beliefs, and respects any one who disinterestedly pursues the ideal. That is why Newman is treated so kindly, and why the Oxford Movement, though some of the medieval, Scholastic nonsense that was associated with it is displayed, is dealt with with understanding, and with a complete appreciation of its spiritual force. The description of the Oxford Movement contrasts sharply in tone with the biting description of the General Council of 1869 at Rome. The two descriptions balance one another and are related by the parallel careers of Newman and Manning. Newman is the central figure in the one, Manning in the other. There was a good deal of nonsense both at Oxford and at Rome ; but the Oxford Movement was disinterested, spiritual, and sincere ; while Manning's group at the General Council, Strachey believes, was pretentious, worldly, and self-seeking. And throughout the biography Newman's many frustrations in the Catholic Church set off like a foil the glittering splendour of Manning's worldly success, obtained through his influence at Rome. One is reminded of the Sawstonian episode in *The Longest Journey*, in which Herbert Pembroke, an organizer whose one test for all things was success, triumphed at Sawston School over a humane master.

The comparison of Manning and Newman culminates in the description of Manning's jealous frustration of Newman's plans for an Oratory at Oxford. "It was the meeting of the eagle and the dove ; there was a hovering, a swoop, and then the quick beak and the relentless talons did their work." In this metaphor and in the subsequent description of Newman in desolate tears at Littlemore, the passion which is a part of the biography—the detestation of Manning and the love of Newman—comes for a moment to the surface.

After his triumph over Newman, which displays to the full the dangerous poverty and egotism of his character, the pretentiousness of Manning's worldly pomp is set free to parade by itself. The sketch given in the introduction of the influential Prince of the Church is filled out in detail. The goal of the biography has been reached ; and the concluding pages are given a further air of finality by the slow, relentless, funereal prose which describes Manning, surrounded by his ecclesiastical subordinates, awaiting death in the robes and biretta of his office. In the final paragraph questions similar to those posed in the introduction are turned over again. Why did Manning make such an impression ? " . . . yet, after all, the impression was more acute than lasting. The Cardinal's memory is a dim thing to-day." And as Strachey takes us down into the vaults of Westminster Cathedral to show us the dust-encrusted Hat of the dead Cardinal, he certainly intends us to remember Newman's *Apologia*, which he has previously praised as a classic, and to ask whether, after all, Manning triumphed over Newman.

Only Manning and Dr. Arnold are as badly treated in *Eminent Victorians* as the popular conception of the book would have it. Florence Nightingale emerges as a much more admirable woman than the sentimental notion of the Lady with the Lamp, which Strachey explicitly sets out to destroy, envisions. And though General Gordon's superstitious fanaticism is displayed, Strachey admires Gordon's courage and his lack of self-interest. Strachey can find nothing admirable, however, either in Manning or in Arnold. As " Cardinal Manning " is an analysis of intense and unscrupulous worldly ambition, " Dr. Arnold " is a study of pomposity. In Strachey's view, which accords with Bloomsbury ethics, these two traits are the worst that humanity may indulge.

But pomposity requires an altogether different treatment

from ambition ; and the biography of Arnold differs widely from that of Manning. Manning's character, established so early in the biography, moves relentlessly through the surrounding circumstances to its goal. His biography has the air of tragedy. Not in such a grand manner as this is pomposity to be treated ; or, if the manner is grand, it must also be humorously ironic. Consequently, " Dr. Arnold " is a comedy. The central figure, in all its transcendent self-importance, is studied within the static environment of Rugby School. Arnold is not to struggle with the world ; he is above the world—even if the world which he rules is only a world of schoolboys. The difference in the presentment is emphasized even in the physical description of the two men —Manning, tall, gaunt, and ascetic ; Arnold, clothed in the flowing robes of a Doctor of Divinity, energetic, earnest, sturdy, his legs a bit too short, a slightly puzzled look upon his face.

The characteristics of Arnold which Strachey emphasizes are his priggishness, his overweening self-confidence, and his righteous preoccupation with Christian morality. These traits are all embodied in a simile which is played upon so successfully that it becomes the centre of the biography : Arnold as Jehovah and his pupils as the Chosen People. " He would treat the boys at Rugby as Jehovah had treated the Chosen People : he would found a theocracy ; and there should be judges in Israel." For this purpose he developed the prefectorial system.

> This was the means by which Dr. Arnold hoped to turn Rugby into " a place of really Christian education ". The boys were to work out their own salvation, like the human race. He himself, involved in awful grandeur, ruled remotely, through his chosen instruments, from an inaccessible heaven. Remotely—and yet with an omnipresent force. As the Israelite of old knew that his almighty Lawgiver might at any moment thunder to him from the whirlwind, or appear before his very eyes, the visible embodiment of power or wrath, so the Rugby schoolboy walked in a holy dread of some sudden manifestation of the sweeping gown, the majestic tone, the piercing glance, of Dr. Arnold. Amòng the lower forms of the school his appearances were rare and transitory, and upon these young children " the chief impression ", we are told, " was of extreme fear ".

The simile reaches its climax of mock-heroic irony when Arnold is described preaching to his schoolboys in chapel, which, Strachey says, was the centre of the school :

> It was not until then, as all who had known him agreed, it was not until one had heard and seen him in the pulpit, that one could fully realize what it was to be face to face with Dr. Arnold. The whole character of the man—so we are assured—stood at last revealed. His congregation sat in fixed attention (with the exception of the younger boys, whose thoughts occasionally wandered), while he propounded the general principles both of his own conduct and that of the Almighty, or indicated the bearing of the incidents of Jewish history in the sixth century B.C. upon the conduct of English schoolboys in 1830.

The same ironic tone is continued as Strachey deals with Arnold's relations with the world outside Rugby School. The long list of Arnold's published works, which might be impressive in another context, is comic in the biography—as comic as Arnold's industry in begetting children. Arnold's Jehovah-like attributes were not forgotten amidst his family or in his writing. He did indeed play with his children. " Yet, we are told, ' the sense of his authority as a father was never lost in his playfulness as a companion '." He was as self-confident in his articles, his pamphlets, and his books as he was in the pulpit at his School. " He had planned a great work on Church and State, in which he intended to lay bare the causes and to point out the remedies of the evils which afflicted society." Yet he was, Strachey makes it clear, rather muddle-headed ; a trait which corresponded to the puzzled look upon his face. He justified his views, from his belief in the value of flogging boys to his opinions on the correct interpretation of the Scriptures, by profound, but vague, references to " general principles ". His stern preoccupation with morals kept him from appreciating beauty in nature and in art ; his pomposity and his lack of humour prevented him from seeing himself. " He advocated the restoration of the Order of Deacons, which, he observed, had long been ' quoad the reality, dead ' ; for he believed that ' some plan of this sort might be the small end of the wedge, by which Antichrist might hereafter be burst asunder like the Dragon of Bel's temple'." With passages of this sort at hand in Arnold's writings, it is often unnecessary for Strachey to exercise his own wit to produce comedy.

Near the end of the biography, however, the comic tone is abandoned. Even in this, the briefest and lightest of Strachey's biographies, the artistic value of death is exploited to the full. Arnold died suddenly, in the prime of life, from angina pectoris ; but to draw his biography to a close, Strachey wants a more intense feeling of approaching death than the mere description of such an end would be likely to give. He creates it by quoting from Arnold's meditations on death, some of which, fortunately for Strachey, Arnold set down in his diary during the last days of his life, and which give a fitting close to the career of the Jehovah of Rugby. And Arnold's death itself, though sudden in life, is described in detail in the short biography.

This transition to a solemn tone enables Strachey to discuss in a straightforward manner in the concluding paragraphs of the biography some of the serious considerations which he has hinted at previously and which underlie the wit and ridicule of his portrait of Arnold. Arnold, he says, effected a change throughout the Public Schools of England. But what kind of change did he effect? He might have introduced a new and more humane curriculum. "The moment was ripe ; there was a general desire for educational changes ; and Dr. Arnold's great reputation could hardly have been resisted." But he adhered with all his strength to the teaching of Greek and Latin grammar. What he did introduce was the prefectorial system —" the system which hands over the life of a school to an oligarchy of a dozen youths of seventeen "—with the result, unforeseen by Arnold, that he " has proved to be the founder of the worship of athletics and the worship of good form ". An earlier passage in the biography, which comments upon Arnold's aim to produce Englishmen and Christians at Rugby, is recalled :

> . . . how was he to achieve his end? Was he to improve the character of his pupils by gradually spreading round them an atmosphere of cultivation and intelligence? By bringing them into close and friendly contact with civilized men,

> and even, perhaps, with civilized women? By introducing into the life of his school all that he could of the humane, enlightened, and progressive elements in the life of the community? On the whole, he thought not.

Bloomsbury is brought to mind. And we remember St. John Hirst, of Virginia Woolf's *The Voyage Out*, with his faith in affection and in education. In no other biography in *Eminent Victorians* does Strachey step forth so clearly to comment.

"Florence Nightingale" might have been as successful in treating heroism as "Dr. Arnold" is successful in treating pomposity. It might have been, but it is not. The first two of the five chapters in the biography, however, which deal with Miss Nightingale's early and persistent devotion to nursing, and with her achievement at Scutari, are completely successful. And the woman who emerges is a true heroine, a heroine in whom we believe entirely, in spite of her seemingly superhuman accomplishment and her almost inhuman strength and devotion to her work. Strachey does not treat her gently. He knows that no hero or heroine will respond to gentle treatment; he shows us the grim determination that was the necessary complement to her success; he gives us no sentimental picture of the Lady with the Lamp. But Strachey's admiration is complete, and his writing rings with the grandeur of the true epic. The horrors of the hospital at Scutari are described in all their intensity; similes from Dante's "Inferno" and from the first Books of *Paradise Lost* are borrowed to describe the sufferings which Miss Nightingale alleviated and the vastness of the task which she undertook. "Miss Nightingale came, and she, at any rate, in that inferno, did not abandon hope."

> Her good will could not be denied, and her capacity could not be disregarded. With consummate tact, with all the gentleness of supreme strength, she managed at last to impose her personality upon the susceptible, overwrought, discouraged, and helpless group of men in authority who surrounded her. She stood firm; she was a rock in the angry ocean; with her alone was safety, comfort, life. And so it was that hope dawned at Scutari. The reign of chaos and old night began to dwindle; order came upon the scene, and common sense, and forethought, and decision, radiating out from the little room

> off the great gallery in the Barrack Hospital where, day and night, the Lady Superintendent was at her task.

The praise could not be higher, and it does not cease here. The Lady with the Lamp is, after all, not forgotten, though it is a real, not a sentimental, vision that we are given of her :

> Wherever, in those vast wards, suffering was at its worst, and the need for help was greatest, there, as if by magic, was Miss Nightingale. Her superhuman equanimity would, at the moment of some ghastly operation, nerve the victim to endure and almost to hope. Her sympathy would assuage the pangs of dying and bring back to those still living something of the forgotten charm of life. Over and over again her untiring efforts rescued those whom the surgeons had abandoned as beyond the possibility of cure. Her mere presence brought with it a strange influence. A passionate idolatry spread among the men : they kissed her shadow as it passed.

But, Strachey emphasizes, in a passage in which there are further reminiscences of *Paradise Lost*, it was not with soft compassion that Miss Nightingale saved the situation at Scutari :

> It was not by gentle sweetness and womanly self-abnegation that she had brought order out of chaos in the Scutari hospitals, that, from her own resources, she had clothed the British Army, that she had spread her dominion over the serried and reluctant powers of the official world ; it was by strict method, by stern discipline, by rigid attention to detail, by ceaseless labour, by the fixed determination of an indomitable will. Beneath her cool and calm demeanour lurked fierce and passionate fires.

Nor did she believe that she had done enough, Strachey tells us, when she had restored order at Scutari and reduced the death rate there from 42 per cent. to twenty-two per 1,000. She inspected the hospitals in the Crimea itself. And she tried to provide for the mental and spiritual, as well as the physical, needs of the men at Scutari.

> She set up and furnished reading-rooms and recreation-rooms. She started classes and lectures. Officers were

> amazed to see her treating their men as if they were human beings, and assured her that she would only end by " spoiling the brutes ". But that was not Miss Nightingale's opinion, and she was justified.

Strachey's sympathy with her is whole-hearted. And although later in the biography he finds the acerbity in her character somewhat distasteful, we feel in these first two chapters that he agrees with her and understands why, as she struggled with inept officials, " The intolerable futility of mankind obsessed her like a nightmare, and she gnashed her teeth against it." These chapters are wonderfully successful in freeing Florence Nightingale from the unreal sentiment that has surrounded her, and in setting the real woman before us in all her heroism. They promise a short biography which will be more than worthy to stand beside " Dr. Arnold " to complement that excellent study of pomposity.

But as Strachey begins to record the rest of Florence Nightingale's life, a certain dislocation is at once evident in the biography. The tone has changed ; the treatment is almost diffuse ; the last three chapters swell incongruously and destroy the symmetry that was apparent in the first two. Even the focus of the biography has altered. In the first two chapters it was fastened securely upon Florence Nightingale. Now it moves about, and is fixed at moments upon Sidney Herbert, or upon Arthur Clough, or upon Lord Panmure. With the introduction of Lord Panmure, early in the third chapter, a new tone (new, at least, to this biography) enters Strachey's voice. He recounts the amusing relations between Lord Panmure and General Simpson, a man who serves no purpose in the biography—except to give Strachey an excuse to introduce two amusing anecdotes which would be suitable enough in an after-dinner conversation, but which are extraneous in " Florence Nightingale ". And to compare with the Miltonic similes in the preceding chapter is the comic metaphor which describes Lord Panmure as " the Bison ", giving way at the War Office, " with infinite reluctance, step by step ", before Miss Nightingale. The slow negotiations by means of which Miss Nightingale and Sidney Herbert reformed the Army Medical Department are followed in some detail. The speed of the earlier chapters is lost ; their force is dissipated. As an inevitable result of the altered focus and of the change in tone and tempo, Strachey's style suffers. The metaphor of the tigress and the stag, used to illustrate the relations between Miss Nightingale and Sidney Herbert, fails as clearly as the metaphor in " Manning " of the eagle and the dove succeeds.

> If Lord Panmure was a bison, Sidney Herbert, no doubt, was a stag—a comely, gallant creature springing through the forest ; but the forest is a dangerous place. One has the image of those wide eyes fascinated suddenly by something feline, something strong ; there is a pause ; and then the tigress has her claws in the quivering haunches ; and then— !

The direct description of Sidney Herbert is equally bad.

> He was a man upon whom the good fairies seemed to have showered, as he lay in his cradle, all their most enviable goods. Well born, handsome, rich, the master of Wilton—one of those great country-houses, clothed with the glamour of a historic past, which are the peculiar glory of England—he possessed, besides all these advantages, so charming, so lively, so gentle a disposition that no one who had once come near him could ever be his enemy.

In the midst of this desert of *clichés* one comes with relief upon Wilton and all that it recalls of Sir Philip Sidney, the Countess of Pembroke, the *Arcadia*—and then the parenthesis, with the tone of an inferior guidebook, dissipates the beautiful mirage. This weakness follows the strength of the first two chapters ; and the sentimentality which is just beneath the surface in these quotations becomes clearly evident in the description of Sidney Herbert's death, which was caused, Strachey believes, by overwork in Miss Nightingale's service. Sentimentality is highly dangerous in any work of art. In a work which begins as an epic it is fatal.

The last three chapters of " Florence Nightingale " combine the method used in " Manning " with the method of " Arnold " —methods which, apart from their dissonance with the method of the first two chapters, are not amenable to combination with one another. On the one hand, Strachey investigates how the exceedingly strong character of Florence Nightingale combined with, or rather, dominated, the weaker characters of Sidney Herbert and Arthur Clough to attain her end of far-reaching reforms in the Army Medical Department. On the other, he indulges in humorous anecdote and comic irony. In pursuing what may be called the " Manning " method, he displays sympathy and tenderness for Sidney Herbert, as he did for Newman. But there was no sentimentality, no excess of sentiment, in the treatment of Newman, because Strachey convinced us that Newman, defeated by Manning's unscrupulous egotism, deserved sympathy : he showed us the tragedy of evil triumphing over good. But there is no question of evil triumphing over Sidney Herbert. Miss Nightingale's motives cannot be questioned, nor does Strachey question them. She worked to save lives and to defeat disease, not only in the British Army, but throughout the world. During most of the fifty years and more that she lived after the Crimean War, Strachey says, though she was bed-ridden as a result of her immense exertions at Scutari, " all the energy and all the devotion of her extraordinary nature were working at their highest pitch. What she accomplished in those years of unknown labour could, indeed, hardly have been more glorious than her Crimean triumphs ; but it was certainly more important." The heroic theme is not entirely forgotten in these last chapters, but it becomes hopelessly lost in the strange mixture that surrounds it, until, at last, it is discarded altogether. Near the end of the biography Miss Nightingale's *Suggestions for Thought to the Searchers after Truth among the Artisans of England* is considered.

> She had long noticed—with regret—the growing tendency towards free-thinking among artisans. With regret, but not altogether with surprise : the current teaching of Christianity was sadly to seek ; nay, Christianity itself was not without its defects. She would rectify these errors. She would correct the mistakes of the Churches ; she would point out just where Christianity was wrong ; and she would explain to the artisans what the facts of the case really were.

" As one turns over these singular pages," Strachey continues, " one has the impression that Miss Nightingale has got the Almighty too into her clutches, and that, if He is not careful, she will kill Him with overwork." The method is the same as the method of "Arnold": the epic has become the mock-epic.

It is melancholy to see what might have been a biography of surpassing excellence spoiled in this way. One feels that Strachey has fallen victim to certain characteristics of his own art, and that at the same time, paradoxical as it may seem, he has become diffuse through a failure to select strictly enough. His penchant for analysis of the interaction of character and circumstance causes him to shift his focus from Florence Nightingale to lesser figures in order to demonstrate how Miss Nightingale accomplished the vast tasks to which she set herself after her experience at Scutari. His love of anecdote and of irony causes a similar uncertainty of purpose, which results, for example, in the irrelevant account of the relations between Lord Panmure and General Simpson, and in the discussion of Miss Nightingale's excursions into theology. In a short biography, especially a biography which begins as this one does, this discussion might much better be left out. Miss Nightingale's book directed to the Artisans of England has little bearing upon either her career or her character. Her mind, as Strachey himself says, was an empirical mind, which was lost when it began to consider large theological problems. This is the only point made in the discussion of her theology which is relevant to the biography. What is needed after the first two economical, heroic, and convincing chapters, one feels, is an equally brief and cogent account of Florence Nightingale's life subsequent to the Crimean episode. There is enough grand achievement in that life to have enabled Strachey to maintain the heroic theme to the end of his biography, and to have created (if the term is not too great a contradiction) a small epic, as perfect in its symmetry as the mock-epic biography of "Arnold".

In "The End of General Gordon", however, Strachey is in complete command of his art. He has a tragedy to describe —Gordon's fate at Khartoum—and he does not swerve from his purpose for a moment. His practice of defining the limits and of indicating the goal of his biography in advance is used, even more surely than in "Manning", to lend an air of certainty to his work. His skill in illustrating the interaction of character and circumstance is subservient to his art in this biography, and helps to make Gordon's tragedy appear inevitable. His interest in the religious superstitions of the Victorians serves the same purpose, since Gordon's superstition was fatalistic. In " Gordon " Strachey's irony is sublimed, as it were, into the irony of Fate. Like the Greek tragedians, he turns the popular knowledge of his story to great advantage : we watch with horror as Gordon moves of necessity to a tragic fate which we can see awaiting him, but of which he himself does not know. And although there are touches of comedy within the tragedy, such as Lord Hartington's comic slowness, they but serve, like the tantalizing comedy of Shakespeare's clown who brings Cleopatra the asp, to add to the intensity of the drama. Wit is almost entirely replaced by humour in this biography ; and humour, with its wider and kindlier vision, is the more suitable of the two to tragedy. The biography as a whole conforms to Roger Fry's notion of tragedy, at which we have previously looked. The essential of great tragedy, Fry has said, is " the vivid sense of the inevitability " of its unfolding. In this respect " Gordon " recalls Forster's *Where Angels Fear to Tread*, though the sense of inevitability is much more vivid in Strachey's biography than in Forster's novel.

It is significant that Strachey chooses men and women of action for his subjects in *Eminent Victorians*. Their inner lives, in which Strachey is interested, express themselves in action ; so Strachey is able to construct biographies which are very much like dramas. It appears paradoxical, at first, that the biography of General Gordon, the most active of these Victorians, should, stylistically, be the least like a drama of any of the four biographies in the book. The style is narrative, bare, historical. The paragraphs are long ; the biography is not divided into chapters. We are not shown numerous scenes, as we are in " Manning ", " Florence Nightingale ", and " Arnold "—Manning at the General Council at Rome ; Newman in tears at Littlemore ; Miss Nightingale at Scutari ; Arnold in his pulpit. The development of the biography is descriptive, not scenic. Strachey even forgoes those metaphors of his which, in a sentence, conjure a situation or a relationship into a scene. Nor does he make the characters in this biography parade before us, even momentarily, in the guise of animals. The events which he has to portray are too numerous and too intricately related to one another to permit any flourishes of this sort if " the vivid sense of the inevitability " of the tragedy is to be retained. He allows the bareness of his style to be relieved only when the actual events of the narrative demand a richer treatment—when he is describing the state of the Mahdi at El Obeid, or the intricacies of Gladstone's character. But when the complicated mechanism of the tragedy is finally set clearly before us, the narrative swells into the great dramatic scene depicting Gordon's last days at Khartoum.

We are, however, shown one scene as the biography begins : Gordon, with his tripping step and his large blue, boyish eyes, walking in Palestine with his Bible in his hand to determine some questions of Biblical history. The time is just before his fatal expedition to the Sudan ; and this simple scene, which introduces the blue eyes and illustrates Gordon's religious preoccupation, complements, with its peacefulness, the great sanguinary scene which ends the biography. Between these two scenes, then, lies the whole biography ; and Strachey looks forward at once to the ultimate scene, sketching, as he does so, the shadow of the tragedy :

> . . . it was not in peace and rest, but in ruin and horror, that [Gordon] reached his end.
>
> The circumstances of that tragic history, so famous, so bitterly debated, so often and so controversially described, remain full of suggestion for the curious examiner of the past. There emerges from those obscure, unhappy records an interest, not merely political and historical, but human and dramatic. One catches a vision of strange characters, moved by mysterious impulses, interacting in queer complication, and hurrying at last—so it almost seems—like creatures in a puppet show to a predestined catastrophe. The characters, too, have a charm of their own : they are curiously English. What other nation on the face of the earth could have produced Mr. Gladstone and Sir Evelyn Baring and Lord Hartington and General Gordon ? . . . As for the *mise-en-scène*, it is per-

fectly appropriate. But first let us glance at the earlier adventures of the hero of the piece.

As Gordon's active, agitated life, so crowded with incident, is reviewed, a pattern begins to emerge. It was a life full of violent action, on the one hand, and religious meditation, on the other. Gordon's religious fanaticism, his fatalism, his acceptance of the Bible as an absolute and irrefutable law, are underlined. Fits of depression, we are told, alternated in Gordon's life with moments of exaltation, when he believed that he had been predestined by Divine Wisdom for a great end. And Strachey gives us a clearer sense of Gordon's periods of fanatical, spiritual intoxication by describing, as well, his addiction to brandy. Gordon's fatalism is used to emphasize the unpredictability of his nature and the violent agitations of his career :

> Fatalism is always apt to be a double-edged philosophy ; for while, on the one hand, it reveals the minutest occurrences as the immutable result of a rigid chain of infinitely predestined causes, on the other, it invests the wildest incoherences of conduct or of circumstance with the sanctity of eternal law. And Gordon's fatalism was no exception. The same doctrine that led him to dally with omens, to search for prophetic texts, and to append, in brackets, the apotropaic initials D.V. after every statement in his letters implying futurity, led him also to envisage his moods and his desires, his passing reckless whims and his deep unconscious instincts, as the mysterious manifestations of the indwelling God.

Gordon's fatalism swells from his personal belief into the outer circumstances of his life, and into the very structure of the biography. In the first great adventure of his career, he leads an army against another religious fanatic, the Chinese Tien Wang, the Celestial King. Both Gordon and the Tien Wang, Strachey tells us, turned to religion after experiencing an attack of illness—so Strachey points the similarity between them. In Gordon's last adventure he again faces a man who is his spiritual peer, the fanatical Mahdi, the divine Mohammedan guide. And his death at the hands of the Mahdi's followers depends upon so many interlinked contingencies

—the alteration of any one of which, so it seems, would have changed the outcome—that it appears to be predestined.

After Gordon's character and the events of his life preceding his last adventure have been set before us, the other components of his tragedy are economically and skilfully assembled. An account is given of the Mahdi's rise, of the weakness of the Egyptian Pashas, of British intervention in Egypt, of Colonel Hicks's disastrous expedition against the Mahdi, of political intrigue and popular sentiment in England—it is small wonder that Strachey is obliged to restrict himself to bare narration throughout most of " Gordon "! Then, after the stage is set and Gordon has reached Khartoum, the three Englishmen, Gladstone, Sir Evelyn Baring, and Lord Hartington, whose characters, besides Gordon's, are to combine with circumstances to produce the final catastrophe, are described and analysed. We are shown their inner lives, the springs of their actions, in three fine portraits in which Strachey probes into the minds of his subjects. Gladstone is described as ambiguous : crafty and agile, yet naïve in some respects, a lover of liberty and a hater of bloodshed, a formidable antagonist—impossible to see to the depths of his strange, involved mind ! Sir Evelyn Baring is a cool diplomat, " cautious, measured, unimpeachably correct ", with a " steely colourlessness, and a steely pliability, and a steely strength ", sure to do nothing that might injure his reputation. " It would be difficult to think of a man more completely the antithesis of Gordon." Lord Hartington is exceedingly slow and ponderous, but he has a persistent conscience, and he is powerful. The characteristics of these men, and of Gordon, are now set in action to produce the catastrophe at Khartoum. Gordon's sense of a divine mission, his feeling of spiritual exaltation, causes him to see himself as the saviour and liberator of the Sudan, though he has been sent, ostensibly, to evacuate Khartoum. He has a " mystic feeling " that he can trust his old enemy, the slave-hunter Zobier. As a result, he champions Zobier as his successor in the Sudan and so disturbs public opinion in England that British troops are withdrawn from the eastern Sudan, and the Mahdi is enabled to surround Khartoum. So the inevitable tragedy proceeds. Gladstone, incensed by Gordon's failure to withdraw, sympathetic to the nationalist rising of the Sudanese, and averse to bloodshed, does not intend to send Gordon relief. Sir Evelyn Baring is aware of the great danger that Gordon is in ; but, having warned his government, he is too cautious to insist that action be taken. Finally, Lord Hartington, who believes himself responsible for Gordon's appointment, begins to be troubled by his conscience ; and the whole tragedy, woven of so many fatal contingencies, hangs tantalizingly at last upon one thing : Lord Hartington's slowness, his ponderous efforts, which succeed just too late, in forcing the agile, ambiguous Gladstone to send relief to Khartoum.

> The fate of General Gordon, so intricately interwoven with such a mass of complicated circumstance—with the policies of England and of Egypt, with the fanaticism of the Mahdi, with the irreproachability of Sir Evelyn Baring, with Mr. Gladstone's mysterious passions—was finally determined by the fact that Lord Hartington was slow. If he had been even a very little quicker—if he had been quicker by two days . . . but it could not be.

And Strachey drives home his slowness by ticking off monotonously, on his fingers, as it were, the " seven stages . . . in the history of Lord Hartington's influence upon the fate of General Gordon ".

It might be supposed after this that little more could be done, or is needful, to achieve a vivid sense of inevitability ; but Strachey uses other touches to contribute to the certainty of his tragedy. As Gordon left England on his fatal mission, he arranged that each member of Gladstone's Cabinet should receive a copy of Dr. Samuel Clarke's *Scripture Promises.* The title, when seen in relation to Gordon's beliefs and to subsequent events, is significant. In the last scene, as we watch Gordon, sunk in a final fit of melancholy, awaiting a doom which we know to be certain, the " strange premonitory rhapsodies " which he committed to his Journal are reviewed.

> The splendid hawks that swooped about the palace reminded him of a text in the Bible : " The eye that mocketh at his father and despiseth to obey his mother, the ravens

of the valley shall pick it out, and the young eagles shall eat it". "I often wonder", he wrote, "whether they are destined to pick my eyes, for I fear I was not the best of sons."

The Mahdi, from his first introduction in the biography, is shown to be Gordon's peer.

> The tall, broad-shouldered, majestic man, with the dark face and black beard and great eyes—who could doubt that he was the embodiment of a superhuman power? Fascination dwelt in every movement, every glance. The eyes, painted with antimony, flashed extraordinary fires; the exquisite smile revealed, beneath the vigorous lips, white upper teeth with a V-shaped space between them—the certain sign of fortune.

In Gordon's Journal, Strachey says, "it is easy to perceive, under his scornful jocularities, the traces of an uneasy respect" for the Mahdi.

> When he heard that the Mahdi was approaching in person, it seemed to be the fulfilment of a destiny, for he had "always felt we were doomed to come face to face". What would be the end of it all? "It is, of course, on the cards," he noted, "that Khartoum is taken under the nose of the Expeditionary Force, which will be *just too late*".

After Gordon's melancholy is ended in the exhilaration of violent death, his head is taken to the Mahdi.

> . . . at last the two fanatics had indeed met face to face. The Mahdi ordered the head to be fixed between the branches of a tree in the public highway, and all who passed threw stones at it. The hawks of the desert swept and circled about it—those very hawks which the blue eyes had so often watched.

Within these sentences, with their grim, Biblical quality, there is a tenderness of a kind that can be achieved, perhaps, only in great tragedy, the same tenderness that we find mixed with horror in some of Shakespeare's greatest passages—as Lear holds the dead Cordelia in his arms, or Cleopatra applies the asp to her breast. Our first meeting with the blue eyes, in the peaceful scene in Palestine, is irresistibly recalled, and is strangely linked, by its prophetic, Biblical flavour, to this terrible scene. Gordon's fate seems now indeed to have been predestined : his mystic fatalism appears to have been wholly justified. This is the final, tragic irony of the biography.

The style of *Eminent Victorians* varies from the incisive, occasionally caustic, style of " Manning " to the suave, suggestive, ironic style of " Arnold " ; from the grandeur of the description of Florence Nightingale's work at Scutari to the bare narration of the events leading up to General Gordon's catastrophe. However, with the exception of the latter part of " Florence Nightingale ", all four biographies move swiftly. The leisurely pace of " Madame du Deffand " is discarded ; and it is evident, moreover, that Strachey is no longer as sure of his audience as he was in that essay. *Eminent Victorians* assumes only at rare intervals the tone of the after-dinner story.

There is flippant wit at times—the house of the Holy Family at Loreto is described as having been " transported thither, in three hops, from Palestine " ; and at times there is quiet, devastating commentary, such as the remark that follows the summary of one of Keble's most extravagant Scholastic flights —" Writings of this kind could not fail of their effect ". Strachey often finds unconscious humour in the writings of the Victorians, as, for example, in Arnold's suggestion, already quoted, that the restoration of the Order of Deacons might lead to the bursting asunder of Antichrist, or in " the celebrated " Mr. Bowdler's comment on a published sermon of Manning's : " ' The sermon ', said Mr. Bowdler, in a book which he devoted to the subject, ' was bad enough, but the appendix was abominable ' ". Again, Strachey may bring a remark into a focus which its originator did not see : " ' No one could know him even a little ', said [a friend of Dr. Arnold's], ' and not be struck by his absolute wrestling with evil, so that like St. Paul he seemed to be battling with the wicked one, and yet with a feeling of God's help on his side ' ". Or he may ask a question with disarming innocence : " [After the succession of Pope Leo XIII] things were not as they had once been : Monsignor Talbot was [in an insane asylum] at Passy, and Pio Nono was—where ? " One is reminded of Strachey's comment on a sentence of Hume's that he admired :

" The sentence is characteristic of Hume's writing at its best, where the pungency of the sense varies in direct proportion with the mildness of the expression ". Strachey's opponents have found his skill at poking fun at venerable Victorians particularly infuriating ; but wit and humour are surely legitimate weapons for the critic of manners and of morals to employ. And Strachey's humour saves his satire from Swiftean bitterness. " Manning " is the most caustic of his biographies, and even " Manning " has the saving grace of humour.

Another quality of Strachey's style helps to keep his satire from becoming bitter : its familiarity. The style of *Eminent Victorians*, even at its most incisive, retains, with the help of its *clichés*, its questions, its easy additions, and its quiet comments, something of the tone of the humble, contemporary observer who watches the actions of the great. Thus, it takes the reader, as it were, into the midst of the events with which Strachey deals. " And yet—why was it ? " Strachey asks after describing Arnold's appearance. " Was it in the lines of the mouth or the frown on the forehead ?—it was hard to say, but it was unmistakable—there was a slightly puzzled look upon the face of Dr. Arnold." The dangers of this style are obvious. At its worst its produces flat, exhausted sentences of the kind that, as we have seen, describe Sidney Herbert. At its best it creates a vivid sense of reality. On the whole, the *cliché*, which Strachey uses so often, serves him well in *Eminent Victorians*. It helps him to keep his passion in check, to be pleasant, to be quiet, to be clear. And Strachey seeks clarity above all else in style. At the same time, he is aware that life is highly complicated. So, in presenting even the most concise view—and, of course, Strachey is usually concise—he qualifies, and defines, and piles adjective upon adjective. Usually his use of adjectives enables him to be precise, to analyse carefully, to give us a sense of the intricacy of things. Sometimes it becomes merely an unfortunate habit, as in this sentence, which comments, in " Gordon ", upon a letter of Rimbaud's :

> So wrote the amazing poet of the *Saison d'Enfer* amid those futile turmoils of petty commerce, in which, with an inex-

plicable deliberation, he had forgotten the enchantments of an unparalleled adolescence, forgotten the fogs of London and the streets of Brussels, forgotten Paris, forgotten the subtleties and the frenzies of inspiration, forgotten the agonized embraces of Verlaine.

Strachey's style in *Eminent Victorians* is by no means simple, in spite of its familiarity, its clarity, and its use of *clichés*. Nor is it flat, except in a few sentences in which Strachey falls victim to the dangers of his own devices. Each of the four biographies is rich in vivid images and fine prose rhythms, which do not exist independently, as mere ornament, but express Strachey's meaning concisely and beautifully. Gladstone's ambiguity, for instance, is emphasized in a resounding phrase : " there was something in his nature which invited —which demanded—*the clashing reactions of passionate extremes*." The impossibility of probing to the depths of his mind is illustrated by means of imagery :

> His very egoism was simple-minded : through all the labyrinth of his passions there ran a single thread. But the centre of the labyrinth ? Ah ! the thread might lead there, through those wandering mazes, at last. Only, with the last corner turned, and the last step taken, the explorer might find that he was looking down into the gulf of a crater. The flame shot out on every side, scorching and brilliant ; but in the midst there was a darkness.

Mental and physical phenomena are closely associated in Strachey's writing, and, as in this instance, the latter is often used to express the former. Manning's character, as we have seen, is displayed by the careful selection of incidents from his early career. When Manning began to intrigue with Monsignor Talbot, he went up a " little winding staircase in the Vatican ". The flowing robes of a Doctor of Divinity which Arnold wore are woven into the simile that compares Arnold to Jehovah and expresses Arnold's inner traits. This technique reaches its height, of course, in Strachey's metaphors ; and it is often in his metaphors that his feelings and his point of view are most clearly expressed. His best metaphors, moreover, demonstrate that the ease and precision of his style is not attained carelessly, or without effort, but by polishing and adjusting until ideas and emotions are conveyed in words that fit them precisely and express them beautifully.

No two works from the pen of the same biographer could differ more profoundly, one would at first imagine, than *Eminent Victorians* and *Queen Victoria*. For the increased scale of the second book is controlled by a broader, a more measured, and a kindlier point of view ; Strachey's irony plays with a more lambent touch and illuminates less starkly, though no less surely ; the Rouveyre caricature has become a Rembrandt portrait ; and the artist finds unlovely neither the weaknesses nor the strength of his sitter. Moreover, though there are clashes and struggles of will within the biography, the presentment as a whole, to change the comparison, is not dramatic. The pace is slower than the pace of drama, the exploration is more complete, the depth greater. But here the differences between *Queen Victoria* and *Eminent Victorians* end. The penetration which served Strachey in his short biographies, the determination to seize the essential spiritual life of his subject and to present that, is no less evident in this long biography. And the ability to select and to present concisely is perhaps even more necessary to Strachey in *Queen Victoria* than ever before, faced as he is with the longest and perhaps the best documented reign in English history.

Strachey's determination to present Victoria's inner history guides his selection of material throughout the biography ; his skill in displaying the inner life both directly and through, as it were, its outer habiliments, helps him to fuse his material into an organic whole. His *point d'appui* amidst the sea of information that surrounds him is Victoria's Journal, which is peculiarly useful to Strachey, because, as he says, when Victoria writes, " What is within pours forth in an immediate, spontaneous rush ", reminding one " of a turned-on tap ". Victoria's inner life is reconstructed, or rather, presented, largely from her Journal and her letters. And the Journal itself gives Strachey the perspective necessary to his biography : he keeps his own point of view, but he selects events and characters, and determines the extent of their presentment, according to their importance, as witnessed in the Journal, in Victoria's life. Many of the events of Victoria's reign, such as her coronation, or the opening of the Great Exhibition of 1851—events which were of the highest emotional importance to the Queen—are described by means of selection and summary from her Journal, so that we see them through the eyes of Victoria herself. The Bedchamber crisis and the Hastings scandal, both of which affected Victoria intimately, are described in detail ; but the Schleswig-Holstein embroilment, though it caused serious differences to arise between Albert and Victoria, on the one hand, and Palmerston, on the other, is described only as " the dreadful Schleswig-Holstein question —the most complex in the whole diplomatic history of Europe ". The political niceties of this question were entirely beyond Victoria's comprehension, and so they are excluded from the biography. Again, the problem of the extent of the royal prerogative in the British Constitution is discussed so thoroughly and so often that it becomes a theme. Victoria's attitude towards this prerogative illustrates the imperious, egotistical traits in her character ; and the extension of the power of the sovereign through Albert's efforts, together with the steady decline of that power after Albert's death, demonstrates Victoria's inability to conceive or execute long-range plans designed to effect her will. But, though this matter is discussed so fully, the great and far-reaching reforms that Gladstone accomplished are little more than mentioned. They appear in the biography as they appeared to Victoria—as the tiresome, annoying activities of that " dreadful man ". Yet Strachey's own point of view is apparent. It is evidenced, sometimes by a comment, placed so carefully in the biography that it is a part of the description of a character or an event ; sometimes by the irony, always gentle in this book, of the presentment. Strachey's point of view informs the whole biography, though the biography is shaped by the inner life of its central character.

The characters of the biography, like the events, are grouped about Victoria. They come and go as they affect, or cease to affect, her. Lord Melbourne and Disraeli, who exercised such strong personal influences upon her, are described at length. Palmerston, who for years pitted his strength against Victoria and Albert's, to become reconciled with them at last during the Crimean War, has as important a rôle. But Peel, whose influence upon the Queen was slight, is correspondingly unimportant in the biography ; and Gladstone, to whom Victoria was unsympathetic and unyieldingly correct, is scarcely more important than Victoria's beloved Scottish servant, John Brown. Here the restraint and self-discipline which Strachey exercises in this book is particularly apparent ; for Strachey is personally fascinated by Gladstone, as both his comparatively long analysis of him in " Gordon " and his brief references to him in *Queen Victoria* testify. But art demands that Gladstone shall have an important rôle in " Gordon ", an unimportant rôle in *Queen Victoria* ; and Strachey obeys.

These characters—Lord Melbourne, Palmerston, John Brown, Gladstone, Disraeli—each came into Victoria's life, early or late, to exercise a passing influence, and then to withdraw for ever. They are described in portraits, long or short, as the case may be, which depict them as they were when Victoria knew them. And in these portraits the experience which Strachey had gained from his essays and from *Eminent Victorians* is especially evident. He presents economically and forcefully ; he selects just what is needed to bring his characters alive, to harmonize them with the other elements in his book, and, above all, to establish clearly their relationship with Victoria. We see Peel as he appeared to Victoria while he urged her to appoint Tory Ladies to wait upon her —uncomfortable, shy, unable in his embarrassment to stand still : " It was in vain that Peel pleaded and argued ; in vain that he spoke, growing every moment more pompous and uneasy, of the constitution, and Queens Regnant, and the public interest ; in vain that he danced his pathetic minuet." Lord Melbourne, an old man when Victoria knew him, an eighteenth-century aristocrat living on in the unsympathetic climate of the new age, is described as an " autumn rose ". And the metaphor is used to illustrate his relation with the young Queen : ". . . cherished by the favour of a sovereign and warmed by the adoration of a girl, the autumn rose, in those autumn months of 1839, came to a wondrous blooming. The petals expanded, beautifully, for the last time." Palmerston's boldness, his verve and apparent recklessness in the conduct of foreign affairs (which so disturbed Albert), and his pride, his imperious dislike of interference from anybody, whatever their station (which so infuriated Victoria), are emphasized in his portrait. " He was very bold ; and nothing gave him more exhilaration than to steer the ship of state in a high wind, on a rough sea, with every stitch of canvas on her that she would carry." While Disraeli's infinite capacity for romantic flattery, which caused Victoria to become so strongly attached to him and made her " intent upon showing her supernal power ", is the significant feature in his portrait.

But there are other characters—the Duchess of Kent, Lehzen, Leopold, Stockmar—who are treated differently. They are not presented in such clear, precise portraits as they enter the biography—in fact, they are in the biography, and a part of Victoria's life, from the beginning, or almost from the beginning. Throughout most of the book they stay quietly, sometimes mysteriously, in the background. The Duchess of Kent, segregated by her daughter's displeasure, remains in her own apartments in the Palace ; Leopold is King of the Belgians ; Lehzen dominates the household of the young Queen, but is finally forced into retirement in Germany by Stockmar and Albert ; Stockmar remains quietly in the Palace for years to guide the destiny of Albert, but he too retires at last to Germany. Yet, though the impact of these characters, both upon Victoria and upon the reader, is less vivid than the impact of Lord Melbourne, or Palmerston, or Disraeli, their influence is more pervasive and more enduring. And there is an uncanny likeness among them, in spite of widely different personal characteristics, in spite of differences of rank, which relates them inextricably, not only to one another, but also to Victoria and to Albert. The Duchess of Kent and Lehzen, with their incessant vigilance and their rigid regimen of education, moulded Victoria in childhood and early youth. Leopold continued her education with instructions, given in his letters, upon the proper conduct of a sovereign ; and he sent Stockmar to her to give her personal guidance. Albert was educated with the same German thoroughness as Victoria. His preliminary examination before being confirmed corresponds to Victoria's examination, on her mother's request, by the Bishops of London and Lincoln. Shortly before Albert's marriage to Victoria, which was forwarded by Leopold, uncle to them both, Albert too came under the tutelage of Leopold and Stockmar; and it was Stockmar's persistent pressure, his advice, his injunction never to relax, which, Strachey says, pushed Albert forward to a dominant position, not only in the royal household, but also in European politics. The careers of Leopold and Albert, Strachey points out, were curiously analogous. They both rose, thanks largely to Stockmar's good management, from the obscurity of Saxe-Coburg to high and powerful positions. Indeed, had the Princess Charlotte, Leopold's first wife and heir-apparent to the British throne, not chanced to die in youth, Leopold would have occupied the very position that Albert filled. From this circumstance grows the theme of fate, which is present in this biography too, and is intimately associated with Albert and with the mysterious German figures who lurk behind him and behind Victoria. It attends the unexpected combination of events that brought Victoria to the throne; and it is emphasized, as these events are recounted, by the Duke of Kent's superstition, and by the prophecies, so strangely fulfilled, which were made to him by a gipsy. It reaches its height in Albert's death, which is preceded by omens—the carriage accident in which Albert narrowly avoided being killed; Albert's melancholy; his remark to Victoria that he would give up life at once if he had a serious illness—and is prefigured in the same year by the death of the Duchess of Kent. Indeed, the whole of Albert's life in England, as Strachey describes it, has a fatalistic quality. When he crossed the Channel for his wedding, he was violently sea-sick, and only his sense of duty enabled him to force himself above deck to bow to the people at Dover. "It was a curious omen: his whole life in England was foreshadowed as he landed on English ground." And his triumph in the highest sphere of British politics, "big with fateful consequences, was itself the outcome of a series of complicated circumstances which had been gathering to a climax for years". His triumph was due, of course, mainly to Stockmar; and Stockmar, who moves "as if in accordance with some pre-ordained destiny", appears in this biography to be the very instrument of Fate. He is even, perhaps, the unwitting cause of Albert's early death; for his lesson of "never relax", which Albert learned so thoroughly, was partly responsible, Strachey infers, for Albert's melancholy and his willingness to relinquish life. May not Stockmar have accomplished too much? Strachey asks. Stockmar's teaching, at any rate, was in accordance with the precepts of Lehzen, of Leopold, and of the Duchess of Kent. The whole weight of the terrible system of education which these four devised fell squarely, thanks to the care of Victoria and Albert, upon the young Prince of Wales, and failed completely because it left him not a moment in which to enjoy himself. The emphasis Strachey gives to this failure is his final comment upon the methods which caused it, a comment which is given added weight by the fact that on Albert's visit to Cambridge to admonish his son—who, given some freedom at last, was beginning to enjoy himself too much—his melancholy was increased and he suffered the "fatal chill" which led to his death.

The arrangement of Stockmar, Lehzen, Leopold, and the Duchess of Kent behind Victoria and Albert, and behind the figures of Lord Melbourne, Palmerston, and Disraeli (who stand so brilliantly illuminated in the public eye and in the eye of their sovereign), is of paramount importance to the success of *Queen Victoria*. These four characters, moving and brooding in the background, give depth and mystery, unity and force, to the book; at times they seem to envelop the whole biography; at other times they seem—in keeping with the formative influence they exercised—to exist only as traits of Victoria's and Albert's minds, to be expressed in their iron wills, in their immense capacities for work, in their ponderous, thorough, methodical habits. Yet, one wonders whether this consummate disposition of characters was achieved by design or by accident. Certainly, Strachey seems to regret that he has not more information to give us about Stockmar and Lehzen, at least. But if we knew more about these characters, if we could see them more clearly, Stockmar would not embody, as he does, the strange potency of Fate ; nor would Lehzen, the grim and silent preceptress, personify the terrors of an inhuman system of education.

Strachey's treatment of Albert combines to some extent the methods used in dealing with the other German figures and in depicting Victoria's Prime Ministers. Albert is introduced early in the book, on his first visit to England ; but we see him only briefly, as he appears in Victoria's Journal. After he has become engaged to Victoria, however, he is described in a portrait that is the most detailed in the biography. For a time he is at the very centre of the biography. Then, he dies ; but his influence endures almost to the end of the book. He is the only character who succeeded in dominating Victoria so completely that he bent her will to his ; and he succeeded, not only because of his determination and his superior intellectual attainments, but because she loved him even to idolatry. So Albert dominates the middle chapters of the biography, as he dominated the middle years of Victoria's life. The focus of the biography has not changed when it is fastened upon Albert and his affairs : Strachey is continuing to follow Victoria's inner life : and her mind was fixed upon Albert. In order to convince us of this fact, and to give his biography unity, Strachey must show us Victoria's passionate, absolute love for her husband. And Victoria's love—her ecstasy at its first awakening ; her delirious joy when the Great Exhibition, Albert's achievement, was opened ; her complete happiness at Balmoral ; and her overwhelming sorrow when Albert died—permeates this part of the book and surrounds Albert.*

* It is curious that Sir Arthur Quiller-Couch should take Strachey to task for probing " Victoria's weakest, most feminine point—her adoration of her husband " in order to produce comedy. It is difficult to agree either that Strachey " contrive[s] it so that Victoria's adoration appears extraordinarily funny ", or that he considers her love of Albert a weak point in her character. One wonders whether *Eminent Victorians* had not made Quiller-Couch unduly suspicious of Strachey. E. M. Forster's view is different : " [Strachey] is always moved by constant affection, and the Queen's love for the Prince Consort, and for his memory, makes [*Queen Victoria*] glow and preserves it from frigidity." (Quiller-Couch, *Studies in Literature*, pp. 289–93 ; Forster, *Two Cheers for Democracy*, p. 289.)

Victoria's happiness is even more apparent because it is set in such sharp contrast to Albert's melancholy, which Strachey also emphasizes. Strachey sees some unconscious humour in Albert's life—in his intense seriousness ; his insistence upon method ; his simple, but sometimes overweening, self-confidence—but he pities Albert's unhappy, lonely destiny. He was " so full of energy and stress and torment, so mysterious and so unhappy, and so fallible, and so very human " ; and no one in England, not even his wife, understood him.

Victoria herself moves steadily and irresistibly through the characters and events that surround her. Her personality grows and asserts itself as the biography develops, yet it is always recognizably the same. In childhood there is the same determination, the same truthfulness, the same piety that characterize the old Queen. The blue eyes flashed brighter lights in youth than in old age, but they are the same eyes. The little mouth, which is mentioned on several occasions throughout the biography, smiles at Albert or crushes the unfortunate person who has sinned against palace etiquette, but it is the same mouth, and expresses the same will. " Through the girl's immaturity ", Strachey says of the young Queen, " the vigorous predestined traits of the woman were pushing themselves into existence with eager velocity, with delicious force." And throughout the biography he gives us the sense of a Queen whose popularity ebbs and flows and ebbs and flows again among her people, who is now influenced by the sceptical urbanity of the dying eighteenth century, and now is " the living apex " of the Victorian Age, who is now young, now middle-aged, now old, but always essentially the same : vigorous, sincere, simple, proud, iron-willed. The " underlying element " of her nature, Strachey says, " was a peculiar sincerity ". It is this that he admires.

> Her truthfulness, her single-mindedness, the vividness of her emotions and her unrestrained expression of them, were the varied forms which this central characteristic assumed. It was her sincerity which gave her at once her impressiveness, her charm, and her absurdity. She moved through life with the imposing certitude of one to whom concealment was impossible—either towards her surroundings or towards herself.

> There she was, all of her—the Queen of England, complete and obvious ; the world might take her or leave her ; she had nothing more to show, or to explain, or to modify ; and, with her peerless carriage, she swept along her path. And not only was concealment out of the question ; reticence, reserve, even dignity itself, as it sometimes seemed, might be very well dispensed with.

It would be impossible for an Apostle and a member of Bloomsbury not to be captivated by such traits as these ; and Strachey, though he is well aware of the limitations and absurdities of Victoria's character, is captivated from the first.

Towards the end of the book, Victoria's association with Disraeli is described, and recalls unmistakably her friendship, so many years before, with Lord Melbourne. " The autumn rose ", it will be remembered, under the influence of the young Queen, " came to a wondrous blooming " in the autumn months of 1839. " The petals expanded, beautifully, for the last time." Disraeli, in his turn, aroused Victoria from her prolonged mourning for Albert. " After the long gloom of her bereavement, after the chill of the Gladstonian discipline," Strachey says, " she expanded to the rays of Disraeli's devotion like a flower in the sun." The rest of the book, too, as it moves forward to Victoria's death, is full of recollections of the past, which give us a sense of finality, of completeness, and of unity. The Duchess of Kent's and Lehzen's religious teaching is recalled. For a moment, as palace etiquette is discussed, we glimpse again Lord Melbourne sitting stiff upon the sofa ; and we are told, as we were told in the chapter describing the young Queen, that " Sometimes the solemnity of the evening was diversified by a concert, an opera, or even a play." The much more distant past is brought to mind, as well, and we remember, for instance, the Duke of Kent's fussy supervision of his household. The old Queen displayed " dreadful displeasure ", Strachey says, if any one was unpunctual : " At such moments there seemed nothing surprising in her having been the daughter of a martinet." These recollections are thickest, of course, in the description of Victoria's amazing collection of statues and statuettes, of Albert's clothes, of every conceivable memento, carefully ordered and docketed to preserve, as it were, the entire past. And this collection illustrates Victoria's iron will, her determination, as it seemed, to defeat time itself.

The simple comparison of life to a day is also used, persistently and with great effect, to give unity to the biography. The first years of Victoria's reign, during which " youth and happiness gild[ed] every hour " are radiant with " the magical illumination of . . . dawn ". The autumnal years are golden with the long serene splendour of evening. Victoria's happiness has returned once more ; and her popularity, which had declined during her mourning, is at its height. Her character, which we have seen influenced in turn by the Duchess of Kent, by Lehzen, by Lord Melbourne, by Disraeli, and, above all, by Albert, finally emerges to stand completely alone. Even Albert slowly receded, Strachey says. " Her egotism proclaimed its rights. Her age increased still further the surrounding deference ; and her force of character, emerging at length in all its plenitude, imposed itself absolutely upon its environment by the conscious effort of an imperious will." Strachey emphasizes the emergence with a formal Character of the Johnsonian type, and with the picture of the Queen-Empress at the Jubilee of 1897. It seems as one reads the biography that it was particularly fortunate for Strachey that this splendour should have been darkened, in the last years of Victoria's reign, by the South African War. But the measure of a biographer is the use that he makes of his materials ; and certainly Strachey draws his book to an effective close. " The evening had been golden," Strachey says ; " but, after all, the day was to close in cloud and tempest." In this last chapter the strength of the Queen's will is again emphasized. We still feel, even as her body fails, the force of her character. And in the famous paragraph in which the old Queen, as she dies, is made young again, the whole method of the biography is summed up. The past is recalled, the biography is reviewed, the continuity of Victoria's life is pointed—and it is all done by an imaginative reconstruction of the Queen's inner life.

It is Strachey's skill in reconstructing the inner life which makes his characters move in *Queen Victoria* with the force of characters in a novel.* The method is vivid, convincing, and economical. It often shows us more in a few lines than paragraphs of description could convey. We are shown Victoria's wilfulness as a child—" From time to time, she would fly into a violent passion, stamp her little foot, and set everyone at defiance ; whatever they might say, she would not learn her letters—no, she *would not* "; and her childhood affections, and reservations of affection—" Warm-hearted, responsive, she loved her dear Lehzen, and she loved her dear Feodora, and her dear Victoire, and her dear Madame de Späth. And her dear Mamma . . . of course, she loved her too ; it was her duty ; and yet—she could not tell why it was —she was always happier when she was staying with her Uncle Leopold at Claremont." The young Queen's annoyance during the Bedchamber crisis is demonstrated—" It was outrageous of the Tories to want to deprive her of her ladies." We are taken into Leopold's mind as he attempts to control English foreign policy through his influence upon Victoria—" What were royal marriages for, if they did not enable sovereigns, in spite of the hindrances of constitutions, to control foreign politics ? For the highest purposes, of course ; that was understood " ; into Victoria's mind as she rebuffs his attempt—" Life flowed on . . . with its accustomed smoothness—though, of course, the smoothness was occasionally disturbed. For one thing, there was the distressing behaviour of Uncle Leopold " ; and into Palmerston's mind to see his opinion of Albert—" Powerful, experienced, and supremely self-confident, he naturally paid very little attention to Albert. Why should he ? The Prince was interested in foreign affairs ? Very well, then ; let the Prince pay attention to *him*. . . . Not that he wanted the Prince's attention—far from it : so far as he could see, Albert was merely a young foreigner, who suffered from having no vices, and whose only claim to distinction was that he had happened to marry the Queen of England." Imagination, tact, and discretion are all required if this method is to be pursued successfully. Strachey keeps his eye on his sources as he reconstructs the inner lives of his characters ; often, indeed, their thoughts are presented directly

* Cf. pp. 78–9 ; Forster, *Two Cheers for Democracy*, p. 288.

from their letters or Journals; and it is only in the last paragraph of *Queen Victoria* that Strachey, after giving due warning, allows his imagination to range above the solid facts. He has to check imagination with careful research; but his imagination must always be active enough to so enliven the material which research provides that that material will seem real. We must be made to believe that Victoria did indeed think and act as her Journal and contemporary accounts testify. It is a difficult balance to maintain, but Strachey maintains it throughout *Queen Victoria.* His skill in quoting his subjects' writings to reveal their thoughts, and in putting himself in their positions to think as they would think, is here at its height.

The style of *Queen Victoria* is less incisive than the style of *Eminent Victorians.* The pace is slower; the irony more gentle; wit is often softened to humour; and the writing is richer. Albert's melancholy is beautifully described:

> Victoria idolized him; but it was understanding that he craved for, not idolatry; and how much did Victoria, filled to the brim though she was with him, understand him? How much does the bucket understand the well? He was lonely. He went to his organ and improvised with learned modulations until the sounds, swelling and subsiding through elaborate cadences, brought some solace to his heart.

In this last sentence the organ may almost be heard through the prose. Strachey's style, in keeping with the dramatic, psychological methods he uses in portraying his characters, varies, as Sir Max Beerbohm has pointed out, from character to character. It is subdued, or mildly tinged with malicious irony, when Albert is dealt with; brisk when Palmerston is on the scene; mellow when Lord Melbourne is present. The simplicity and vigour of the style of Victoria's Journal is often echoed when she is described. And the description of Disraeli's flattery contains the richest and most complicated writing in the book:

> The strain of charlatanism, which had unconsciously captivated [Victoria] in Napoleon III, exercised the same enchanting effect in the case of Disraeli. Like a dram-drinker, whose ordinary life is passed in dull sobriety, her unsophisticated

> intelligence gulped down his rococo allurements with peculiar zest. She became intoxicated, entranced. Believing all that he told her of herself, she completely regained the self-confidence which had been slipping away from her throughout the dark period that followed Albert's death. She swelled with a new elation, while he, conjuring up before her wonderful Oriental visions, dazzled her eyes with an imperial grandeur of which she had only dimly dreamed.

Queen Victoria recalls a part of the Victorian Age that Strachey, as he views it in retrospect, regrets losing. He sees a vision, surrounded though it is by " prim solidity ", towards which he feels pleasantly affectionate. As a result, his style is mellow, and somewhat nostalgic.

Strachey's last book, *Elizabeth and Essex*, curiously resembles the two early essays at which we have looked, " Mademoiselle de Lespinasse " and " Madame du Deffand ". In each of these three compositions, Strachey portrays a love story which, because of peculiarities of circumstance and character, ends tragically. Moreover, the Elizabethan Age is used as *décor* in *Elizabeth and Essex*, as the eighteenth century was used in " Madame du Deffand "; and the narration of Elizabeth and Essex's story is almost as straightforward and unornamented as " Mademoiselle de Lespinasse ". But Strachey does not seize this story as passionately as he seized the tragic history of Mademoiselle de Lespinasse, nor does he set it forth with the ease and brilliance of " Madame du Deffand ". *Elizabeth and Essex*, of course, is much longer than either of these two essays. Had Strachey shortened it, it might have been more fortunate than it is.

In writing *Elizabeth and Essex* Strachey was confronted with a problem the very opposite of the problem which faced him as he wrote *Queen Victoria*. In the latter book he dealt with a Queen whose innermost thoughts were expressed and preserved in her Journal, and whose reign is recorded in a horde of contemporary books and documents. He was, if anything, embarrassed by the immense quantity of information at his disposal. But Elizabeth's inner life was a mystery even to those who were nearest to her ; she left behind her no record of her thoughts ; and there are gaps in our knowledge of her reign. It would be impossible to write a biography of her comparable to *Queen Victoria* : circumstances, as well, perhaps, as inclination, dictated that Strachey should concern himself with the romantic, tragic history of Elizabeth and Essex. And of course, this history is not to be treated in the same way as the life of Queen Victoria. *Queen Victoria*, in which Strachey reconstructs the inner lives of his characters so carefully and so satisfactorily, resembles a novel—a novel, moreover, in which the story, the arrangement of events according to their sequence in time, is unimportant. Certainly, Victoria's life is followed from childhood to old age ; but as we look back at the book after reading it, we see, not a sequence of events, but a group of solidly realized characters, arranged with consummate art around the central figure of the Queen. In *Elizabeth and Essex*, on the contrary, the story dominates the book.

But Strachey wishes to do much more in *Elizabeth and Essex* than merely tell a story. As he portrayed the end of General Gordon in an inevitable, tragic, drama ; as he set forth the history of Madame du Deffand on a miniature stage with the eighteenth century as scenery ; so he wishes to present the story of Elizabeth and Essex in a form akin to the dramatic. He casts his narration of their story in the loose, episodic form of the Elizabethan drama, which is suitable, not only to the age with which he deals, but to the nature and development of the story itself, in which the scene shifts rapidly from Hampton Court to the Escurial, from the Azores to Ireland, from the splendours of Elizabeth's court to the horrors of Tyburn, and from the fervid, puerile plotting at Essex House to the cold competence of Cecil at Whitehall. In the first two chapters of the book, he creates the stage, as it were, upon which the action that is to follow will take place. At the same time, he introduces the two central characters. He describes Essex briefly ; he analyses Elizabeth in a long portrait ; and he sets both of them in the Elizabethan Age—as he set Madame du Deffand in the eighteenth century—telling us exactly what aspects of their Age each represents. The style of these two chapters is completely different from the style of the rest of the book. It is rich, involved, scattered thick with metaphors, and crowded with baroque ornament. The rest of the book is written in a style at least as bare as the style of " Gordon ". The first two chapters provide, in effect, the *décor* for the drama which follows.

The plan of *Elizabeth and Essex* appears to be excellent; but Strachey's execution of his plan is only partially successful. He is fascinated by the Elizabethan Age, but he is unable to come to grips with it as he came to grips with the eighteenth century and with the Victorian Age. There is an incompleteness of vision and an uneasiness of presentation in *Elizabeth and Essex* that is evident in no other work of Strachey's. For the first time, he talks about his art. He speaks of the virtual impossibility of reaching " an imaginative comprehension of those beings of three centuries ago ", and of the difficulty of chronicling " the ambiguous age ". At the beginning of the portrait of Bacon, this sentence occurs : " Francis Bacon has been described more than once with the crude vigour of antithesis ; but in truth such methods are singularly inappropriate to his most unusual case." Bacon " never dreamt ", Strachey remarks a page or two later, " how intensely human he was. And so his tragedy was bitterly ironical, and a deep pathos invests his story ". It is only necessary to transpose these sentences to any portrait in *Queen Victoria* to realize how much more intense Strachey's inspiration is in that book. *Queen Victoria* is informed throughout by Strachey's intellect and emotion ; but in *Elizabeth and Essex* there are, as it were, empty spaces, where his imagination has failed, and where, instead of creating, he talks to us.

As a result, the shape of the book, admirable as it is in its conception, seems to be imposed externally, and fits loosely enough in places. It is not always filled out with suitable material. Parts of the book do succeed, however, and give us a glimpse of what the whole would have been had Strachey been able to realize his vision completely. The account of Elizabeth and Essex's first quarrel, which is actualized by the description of Sir Walter Raleigh standing on guard outside the Queen's chamber, while the quarrel, in which Raleigh's name is involved, rages on the other side of the door, holds the reader's interest and attention throughout. The success of this scene is due, not only to the vivid picture of Raleigh, but also to the speed with which it moves and to its position in the book. It is the third chapter, and the bare style in which it is written contrasts strikingly with the involved ornament of the first two chapters. This chapter, depicting one event, is followed by a chapter which moves as swiftly, but which is crowded with action—the raid on Corunna and Lisbon; Essex's duel with Charles Blount; his financial negotiations with the Queen; his marriage; and his expedition to France in command of a force sent to assist Henry IV. Then, the pace slows somewhat as an account is given of Essex's long negotiations with the Queen on Francis Bacon's behalf, an account which is enlivened with some of the most vivid incident in the book—with Lady Bacon's letters, with the dialogue between the Queen and her carter, and with the words that passed between Essex and Sir Robert Cecil as they rattled one day in a coach through the city. And the account of these petty domestic and court squabbles, upon which hangs only Francis Bacon's position in the world, is succeeded at once by the superb, economical account of the intrigue, in which Essex was equally involved, that brought about Dr. Lopez's hideous execution. But much of the rest of the book is dull and uninteresting. One finds oneself wishing as one reads that Strachey would bring his story to its climax more quickly, and that he would not inflict upon us such a detailed, historical account of events. A description of Essex's military fortunes and misfortunes is no doubt needed to elucidate the course of his relationship with the Queen and to display his character—to illustrate his chivalry, his impetuosity, his quick pride, and his obstinate temper which was fatally combined with an inability to decide upon and follow a settled course of action. But could not the description be more brief than it is? Need we follow quite so closely the expedition to Cadiz, the Islands Voyage, Essex's Irish campaign, the fluctuations of his ineffectual intrigue to gain control of the Court by force? Indeed, the accounts of these episodes seem to fall between two stools: they are not vivid enough to arouse our interest in the episodes themselves, but they are detailed enough to distract our attention from the subject of the book—the relationship between Elizabeth and Essex. For Strachey does not accomplish his purpose in these episodes : he illustrates to his own satisfaction neither Essex's character nor the Queen's suspicion of Essex. At the height of Essex's career, after he has returned from Cadiz, Strachey pauses to discuss his character at length ; and later in the book, after the Queen has boxed Essex's ears, Strachey analyses their quarrel. He tells us what he has been unable to show us.

The main cause of Strachey's difficulties in *Elizabeth and Essex* is a lack of intimate information. He is unable to take us into the minds of his characters as often as he does in *Queen Victoria* ; and when he does reveal their inner lives, the revelation is not always convincing. His account of Elizabeth's sexual maladjustment, for instance, is pertinent enough—if it is correct. But Strachey has to base his account largely upon conjecture ; and his information is not complete enough to convince us that Elizabeth's maladjustment, even if it existed and was as Strachey believes, contributed towards Essex's fate. As a result, the sexual discussion in the book, which is introduced in the portrait of Elizabeth, degenerates into a theme which does not affect the action, and which may cause the reader to suspect that Strachey's interpretation of this aspect of Elizabeth's life is subjective. Again, Strachey's use of omens, which was so successful in " Gordon " because it was closely related to Gordon's inner life, fails almost completely in *Elizabeth and Essex*, because the omens, such as the tempest which Essex's expedition against Ferrol encountered, and which Strachey describes as " only an ominous prologue " to Essex's final disaster, are nearly all mere devices—Senecan devices of the sort that Shakespeare employs in *Richard III* and *Julius Caesar*, which may be effective enough on the stage, but which are ineffective in Strachey's book because they are unassociated with the inner lives of his characters. Sources which reveal the minds and the thoughts of his subjects are indeed indispensable to Strachey's type of biography. He must make constant reference to facts as he imaginatively reconstructs the inner lives of his characters ; for biography must satisfy the demands both of art and of life. It is no accident that Francis Bacon, in spite of weaknesses in his portrait, is the most convincing figure in the book, nor that Bacon's warning and advice to Essex is the most successful of the omens that Strachey uses. Bacon's character is revealed to posterity more fully, thanks especially to his essays and his letters, than the character of any other of the Elizabethans with whom Strachey is concerned, and the letter in which he warned Essex may still be read, and is quoted from by Strachey. There can be little doubt that *Elizabeth and Essex* would have been more successful if Strachey had had more material of this sort at his disposal. As it is, the central characters are dim; and their story is not told quickly enough to hold our interest, as our interest is held, for example, by "Mademoiselle de Lespinasse". We are moved more by the fate of Dr. Lopez, whose story is told briefly and economically, than by the execution of Essex—the climax of the book—or by the miserable death of Elizabeth.

The uncertainty which characterizes the book is evident in its style. In the first two chapters Strachey is intent upon achieving a rich and striking effect. At moments he succeeds. A splendid sentence describing Elizabeth's childhood combines magnificently the image of Henry VIII dressed in yellow, the sound of trumpets, and the religious recollections which the word Mass arouses:

> It is possible that she could just remember the day when, to celebrate the death of Katherine of Aragon, her father, dressed from top to toe in yellow, save for one white plume in his bonnet, led her to Mass in a triumph of trumpets, and then, taking her in his arms, showed her to one after another of his courtiers, in high delight.

The description of Essex's estate of Chartley, though less inspired, is as rich:

> . . . the ancient house, with its carved timber, its embattled top, its windows enriched with the arms and devices of Devereux and Ferrers, stood romantically in the midst of the vast chase, through which the red deer and the fallow deer, the badger and the wild boar, ranged at will.

But there are numerous sentences in these chapters in which Strachey strains too hard. The description of Elizabeth's manner of speaking in public succeeds, but we are uncomfortably aware of the effort that has gone into its composition :

> . . . the splendid sentences, following one another in a steady volubility, proclaimed the curious workings of her intellect with enthralling force ; while the woman's inward passion vibrated magically through the loud high uncompromising utterance and the perfect rhythms of her speech.

While Strachey's comment on the Spanish ambassadors' opinion of Elizabeth is barely intelligible : " They had come into contact with those forces in the Queen's mind which proved, incidentally, fatal to themselves, and brought her, in the end, her enormous triumph." And his attempt to foreshadow the history of Elizabeth and Essex surpasses the limits of effective hyperbole :

> When two consciousnesses come to a certain nearness the impetus of their interactions, growing ever intenser and intenser, leads on to an unescapable climax. The crescendo must rise to its topmost note ; and only then is the preordained solution of the theme made manifest.

In these sentences Strachey's style appears to have gone to seed.

But in the rest of the book he makes a determined attempt to prune his style. There is virtually no rich description ; the narration is bare ; metaphors are sparingly used ; and, most surprising of all, there is very little irony or humour. A decided advantage to the structure of *Elizabeth and Essex* might have been gained by this Spartan discipline if it had increased the speed of the book ; but only occasionally, in the description of Elizabeth and Essex's first quarrel, for instance, does it have this effect. In spite of the restraint that Strachey exercises—perhaps, indeed, owing to this restraint—the pace of his sentences is unincreased. He moves gingerly, not boldly ; the narration is as bare as the narration of " Gordon ", but the sentences are far less incisive. And, uninformed as they are by critical wit, they are often flat and uninteresting : " The state of affairs in Ireland was not quite so bad as it might have been "—" The Government had never been in any danger, though there must have been some anxious moments in Whitehall "—" On the whole, it seemed certain that with a little good management the prosecution would be able to blacken the conduct and character of the prisoners in a way which would carry conviction—in every sense of the word."

Strachey appears to be consciously experimenting in *Elizabeth and Essex* ; and deliberate experiment seldom results in a highly successful work of art. It may, however, give the artist valuable experience ; and Strachey's art might conceivably have taken a new departure if he had lived to write another book after *Elizabeth and Essex.* One wonders whether this would have been the case, or whether the restraint of the style of most of the chapters of *Elizabeth and Essex* merely indicates that Strachey had listened too carefully to the cries of his critics.

CHAPTER VII

VIRGINIA WOOLF

VIRGINIA WOOLF began her literary career with the same care and deliberation that characterizes her novels, and she pursued it with unhurried industry. She began to review books before she left Hyde Park Gate, and for many years she wrote reviews for *The Times Literary Supplement*. As we have seen, she started her first novel, *The Voyage Out*, in the early years of Bloomsbury—and took seven years to finish it. " The time she gave to her writing ", Duncan Grant, her Bloomsbury neighbour, tells us, " was two and a half hours in the morning. She never, I believe, wrote for more than this time, but very regularly ".* *The Voyage Out* was published in 1915, and was followed four years later by *Night and Day*. A significant little volume of short stories, *Monday or Tuesday*, appeared in 1921, and proved to be a prelude to *Jacob's Room*, which came out a year later, and made use of the highly individualistic techniques of the short stories. This book announced that a novelist of great originality was beginning to find her strength ; and in the next decade, the greatest of Virginia Woolf's career, the promise of *Jacob's Room* was fulfilled. Three novels, *Mrs. Dalloway* (1925), *To the Lighthouse* (1927), and *The Waves* (1931), which deserve to stand in the front rank of English fiction were published ; as well as a fourth novel, *Orlando* (1928), a light, beautifully written, *tour de force* ; a Feminist book, *A Room of One's Own* (1929)—which contains, incidentally, a discussion of the novelist's art ; and the two volumes of essays entitled *The Common Reader* (1925 and 1932). In the decade that followed this burst of creative energy, Virginia Woolf wrote two more novels, *The Years* (1937) and *Between the Acts* (which was completed shortly before her death in 1941), another Feminist book, *Three Guineas* (1938),

* *Horizon*, III, June 1941, 403.

and two biographies—one light, one serious—*Flush* (1933) and *Roger Fry* (1940). Meanwhile, she continued to write essays and short stories, which have appeared in four volumes, published posthumously. Her career, unhurried as it was, was prolific, and demonstrates a single-minded devotion to her art, which was made possible, of course, by her financial independence, and was strengthened by her association with Bloomsbury.

We have already seen something of Virginia Woolf's first two novels, *The Voyage Out* and *Night and Day*. They are more subjective than her other novels, in the sense that they are less clearly set apart from their author. They interpret, or at least examine, Virginia Woolf's own experiences, they consider problems that she herself faced ; and although all Virginia Woolf's novels do this, *The Voyage Out* and *Night and Day* do so more intimately than the rest. The novelist is in the midst of the life she is seeking to understand ; she is living it even as she writes ; she is not looking back, as in *To the Lighthouse*, upon experiences that are past ; and though she tries to give life the order of art, she is unable to stand far enough from it to fashion it in a form that is completely autonomous. As one reads these novels; one enters the mind of the shy young woman who had recently come to Bloomsbury from Hyde Park Gate, to whom, though her sensations were so intense, her new existence was only slowly " coming alive ", who was so aware of both the beauty and the horror of life, who had to adjust the old life to the new, who had to co-ordinate the dreamy contemplative self who loved solitude with the eager active self who craved company, who had to seek a balance between intellect and emotion, who had to range in order a chaos of sensations so vivid as to be sometimes overpowering—who had, in short, to find her own personality before she could attempt to see life clearly. Rachel Vinrace and Terence Hewet, of *The Voyage Out*, who become engaged to one another and achieve complete and perfect union for a moment as Rachel dies,* express the two different sides of their creator's character—her dreamy, sensitive, intuitive

* p. 149.

femininity ; and her active, companionable, intellectual masculinity. These two selves are merged in Katharine Hilbery of *Night and Day*, the tall young woman who strides through the streets of London absorbed in her own thoughts, who returns to a literary home in Chelsea to pour tea for her mother's guests, who dreams, and studies mathematics in secret, who loves to gaze at the stars until her being seems to spill over their " ledges . . . for ever and ever indefinitely through space ". Katharine's cousin Henry, a musician, makes almost the same remark about Katharine that Duncan Grant has made about Virginia Stephen : " Katharine hasn't found herself yet. Life isn't altogether real to her yet. . . ." * " Circumstances had long forced [Katharine]," Virginia Woolf tells us, " as they force most women in the flower of youth, to consider, painfully and minutely, all that part of life which is conspicuously without order ; she had had to consider moods and wishes, degrees of liking or disliking, and their effect upon the destiny of people dear to her ; she had been forced to deny herself any contemplation of that other part of life where thought constructs a destiny which is independent of human beings." And Rachel Vinrace, as she sails away from England and from her aunts' home in Richmond, is excited by the idea that she can now be " a person on [her] own account " : " The vision of her own personality, of herself as a real everlasting thing, different from anything else, unmergeable, like the sea or the wind, flashed into Rachel's mind, and she became profoundly excited at the thought of living ".

It is exactly because Virginia Woolf found divisions and forceful contradictions both in her outer life and within herself, and because her senses brought her evidence which, though chaotic, seemed vividly to testify to a greater reality outside herself, that she is so concerned with " Mrs. Brown " (who personifies the inner life), with her own personality and its relation to the rest of reality, and with the attempt to find a pattern in her experience of life. In *The Voyage Out* and in *Night and Day* she is occupied primarily with discovering her own personality—this is the greatest achievement of the

* Cf. pp. 7 and 131–2.

heroine of each novel—but she is not forgetful of the other problems with which she was faced. She considers the active life—represented in *The Voyage Out* by Richard Dalloway and in *Night and Day* by Mary Datchet—and decides that it is necessary, but inferior. As we have seen, love, friendship, and art (especially love, in these first two novels) help her characters to see the pattern in life and to glimpse reality. And indeed, these were the things—the friendship she found in Bloomsbury, the love of her husband, and her devotion to art—which assisted her in life. It was not only the security she found in marriage and the care and consideration she received from her husband that warded off for years the recurrence of her mental illness. It was also her ability to fix her experience in a work of art, to order in a novel the chaos of sensations and thoughts and emotions that crowded upon her, to orient herself, by means of art, with the rest of reality. Her comment upon the rôle of art in Roger Fry's life is pertinent in this respect. Fry's belief that the " special spiritual activity of art ", though open at times to influences from life, is in the main self-contained, " helps to explain ", Virginia Woolf says, " how it was that he survived the war, and not with his intellect merely ". She describes a visit to his crowded, untidy studio in 1918. It was cold and littered. " But on the table, protected by its placard [' Do not touch '], was the still life—those symbols of detachment, those tokens of a spiritual reality immune from destruction, the immortal apples, the eternal eggs." *The Voyage Out* and *Night and Day*, as their titles indicate, are quests for reality ; and the same is true of the rest of Virginia Woolf's novels.

She is too concerned with life in these first two novels to have much time for experimentation with art. She is, moreover, learning her art ; and she is content, on the whole, with the tools of the Edwardian novelists. Some of her own techniques, however, may be seen in embryo. The characters of *The Voyage Out* are isolated, first on a ship and then in the remote South American seaside village of Santa Marina, as the characters of *To the Lighthouse* are isolated on an island. The characters of *Night and Day* move about the West End of London in somewhat the same way as the characters of *Mrs.*

Dalloway. Scenes and circumstances are not always directly described by the author in *The Voyage Out*. We discover incidents and situations as we read on ; we are taken, as it were, on the voyage with the characters of the book. (This method is less used, however, in *Night and Day*, in which there is a good deal of direct, " realistic " description.) Similarly, Rachel Vinrace and Katharine Hilbery, the heroines of the two books, are not revealed to us directly ; we discover them gradually, as we read the book ; they are, so to speak, created from the inside out, rather than from the outside in. It is possible that this method, so important in Virginia Woolf's novels, was discovered almost unwittingly ; for it is a natural, even a naïve, way of treating characters who are closely identified with their author. Rachel and Katharine, as it were, are Virginia Woolf, moving through her novel. The thoughts and emotions of these two characters are revealed to us ; and we enter the minds of other characters as well. There are occasional passages in each of these novels which might be found, so far as technique is concerned, in *Jacob's Room* or in *Mrs. Dalloway*. Helen Ambrose leans over the Thames, weeping, as she is about to leave London, while her husband paces on the Embankment behind her, declaiming Macaulay's poetry :

> . . . the only thing she had seen, since she stood there, was a circular iridescent patch slowly floating past with a straw in the middle of it. The straw and the patch swam again and again behind the tremulous medium of a great welling tear, and the tear rose and fell and dropped into the river. Then there struck close upon her ears—
>
> Lars Porsena of Clusium
> By the nine Gods he swore—
>
> and then more faintly, as if the speaker had passed her on his walk—
>
> That the Great House of Tarquin
> Should suffer wrong no more.
>
> Yes, she knew she must go back to all that, but at present she must weep.

Or Katharine Hilbery walks from Bond Street towards the

Strand, reflecting, as she goes, upon her fiancé, William Rodney:

> There were many more things in him than she had guessed until emotion brought them forth—strength, affection, sympathy. And she thought of him and looked at the faces passing, and thought how much alike they were, and how distant, nobody feeling anything as she felt nothing, and distance, she thought, lay inevitably between the closest, and their intimacy was the worst pretence of all. For, "Oh dear," she thought, looking into a tobacconist's window, "I don't care for any of them, and I don't care for William, and people say this is the thing that matters most, and I can't see what they mean by it".

But perhaps the clearest indication in these books of what is to follow is the extensive, detailed examination of moods, of thoughts, and of emotions—an examination, in fact, of the experience of living. The strongest impression that is obtained from *The Voyage Out*, and even from *Night and Day*, encumbered though this book is with pages of "realistic" description which contribute little to its author's purpose, is an impression of what life was like for the heroine.

Both novels have form. *The Voyage Out* follows Rachel's steady progression towards, and final attainment of, reality.* This progression, the essential voyage of the novel, is set in motion, as it were, by the actual voyage from London to South America. And Rachel's attainment of reality through death is similarly emphasized by another event in the world of time and space—the thunderstorm which rages over Santa Marina in the last pages of the book, and then subsides into the vast sea of air, as Rachel, after hectic days of troubled delirium during her illness, subsided into the sea of reality. Helen Ambrose's embroidery, which recurs in the book and depicts in advance the tropical river where Rachel likely contracted her fever, helps to hold the novel together by slowing the stream of time and merging the present with the future. It is the first device that Virginia Woolf uses in her novels to help her escape from the tyranny of the time sequence. And moreover, it lends inevitability to the story itself. As

* p. 149.

Helen embroidered, her " figure possessed the sublimity of a woman's of the early world, spinning the thread of fate ". It is a quiet touch, which might have been made as effective as the omens that Strachey uses in " Gordon ". But it is not driven home as those omens are : when Rachel becomes ill Helen's embroidery is forgotten, and does not reappear in the novel.

Night and Day dangerously resembles the well-made novels of Arnold Bennett. Mary Datchet and Ralph Denham, Katharine Hilbery and William Rodney, change positions, so far as their relationships with one another are concerned, with a precision that is almost too perfect. The symmetry is finally relieved by the introduction of Cassandra Otway and the relegation of Mary Datchet, who devotes herself wholly to social and political work. Katharine, who was originally engaged to William, marries Ralph, who had nearly become engaged to Mary, and William marries Cassandra—or at least, these marriages are about to take place as the novel ends. Amidst this somewhat monotonous balance, however, there is a progression, similar to the progression in *The Voyage Out*, from confusion in the minds of the central characters —especially in the mind of Katharine Hilbery—to a knowledge of themselves and an understanding of life, from unreality to reality, from night to day. And there are significant moments, moments when the pattern of life can be clearly seen, when sorrow becomes joy and ugliness gives way to beauty, which vary the speed and texture of the novel and reach a climax at last in the happiness that Katharine and Ralph know at the end of the novel, when, finally secure in their love for one another, they have a vision of an orderly world. Similar moments, charged with significance, occur in *The Voyage Out*, and reach a climax at Rachel's death, at which, as we have seen, Rachel's mind merges for a time with Hewet's, and they feel that they have achieved complete union and happiness. Both novels are completed by a final touch—like the last stroke an artist gives to a painting—*The Voyage Out* by Rachel's death ; *Night and Day* by Katharine's realization that she loves Ralph, a realization which ends the confusion she experienced throughout the novel, and puts in her hands " for one brief moment the globe which we spend our lives in trying to shape, round, whole, and entire from the confusion of chaos ".* The resolution of *Night and Day*, though achieved so differently, is similar to the resolutions of *Howards End* and *A Passage to India*. It is complete, but we are aware that it will not endure : the order of life may be destroyed and chaos may reign again at any moment. The resolution of *The Voyage Out* is brief for Hewet—it lasts, it will be remembered, only until his friends enter the room after Rachel's death and recall him to the world of time and space—but it is everlasting for Rachel.

In *Monday or Tuesday*, a collection of short stories which are really exercises in preparation for *Jacob's Room*, Virginia Woolf turns from the conventional methods she used in *Night and Day* to attempt for the first time to put into practice the theory which she outlines in " Modern Fiction " and in *Mr. Bennett and Mrs. Brown*. She tries in the title story and in " The String Quartet " (from both of which quotation has already been made) to " record the atoms as they fall upon the mind in the order in which they fall " ; and in " The Mark on the Wall " she follows her consciousness whither it will take her, as she sits by the fireside on a January evening.† In " Kew Gardens " she experiments in a way which is not mentioned in either of her two essays on fiction, but which is equally important to the novels which follow : she attempts to give us a total impression of Kew Gardens, and of the people there, by means of direct, vivid description, and by following, in order to record their conversation and thoughts, several groups of people who pass a certain flower-bed. The form of these stories differs completely from the form of the traditional short story. In fact, they are not stories, properly so called, at all, but sketches ; and as one reads them, the problem which faced Virginia Woolf as an artist is immediately apparent : how is she to remain true to her vivid impressions, sensations, and emotions—which are inevitably chaotic—and yet order them in a work of art? Clearly, since the sequence of events in the inner life is not logical, and even thoughts themselves

* Above, p. 147. † Above, pp. 133 and 137–8.

are often discontinuous and inconclusive, the old apparatus of story and plot will not serve her. Some other kind of formal organization is required ; and in these short stories Virginia Woolf is seeking it. " Monday or Tuesday " is rather disjointed ; but, since it is only a page in length, some sort of unity is imposed on it by the image, with which it begins and ends, of the heron flying lazily through the sky. The normal progress of a concert, and the frame, as it were, of a concert-hall, shapes the thoughts and impressions of which " The String Quartet " is composed. Virginia Woolf's musings in " The Mark on the Wall " are centred around the mark itself, which set them off. Similarly, in " Kew Gardens ", in which the problem of organization is most successfully solved, the flower-bed, so vividly and closely described, is the centre around which vaguer, less co-ordinated impressions are grouped ; while the snail in the flower-bed is, so to speak, a clock : his laborious journey, which is the story of the sketch, links together in time the different groups of people who pass him, as the flower-bed unites in space the impressions of the Gardens.

It is, of course, much harder to unify a novel than a short story ; and *Jacob's Room*, so far as its form is concerned, is midway between the short stories, unrelated to one another, which *Monday or Tuesday* contains, and the beautifully coherent wholes of *Mrs. Dalloway* and *To the Lighthouse*. It is episodic ; and although the episodes are linked together, the relations between them are not always close or inevitable. The episodes themselves, however, are often astonishingly beautiful and effective. The first triumphs of a new technique, they have the freshness of the morning upon them.

The scene on the Cornish beach as the book begins, and the impressions of Scarborough, of Cambridge, and of London, are similar to " Kew Gardens " ; the direct accounts of Jacob's thoughts and impressions as he works on his butterfly collection, or attends a service in King's College Chapel, are like " The String Quartet " and " The Mark on the Wall ". In these parts of the novel, which are finer and more organic than the short stories, a beauty and economy of a kind previously unknown to fiction is attained. We suddenly find ourselves, without preamble, on a beach in Cornwall ; and as we move from Betty Flanders' mind to Charles Steele's and to Jacob's, while, at the same time, we are enabled, by brief touches of objective description, to see, as it were, around these figures ; as we watch, through Betty Flanders' tears, the mast of Mr. Connor's little yacht " bending like a wax candle in the sun ", and look with Charles Steele at his painting, and with Jacob at a crab on the sandy bottom of a pool in the hollow of a rock—as we do all this, and much more, in less than four pages, time stands still for a space, and the scene which Virginia Woolf sets before us has the substance, the clarity, and the certainty (a " rightness " unknown in life) of a Seurat painting. Jacob's thoughts, as he works on his butterfly collection and recalls how he caught the different trophies there, give us in two pages a series of pictures of his childhood that would require a chapter if they were described in the way that Katharine Hilbery's life in her Chelsea home is described in *Night and Day*. And in other episodes, in the scene in King's College Chapel, in the impressions of Cambridge, or of St. Paul's Cathedral, Virginia Woolf recalls the very feelings one has in these places, and so, with the least description, creates the places themselves—though one must be familiar with them if her brief, allusive suggestions are to achieve their full effect.

> Dim it is, *she says as she takes us into St. Paul's*, haunted by ghosts of white marble, to whom the organ for ever chaunts. If a boot creaks, it's awful ; then the order ; the discipline. The verger with his rod has life ironed out beneath him. Sweet and holy are the angelic choristers. And for ever round the marble shoulders, in and out of the folded fingers, go the thin high sounds of voice and organ. For ever requiem—repose.*

One feels that Virginia Woolf, like the plein-airist painters, has gone directly to St. Paul's, to a Cornish beach, to King's College Chapel, in order to write of these places on the spot. And indeed, her impressions of London, of Cornwall, and of Cambridge, which she knew so well, are more successful than

* p. 64.

her impressions of Scarborough, with which she was less familiar.

Particular portions of time—as well as segments of space such as the Cornish beach—are also vividly recorded in *Jacob's Room*. The bag of cherries from which Timmy Durrant eats, as he lies in a punt at Cambridge, becomes empty and is thrown away. The steady march of the hours of an evening at sea are described as Timmy and Jacob sail around Land's End. A bumble-bee sucks honey from a foxglove, and then, having sucked its fill, flies away (relating in space as it does so, by the line of its flight, the human figures in the scene—Mrs. Pascoe and the tourists in her garden). And as Jacob, facing a window that overlooks the sea, eats dinner with the Durrants, a ship sails across the window, and a light comes on to mark the end of the pier.

The brief portions of time and limited segments of space so clearly depicted are enveloped, as it were, by eternity, and surrounded by all space. For besides creating vivid scenes in *Jacob's Room*, Virginia Woolf ranges at will through space and time. Amidst the impressions of Cambridge we are given glimpses of Turkey and of the Indian Ocean. As night falls on Jacob and Mrs. Williams in Greece, we leave them there, and are taken over much of Europe and the Middle East, to come, finally, to London to watch the new day begin. We are taken back through the centuries in the impressions of Scarborough. And as Mrs. Flanders and Mrs. Jarvis pause one evening at the Roman camp above the town, relics of the centuries which the earth has accumulated—the bones, the rusty swords, the garnet brooch that Mrs. Flanders lost—are considered in a passage that recalls Forster's descriptions of the countryside ; the nearby church with its dead is described as " a ship with all its crew aboard " ; and the eternal moors, " motionless and broad-backed " in the moonlight, stand in the background of the scene. Meanwhile, present time flows on, and is measured by the church clock, which strikes the hours and the quarter-hours. And we are taken up, as well as down, the stream of time in *Jacob's Room*. Before the First World War has occurred in the book, we are told of Jimmy, who did not propose to the girl who loved him. " And now ", their brief story ends, " Jimmy feeds crows in Flanders and Helen visits hospitals." Again, near the beginning of the book, when Jacob is still a boy, we are told of the Rev. Mr. Floyd who taught him Latin, and we leave the realm of present time to follow Mr. Floyd's life into the future. He left Scarborough, and after a successful career retired to Hampstead. " Meeting Jacob in Piccadilly lately," the episode concludes, " he recognized him after three seconds. But Jacob had grown such a fine young man that Mr. Floyd did not like to stop him in the street." We return to Jacob's boyhood to take up again the normal progress of time ; and in the last pages of the book, when Jacob is indeed a young man, this incident, which was described so early, occurs, or rather, is described again : Mr. Floyd recognizes Jacob in Piccadilly, but does not stop him.

Apparently, Virginia Woolf wished to emphasize, and in a sense to frame, the vivid scenes in her novel by giving us an impression of the vast realms of space and time which surround them. In the same way, in the smaller scale of " Kew Gardens ", she surrounded the flower-bed, so closely described, with vaguer, more generalized impressions of the Gardens as a whole. But this method of composition is only partially successful in *Jacob's Room*. Certain scenes—the scene between Mrs. Flanders and Mrs. Jarvis in the Roman camp, in which the past envelops the present ; or the Guy Fawkes festivities, in which, after ranging about London and glimpsing incidents at Scarborough and in the eighteenth century, we concentrate upon a particular point in space and a given moment of time—are undoubtedly intensified. It is only seldom, however, that scenes are so well co-ordinated with the realms of space and time which surround them ; Virginia Woolf's exploration of time and space often becomes an end in itself—a search, so it seems, for reality ; and there is, in consequence, a division in the book between the particular and the general impressions which it contains. The flow of present time, moreover, is not consistently or continuously recorded. The snail in " Kew Gardens " moved steadily through the flower-bed, and linked the discontinuous episodes in the sketch. But the bag of cherries, the bumble-bee, the ship, the church clock, in *Jacob's Room* are unrelated to one another, and the time which they record is fragmentary. Their very vividness, in fact, detracts from the unity of the novel; for they are more clearly seen than Jacob himself—whose life is the only continuous time sequence; and so they tend, as it were, to break his life into fragments. The hints of approaching war restore the situation somewhat; but they are introduced late in the book; they do not increase noticeably after their introduction; and they are an external device, depending, as they do, upon historical knowledge.

It is apparent in *Jacob's Room*—and indeed it was apparent in "Kew Gardens" too, for without the snail the episodes in that sketch would be unrelated in time—that when Virginia Woolf ceases to tell stories and construct plots, a clear, continuous record of the time sequence is essential to the unity of her compositions. Paradoxically enough, it appears that in order to escape from the time sequence, she must first record present time clearly.

As the use of Mr. Floyd's recognition of Jacob in Piccadilly testifies, Virginia Woolf attempts to gain a great advantage in *Jacob's Room* from her journeys up and down the stream of time. She wishes to convince us that the whole of Jacob's life, from the scene on the Cornish beach to the final scene in Jacob's room (which are related by the reiterations of Jacob's name, and by the presence of Mrs. Flanders, worried and helpless), existed from the beginning in the real world—which is outside the limitations of time and space—and only remained to be fulfilled in present time. This conception, which accords with Virginia Woolf's view of life, attracts by its very daring: if it could be accomplished, Jacob's life would be given an inevitability that would be absolute. But the most that the artist can do in this respect, so it seems, is to foreshadow, as Strachey does in his biographies, the future course of events. And this is fortunate; for art, though it may aim at the absolute, should never attain it: if it did, it would be too far removed from life. At any rate, when the incident in Piccadilly is described for the second time, and when sentences from earlier descriptions of Jacob's rooms at Cambridge and in Bloomsbury are repeated verbatim in the last chapter, we may have for a moment the feeling, which we sometimes know in life, that all this has happened before—but only for a moment: then we see through the device, and reflect upon the mechanics of the novel, rather than upon the inevitability of Jacob's life.

Virginia Woolf's treatment of time and space in *Jacob's Room* affords an instructive comparison with Forster's method in *A Passage to India.* The scenes and characters in that book too, as we have seen, are surrounded by infinite realms of space and time; or rather—and perhaps this is a vital difference—they reach out towards those realms. Forster's conception of the universe is less sensational and impressionistic, more intellectualized and mystic, than Virginia Woolf's. So he is able to make the vastness of India and of the universe, and the aeons of geological history, a part of the philosophy and religion of his novel. And through philosophy, religion, mystic feelings, and the echo in the Marabar Caves (which is a manifestation of the supernatural), aspects of the universe enter the minds of his characters, though the characters remain intensely themselves, and are never merged or confused with the universe so long as they are alive. It is only after her death that Mrs. Moore becomes a part of India.

But Jacob, from the time that he wanders on the beach in Cornwall and views nature with the single, unanalytical vision of a child, is never clearly differentiated from his environment. He marvels that he should exist as a separate entity in the world of time and space. As he goes through Italy on his way to Greece, he thinks that "It is a strange reflection that by travelling two days and nights you are in the heart of Italy . . . there is a lonely hill-top where no one ever comes, and yet it is seen by me who was lately driving down Piccadilly in an omnibus." And at the Acropolis, "looking up and seeing the sharp outline, his meditations were given an extraordinary edge; Greece was over; the Parthenon in ruins; yet there he was". When we learn from Mrs. Flanders and Richard Bonamy, who are in Jacob's room, that Jacob has been killed, we miss him scarcely at all; for he has been a part of his room from the first, and his room is the whole world. He is like a pebble which is dropped into a pool. The rings move out from it and encounter reeds in the water;

we see them from the point of view of the reeds, from the point of view of the pebble ; we even feel the sensations of the pebble ; but as for the pebble itself—we cannot grasp it. And this is a serious weakness in the novel ; for its centre, the character who might unite all its various scenes, is—not there. His sensations and some of his thoughts are there ; his effects upon others are there ; but he himself is absent. The impressions of him that we are given are not co-ordinated into a whole. Virginia Woolf's theory about character—that it is impossible to sum a person up, that there is nothing more ludicrous than one person's opinion of another person—which is reiterated throughout *Jacob's Room*, is put into practice. And there are other causes which conspire to effect this weakness in the novel. The logical extreme of sensationalism is an inability to distinguish between one's self and one's surroundings ; and the only definite characteristic that Jacob displays throughout the novel—if one excludes such banalities as his awkwardness and his distinguished appearance—is a determination to retain, so far as possible, the unconceptual vision and sensations of childhood. " We start transparent, and then the cloud thickens. All history backs our pane of glass. To escape is vain." But Jacob tries to escape, none the less. He wants to be what he is and remain unchanged, to prevent " the world of the elderly " from coming between him and " the reality ", " to have—positively—a rush of friendship for stones and grasses, as if humanity were over " —" there is no getting over the fact ", Virginia Woolf says, " that this desire seizes us pretty often ". The thoughts and feelings that Jacob has are, for the most part, Virginia Woolf's ; yet she set out to create a young man of the sort that she knew in Bloomsbury. She is aware herself of the discrepancy ; and after filling Jacob momentarily with her own feelings, she halts, and, with a comment, almost denies what she has done. As a result, there is a queer lack of focus in her treatment of Jacob, which contributes to his elusiveness.

There is a similar uncertainty of method in the structure of the novel as a whole. Beside the impressionistic scenes and the presentations of the characters' inner lives, there are interludes in which character, life, literature, letters, and the difficulty of communicating are discussed : the philosophy in the book is by no means entirely subsumed by its form. As the novel proceeds Virginia Woolf is unable to maintain the high pitch of inspiration with which it began ; her method is new and strenuous, and it is not surprising that she should flag at times. Sentences such as her comment upon the relationship between Helen Aitken and Jimmy—" For my own part, I find it exceedingly difficult to interpret songs without words "—are indications of a method which is at variance with the method consistently used in the first four or five chapters. In the episode in Greece *Jacob's Room* becomes almost a travel book ; while the description of the Parthenon might have come straight out of one of Roger Fry's lectures. And the scenes in Paris are mechanically related to one another, and introduced off-handedly : " For example, take this scene " —" Then here is another scrap of conversation ; the time about eleven in the morning ; the scene a studio ; and the day Sunday "—" And then, here is Versailles "—" And finally under the arc lamps in the Gare des Invalides. . . . "

The impressionistic episodes in *Jacob's Room* are not united in a satisfactory composition, but there are indications of what is to follow in later books. The scene on the beach in Cornwall is so successful because the different elements in it are carefully and organically related to one another—in this scene the composition is completely satisfying. Mrs. Flanders looks up from her letter and across the bay ; Archer comes to her and she sends him in search of Jacob ; she moves, and disturbs Charles Steele, who is painting her in his landscape ; Archer runs past Steele shouting Jacob's name, and Steele, though exasperated by the noise, points Jacob out to Archer ; we move on to Jacob, the object of the search ; and finally, he and Archer return to Mrs. Flanders, and the composition is complete. In the penultimate chapter of the book, Virginia Woolf begins for the first time to relate scenes to one another as consistently as the different elements of the scene on the beach are related. We range over much of the West End of London, and glimpse Cornwall, Greece, and Scarborough ; but each new scene is related to the last by an incident, an action, a thought, or a conjunction in time or space. The part of this chapter which takes place in London is almost a miniature of *Mrs. Dalloway* ; and the germs of *To the Lighthouse* and *The Waves* may also be found in *Jacob's Room*. *To the Lighthouse* is inescapably suggested by the chapter which depicts Jacob's and Timmy Durrant's voyage around Land's End, and describes the dinner and the guests at the Durrant's house in Cornwall.* And Virginia Woolf's greatest book, *The Waves*, describing as it does the life experience of six characters who might all have met in Bloomsbury, deals with the subject of *Jacob's Room* on a larger canvas, and with mature wisdom and art.

In *Mrs. Dalloway* Virginia Woolf's artistic problem is solved for the first time. Impressions, records of the inner life, exploration of time and space, the search for reality, are ordered and combined in a work of art that is disciplined, consistent, and almost completely set apart from its author. This novel is as coherent as *Jacob's Room* is diffused. When we look back on *Jacob's Room*, we see a number of vivid but loosely related episodes, surrounded, sometimes separated from one another, by vast and indefinite tracts of time and space. Any one of these episodes, so it seems, might be lifted cleanly from the book. But *Mrs. Dalloway* brooks no division ; it is not even divided into chapters ; and no scene could be taken from it without mutilating the whole. It is, as it were, a solid, clearly defined block of space and time ; contained by the West End of London, encompassed by a day in June, 1923—a day which, though past, is held steadily before us in the work of art. There is no wanton wandering in space or time ; but as the characters move to and fro in the West End, a design is drawn ; and upon this day in June, as it progresses steadily to its close, is the pressure of all the other days they have experienced. So, while remaining in London and following the sequence of the hours of a day, the novel shows us, in the minds of the characters, other scenes from years long past.

* The descriptions both of this house and of the Ramsays' summer home in *To the Lighthouse* are apparently based on Talland House, St. Ives, where the Stephens spent many of their summer vacations. There is a picture of Talland House in N. G. Annan's *Leslie Stephen*.

The formal organization of *Mrs. Dalloway* is not unlike the organization of " Kew Gardens ". Both compositions are impregnated with space, and the space with which each is concerned is clearly defined. The flow of time is recorded in " Kew Gardens " by the movements of the snail ; it is recorded in *Mrs. Dalloway* by Big Ben, which, standing near the Dalloways' home in Westminster, and assisted by the other clocks of London, irrevocably strikes the hours. But the scenes in *Mrs. Dalloway* are more closely co-ordinated than the episodes in " Kew Gardens ". They are related to one another throughout the novel as carefully and surely as are the elements of the beach scene in *Jacob's Room.*

Mrs. Dalloway leaves her home in Westminster, as Big Ben strikes ten, to walk to Bond Street to buy flowers for her party. In the flower-shop she is startled by an explosion from a large motor car, which, carrying some famous person mysteriously withdrawn behind its blinds, stops in the street for a moment and causes a crowd to collect. Septimus Warren Smith and his wife, Lucrezia, are delayed by the crowd. The car drives away ; we follow it, and watch the ripple of excitement that it causes, as it crosses Piccadilly, goes down St. James's Street, and proceeds towards Buckingham Palace. As it enters the gates of the Palace, the attention of the crowd gathered there is distracted from it by an aeroplane writing advertisements in the sky. The aeroplane gives Virginia Woolf an opportunity to range over the scene of her novel : we are shown numerous people watching the aeroplane from different parts of London. Septimus and Lucrezia see it from Regent's Park, which they have now reached ; Mrs. Dalloway, back from Bond Street, sees people looking up at it as she re-enters her house. Soon after she has returned, Peter Walsh calls on her. Then he walks to Regent's Park, where he is seen by Septimus, becomes a part of Septimus's hallucination, and wonders why Septimus and Lucrezia look so desperate. So the scenes are related as the novel develops : each movement from one place to another, each shift in the point of view, is carefully prepared and surely made. And throughout all the scenes the position of the characters in time and in space is clearly indicated by the striking of clocks and by the names of streets and parks in the West End. In fact, to appreciate *Mrs. Dalloway* to the full, an acquaintance with London is required, just as a familiarity with St. Paul's or with King's College Chapel is necessary if the impressions of these places in *Jacob's Room* are to have their full effect. The West End is indeed a part of *Mrs. Dalloway*. Its buildings, its shops, its traffic, its people, its squares, and its parks blend with the thoughts and emotions of the characters and become a part of their spiritual experiences. In no other book, perhaps, is the atmosphere of the West End in the twentieth century so surely captured. And, after all, one is taken there by *Mrs. Dalloway* whether one has ever been there in life or not. The novel has an added savour, and its spatial relations are clearer, if the reader knows the West End ; but it exists, nevertheless, as a self-contained work of art which is independent of this outside knowledge.

Most of the action of the novel, if one may call it " action ", takes place in the minds of the characters, or is seen from their various points of view. The whole " reality " of the June day is created by collocating the experiences of different personalities. They go about London ; they meet ; they reflect upon the past ; and as they do so, their impressions, their emotions, and their thoughts are recorded. As we move from mind to mind—and the essential transitions of the novel are from one mind to another—we meet directly, without the author's intervention, each of the major characters, and many of the minor ones ; and we see their reactions to, and their conscious opinions of, one another. Moreover, some of them go back in memory to the same events in the past, enabling us to see those events from different points of view. So the characters are oriented and related to one another psychologically and spiritually, as well as in time and space ; we are able to see them and to see around them, to see events and to see around those events—in rather the same way (though Virginia Woolf's method is much more economical) as we see Franceschini's crime in Browning's *The Ring and the Book* ; and the novel, with little direct intervention on the part of the author, is given an astonishing depth.

Virginia Woolf's belief that it is impossible to sum a character up is an advantage in *Mrs. Dalloway*, and contributes to the sense of depth that the novel gives us. It helps her to withdraw from the novel, and to present different views of the major characters ; yet it is not carried to an extreme. The unhesitant presentation of Mrs. Dalloway's inner life demonstrates that Virginia Woolf had a clear conception of her before she began to write—even though she does not sum Mrs. Dalloway up—and provides a centre, which was lacking in the presentation of Jacob Flanders, around which are co-ordinated the various impressions of Mrs. Dalloway that we see in the minds of others—and, indeed, in Mrs. Dalloway's own mind, as well. The result is a character whom we can sum up no more than Virginia Woolf can, but who is completely convincing, because she has about her the reality, the infinite diversity, and, beneath diversity, the essential unity, of life.

Around the central figure of Clarissa Dalloway, the other characters in the novel are grouped, according to the extent and method of their presentment, in somewhat the same way as the characters in Strachey's *Queen Victoria* are grouped about the Queen. Peter Walsh and Richard Dalloway are created in the same way as Mrs. Dalloway, though we are given rather fewer and less variable impressions of them in the minds of other characters, and their inner lives are not explored so extensively as Clarissa's. Their thoughts are mainly concerned with Clarissa ; and thus they direct our attention back towards her. Of the two, Richard is, if one may use the term, a less organic character than Peter, and his rôle in the novel is less important. The variations among the impressions which others have of him are so few that he can be summed up—as a conscientious, likeable politician of no more than average intelligence, but with a great amount of good will, who would be happier if he were farming in his native county of Norfolk. The fact that he can be described in a sentence emphasizes how much less complex he is than Clarissa. And as one moves, as it were, from the inner to the outer characters in the novel, one finds that they become less and less complex, and that Virginia Woolf's method of creating them changes almost imperceptibly from the method used in creating Clarissa to the more conventional method of direct description. Hugh Whitbread is just outside the central group of characters, and his inner life is not revealed. We only enter his mind perfunctorily for a moment as he stands under Messrs. Rigby and Lownde's clock, and in the same scene there are a few sentences of direct description. We see him almost entirely through the minds of Clarissa, Richard, Sally Seton, and Peter Walsh ; and although Clarissa likes him, while Peter and Sally loathe him, and Richard cannot endure him for long, a clear picture of him emerges. He is a pompous, insensitive, unintelligent, but kind-hearted man, whose main purpose in the novel is to illustrate the characters of the four who observe him. Elizabeth Dalloway is an even simpler character than her father. A withdrawn, erect, beautiful girl, she is created from two or three vivid traits of adolescence ; and her characterization, achieved by touches of direct description, by the occasional use of the views of others, and by recording some of her thoughts, is completely consistent throughout. In the presentation of Doris Kilman, which is not unlike a Stracheyean portrait, direct description and a reconstruction of the inner life are almost inextricably mixed, and irony is added. Finally, we find that Sir William Bradshaw and Dr. Holmes are presented almost entirely by means of direct description, and with trenchant irony. Yet, even in the presentation of these last three characters, the method used in creating Clarissa Dalloway is not entirely discarded. We see the reactions of Mrs. Dalloway and Elizabeth to Doris Kilman, the reactions of Septimus and Lucrezia Smith and of Mrs. Dalloway to Sir William Bradshaw (which, however, are almost identical), the reactions of the Smiths to Dr. Holmes. And the description of Holmes is so skilfully managed that one is, as it were, in the room with the Smiths, watching him as he comes to see Septimus.

Among these characters, then, the central group of Clarissa, Peter, and Richard are created, as it were, in depth, and without the intervention of the author ; Bradshaw and Holmes are oreated by the author's direct description, with the result that we cannot " see around " them ; and Elizabeth Dalloway, Hugh Whitbread, and Doris Kilman, so far as the methods used to create them are concerned, stand at intermediate points between these two groups. But there is another character,

Septimus Warren Smith, who, though he is second in importance in the novel only to Mrs. Dalloway herself, is not created in such depth. Because he is unknown to the Dalloways and their friends, he cannot be set before us in the way that Clarissa is. With the exception of the occasional glances of passers-by, we see him through no other eyes but those of his wife (for the medical opinions which Bradshaw and Holmes give have nothing to do with his character), and she is unable to understand him. So the author has to intervene directly to narrate Septimus's history and describe the growth of his mental illness ; and when she does so, one has an uncomfortable feeling, as one reads the novel, that her method has changed. The direct description of Sir William Bradshaw does not jar in the same way (though even here one wishes that Virginia Woolf had adjusted it to her method as she adjusts the description of Holmes) because Bradshaw's rôle is a relatively simple one. But Septimus's rôle is too important to allow him, without some weakness, to be treated descriptively in a novel in which the other major characters are set before us so differently. We have to depend upon the author for a good deal of information about Septimus, while all our knowledge of Clarissa, Peter, and Richard is obtained, so to speak, directly from the work of art. As a result, one feels —though only, of course, because *Mrs. Dalloway* is created according to the dictates of a high and strict aesthetics—that in this respect the novel is not completely set apart from its author. This is perhaps the only definite weakness in the structure of the book, and it is not evident for long as one reads, for Virginia Woolf gives us in her description of Septimus one of the finest and most sympathetic analyses in fiction of insanity. And of course, Septimus is by no means entirely created by descriptive methods. We are shown the workings of his mind ; we see his hallucinations, and feel ourselves, at moments, his intense sensations and his fears. The presentation of his consciousness, which is followed as closely as that of Mrs. Dalloway herself, is one of the finest things in the novel.

Mrs. Dalloway and Septimus, as Virginia Woolf tells us in her introduction to the Modern Library edition of *Mrs. Dalloway*, are " one and the same person ". Like Rachel

Vinrace and Terence Hewet in *The Voyage Out*, they are opposite sides of the same personality. Septimus is dominated by the horror in life ; Clarissa is surrounded by life's beauty. Yet, amidst her enjoyment of life, Clarissa is aware of life's horror and danger ; and there are moments, even amongst his hallucinations, when Septimus is overwhelmed by the beauty of the world. Clarissa saw her sister killed before her very eyes by a falling tree ; Septimus was with his best friend, Evans, when Evans was killed in the War. Each thinks often of death. Septimus threatens to kill himself to end the horror he experiences. Clarissa regrets that death must end her happiness. She remembers once throwing a shilling into the Serpentine ; then, she wonders whether one ceases completely to exist after death, or if one is borne up, like mist on the branches of trees, about the people and places one has known. And throughout the novel Septimus and Clarissa are more and more closely associated, until they are merged, at last, as Rachel and Hewet are merged in *The Voyage Out*.

Clarissa's musings upon death are associated with the Shakespearian lines,

> Fear no more the heat o' the sun
> Nor the furious winter's rages,

which become, as the novel develops, a comment upon Septimus and upon his suicide. These lines enter Clarissa's mind as she walks to Bond Street, and shortly afterwards we are shown Septimus there, with a look of apprehension in his eyes. " The world has raised its whip ; where will it descend ? " In Regent's Park Septimus thinks of death, and believes that he sees Evans amongst the dead behind the Park railings. A few pages later, when Clarissa is saddened by Lady Bruton's luncheon invitation to Richard, she too thinks of death, and the Shakespearian refrain recurs in her mind, indirectly expressing sympathy for Septimus. Then, Clarissa begins to sew her green dress, and its folds insensibly become the sea, and the sea becomes the reality which one enters at death :

> Quiet descended on her, calm, content, as her needle, drawing the silk smoothly to its gentle pause, collected the

> green folds together and attached them, very lightly, to the belt. So on a summer's day waves collect, overbalance, and fall; collect and fall; and the whole world seems to be saying, "that is all" more and more ponderously, until even the heart in the body which lies in the sun on the beach says so too, that is all. Fear no more, says the heart. Fear no more, says the heart, committing its burden to some sea, which sighs collectively for all sorrows, and renews, begins, collects, lets fall. And the body alone listens to the passing bee; and the wave breaking; the dog barking, far away barking and barking.

Septimus has the same sensations shortly before his suicide, when, as he lies on his sofa, the reality which surrounds him seems already to beckon:

> Going and coming, beckoning, signalling, so the light and shadow, which now made the wall grey, now the bananas bright yellow, now made the Strand grey, now made the omnibuses bright yellow, seemed to Septimus Warren Smith lying on the sofa in the sitting-room; watching the watery gold glow and fade with the astonishing sensibility of some live creature on the roses, on the wall-paper. Outside the trees dragged their leaves like nets through the depths of the air; the sound of water was in the room, and through the waves came the voices of birds singing. Every power poured its treasures on his head, and his hand lay there on the back of the sofa, as he had seen his hand lie when he was bathing, floating, on the top of the waves, while far away on shore he heard dogs barking and barking far away. Fear no more, says the heart in the body; fear no more.
>
> He was not afraid.

The scene which follows, and which reaches its climax in Septimus's suicide, has the quality of great tragedy. For Septimus is sane for a time; he and Lucrezia, after weeks of anxiety and terror, have never been happier; the odds and ends of existence have come together to make "a centre of peace and satisfaction", which Lucrezia, in her joy, believes will last, though the reader knows that doom is impending.* The line from *Othello*, "If it were now to die, 'twere now to be most happy", which has occurred, pages before, in Mrs.

* See p. 147.

Dalloway's mind, is a comment upon this scene and, like the other Shakespearian lines, upon Septimus's suicide. After his death we follow, through Lucrezia's mind, his journey to reality, in much the same way as we discovered Rachel's happiness at death through Hewet's mind. Lucrezia has been given a sleeping-draught by Dr. Holmes, and she is losing consciousness :

> She put on her hat, and ran through cornfields—where could it have been ?—on to some hill, somewhere near the sea, for there were ships, gulls, butterflies ; they sat on a cliff. In London, too, there they sat, and, half dreaming, came to her through the bedroom door, rain falling, whisperings, stirrings among dry corn, the caress of the sea, as it seemed to her, hollowing them in its arched shell and murmuring to her laid on shore, strewn she felt, like flying flowers over some tomb.

That night, after Septimus has become a part of the sky, of the sea, of the air which he had seen flowing through the leaves outside his room (as Clarissa had imagined that she would be upheld like a mist on the branches of trees after her death), Sir William Bradshaw brings the news of Septimus's suicide to Clarissa's party, and Clarissa's identification with Septimus is completed. He threw himself from the window because Sir Willaim Bradshaw wished to lay hands upon his soul ; and Clarissa, who dislikes Bradshaw instinctively, realizes why he did it. In the scene depicting the suicide, we were taken into Septimus's mind as he sat on the window-sill, and then threw himself to the ground : " Coming down the staircase opposite an old man stopped and stared at him. Holmes was at the door. ' I'll give it you ! ' he cried, and flung himself vigorously, violently down on to Mrs. Filmer's area railings." Now, at Clarissa's party, Septimus's fall is completed in Clarissa's consciousness : " He had killed himself—but how ? Always her body went through it, when she was told, first, suddenly, of an accident ; her dress flamed, her body burnt. He had thrown himself from a window. Up had flashed the ground ; through him, blundering, bruising, went the rusty spikes. There he lay with a thud, thud, thud in his brain, and then a suffocation of blackness. So she saw it." Moreover, as Septimus saw an old man opposite him before he leapt, Clarissa sees from her window, as she thinks of Septimus's death, the old lady opposite, whom Clarissa has previously associated with the privacy and dignity of the soul—in the protection of which Septimus died. And Clarissa feels unaccountably happy. " Odd, incredible ; she had never been so happy." She recalls the Shakespearian refrain, the line from *Othello*, the shilling she once threw into the Serpentine—as Septimus threw away his life. Death, she thinks, is " an attempt to communicate" ; and she believes that the sky above Westminster holds " something of her own in it ".

Rachel's union with Hewet as she died completed the pattern of *The Voyage Out* ; but *Mrs. Dalloway* is much more complicated than that novel ; and there are other touches besides Clarissa's identification with Septimus—though that is the most important touch—which complete its design. Throughout the day, as time has flowed steadily on, we have followed Septimus and Lucrezia's story ; we have looked forward with anticipation to Clarissa's party ; we have looked back with Clarissa, Peter, and Richard to Clarissa's youth at Bourton ; and we have seen, in their minds, her old love affair with Peter Walsh. In the last scene of the novel, at Clarissa's party, in which she had wished to bring people together from all parts of London, " to combine, to create ", all these threads are brought together. The characters whom we have seen in the past at Bourton—Clarissa, Richard, Peter, Hugh Whitbread, Sally Seton, even Aunt Helena, whom Peter had thought dead—are all at the party. And other characters whom we have seen throughout the day—Lady Bruton, the Bradshaws, the Prime Minister, whose car perhaps it was that Clarissa and the Smiths saw in Bond Street—are there too. Big Ben strikes for the last time in the novel as Clarissa's identification with Septimus is completed ; Sally and Peter discuss Clarissa as they were wont to do at Bourton ; Peter feels again his old love for Clarissa as the party ends ; and the unity of the novel is complete.

The framework of *Mrs. Dalloway* is rather rigid ; but the novel is saved from stiffness because it is permeated by the author's sensibility, by changes of mood and of pace which are expressed in a beautiful style. Clarissa's walk to Bond Street is bright and full of movement. It contrasts in pace and mood with her darker, slower, deeper reflections as she changes her clothes after returning home. The scene between Peter and Clarissa which follows is remarkable for the extraordinary range of shifting emotions it portrays. When Peter leaves her, his agitated thoughts are expressed in short rhythms, which are varied occasionally by a long breathless sentence giving vent to his emotions. Then, a cloud passes over the sun, Peter becomes pensive, and the style slows immediately. It gradually quickens, with a military rhythm, as Peter walks up Whitehall, is passed by marching troops, and is filled with a wonderful feeling of happiness. Peter's whimsical adventure with the unknown young lady follows; and then, after experiencing such a gamut of emotions, he sleeps in Regent's Park, and the sentences become long, soft, and soothing. There are also perceptible changes in style in different parts of the day. The style is brisk in the morning, the hours are crowded with action; it is slower about midday, the hours are less crowded, the mood is drowsy; in the evening the mood tends to be contemplative, the style becomes more analytical, and the hours are unhurried. Throughout the novel, the style, whether it is following the unpredictable movements of Mrs. Dalloway's wayward thoughts, or depicting Septimus's suicide with direct, vivid force, is sensitive, completely organic, and inseparable from the material of the book. And as always, Virginia Woolf has a sharp eye for beauty. It is there in profusion in the description of Mulberry's flower-shop; but there is finer beauty in the tragic scene before Septimus's death, beauty which is created with perfect simplicity and sometimes from the slightest materials. Septimus is sane again, and he wishes to burn the things he wrote while he was mad. "But Rezia laid her hands on them. Some were very beautiful, she thought. She would tie them up (for she had no envelope) with a piece of silk."

As Virginia Woolf expands a day into nearly a lifetime in *Mrs. Dalloway*, so she contracts ten years into the pattern of a day in *To the Lighthouse*—in somewhat the same way as

Forster gives *A Passage to India* the shape of an Indian year. And closely co-ordinated as *Mrs. Dalloway* is, the structure of *To the Lighthouse* is even more compact. Instead of moving about the West End of London, our attention is fixed unremittingly upon the Ramsays' summer home and the little cosmos of land and sea and sky which surrounds it. There are two groups of characters in *Mrs. Dalloway*, and each group has its central character—Septimus and Clarissa. In *To the Lighthouse* there is only one group, with Mrs. Ramsay at its centre. The past which the characters look back upon in *Mrs. Dalloway*—Clarissa's youth at Bourton—is, in a sense, an addition to the solid structure of the book : it is outside both the West End and the June day. But, with the exception of Mrs. Ramsay's amazed recollections of the Mannings as William Bankes brings them to her mind for the first time in twenty years—the exception which proves the rule—the characters of *To the Lighthouse* do not look back at all until the third, and last, Part of the novel, and then they look back upon the scene which has been depicted in the first Part—with the result that the novel is completely self-contained. This unique kind of unity is made possible, of course, largely by the way in which the time sequence is handled in the second Part, "Time Passes", which, by focusing on the empty house and describing its decay, records the passage of ten years without a change of scene, and, while giving us a vivid sense of the passage of time, and informing us of the deaths of Mrs. Ramsay, Andrew, and Prue, contracts the ten years, in effect, into one night. For the characters whom we have seen in the afternoon and evening of the first Part, "The Window", have just gone to bed as "Time Passes" begins, and those who return to the Ramsays' summer home ten years later, awake as "Time Passes" ends, to begin the action of the morning that is depicted in the last Part, "The Lighthouse". It is therefore perfectly natural that they should look back upon the scene of the first Part, when, ten years before, they were last at the summer home. Time has passed, but numerous scenes have not intervened between the two Parts ; and so the full force and significance of the relations between them is felt ; and the novel is given an astonishing unity, accomplished so naturally and with such apparent ease that *To the Lighthouse* realizes the ideal which Lily Briscoe holds before her as she paints her picture : " It was to be a thing you could ruffle with your breath ; and a thing you could not dislodge with a team of horses." Roger Fry's aesthetics is behind Lily's theory of painting ; and it is behind the structure of *To the Lighthouse*, as well. Fry, who regretted, it will be remembered, that " comparatively few novelists have ever conceived of the novel as a single perfectly organic aesthetic whole ", must have been peculiarly satisfied by this novel ; for it accords with his theory of art.

The solidity of the structure of *To the Lighthouse* gives Virginia Woolf a freedom that is unknown in *Mrs. Dalloway*. Much of her creative energy had to be used in that book to relate scenes to one another in time and space ; but within the compact structure of *To the Lighthouse*, with only one group of characters and such a limited and uncomplicated cosmos, this problem is much more easily solved. The scene may be transferred from Mr. and Mrs. Ramsay, out for a stroll, to Lily Briscoe and William Bankes when Mrs. Ramsay sights the latter couple ; or from Lily Briscoe, painting on the lawn outside the house, to Mr. Ramsay, Cam and James in a boat on the bay when Lily looks up from her painting and sees them raising their sail. The characters are literally within sight and sound of one another, and the links between the scenes are consequently less obtrusive and more organic than the links in *Mrs. Dalloway*. Moreover, the spatial relations —and *To the Lighthouse* is as thoroughly impregnated with space as *Mrs. Dalloway* is—do not depend in the least upon outside reference : the window, the terrace, the hedge, the gap between the clumps of red-hot pokers, the town, the bay, and the lighthouse exist within the novel in a way that the streets and parks of the West End do not exist in *Mrs. Dalloway*. Similarly, the flow of time is measured in " The Window " and " The Lighthouse " by the natural events of a day—by Mrs. Ramsay's trip to and from the town, by her knitting which she tries to finish before night, by dinner, by bedtime, by the movement of the boat from the bay to the lighthouse, by the newly-caught fish that flop on the bottom of the boat and then lie still—events which are not external to the action, as the striking of Big Ben is, to some extent, external to the action of *Mrs. Dalloway*. The method Virginia Woolf uses in the first and last Parts of *To the Lighthouse* reaches its height in the dinner scene, in which she moves, without preamble, from mind to mind, presenting the scene from various points of view, while the passage of time is marked by the normal progress of the meal, by the gathering darkness, and the lighting of the candles.

Most of the scenes of the novel are created by this easy, fluid method ; and direct description is mingled more freely with the characters' thoughts than is the case in *Mrs. Dalloway*. Sometimes touches of description enable us to see a character at the same time as we see into his mind ; and often Virginia Woolf's point of view is so closely adjusted to her character's that it is difficult to distinguish between the two. This too contributes to the ease and fluidity of the novel, and it gives Virginia Woolf some of the advantages both of objective description and of the direct presentation of her characters' inner lives. But some sacrifice attends this gain : no character's consciousness in *To the Lighthouse* is presented quite as vividly and directly—for its own sake, as it were—as the consciousness of Clarissa or Septimus in *Mrs. Dalloway*. Of all the characters in the book, Mrs. Ramsay's mind is most thoroughly explored ; but one is aware at moments, as one is not in the case of Mrs. Dalloway, that the author is creating this mind by selecting, as it were, from the experiences of a lifetime, rather than of a day, that the method, in other words, is historical, not immediate. Lily Briscoe's inner life is presented only seldom for its own sake : her mind is a medium through which we look back, in the last Part, upon the scene which has passed. And Mr. Ramsay's inner life is not presented directly at all. We are given a stylized account of it ; we do not get inside his mind, but see him from the points of view of other characters, or, more often, from the author's point of view.

Undoubtedly, the presentation of *To the Lighthouse* is influenced, even more intimately than is usually the case in a work of art, by the experience from which the book is shaped. For in this novel Virginia Woolf is looking back across the years to her childhood and youth, as, on the voyage to the lighthouse, Cam looks back across the sea to the island she has left. Mr. Ramsay, like Ridley Ambrose in *The Voyage Out*, has Leslie Stephen as his original in life ; Mrs. Ramsay is Virginia Woolf's mother ; and the house at St. Ives where the Stephens spent many summer vacations is transferred to the Isle of Skye, as though Virginia Woolf wished to place it as far distant in space as it was in time.* It is because the past of which she writes is so far removed from her, because Bloomsbury, her marriage, the War, and her success as a novelist have filled the years which lie between, that she is able to see it so clearly as a whole. " Already ", Cam thinks as the boat puts out upon the bay towards the lighthouse, " the little distance they had sailed had put them far from it and given it the changed look, the composed look, of something receding in which one has no longer any part." And yet, Virginia Woolf's part in the past inevitably determines the way in which she treats the characters in *To the Lighthouse*. With the exception of Cam in " The Lighthouse " and of Prue, as we see her for a moment admiring her mother in " The Window ", she looks at them almost always, we are aware, from the outside. Her point of view, subtly adjusted as it is with the points of view of her characters, is seldom completely merged with theirs. Mrs. Ramsay's inner life is reconstructed from Virginia Woolf's girlhood impressions of her mother, and from some of Virginia Woolf's own characteristics—her awareness of the danger and horror of life, her love of beauty, and her ability to sink down into the subconscious, and so to come, as she believed, into contact with reality—characteristics which she attributes to her mother. The forceful character of Mr. Ramsay is created from the strong impression that Leslie Stephen made upon his daughter ; but she is unable to see into his mind as she sees into Mrs. Ramsay's. His strong intellectual bias and his lack of intuitive powers are alien to her ; his philosophical flights are beyond her, and she has to represent them by the image of the kitchen table which comes into Lily Briscoe's mind, or by comparing

* See Annan, pp. 97–109.

thought to an alphabet which Ramsay can run over easily as far as Q, from where he strives to reach the remaining letters. And Ramsay is something of an enigma to his creator in other respects as well. He is so rational when he looks out beyond himself, yet so irrational when he looks inward ; so insensitive to the feelings of others, so easily hurt himself ; " so brave a man in thought . . . so timid in life ; how strangely he was venerable and laughable at one and the same time." These contradictions in the man himself are complemented by contradictory feelings which he aroused in his daughter, feelings of love and hate, which every child, perhaps, has for a parent, but which were inevitably more intense than usual in this case. Cam admires Ramsay's intellect, but she hates his lack of consideration for the feelings of others. He gives her a peculiar sense of security, and she loves his strength ; but that very strength has often been turned upon her, to her cost. She looks at him in the boat :

> Her father was feeling in his pockets ; in another second, he would have found his book . . . no one attracted her more ; his hands were beautiful to her and his feet, and his voice, and his words, and his haste, and his temper, and his oddity, and his passion, and his saying straight out before every one, we perish, each alone, and his remoteness. (He had opened his book.) But what remained intolerable, she thought, sitting upright, and watching Macalister's boy tug the hook out of the gills of another fish, was that crass blindness and tyranny of his which had poisoned her childhood and raised bitter storms, so that even now she woke in the night trembling with rage and remembered some command of his ; some insolence : " Do this ", " Do that ", his dominance : his " Submit to me ".

As this quotation indicates (for its point of view is the author's, as well as Cam's) Virginia Woolf's theory of character has little influence upon her characterization in *To the Lighthouse*. She still pays it lip-service. Lily Briscoe would like " fifty pairs of eyes to see with " as she tries to paint Mrs. Ramsay. " Fifty pairs of eyes were not enough to get round that one woman with, she thought." And certainly we see Mrs. Ramsay, and many of the other characters in the novel, from various points of view. But the different views complement one another ; they fill out, as it were, a single conception of each character ; there is virtually no contradiction amongst them. The characters are created according to Virginia Woolf's youthful vision of them ; a vision which the passage of the years has refined and the experience of life has completed ; a vision, above all, which is sure, unhesitant, and informed with strong feelings. As a result, the characters in *To the Lighthouse*, though none of them, perhaps, is as complete as Clarissa Dalloway, are more vivid than the characters in any other of Virginia Woolf's novels.

And for the first time she relates her characters consistently and thoroughly to one another—as Forster does in his novels—by means of similarities and dissimilarities, analogies and contrasts, amongst them. Mrs. Ramsay's intuitive search for reality is complemented by Mr. Ramsay's intellectual search ; and her selflessness and constant concern for the well-being of others is the exact opposite of his egotism and lack of consideration for those around him. William Bankes also pursues truth intellectually, but his disinterestedness contrasts with Ramsay's desire for fame. Moreover, Ramsay is a family man with eight children ; Bankes is a widower who will allow no one to disturb the carefully planned routine of his existence. He remembers Ramsay pointing fondly once, on a Westmorland road, at a hen with a covey of chicks—" an odd illumination into his heart, Bankes had thought it, which showed his simplicity, his sympathy with humble things ; but it seemed to him as if their friendship had ceased, there, on that stretch of road." Mr. Carmichael, who is almost continuously sunk in " a grey-green somnolence ", and who is remarkably self-sufficient, is a reproach to Mrs. Ramsay ; for she too knows that one loses " the fret, the hurry, the stir ", and finds the limitless horizon of reality when one sinks down into the subconscious, but she is too much occupied with human relations to seek reality often in this way ; and Carmichael, who stands in the same relation to her as William Bankes does to Ramsay, causes her to question her motives for helping others. Lily Briscoe creates in paint as Mrs. Ramsay creates in life. She admires Mrs. Ramsay's ability to bring order out of chaos in human relations, while Mrs. Ramsay, for her part, instinctively appreciates beauty in art. Lily shares, in so far as her art is concerned, Mrs. Ramsay's selflessness ; and she opposes Ramsay's egotism, as he descends upon her while she paints, bringing chaos with him. But in life Lily Briscoe is determined to be herself. She will not marry, though Mrs. Ramsay believes every one should ; she gives sympathy only reluctantly to Charles Tansley—Ramsay's awkward disciple who is as sensitively egotistical as Ramsay himself—in order to help Mrs. Ramsay establish harmony at the dinner ; later she refuses to sympathize with Ramsay, to whose requests for sympathy Mrs. Ramsay had always responded. In this manner the characters are related to one another in a fine and complicated harmony of a kind that a novelist can attain only when he clearly defines the distinctive traits of his characters.

As in *Mrs. Dalloway*, various threads are pursued throughout *To the Lighthouse* (or rather, throughout the first and last Parts), and they are all brought together in the final resolution which completes the design of the novel. The voyage to the lighthouse is proposed as the book begins ; it is accomplished, ten years later, as the book ends. James's resentment against his father, aroused because Ramsay predicted, in the first Part, that the weather would prevent the voyage, is banished as the lighthouse is reached. At the same time Ramsay escapes for a moment from his preoccupation with himself. Responding for once to the emotional needs of others, he praises James's skill as a sailor ; and he and James and Cam are in complete accord. On shore, at the same moment, Lily Briscoe completes the painting of Mrs. Ramsay and James seated in the window, which she began ten years before and has had in her mind ever since.

But this is only to begin to describe the consummate resolution with which *To the Lighthouse* ends. Throughout the novel, as in *The Voyage Out* and *Night and Day*, there are significant moments, moments of intense reality, when things come together in peace, and the characters find that their vision is abnormally clear. Lily Briscoe knows a moment of this sort when she sees Mr. and Mrs. Ramsay walking together and then watches the flight of the ball that Prue throws high into the air. Nancy has a similar experience when Minta Doyle takes her hand and Nancy sees " the whole world spread out beneath her ". When Mrs. Ramsay sinks down into the subconscious, " There were all the places she had not seen ; the Indian plains ; she felt herself pushing aside the thick leather curtain of a church at Rome." These moments reach a climax in the first Part at the dinner, which Mrs. Ramsay creates so successfully that she believes it partakes of eternity, and at which Lily Briscoe glimpses for the first time the solution to the composition of her painting. When the last Part of the novel begins, the scene seems unreal and chaotic to Lily. She feels that she is in a house of unrelated things, amidst a family whose passions are unrelated ; for Mrs. Ramsay is dead, and, like Mrs. Wilcox in *Howards End*, she was a unifier who prevented strife. But from this unpromising beginning we move steadily to the complete resolution of differences which concludes the novel and which is the most significant, and intensely real, moment in it ; for Mrs. Ramsay's influence, like that of Mrs. Wilcox and of another Forsterian character, Mrs. Moore of *A Passage to India*, is pervasive even after death. Mr. Ramsay undertakes the voyage in her memory, and he and Cam and James move off across the sea into space and towards reality. " Distance had an extraordinary power," Lily Briscoe thinks as she watches them go ; " they had been swallowed up in it, she felt, they were gone for ever, they had become part of the nature of things." Meanwhile, Cam and James go back in memory to the past, and dip down into the subconscious. Lily Briscoe does likewise, and she tries to submerge her individual personality completely in order to create as an artist. Mr. Carmichael, as usual, is sunk deep in the subconscious. So, in various ways, they all reach out towards reality, and in doing so they come into contact with Mrs. Ramsay (who, being dead, is at one with reality) and with one another.* Lily Briscoe sees Mrs. Ramsay seated in the window, and so she is able to complete her painting ; and both she and Mr. Carmichael know when the Ramsays have reached the lighthouse, though their boat has melted away

* Analogies with *A Passage to India* are obvious. See, especially, pp. 261–2 above.

into the blue haze of the distance. They are all part of "a pool of thought, a deep basin of reality". Moreover, there is a suggestion that all their experience has existed from the beginning, that, as Mrs. Ramsay thought, looking back on her dinner, "it seemed always to have been, only was shown now, and so being shown struck everything into stability". And this suggestion has more force than the similar suggestion in *Jacob's Room*: for the experience of ten years has been traversed, as it were, in a day; the flow of time has been slowed; the past has come forward into the present; Mrs. Ramsay sits in the window as she did ten years before; and the vision of her is fixed for ever in Lily's painting. In *To the Lighthouse* Virginia Woolf succeeds, after all, in lending, by means of her treatment of time, a greater sense of inevitability to her novel than the mere foreshadowing of the future could give it.

The style of *To the Lighthouse* is not as varied as the style of *Mrs. Dalloway*, but it contributes as much to the unity of the novel. In the first and last Parts it has, as it were, an atmospheric quality, which blurs the edges of things, and gives the unity of a suffused tone to the whole composition. Yet, when details of a scene are described, they are often astonishingly vivid, perhaps because they contrast with the fluid thoughts and emotions which surround them:

> [Lily Briscoe and William Bankes] came there regularly every evening drawn by some need. It was as if the water floated off and set sailing thoughts which had grown stagnant on dry land, and gave to their bodies even some sort of physical relief. First, the pulse of colour flooded the bay with blue, and the heart expanded with it and the body swam, only the next instant to be checked and chilled by the prickly blackness on the ruffled waves. Then, up behind the great black rock, almost every evening spurted irregularly, so that one had to watch for it and it was a delight when it came, a fountain of white water; and then, while one waited for that, one watched, on the pale semicircular beach, wave after wave shedding again and again smoothly a film of mother-of-pearl.*

In this description the abstract—"the pale semicircular beach"—and the particular—"the prickly blackness on the

* p. 36.

ruffled waves"—are freely mingled; the refluent motion of the waves on the beach is caught in the rhythm of the last phrase; and the effect of the scene upon the observer is recorded, so that the reader is placed at a viewpoint overlooking the bay. The danger of such a style is that it may become monotonous; and this danger is increased in *To the Lighthouse* because the cosmos of the novel is so small. The style of "The Window" and "The Lighthouse" is interrupted and varied, however, by the slower, contemplative, more intellectual style which records the passage of the years in the middle Part, and which moves with a firm tread in sentences that follow a logical pattern. So monotony is avoided; and the fluid, impressionistic style of the first and last Parts, while moving on steadily, sets things firmly in their place, and contributes to the sense of permanence and finality that the novel gives us.

Orlando must have given Virginia Woolf a welcome period of relaxation after the strenuous work of writing *Jacob's Room*, *Mrs. Dalloway*, and *To the Lighthouse*. Under the guise of biography, and with some reference to Victoria Sackville-West and her ancestry, it creates the remarkable character who is a man in the first half of the book and a woman in the second, and recounts this character's experiences, from the Elizabethan Age to the year 1928, in England and Turkey and Persia, in London and at his (or her) country house, as Elizabethan courtier, English Ambassador to the Court of the Sultan, gipsy, and Victorian matron. All Virginia Woolf's interests, so it seems, are to be found in the book: her antiquarian and historical interests (which are evident also in many of her essays), her interest in literature, her love of gossip, her Feminism and her desire that sex should be treated more openly and honestly; her ever-present concern with the relations of time, space, and personality to one another. But none of these matters is very seriously considered in *Orlando*. The book is spirited and light-hearted. It is distinguished for its wit and humour; for its style, which varies from the downright Elizabethan vigour of the description of the Great Frost, to the sensitive, impressionistic style, typical of the preceding novels, which depicts Orlando motoring from London to her country estate and then recalling the past; and for its nicely adjusted changes of mood, as it describes, for example, without a trace of a smile, Orlando rummaging amongst the skeletons of his ancestors while musing upon the writings of Sir Thomas Browne, or creates the portentous dampness of the Victorian Age. It is the book of a novelist who, after long subjection to a severe artistic discipline, casts care aside for a moment, and revels in her freedom.

After this frolic, discipline is supreme once more and Virginia Woolf's purpose is completely serious in *The Waves*. *The Waves* is her highest achievement, and never, perhaps, has a novel been conceived and written with greater integrity and consistency. In the italicized interludes which frame and unite the different sections of the book, the progress of a day at the seaside (a generalized, abstract seaside, which no one has visited, and yet every one has visited), the journey of the sun from dawn to night, the motion of the waves as they break on the shore, the movements of the birds in the trees beside a house, is followed surely and steadily, without any deviation or turning aside from the purpose of the interludes, which is, so it seems, simply to describe a day. In the rest of the book there is not a sentence of direct description; we are always inside the minds of the six characters, Bernard, Louis, Neville, Rhoda, Susan, and Jinny; there is no departure from the restrained, formalized style of their interior monologues; the point of view is never the author's. And yet, through complete submission to the demands of art, Virginia Woolf gains a freedom hitherto unknown to her, beside which the freedom of *Orlando* seems paltry. The day she describes becomes, easily, naturally, a lifetime; the lifetime becomes eternity. The interludes, far from holding the novel rigidly within a frame, merge the lives of the six characters with the vast and eternal sea of reality. The restrained, formal style which depicts their inner lives allows us to look through their conscious minds into the depths of their souls, because, turning its back on ornament and glitter, it refuses all but the essential. And though Virginia Woolf's point of view is not stated, it shapes the whole composition, and is present in the heightened consciousnesses, the preferences, and the judgments of the characters. Her prejudices are discarded, her personality is submerged in the work of art; but her values and her deepest view of life are expressed so thoroughly as to make the prejudices and interests directly stated in *Orlando* appear querulous and trivial in comparison. *Orlando* comes from the surface personality; *The Waves* is drawn from the depths. In it Virginia Woolf's art presents her vision of life without any distortion, with the result that "there is throbbing under [*The Waves*]", as Lowes Dickinson wrote to her after reading the novel, "the mystery which all the poets and philosophers worth mentioning have felt and had their little shot at".*

The greatest thing in *The Waves*, the essential thing without which it would not exist, is the experience of life, the experience of living from childhood to maturity, which it presents through the minds of the six characters. The record of their experiences is more complete than that of the experiences of Clarissa Dalloway or of Septimus Smith; for not only does it extend farther—from childhood to age, rather than from morning to evening—but it goes deeper, it is more profound. Only articulate thoughts and clearly felt sensations and emotions have a place in Clarissa's mind as she walks to Bond Street, muses in her bedroom, or thinks of Septimus's death. There is nothing in the presentation of her inner life which she might not have said to herself or experienced directly and consciously. But the interior monologues of the six characters in *The Waves* express much that is inarticulate, or of which one is only partially aware, in life. The children in the first section could not in life, of course, describe their experiences as they do in the novel. But we are convinced that if they could set before us, with the vision of an artist and in the language of adults, the whole complex of newly-born thoughts, sensations, and emotions (some of them sharp and clear, others strange, distant, and only to be glimpsed in the twinkling of an eye) which make up their lives, this, surely, is what they would tell us. And similarly, when they are adults, we are shown much more than their immediate consciousnesses; we look

* G. L. Dickinson to V. W., 23 Oct. 1931 (quoted by Forster, p. 231).

beneath the surface to the springs of their desires and their fears ; we see the forces which mould their characters. If a work of art is to be judged by its capacity for increasing our awareness of life and of ourselves—and this is the ultimate measure for all works of art—then *The Waves* is eminently successful.

The characters of *The Waves* are related to one another in an even closer harmony than that which unites the characters of *To the Lighthouse*. Each of them is a distinctive type (Virginia Woolf's theory of character seems, at first sight, to be completely discarded in *The Waves*) ; and they radiate out, as it were, like the spokes of a wheel, from Percival, the character whom they all observe and admire, but who is completely silent in the novel, and whose mind we do not enter. Percival—for we see him clearly through the minds of the others—is a Forsterian character, a better educated Stephen Wonham, a happier, calmer George Emerson. He lives easily, naturally, instinctively ; he plays cricket and reads detective novels, but he appreciates Shakespeare and Catullus when Neville reads them to him ; he is beautiful, pagan, " monolithic ". He is " a great master of the art of living ", who " understands everything ", and is, so to speak, a centre of reality, a perfectly adjusted person, around whom the six are grouped.

Percival's nearest relation in the book is Susan, whom he wishes to marry, whose home is the countryside, who feels sometimes that she is the field, the barn, the trees, the seasons, " the mud, the mist, the dawn ", and who, after she refuses Percival and marries a farmer, satisfies her intense desires by occupying herself with child-bearing, and thus becomes a part of the fertile cycle of the countryside. The sensuous Jinny, whose " imagination is the body's ", is Susan's opposite in some respects ; for she loves London as Susan loves the countryside ; she lives for parties and for love ; she does not want to tie herself to one man, nor to burden herself with children. Yet, both Susan and Jinny are guided by the desires of the body, which each satisfies in her own way. Rhoda is Jinny's real opposite. She is as timid and fearful as Jinny is confident and courageous ; and while Jinny sees nothing that is not there, and is always absorbed in the immediate sensations of her body, Rhoda looks between the shoulders of the others at dinner to a landscape " beyond India " ; her mind is wont to leave her body to wander in space, and it is only with difficulty that she can recall it and so return to the hated life to which her body commits her. Louis is her ally ; for, though so successful in business, so neat, and so correctly dressed, he too is timid. He thinks of himself, as Rhoda thinks of herself, as the youngest, the most naked, of the group. Moreover, as Rhoda's mind wanders in space, so Louis's mind moves down the stream of time. He feels that he has lived " many thousand years ", and he sees women carrying red pitchers to the Nile in the time of the Pharaohs. These two commune with one another silently at each of the two reunions ; and for a time they are lovers. Louis, in keeping with both his vivid sense of the past and his timidity, is a traditionalist ; and in this respect he is Neville's exact opposite. From Neville, Bernard says as he " sums up " in the last section of the novel, the group " derived some of those persistent habits of thought which make us irredeemably lop-sided—for instance about crucifixes, that they are the mark of the devil ".* Neville hates, moreover, " the mediocrity of this world " ; Louis, proud of his company's ships which ply the seas complete with gymnasiums and toilets, is devoted to it. In other respects, however, Louis and Neville are not so different from one another. They are both neat, and precise in their habits. Neville's intelligence is remarkably clear and strong, but Louis's intellect compares not unfavourably with his. Neville pursues truth calmly, steadily, amongst his books. Louis is occupied each day in his office ; but, retiring to his attic room after the day's business is over, he too seeks truth, and he " has formed unalterable conclusions ", Bernard thinks, " upon the true nature of what is to be known ". " When Louis is alone he sees with astonishing intensity, and will write some words that may outlast us all." And though Neville's intellect is so splendid and brave, he too is timid in some respects. He is very like St. John Hirst of *The Voyage Out*. His body is ugly, and, he fears, disgusting. He wonders whether he is " doomed always to cause repulsion in those [he] loves ".

* This sentence recalls Keynes's Memoir, " My Early Beliefs ".

He loves Percival, who is so intensely his opposite, with an " absurd and violent passion ", which he is afraid to expose to Bernard or Louis ; for he is one of those who love men more than women. At moments his emotions inspire him to write poetry, but then his intellect draws him up short, and ends his inspiration. Bernard, the phrase-maker, the story-teller of the group, is not troubled by such divisions within himself. He possesses " the double capacity to feel, to reason ".* He sees life with an artist's vision, and seeks continually to integrate the phrases in his note-book into a whole which will express the truth about life. In this respect he is opposed to Neville, whose mind " falls like a chopper on a block " ; and the difference between them is emphasized by Bernard's untidiness, of which Neville disapproves. " . . . how I distrust neat designs of life that are drawn upon half-sheets of note-paper," says Bernard. " . . . I begin to seek some design more in accordance with those moments of humiliation and triumph that come now and then undeniably." And, like Virginia Woolf herself, he sometimes finds reality, as he walks about the streets of London, by sinking " down, deep, into what passes, this omnipresent, general life ". " . . . beneath these pavements ", he reflects, " are shells, bones and silence ".

But closely as the six characters are related to one another —and there are, of course, many more relations between them than can be indicated here—unity is established among them mainly through their several relationships with Percival. It is not only that they all admire him, but also that each of them reaches out in his or her own way to the reality which Percival enjoys instinctively in life and with which he is merged after his death in India. Susan finds reality in the countryside and in helping to fulfill nature's task ; Jinny finds it in the intense sensations of her body ; Rhoda glimpses it when her

* When opening a posthumous exhibition of Roger Fry's paintings, Virginia Woolf spoke of the union in Fry " of two different qualities—his reason and his sensibility. Many people have one ; many people have the other," she said. " But few have both, and fewer still are able to make them work in harmony. But that was what he did. While he was reasoning he was seeing ; and while he was seeing he was reasoning. He was acutely sensitive, but at the same time he was uncompromisingly honest " (*The Moment*, p. 85).

mind wanders in space, and she attains it, at last, through suicide ; Louis sees it when his mind goes back through the centuries ; Neville seeks it—as Louis does too, when he has time—through the intellect ; Bernard through the artist's vision. They are all seeking the same thing ; and this is why they are grouped about Percival, as Rhoda thinks during their dinner with him, like minnows round a stone which has fallen into a pond. This is also why they have a vivid sense of reality and of union with one another at the dinner, and again at the second reunion—when Percival, though dead, is present in the memories of them all. " It is Percival ", Louis thinks, " . . . who makes us aware that these attempts to say, ' I am this, I am that ', which we make, coming together, like separated parts of one body and soul, are false."

Some critics, indeed, believe that the six characters are " different facets of a single person ".* And certainly many traits of Virginia Woolf herself may be found in them. Jinny shares her creator's courage and responsiveness to the animal sensations of the body ; Susan her affinity with the impersonal world of nature ; Rhoda her awareness of the terror of life ; Louis and Rhoda together her sense of the vast realms of time and space which exist beyond the individual's immediate consciousness ; Bernard her aesthetic theories and her artist's vision. But there is also something of Roger Fry in Bernard ; there is much of Lytton Strachey in Neville ; Louis suggests Maynard Keynes at moments, different though he is from Keynes in many respects. Each of the characters is conceived as an individual ; and it is as individuals that they are related and contrasted to one another. At the same time, they all merge in the deep sea of the subconscious, from which, as it were, they speak to us. " Let us hold it for one moment," Jinny says as the dinner with Percival ends ; " love, hatred, by whatever name we call it, this globe whose walls are made of Percival, of youth and beauty, and something so deep sunk within us that we shall perhaps never make this moment out of one man again." There is something so deep sunk within every one, Virginia Woolf implies, that we are all, in a sense, one person. It is this view of life that enables her to create

* Deborah Newton, *Virginia Woolf*, p. 51.

each of the characters in *The Waves* so consistently without, after all, repudiating her belief that there are no " circles of chalk between people's feet ".* Beneath the personalities that she creates, beneath the individual waves, she shows us an infinite and inscrutable sea.

The form of *The Waves*, in so far as its form may be considered apart from the relations between the characters, has something in common with the form of Virginia Woolf's previous compositions. Bernard, in his " summing-up ", looks back upon the action of the preceding sections as the characters in the last Part of *To the Lighthouse* look back upon the action of the first Part. The two reunions recall the dinner in that book. Once more the novel is contained by the time sequence of a day. And time is measured in essentially the same way as in " Kew Gardens " : the interludes in *The Waves* are a development, so to speak, of the description of the flower-bed and the journey of the snail in that short story.

Besides recording the passage of time, the interludes serve as premonitory choruses. At noon, when life is at its height, forms are sharp and individual in the sunlight ; the birds sing " passionate songs addressed to one ear only " ; the waves beat steadily on the shore " like the thud of a great beast stamping ". At nightfall, when death is near, darkness merges everything together ; there is " no sound save the cry of a bird seeking some lonelier tree " ; the waves, after breaking on the shore, roll back " sighing over the shingle ". The interludes are related to the interior monologues of the characters by means of imagery, especially by the wave imagery which recurs again and again in their thoughts, but also, for example, by Bernard's comparisons of the six to birds, or by the plates and cutlery which Rhoda sees in the first section, which recur in several of the interludes, and which are related to the coffee-cup, the knife, and the fork, " things in themselves ", with which Bernard communes in the last section of the novel. And the sea that the interludes describe becomes the eternal sea from which the lives of the children were drawn, and into which we see Bernard subside at death.

The transitions from mind to mind are sometimes effected

* p. 128.

in the same manner as the transitions in previous novels. In the first section Jinny runs past Louis and kisses him ; Susan sees them, is jealous, and goes away to cry in the beech-wood ; she passes Neville and Bernard ; Bernard follows her ; and so we move from one child to another. But as they grow older and Virginia Woolf becomes more and more concerned with the spaceless, timeless world of the deeper layers of the mind, such relations become unnecessary ; she need concern herself only with the emotional appropriateness of her transitions, without regard to the relations of her characters to one another in space. And the effects that she achieves as she moves, for example, directly from Susan, communing with the earth, to Jinny, confidently exercising all her charms at a party, and then to Rhoda, sensitive and fearful, trying to hide herself at perhaps the same, perhaps another, party, are accomplished with greater ease than the effects attained by the transitions in previous novels. In no other respect, perhaps, may Virginia Woolf's steadily increasing mastery of her art from *Jacob's Room* to *The Waves* be more clearly seen.

Images and phrases which have an emotional significance recur in the minds of the characters to make a pattern in the novel. Rhoda's repeated statement, " I have no face ", expresses her timidity. Louis's image of women carrying red pitchers to the banks of the Nile and his reiterated remark that " the chained beast stamps on the beach " express his awareness of the past and of the flow of time. Jinny's visions of herself seated in a billowing dress upon a gilt chair inform us, while she is still at school, of her gifts and propensities. These are more or less arbitrary symbols ; but often we see a significant image coming into being in the mind of a character, as the emotion which he feels accretes round some external object. Jinny sees leaves moving as she dashes past the hedge in the first section, and later the image of a dancing leaf expresses her vivacity. As Louis stands in the garden beside the hedge he feels that his roots " go down to the depths of the world ", and this feeling recurs in later sections to emphasize his traditionalism. Again in the first section, as Neville comes through a swing-door to ascend the stairs, he hears the servants speaking of a dead man who was found lying in a gutter with his throat cut. The shock of this news causes him to halt ; for a moment he is unable to ascend the stairs ; and the apple-tree outside the window becomes " immitigable ", " implacable ". At the first reunion Neville arrives early and waits for Percival to come through a swing-door. When he learns, in the next section, of Percival's death, he recalls his childhood experience. And the " immitigable tree " recurs in his mind in other sections, as well, when he thinks of death. Swing-doors appear and reappear throughout the novel, and are always associated with the transitoriness of life. These images, it should be pointed out, differ from Forster's " rhythms ". With the exception of the swing-door, they are private symbols, specifically attached by a given character to a certain emotion. And even the swing-door is too closely associated with one well-defined meaning to take on a life of its own. Similar images occur in *Jacob's Room*, *Mrs. Dalloway*, and *To the Lighthouse*, but they are not used consistently enough in those novels to form a pattern of the sort that is found in *The Waves*.*

As in *The Voyage Out*, *Night and Day*, and *To the Lighthouse*, there are in *The Waves* a number of moments charged with reality which culminate as the novel ends. Each of the characters, as we have seen, experiences individually moments of intense reality ; and the two dinners of reunion are, as it were, nodes of reality in which they all participate. The shock of the news of Percival's death enables both Bernard and Rhoda to step outside the everyday sequence of life for a short time ; and art, which is concerned with reality, brings each of them closer to Percival.

> I will . . . submit myself to the influence of minds like mine outside the sequence, [Bernard thinks as he enters the National Gallery]. . . . Here are pictures. Here are cold madonnas

* As Bernard sums up, he describes the way in which an object may come to be associated with an emotion : " On the outskirts of every agony sits some observant fellow [in the mind] who points . . . [He directs us] to that which is beyond and outside our own predicament ; to that which is symbolic, and thus perhaps permanent, if there is any permanence in our sleeping, eating, breathing, so animal, so spiritual and tumultuous lives." The experiences of childhood, Bernard says, " happen in one second and last for ever " (pp. 170 and 176).

> among their pillars. Let them lay to rest the incessant activity of the mind's eye, the bandaged head [of Percival], the men with ropes, so that I may find something unvisual beneath. Here are gardens ; and Venus among her flowers ; here are saints and blue madonnas. Mercifully these pictures make no reference ; they do not nudge ; they do not point. Thus they expand my consciousness of him and bring him back to me differently. I remember his beauty. " Look where he comes," I said.

Rhoda enters a concert-hall and submits herself to music :

> " Like " and " like " and " like "—but what is the thing that lies beneath the semblance of the thing ? Now that lightning has gashed the tree and the flowering branch has fallen and Percival, by his death, has made me this gift, let me see the thing. There is a square ; there is an oblong. The players take the square and place it upon the oblong. They place it very accurately ; they make a perfect dwelling-place. Very little is left outside. The structure is now visible ; what is inchoate is here stated ; we are not so various or so mean ; we have made oblongs and stood them upon squares. This is our triumph ; this is our consolation.*

Then Rhoda goes to the Thames at Greenwich, from whence ships sail to India. " Into the wave that dashes upon the shore," she says, " into the wave that flings its white foam to the uttermost corners of the earth, I throw my violets, my offering to Percival." In the last section of the novel, Bernard, having lost his awareness of himself as a distinct individual, is able to step outside the sequence of life almost at will. " [My being] lies deep, tideless, immune," he says, " now that he is dead, the man I called ' Bernard ' . . . The shock of the falling wave which has sounded all my life, which woke me [in childhood], no longer makes quiver what I hold." Hence

* " It is when [the elemental forms of architecture] are combined," Roger Fry says, " when the superposition or interpenetration of two or more rectangular blocks, or of blocks with sections of cylinders, and so forth, is devised in relation to the earth surface and its possible plastic arrangement, that we begin to get the essentially aesthetic quality of architecture. Or, rather, when such interplay of these elemental forms is perfectly adjusted to the expression of an idea " (*Architectural Heresies*, p. 29). Cf. p. 148 above, and *The Waves*, p. 162.

he is able to sum up for the others ; he feels that he is the others ; he shares the experiences that they have had ; and the imagery of their thoughts and emotions recurs in his monologue. But while he is still alive he cannot escape wholly from the sequence of life. He is recalled to himself when he fears that the stranger to whom he has talked in a restaurant may think him a fool ; he is recalled again when the head waiter ostentatiously prepares to close the restaurant. Finally, a last spasm of self-assertion is required of him in order to meet death courageously ; and then his wave breaks on the shore, and is drawn back for ever into the sea.

The style of *The Waves* is more impersonal and restrained than the style of any other of Virginia Woolf's novels. The interludes are full of beautiful description ; but, in keeping with the eternal scene which they depict, they are more abstract than, for example, the description of the bay in *To the Lighthouse* ; and the emotions and thoughts of the characters are not mixed with them. In fact, the style of the novel as a whole contrasts sharply with the fluid style of *To the Lighthouse*. The subdued, uninvolved, almost halting sentences of the monologues, which do not change in style as we move from one character to another, give a uniform texture to the novel and remind us that we are beneath the layer of the mind which expresses itself fluently in speech. Yet these sentences, though restrained, are wonderfully expressive. Neville describes Bernard's nature in an exquisite phrase : " a moth-like impetuosity dashing itself against hard glass." Jinny's breathless exhilaration after dancing is caught in perfect rhythms :

> Suddenly the music breaks. My blood runs on but my body stands still. The room reels past my eyes. It stops.
>
> Come, then, let us wander whirling to the gilt chairs. The body is stronger than I thought. I am dizzier than I supposed. I do not care for anything in the world.

Fear breaks through the furtive sentences of Rhoda's monologue:

> " I shall edge behind them," said Rhoda, " as if I saw someone I know. But I know no one. I shall twitch the curtain and look at the moon. Draughts of oblivion shall quench my agitation. The door opens ; the tiger leaps. The door opens ; terror rushes in ; terror upon terror, pursuing me."

And the sweeping lines of a Titian painting are described in a sentence that might be measured out, so it seems, against the painting itself: " No doubt he rose with the great arms holding the cornucopia, and fell, in that descent ". In passages such as these Virginia Woolf's style reaches a height that can be attained only by an artist who, like Racine and Stendhal, for instance, submits himself to a classical discipline.

Virginia Woolf's last two novels are not as successful or as solidly constructed as *Mrs. Dalloway*, *To the Lighthouse*, and *The Waves*. In *The Years* she returns to a narrative, descriptive method (though not to the construction of plot), a method which, as the title of the book indicates, is in keeping with her subject; for in this novel she records the passage of the years, as in *The Waves* she records the experience of living from childhood to age. Indeed, *The Years* is in some respects curiously the reverse of *The Waves*. The experiences of individuals are no longer Virginia Woolf's primary concern: she is interested rather in the mass of humanity, from which she chooses the Pargiter family as a typical group. The purpose of the novel is to describe the flow of time and the changes in human life from 1880 to 1937: the time sequence, from which Virginia Woolf has tried to escape as far as possible in her previous novels, is the *raison d'être* of *The Years*. And as the interior monologues in *The Waves* are framed by interludes which record the passage of time, so each year from which scenes are described in *The Years* is introduced by a passage which gives us spatial impressions of the English countryside and of London. Moreover, as the height of the sun in each interlude in *The Waves* becomes a significant part of the succeeding section because it indicates the age of the characters, so the rain, the smoke, the moonlight, the wind, the snow, the mist, which are used, each in turn, to emphasize space in the various introductory passages in *The Years*, become, respectively, part of the succeeding scenes. It is as though Virginia Woolf wished to frame the time sequence of *The Years* with space—we have seen a somewhat similar attempt in *Jacob's Room*. But space cannot tie things up as neatly as time: it has no cycles—of a day, of a year—as time has. And the time sequence of

The Years is not itself a cycle : it is only a section, taken, as it were, from the stream of time, open at both ends. There is no reason why it should begin in 1880 or end in 1937, except that this is the particular portion of time with which its author is acquainted. Consequently, *The Years* is not a coherent, self-contained whole. The scenes in it are often beautifully linked together ; the two branches of the Pargiter family are followed in skilfully arranged sequences, within which Lady Lasswade and the servant Crosby—at opposite extremes of the social scale—are included ; objects that stand like stones amidst the flow of time—the chair with gilt claws, the Italian glass, the portrait of Mrs. Abel Pargiter, the statues in Whitehall—give some pattern to the novel, in rather the same way, though the pattern is not as pronounced or as fine, as recurring images form a pattern in *The Waves* ; and hammering—Jo Robson hammering nails in a hencoop, the hammering in *Siegfried*, a drunken man hammering on a door near Sara and Maggie Pargiter's flat—develops into a modest " rhythm ". But there is no centre around which the whole novel coheres, no principle of organization which sets it apart from life as a self-supporting work of art.

Indeed, Virginia Woolf is not, on the whole, seeking in *The Years* to impose a pattern on her experience of life. Instead, she is examining life, interrogating life, in the hope that a pattern will emerge. And her examination reveals many unpleasant things. She is more aware of the horror of life than of its beauty in this novel, and the horror that she sees is pervasive ugliness, pervasive misery, not the sudden terror that strikes into the heart of Rhoda or of Septimus Warren Smith. The book is crowded with sordid details. Colonel Pargiter's hand, which has lost two fingers and has withered into a claw, fumbles amongst silver to extract a sixpenny-bit, fumbles about the neck of his frowzy mistress. Rose, when a little girl, barely escapes from a horrible sexual pervert as he unbuttons his clothes. Martin buys violets from a flower-girl, catches sight of her face beneath the hat pulled low to obscure it, and sees that she has no nose. The aged Crosby cries out, when she is alone, against the " dirty brute " who spat in the bath she has to clean ; a Jew leaves hairs and a greasy ring in the bath which Sara must use in her cheap lodging-house. " How terrible old age was," Eleanor thinks as she watches her father ; " shearing off all one's faculties, one by one, but leaving something alive in the centre. . . ." And beyond these intimate, personal miseries, there is the constant threat to civilization ; there is War ; there is the " tyranny, brutality, torture " rife in Europe in the 'thirties.

Yet, there is poetry too in the novel, as though pain must find an outlet in beauty, and courage must sing. The deformed Sara, like the characters in O'Casey's later plays, though less bitterly than they, expresses herself in poetry : amidst the squalor in which she lives, she breaks continually into song, even though her voice is cracked. Moreover, faith in the essential goodness of humanity remains. " I'm not despondent," says Eleanor, who has devoted much of her life to social service ; " no, because people are so kind, so good at heart. . . . So that if only ordinary people, ordinary people like ourselves . . . " And she says in 1937 that things have changed for the better since she was a girl. " What I mean is, we've changed in ourselves. We're happier—we're freer." The Bloomsbury ideals of self-knowledge, courage, tolerance, and freedom must be trusted to, *The Years* indicates, if civilization is to survive. The mysterious Nicholas, a man whom our laws would imprison for his homosexual tendencies, but whose fine qualities Eleanor appreciates, expresses these ideals. " If we do not know ourselves, how then can we make religions, laws, that fit ? " he asks. If the world is to improve, we must cease to live, each of us, " screwed up into one hard little, tight little—knot ", he says in his halting English. " The soul —the whole being . . . wishes to expand ; to adventure ; to form—new combinations." He is always on the point of making a speech about the New World of the future. The speech is never made ; the song of the new generation, the caretaker's children whom Delia brings up from the basement into the midst of her party, is unintelligible ; but the novel ends on a note of hope as a new day dawns.

Between The Acts has all the outer trappings of success. The narrative, descriptive method of *The Years* is combined so tactfully in this novel with the technique of presenting scenes through the minds of the characters that the advantages of both methods are gained and the disadvantages of each are eliminated. Poetry, which was quietly introduced in *The Years*, is a dominant and beautiful feature of *Between The Acts*. The pageant, around which the novel centres, is almost all in verse ; Isabella Oliver's thoughts run naturally into lines of poetry which she composes and murmurs to herself ; the impressions of the audience as they behold the pageant are often expressed in doggerel lines that rime with a satiric jingle. And the novel has form. Like Virginia Woolf's three most successful novels, it is contained within the time sequence of a day. Moreover, prehistoric time, historic time, and present time are merged with one another to become integral parts of *Between the Acts*. The first is introduced by Mrs. Swithin's musings as she reads her Outline of History ; the second by the description of Pointz Hall and of the countryside around it, which has been moulded by the generations of the past ; and the three periods of time are brought together in the pageant. The pageant reviews the history of England ; it is saved from failure during an awkward pause in its production by the bellowing of cows behind the outdoor stage—by " the primeval voice sounding loud in the ear of the present moment " ; and it ends with " ten minutes of present time " and with a scene in which the audience are shown themselves in mirrors held up by the actors. As the novel concludes, Pointz Hall is covered by darkness. " The house had lost its shelter. It was night before roads were made, or houses. It was the night that dwellers in caves had watched from some high place among the rocks." And Giles and Isabella Oliver are about to fight and then embrace, " as the dog fox fights with the vixen, in the heart of darkness, in the fields of night ". So the cycle of twenty-four hours which the novel describes is merged with the universal and the eternal. Furthermore, Virginia Woolf's sense of the vast areas of space upon the earth's surface is made a coherent part of the novel—more successfully, perhaps, than ever before. Mrs. Swithin thinks of the swallows who come each year from Africa ; she becomes, as she watches them, almost the swallows herself, so that her brother Bartholomew calls her " Swallow, my sister, O sister swallow " ; and as she gazes at the lily-pond she sees the world spread out beneath her : " She fluttered her eye over the surface, naming leaves India, Africa, America. Islands of security, glossy and thick." These musings of hers are not extraneous or capricious, but a part of her vague, diffuse, but vital character, which continually seeks unity amongst the many. " . . . she was given to increasing the bounds of the moment by flights into the past or future ; or sidelong down corridors and alleys. . . ."

And yet, in spite of these merits, *Between the Acts* hits only the surface of the mind. Part of the trouble is that Virginia Woolf, though she loves the beauty of the countryside, is not strongly attached to the countryside by deep emotions, as Forster, for instance, is ; and she does not understand its people as he does. Nor has she a strong historical sense, though she has a strong sense of time. The scenes of the pageant catch the mannerisms, not the spirit, of the Ages they review. However, the main subject of *Between the Acts* is not the countryside or England's past, but the impending catastrophe of war which overshadowed England, which overshadowed civilization, in the summer of 1939. And this, undoubtedly, is a subject with which Virginia Woolf was deeply concerned. Nevertheless, her concern is not forcefully expressed in the novel, though the Battle of Britain was being fought as she completed it. It is as though the pain would be too great if she looked directly at the world ; and so she averts her eyes. Giles Oliver, the character most aware of the terror and danger in Europe, feels that he is " manacled to a rock . . . and forced passively to behold indescribable horror ". But his suffering is not convincing. He remains in character what he is in appearance : a cricketer who is rather uncomfortable, rather annoyed. His actions when he stamps on the snake which is gorging itself with a toad are histrionic ; the blood on his shoes is not real ; it is not envisioned by the author as the greasy ring on the bath in *The Years* is envisioned ; and as a result, it does not sink into the mind of the reader. Indeed, as *The Years* would be a better novel if it were more detached from life, so, conversely, *Between the Acts* would be better if it were less detached. It presents the view of one who is already beginning to withdraw from the scene, who, like Isabella Oliver, wonders if she would "mind not again to see may tree or nut tree? Not again to hear on the trembling spray the thrush sing, or to see, dipping and diving as if he skimmed waves in the air, the yellow woodpecker?" And though it has the strange still beauty of this withdrawal, the emotional material of which it is made is in other respects very slight.

Miss La Trobe, the author and producer of the pageant in *Between the Acts*, is associated with Virginia Woolf the artist in the same indefinable way that Solness, the Master Builder, is associated with Ibsen. Miss La Trobe is concerned above all to create a work of art which will hold the attention of the audience and make them understand. She wants no thanks; she will not come forward to explain her meaning. After every one else has left the scene of the pageant, she remains for a moment.

> She could say to the world, You have taken my gift! Glory possessed her—for one moment. But what had she given? A cloud that melted into the other clouds on the horizon. It was in the giving that the triumph was. And the triumph faded. Her gift meant nothing. If they had understood her meaning; if they had known their parts; if the pearls had been real and the funds illimitable—it would have been a better gift. Now it had gone to join the others.

Then she strides off across the lawn into the gathering darkness.

> The house was dormant; one thread of smoke thickened against the trees. It was strange that the earth, with all those flowers incandescent—the lilies, the roses, and clumps of white flowers and bushes of burning green—should still be hard. From the earth green waters seemed to rise over her. She took her voyage away from the shore, and, raising her hand, fumbled for the latch of the iron entrance gate.

So Virginia Woolf takes her leave.

CONCLUSION

BENEATH the individual differences among the works of art of Forster, Strachey, and Virginia Woolf there is essential agreement. There is a common respect for the things of the spirit ; a belief that the inner life of the soul is much more important than the outer life of action or the outer world of material things ; an admiration for the individual and for the virtues of courage, tolerance, and honesty ; a desire that man shall be whole and express himself emotionally as well as intellectually ; a love of truth and of beauty. And the integrity and careful composition of their books demonstrate a profound respect for art, and a conviction that form is as important to a work of art as content ; that, indeed, the two are inseparable since the artist cannot express emotions and ideas adequately except in significant form.

Moore's philosophy, with its insistence upon the intrinsic value of good states of mind, and its emphasis upon the importance of good taste and of an adequate response to all the various kinds of beauty, undoubtedly helped to form the values of these three writers and of the rest of Bloomsbury. But even more important to Bloomsbury than Moore's philosophy was the Cambridge humanism which is behind that philosophy, and which is expressed, as well, in the writings of such men as Lowes Dickinson, John Ellis McTaggart, and Leslie Stephen. To this spiritual, idealistic strain of humanism, Roger Fry's aesthetics and his appreciation of the visual arts were added in Bloomsbury.

Fry's contribution to Bloomsbury was of crucial and incalculable importance. An appreciation of beauty in visual form and colour, and an aesthetics which embraced all the arts, were exactly, as Clive Bell and Strachey knew, what Cambridge lacked. Fry made this deficiency good in Bloomsbury ; he insisted that " the aesthetic pursuit is as important in the long run for mankind as the search for truth " ; * and if there was any tendency in Bloomsbury—as there was at Cambridge—to allow intellect to repress sensibility, Fry's influence averted this danger. Moreover, his lucid, definitive statement of the relationship between art and life helped Bloomsbury's artists to express their values clearly in works which are solidly constructed from materials drawn directly from life.

These works of art are Bloomsbury's main contribution to the world. They set forth Bloomsbury's beliefs and ideals in permanent form, and disseminate them quietly, but surely. How far Bloomsbury's values have spread, and how far they will spread, cannot, of course, be estimated. What is certain is that Bloomsbury has exerted its influence in an attempt to increase and to improve the public knowledge of art, to combat prudery and to encourage clear and honest thought, to gain a sympathetic understanding for those who are mentally or sexually abnormal, to help man to be an individual and to foster his creative emotions. Bloomsbury has attempted, in other words, to spread civilization. Turning their backs upon materialism and upon conventional religion, the members of the group have carried forward some of the highest and most spiritual ideals of the past into a century which has paid scant attention to the things of the spirit. And, above all, they have been individuals in a world in which individualism is threatened daily.

* *Architectural Heresies*, p. 47.

BIBLIOGRAPHY

Note : The dates given are the dates of the editions used. Books are listed under each author in the order of their first publication.

I

SOURCES

A. *Direct*

BELL, CLIVE. *Art.* London, Chatto & Windus, 1914.

Since Cézanne. London, Chatto & Windus, 1929.

Landmarks in Nineteenth-Century Painting. London, Chatto & Windus, 1927.

Civilization, an Essay. London, Chatto & Windus, 1928.

Proust. London, Hogarth Press, 1928.

An Account of French Painting. London, Chatto & Windus, 1931.

Enjoying Pictures : Meditations in the National Gallery and Elsewhere. London, Chatto & Windus, 1934.

Victor Pasmore (Penguin Modern Painters). Harmondsworth, Penguin Books, 1945.

DICKINSON, G. L. *The Greek View of Life.* London, Methuen, 1947.

The Meaning of Good : A Dialogue. Glasgow, Maclehose, 1901.

Letters from John Chinaman, and other Essays. London, Allen & Unwin, 1946.

After Two Thousand Years : A Dialogue Between Plato and a Modern Young Man. London, Allen & Unwin, 1930.

J. McT. E. McTaggart (with chapters by Basil Williams and S. V. Keeling). Cambridge University Press, 1931.

FORSTER, E. M. *Where Angels Fear to Tread.* London, Arnold, 1947.

The Longest Journey. London, Arnold, 1947.

A Room with a View. London, Arnold, 1947.

Howards End. London, Arnold, 1947.

Alexandria : A History and a Guide. Alexandria, Whitehead Morris, 1938.

Pharos and Pharillon. London, Hogarth Press, 1926.

A Passage to India (with an introduction by Peter Burra and some notes by the author). London, Dent, 1948.

Aspects of the Novel. London, Arnold, 1937.

Goldsworthy Lowes Dickinson. London, Arnold, 1934.

Abinger Harvest. London, Arnold, 1936.

England's Pleasant Land : A Pageant Play. London, Hogarth Press, 1940.

Nordic Twilight (Macmillan War Pamphlets). London, Macmillan, 1940.

Collected Short Stories. London, Sidgwick & Jackson, 1947.

Two Cheers for Democracy. London, Arnold, 1951.

FRY, ROGER. *Giovanni Bellini.* London, Unicorn, 1899.

Discourses delivered to the students of the Royal Academy by Sir Joshua Reynolds, Kt., with introductions and notes by Roger Fry (ed.). London, Seeley, 1905.

Vision and Design. London, Chatto & Windus, 1920.

Architectural Heresies of a Painter : A Lecture delivered at the Royal Institute of British Architects, May 20th, 1921. London, Chatto & Windus, 1921.

A Sampler of Castile. London, Hogarth Press, 1923.

The Artist and Psycho-Analysis : A Paper read to the British Psychological Society. London, Hogarth Press, 1924.

Transformations : Critical and Speculative Essays on Art. London, Chatto & Windus, 1926.

Cézanne : A Study of his Development. London, Hogarth Press, 1927.

Flemish Art : A Critical Survey. London, Chatto & Windus, 1927.

Henri Matisse. London, Zwemmer, n.d.

"The Arts of Painting and Sculpture", *An Outline of Modern Knowledge.* London, Gollancz, 1931.

Words Wanted in Connexion with Arts. Society for Pure English, Tract 31, n.d.

Characteristics of French Art. London, Chatto & Windus, 1932.

Reflections on British Painting. London, Faber & Faber, 1934.

Last Lectures (with an introduction by Kenneth Clark). Cambridge University Press, 1939.

GRANT, DUNCAN. "Virginia Woolf", *Horizon,* III (June 1941).

KEYNES, J. M. *The Economic Consequences of the Peace.* London, Macmillan, 1920.

Essays in Biography. London, Macmillan, 1933.

Two Memoirs (with an introduction by David Garnett). London, Hart-Davis, 1949.

MAURON, CHARLES. *The Nature of Beauty in Art and Literature* (translated from the French by Roger Fry). London, Hogarth Press, 1927.

Aesthetics and Psychology (translated from the French by Roger Fry and Katherine John). London, Hogarth Press, 1935.

MOORE, G. E. *Principia Ethica.* Cambridge University Press, 1922.

Ethics, London, Butterworth, 1936.

Philosophical Studies. London, Paul, Trench, Trubner, 1922.

STRACHEY, LYTTON. *Landmarks in French Literature.* London, Chatto & Windus, 1948.

Eminent Victorians. London, Chatto & Windus, 1948.

Queen Victoria. London, Chatto & Windus, 1948.

Elizabeth and Essex : A Tragic History. London, Chatto & Windus, 1948.

Literary Essays. London, Chatto & Windus, 1948.

Biographical Essays. London, Chatto & Windus, 1948.

WOOLF, LEONARD. *The Village in the Jungle.* London, Hogarth Press, 1931.

Hunting the Highbrow. London, Hogarth Press, 1927.

Essays on Literature, History, Politics, etc. London, Hogarth Press, 1927.

After the Deluge : A Study of Communal Psychology. 2 vols. London, Hogarth Press, 1931 & 1939.

Barbarians at the Gate. London, Gollancz, 1939.

The Hotel. London, Hogarth Press, 1939.

WOOLF, VIRGINIA. *The Voyage Out.* London, Hogarth Press, 1949.

Night and Day. London, Hogarth Press, 1950.

Monday or Tuesday (with woodcuts by Vanessa Bell). London, Hogarth Press, 1921.

Jacob's Room. London, Hogarth Press, 1949.

Mrs. Dalloway. London, Hogarth Press, 1950.

The Common Reader. London, Hogarth Press, 1925.

To the Lighthouse. London, Hogarth Press, 1949.

Orlando : A Biography. London, Hogarth Press, 1949.

A Room of One's Own. London, Hogarth Press, 1929.

The Waves. London, Hogarth Press, 1950.

The Common Reader, Second Series. London, Hogarth Press, 1932.

Flush : A Biography. London, Hogarth Press, 1933.

The Years. London, Hogarth Press, 1951.

Three Guineas. London, Hogarth Press, 1938.

Roger Fry: A Biography. London, Hogarth Press, 1940.
Between the Acts. London, Hogarth Press, 1947.
The Death of the Moth and other Essays. London, Hogarth Press, 1942.
A Haunted House and other Short Stories. London, Hogarth Press, 1947.
The Moment and other Essays. London, Hogarth Press, 1947.
The Captain's Death Bed and other Essays. London, Hogarth Press, 1950.

B. *Indirect*

ANNAN, N. G. *Leslie Stephen: His Thought and Character in Relation to his Time.* London, MacGibbon & Kee, 1951.
BEERBOHM, MAX. *Lytton Strachey* (The Rede Lecture, 1943). Cambridge University Press, 1943.
ELIOT, T. S. "Notes on Virginia Woolf", *Horizon*, III (May 1941).
HARROD, R. F. *The Life of John Maynard Keynes.* London, Macmillan, 1951.
KEYNES, F. A. *Gathering Up the Threads: A Study in Family Biography.* Cambridge, Heffer, 1950.
King's College Council. *John Maynard Keynes, 1883–1946, Fellow and Bursar.* Cambridge University Press, 1949.
MAITLAND, F. W. *The Life and Letters of Leslie Stephen.* London, Duckworth, 1906.
MORTIMER, RAYMOND. *Duncan Grant* (Penguin Modern Painters). Harmondsworth, Penguin Books, 1948.
ROBINSON, E. A. G. *John Maynard Keynes, 1883–1946.* Cambridge University Press, 1947.

II

ADDITIONAL READING

BANTOCK, G. H. "The 'Private Heaven' of the 'Twenties", *The Listener*, 15 March 1951.
BEACH, J. W. *The Twentieth-Century Novel: Studies in Technique.* New York, Appleton-Century, 1932.
BENNETT, JOAN. *Virginia Woolf: Her Art as a Novelist.* Cambridge University Press, 1945.

BIBLIOGRAPHY

BLACKSTONE, BERNARD. *Virginia Woolf: A Commentary.* London, Hogarth Press, 1949.

BOAS, GUY. *Lytton Strachey.* The English Association, Pamphlet No. 93 (November 1935).

"Lytton Strachey—Dramatic Critic", *English,* VIII (Spring 1950).

BROWER, R. A. *The Fields of Light: An Experiment in Critical Reading.* New York, Oxford University Press, 1951. (Chapters on *Mrs. Dalloway* and *A Passage to India.*)

BROWN, E. K. *Rhythm in the Novel.* University of Toronto Press, 1950.

BULLETT, GERALD. *Modern English Fiction: A Personal View.* London, Jenkins, 1926.

BURRA, PETER. Essay on E. M. Forster, reprinted as an introduction to the Everyman edition of *A Passage to India.* London, Dent, 1948.

CHAMBERS, R. L. *The Novels of Virginia Woolf.* Edinburgh, Oliver & Boyd, 1947.

CONNOLLY, CYRIL. *Enemies of Promise.* London, Routledge, 1938.

DAICHES, DAVID. *The Novel and the Modern World.* University of Chicago Press, 1939.

Virginia Woolf. London, Editions Poetry, 1945.

DELATTRE, FLORIS. *Le Roman Psychologique de Virginia Woolf.* Paris, Vrin, 1932.

DOBRÉE, BONAMY. *The Lamp and the Lute: Studies in Six Modern Authors.* Oxford, Clarendon, 1929.

"Lytton Strachey", *The Post Victorians* (W. R. Inge, ed.). London, Nicholson & Watson, 1933.

Modern Prose Style. Oxford, Clarendon, 1934.

HOARE, D. M. *Some Studies in the Modern Novel.* London, Chatto & Windus, 1938. (Chapters on Virginia Woolf and E. M. Forster.)

HOLT, L. E. "E. M. Forster and Samuel Butler", *PMLA,* LXI, (September 1946).

HOLTBY, WINIFRED. *Virginia Woolf.* London, Wishart, 1932.

IYENGAR, K. R. S. *Lytton Strachey: A Critical Study.* London, Chatto & Windus, 1939.

LONGAKER, MARK. *Contemporary Biography.* Philadelphia, University of Pennsylvania Press, 1934.

LUBBOCK, PERCY. *The Craft of Fiction.* London, Cape, 1922.

MACAULAY, ROSE. *The Writings of E. M. Forster.* London, Hogarth Press, 1938.

McTaggart, J. M. E. *The Relation of Time and Eternity.* Berkeley, University of California Press, 1908.

Maurois, André. *Aspects of Biography* (translated from the French by S. C. Roberts). Cambridge University Press, 1939.

Poets and Prophets (translated from the French by Hamish Miles). London, Cassell, 1936.

Muir, Edwin. *The Structure of the Novel.* London, Hogarth Press, 1932.

Murry, J. Middleton. *The Problem of Style.* Oxford, Milford, 1922.

Newton, Deborah. *Virginia Woolf.* Melbourne University Press, 1946.

Nicolson, Harold. *The Development of English Biography.* London, Hogarth Press, 1927.

O'Connor, W. V. (ed.) *Forms of Modern Fiction : Essays Collected in honor of Joseph Warren Beach.* Minneapolis, University of Minnesota Press, 1948.

Plomer, William. " Notes on Virginia Woolf", *Horizon,* III (May 1941).

Pryce-Jones, Alan. " The Frightening Pundits of Bloomsbury ", *The Listener,* 1 March 1951.

Quiller-Couch, Sir Arthur. " The ' Victorian Age ' ", *Studies in Literature, Second Series.* Cambridge University Press, 1922.

Read, Herbert. *English Prose Style.* London, Bell, 1928.

The Meaning of Art. London, Faber & Faber, 1931.

Richards, I. A. *Principles of Literary Criticism.* London, Paul, Trench, Trubner, 1938.

Roberts, J. H. " ' Vision and Design ' in Virginia Woolf", *PMLA,* LXI (September 1946).

Russell, Bertrand. " Portraits from Memory—II " (Maynard Keynes and Lytton Strachey), *The Listener,* 17 July 1952.

Russell, John. " Lytton Strachey ", *Horizon,* XV (February 1947).

Sanders, C. R. " Lytton Strachey's Conception of Biography ", *PMLA,* LXVI (June 1951).

Savage, D. S. *The Withered Branch : Six Studies in the Modern Novel.* London, Eyre & Spottiswoode, 1950.

Schilpp, P. A. (ed.) *The Philosophy of G. E. Moore.* Evanston, Northwestern University Press, 1942.

Smyth, Charles. " A Note on Historical Biography and Mr. Strachey ", *The Criterion,* VIII (July 1929).

TRILLING, LIONEL. *E. M. Forster: A Study*. London, Hogarth Press, 1944.
WEITZ, MORRIS. *Philosophy of the Arts*. Cambridge, Mass., Harvard University Press, 1950.

III

RECENTLY PUBLISHED

FORSTER, E. M. *The Hill of Devi*. London, Arnold, 1953.
WOOLF, LEONARD (ed.). *A Writer's Diary: Extracts from the Diary of Virginia Woolf*. London, Hogarth Press, 1953.

DATE DUE
